T0407234

A HISTORY OF FOOD IN LITERATURE

When novels, plays and poems refer to food, they are often doing much more than we might think. Recent critical thinking suggests that depictions of food in literary works can help to explain the complex relationship between the body, subjectivity and social structures. *A History of Food in Literature* provides a clear and comprehensive overview of significant episodes of food and its consumption in major canonical literary works from the medieval period to the twenty-first century. This volume contextualises these works with reference to pertinent historical and cultural materials such as cookery books, diaries and guides to good health, in order to engage with the critical debate on food and literature and how ideas of food have developed over the centuries.

Organised chronologically and examining certain key writers from every period, including Chaucer, Shakespeare, Austen and Dickens, this book's enlightening critical analysis makes it relevant for anyone interested in the study of food and literature.

Charlotte Boyce is Senior Lecturer in English Literature at the University of Portsmouth, UK.

Joan Fitzpatrick is Senior Lecturer in English at Loughborough University, UK.

A HISTORY OF FOOD IN LITERATURE

From the Fourteenth Century to the Present

Charlotte Boyce and Joan Fitzpatrick

Routledge
Taylor & Francis Group

LONDON AND NEW YORK

First published 2017
by Routledge
2 Park Square, Milton Park, Abingdon, Oxon OX14 4RN

and by Routledge
711 Third Avenue, New York, NY 10017

Routledge is an imprint of the Taylor & Francis Group, an informa business

© 2017 Charlotte Boyce and Joan Fitzpatrick

The right of Charlotte Boyce and Joan Fitzpatrick to be identified as
authors of this work has been asserted by them in accordance with
sections 77 and 78 of the Copyright, Designs and Patents Act 1988.

All rights reserved. No part of this book may be reprinted or
reproduced or utilised in any form or by any electronic, mechanical,
or other means, now known or hereafter invented, including
photocopying and recording, or in any information storage or
retrieval system, without permission in writing from the publishers.

Trademark notice: Product or corporate names may be trademarks or
registered trademarks, and are used only for identification and
explanation without intent to infringe.

British Library Cataloguing in Publication Data
A catalogue record for this book is available from the British Library

Library of Congress Cataloging in Publication Data
Names: Boyce, Charlotte author. | Fitzpatrick, Joan author.
Title: A history of food in literature : from the fourteenth century to
the present / Charlotte Boyce and Joan Fitzpatrick.
Description: Milton Park, Abingdon, Oxon; New York, NY :
Routledge, 2017. | Includes bibliographical references and index.
Identifiers: LCCN 2016053821 | ISBN 9780415840514 (harback : alk.
paper) | ISBN 9780415840521 (pbk : alk. paper) |
ISBN 9781135022075 (web pdf) | ISBN 9781135022051 (mobi/kindle)
Subjects: LCSH: Food in literature. | Food habits in literature. |
English literature–History and criticism.
Classification: LCC PR149.F66 B89 2017 | DDC 820.9/3559–dc23
LC record available at https://lccn.loc.gov/2016053821

ISBN: 978-0-415-84051-4 (hbk)
ISBN: 978-0-415-84052-1 (pbk)
ISBN: 978-0-203-76708-5 (ebk)

Typeset in Bembo
by Keystroke, Neville Lodge, Tettenhall, Wolverhampton

CONTENTS

INTRODUCTION

Charlotte Boyce and Joan Fitzpatrick

In a recent review of the exhibition *Painting Paradise: The Art of the Garden* at the Queen's Gallery, Buckingham Palace, Nicola Shulman considers a painting from the seventeenth-century British School entitled *Charles II Presented with a Pineapple* (*c.* 1677). The same painting had featured in the exhibition *The Art of Tudor and Stuart Fashion* the year before, where it 'was a prime exhibit . . . for the sake of the principals' costumes' but now, as Shulman wryly notes in her review, 'it's on show for the pineapple'. Shulman observes that the juxtaposition of monarch and fruit in the image is by no means straightforward:

> What is going on here? Not what we think. Scholarship has revealed that Charles II was perfectly familiar with pineapples by 1677, so it's not his first pineapple. It has also established that the painting does not represent his gardener, John Rose, presenting him with the first pineapple grown in England, because both men were dead by then. The accompanying [exhibition] essay concludes that 'the presentation of the first pineapple that the painting reputedly celebrates is entirely fictitious', but has no answer for the question now arising: why was 'The King's Gardener Hands Him an Imported Pineapple' an event for commemoration on this scale?
>
> *Shulman 2015, 7*

What *is* going on here? The textual history of the pineapple gives us some clue. Although Columbus had first introduced the fruit to European society in 1496, a century and a half later it was still deemed a wondrous curiosity, 'far beyond . . . our choisest [*sic*] fruits of *Europe*' (Ligon 1657, 84). Hothouse pineapples were not successfully cultivated in England until the early eighteenth century, so the example presented to the king in the painting would likely have been imported from the Caribbean, a climatic translocation that few such fruits survived.[1] Indeed, so uncommon was the pineapple in England in the mid-seventeenth century, its appearance at court merited special mention in contemporary diary accounts: in an entry dated 9 August 1661, the courtier John Evelyn wrote that he had seen a 'Queen-pine brought from Barbados presented to his Majestie', and again, some seven years later, he recorded seeing 'that rare fruite called the King-Pine' at a royal banquet (Evelyn 1995, 122, 168). It is in the light of this context of rarity and exoticism that the (actually rather modest-looking) pineapple in the painting can be understood as a status symbol on a par with the other visual signifiers of wealth and prestige represented: the grand house and landscaped gardens, the fountains and statuary.[2]

Yet, while undoubtedly signalling the economic and imperial power of Charles II, the pineapple depicted here may also encompass a secondary set of coded meanings. Noting that the gardener in the painting, John Rose, was employed by the family of the Duchess of Cleveland (one of the king's mistresses), Kaori O'Connor speculates that the image may be read as 'an allegory in which the luscious fruit, representing the duchess, was being offered to the king, whose affectionate term for her was said to be "my pineapple"' (O'Connor 2013, 21). Whether historically accurate or not, this reading intersects intriguingly with the pineapple's long-standing cultural association with temptation and sensual longing. In a 1638 letter to his father, Thomas Verney (an English colonist in Barbados) refers to the myth of the pineapple as 'the apple that Eve cosned [cozened] Adam with', before finding himself overcome by a wave of appetitive desire: 'I might speak much more of this pine, but whilest I am a writing the description of it makes me long after it' (Bruce 1853, 194). Verney's craving for the fruit finds its literary echo in Amelia Opie's novel *Adeline Mowbray* (1805), where a feverish Frederic Glenmurray declares it the 'only thing for weeks that I have wished for' (Opie 2010, 170), and in the musings of Romantic essayist Charles Lamb, where it is described as 'almost too transcendent – a delight, if not sinful, yet so like to sinning, that really a tender-conscienced person would do well to pause' (Lamb 2005, 132). The tantalizing, Edenic connotations of the pineapple alluded to by Verney and Lamb seem also to inform its representation in Tobias Smollett's *The Adventures of Peregrine Pickle* (1751): here, the pineapple is a 'fatal fruit', which arouses the 'curiosity and desire' of the pregnant Mrs Pickle and the anxiety of her sister Mrs Grizzle, who deems it an 'unnatural' production, 'extorted by the force of artificial fire, out of filthy manure' (Smollett 1964, 21–22).

Pineapples would retain something of their exotic, sensory appeal in nineteenth-century literature and culture; Dickens's David Copperfield is fascinated by the examples on view in Covent Garden, for instance (see Chapter 5). However, by the end of the Victorian period, advances in transportation and packaging had transformed the pineapple into a rather more quotidian commodity. An 1873 cartoon in *Punch* pokes fun at the fruit's growing democratization – a working-class man offers a grocer ''arf a sovereign' for one 'if yer'll *only tell us 'ow to cook 'un!*' (Anon. 1873) – while, in Jerome K. Jerome's *Three Men in a Boat* (1889), the pineapple that J., George and Harris take on their river journey is of the tinned variety. Yet, despite this trajectory of growing accessibility and loss of social prestige, the pineapple maintains something of its earlier allure: when George retrieves the tinned fruit from the bottom of the hamper in Jerome's novel, the narrator (J.) observes 'we felt that life was worth living after all' (Jerome 1889, 194). Later, in Wallace Stevens's poem 'Someone Puts a Pineapple Together' (1947), the fruit's exceptional form is a stimulus to poetic imagination, while in Jeanette Winterson's *Sexing the Cherry* (1989) – a novel that imagines the pineapple's first arrival in England and makes ekphrastic reference to the painting of Charles II and John Rose – the fruit is an object of fascination to young Nicolas Jordan, who associates it with a quasi-magical spirit of discovery in a world where 'there's so little wonder left' (Winterson 2001, 113).

As the fluid, kaleidoscopic literary history of the pineapple shows, food in literature is often part of a bigger story and in the texts considered in this volume it is invariably an essential part. We here attempt to explore the interest literary authors, from a range of historical periods, have shown in food and to examine how and why specific foodstuffs – as well as the context in which they are consumed – have proved such a significant point of interest. For the literary authors here considered, food and its consumption operate as potent and multi-faceted symbols. Food is sometimes present simply as what gets eaten but more often (like Charles's pineapple) it functions as a conduit for something else, signalling wealth or poverty, cultural difference or a sense of belonging, status and identity in terms of rank, gender and moral standing, and sometimes (but never simply) fashion.

How does food feature in the stories told by Chaucer's pilgrims? How prevalent is food in Dickens's novels and what kind of food and eating is it? Why is cannibalism a recurring feature of fiction across historical periods? The aim of this book is to answer these questions and many more that pertain to food in literature. This is the first volume to offer a comprehensive, critical overview of significant episodes on food and its consumption in major canonical and a selection of marginal English literary works from the medieval period to the twenty-first century; to contextualize those texts with reference to pertinent (and sometimes hitherto neglected) historical and cultural materials; and to engage with the critical debate on food in literature. (Here 'English' means works commonly studied in university departments of English, including broadly anglophone material). In such a project the choice of where to begin is necessarily arbitrary and driven by some practical concerns. As Henry Fielding implies in his famous description of Homer's *Odyssey* as 'that eating Poem' (Fielding 1996, 440), the history of food in literature is an extensive one, which reaches far beyond the period here considered. The sheer size of a study charting culinary representation from classical culture to the modern day would likely deter even the most enthusiastic reader; we have therefore chosen to begin with William Langland's medieval poem *Piers Plowman* because it remains reasonably well known and its preoccupation with food and eating would influence later literary works in the medieval period and beyond.

The use of food in novels, plays, poems and other works of literature can help explain the complex relationship between the body, subjectivity and social structures regulating consumption. By contextualizing references to food and its consumption in literary texts via texts traditionally surveyed by historians – cookery books, dietary literature, diaries, pamphlets, newspaper reports – we can engage more fully with what might otherwise remain obscure references to, and attitudes towards, food. When authors refer to food, they are usually telling the reader something important about narrative, plot, characterization or motives; we can also explore significant current issues that are connected to food in subtle or complex ways, for example gender, religion, poverty and empire. The consumption of food in literature is grounded in the period within which the work was written but also evident are issues of transhistorical significance such as hunger, desire, revulsion and struggles for survival. This study will enable readers to trace the intersecting, overlapping and sometimes contradictory meanings that inhere in representations of food in works of English literature from the medieval period to the present.

Recent criticism has done much to elucidate the social, historical and cultural importance of food in literary representation. As well as a wealth of individual essays and articles exploring eating and drinking in specific texts and contexts, the last thirty years have seen the publication of various book-length studies on food and its associated practices in works of literature. Typically, though, the scope of these studies is much narrower than that of the present volume. Many existing critical works consider representations of food in specific literary periods (for example Adamson 1995; Morton 2004; Appelbaum 2006; Cozzi 2010; Fitzpatrick 2010) or national and transnational literatures (Aoyama 2008; Xu 2008; Mannur 2010; Carruth 2013). Others examine the manifestation of alimentary themes in the output of an individual author, notably Dickens (Houston 1994), Woolf (Glenny 1999) and Shakespeare (Fitzpatrick 2007), or adopt a particular critical perspective, such as psychoanalysis (Skubal 2002), postcolonialism (Roy 2010) or eco-criticism (Archer *et al.* 2014). The gendered politics of consumption (and non-consumption) have attracted especial critical notice in recent years; female relationships to food have been extensively theorized in a number of works (for example Gutierrez 2003; Mazzoni 2005; Adolph 2009; Moss 2009), while Gwen Hyman (2009) explores the depiction of gentlemanly appetites in the nineteenth-century British novel. Other pertinent critical themes to have emerged in the scholarship on food and literature include vegetarianism (Adams 2010) and cannibalism (Kilgour 1990; Guest 2001), while the significance of eating in children's literature has also been analyzed by Carolyn Daniel (2006) and Kara Keeling and Scott Pollard (2009).

The present volume draws on much of the important scholarly work outlined above in order to produce a comprehensive overview of food in literature from the fourteenth century to the present, enabling readers to find in one place critical readings of the most important references to food in the great works of English literature and the relevance of these references. Unlike existing surveys of food in literature, such as Sandra M. Gilbert's *The Culinary Imagination* (2014), our book is organized chronologically. Each chapter contains an essay on the role of food in several important texts from the period under consideration, which engages with current scholarly debate and incorporates hitherto neglected contextual material that situates the literary text squarely within the period and culture in which it was written. The reader will be able to identify the change in representations of food from age to age and the common concerns that emerge about food across the centuries: for example the manner in which eating too much is consistently condemned but has developed from being a sin (in medieval and early modern society) to become a matter of social responsibility and aesthetics (in modern society). More nuanced variations also emerge: although medieval and early modern people shared a sense of overeating as sin, they differed in the finer aspects of what constituted gluttony with the shift from Catholicism to Protestantism.

Other thematic connections across the book include the relationship between food and the body and a shared horror of cannibalism. There are also distinct differences across periods: for example a change in attitudes towards vegetarianism and the emergence of new foodstuffs from the colonies and other lands abroad. The reader may wish to consult individual sections of the book to learn about a particular text or period (found from the comprehensive index and detailed table of contents) or else read the entire book from start to finish to learn how representations and uses of food develop across the centuries. There is, however, no one story of food's depiction that emerges from this book's conspectus, but rather a series of stories about particular kinds of food, appetites, moralities and human tastes in their various and highly distinct historical contexts.

In Chapter 1, William Langland's important late medieval poem *Piers Plowman* juxtaposes the industrious and Christ-like Piers with the wealthy and gluttonous amongst whom he lives and works. For Langland eating and drinking to excess is a sin but also a social ill, with its consequences roundly condemned from the pulpit, and there is a clear sense that those who take more than their fair share are responsible for the hardship of others. In the anonymous poem *Sir Gawain and the Green Knight* we encounter a very different world from that of the ordinary workers, and shirkers, familiar to Piers. The *Gawain* poet presents life at court and a mysterious Green Knight who presents a challenge accepted by Gawain who is then tested and feasted in sumptuous surroundings with extravagant dishes of all kinds. In *The Canterbury Tales* Chaucer's pilgrims meet at the Tabard Inn and the prize for telling the best tale is dinner. Food frames the tales and permeates them also, with references to food, its preparation and consumption indicating medieval attitudes to hygiene, feasting and sin, amongst other topics. *The Book of Margery Kempe* is an autobiography that offers an insight into medieval attitudes to food and fasting. Margery's rejection of materialism for a life of devotion to Christ causes her difficulties when she is surrounded by others who wish to eat, drink and be merry in company. Contexts are provided by religious writings such as the Bible and the 'Rule of Saint Benedict' as well as medieval dietary literature indicating what one should eat, when and why, and cookery books containing ingredients and recipes relevant to the literature.

There is a clear distinction between the late medieval (principally Catholic) and early modern (principally Protestant) attitudes towards monastic fasting considered in Chapter 2, whereby feeding to excess, or finding too much pleasure in food, is bad but so is not feeding at all. As in some medieval literature considered in

Chapter 1 so too in Spenser's sixteenth-century epic poem *The Faerie Queene*, eating and drinking have a spiritual dimension: Redcross drinks from the Well of Life to restore his faith and Gluttony is one of the seven deadly sins that parade in Lucifera's court. Spenser's rebel leader Maleger is lean and hungry, yet strong, and his knights, overcome by sexual desire, neglect their bellies in order to feed their lust; sexual excess is also a feature of the cannibals who prey upon women in the poem. Shakespeare's plays are full of references to food – many of them made by or about the gluttonous English knight Sir John Oldcastle (Falstaff) – and he also engages with the concept of fasting, including fasting women. Shakespeare's treatment of Italy reveals his engagement with aspects of religious and national identity that pertain to food and eating; also considered here is Shakespeare's influence upon Francis Beaumont and John Fletcher in their play *The Woman Hater* that portrays the Falstaffian Italian glutton Lazarello. Jonson's treatment of food is visceral and fecund and often acquisitive. In *The Alchemist* Epicure Mammon delights in the extraordinary, as much interested in conspicuous consumption as taste, and those who gravitate towards Bartholomew Fair in the play of the same name desire the consumption of food (pork, gingerbread, fruit) at the same time others wish to police its consumption. Ubiquitous references to the preparation and consumption of food reveal Jonson's interest in food and the hypocrisy of the society at which he aimed his satire; in *Volpone* much of the deceit that involves a desire for sex, money or power also involves food. Contexts here include sermons against gluttony and drunkenness, and we see the growing popularity of dietary literature and cookery books.

Chapter 3 brings us to the early seventeenth century where, in *Paradise Lost*, Adam and Eve share a meal with the angel Raphael before eating the apple that will bring death to the world, and in *Paradise Regained* Satan's bread and banquet temptations are firmly refused by a hungry Christ whose patience is rewarded with food in heaven. In *Robinson Crusoe* it is clear that, *in extremis*, money and gold are useless and it is food that counts. How does Crusoe feed himself on the island, what modifications to his diet is he forced to make, and how would this have struck a contemporary reader? Swift's Gulliver has much to say about the culinary habits of the remote nations he has encountered and inverts the usual assumptions about savage natives when hinting at his own cannibalistic desires, a feature also of later cannibal narratives. In *Joseph Andrews* and *Tom Jones* Fielding presents us with food as a context for vice and virtue (a recurrent dichotomy in the book): it plays its part in seduction as well as the kind of prelapsarian innocence witnessed in *Paradise Lost* and, as in the medieval literature considered in Chapter 1, we again encounter hypocritical clergy as well as hunters who are less noble than those described earlier in the volume. The Bible is an important context in this chapter, especially for Milton's poems, whilst attitudes to dietary health and fashion are evident from various sources, including the *The Diary of Samuel Pepys* and cookery books from the period.

Chapter 4 turns to food's role in the luxury debates that raged in eighteenth- and early nineteenth-century culture. Satirical texts such as *The Tryal of the Lady Allurea*

Luxury and *The Expedition of Humphry Clinker* promote plain but hearty English fare over refined, Frenchified dishes, arguing that luxurious consumption (which is typically characterized as 'foreign') has a deleterious effect on the moral and physical health of the nation. Similar anxieties regarding culinary transculturation emerge in the poetry of Robert Fergusson and Robert Burns, where traditional foodstuffs play a crucial part in the maintenance of Scottish national identity and cultural heritage. During the 1790s, both Charlotte Smith and Hannah More critique the alimentary excesses of the middle orders and aristocracy in an echo of earlier literary invectives against the immorality of gluttony; however, whereas More's texts suggest that domestic economy can mitigate the effects of dietary inequality, Smith's *Desmond* indicates that a more radical reorganization of social hierarchies is required if everyone is to have enough to eat. The issue of hunger takes on a different dimension in the novels of Jane Austen, where female characters invariably respond to romantic disappointment – a direct index of their social powerlessness – by refusing to eat. Asceticism is celebrated, by contrast, in the epic verse of Lord Byron, where abstemiousness functions as a measure of heroic masculinity. Ethical concerns around food emerge repeatedly in the texts considered in this chapter: Romantic writers such as Percy and Mary Shelley expand on earlier critiques of luxurious consumption in their advocacy of vegetarianism (a diet which they associate with the prelapsarian Eden of Milton's *Paradise Lost*, a poem discussed in Chapter 3), while Mary Birkett's *Poem on the African Slave Trade* sponsors abstention from sugar as a form of consumer protest against Caribbean slavery, an industry at the heart of Defoe's *Robinson Crusoe*, also discussed in Chapter 3. Yet in the poetry of John Keats it is aesthetics, rather than ethics, that predominates; the representation of eating in works such as *The Eve of St Agnes* and *The Fall of Hyperion* emphasizes the sensuality of consumption, which can engender feelings of pleasure but also of disgust.

The long-standing literary interest in questions of access and entitlement to food re-emerges with particular urgency in Chapter 5. The material hunger of the Victorian lower classes is a key component of the social critique found in the works of Charles Dickens, where representations of famishment and exigency co-exist with depictions of culinary plenty and commensal feasting. Physical hunger is also a matter of concern in the novels of the Brontës and, later in the century, Sarah Grand; however, these texts arguably take a greater interest in the metaphorical hungers of middle-class women, whose dissatisfactions with the gendered inequalities of Victorian culture manifest themselves via a variety of food-refusing behaviours, recalling the abstemious practices of Jane Austen's heroines in Chapter 4. Male excess is a further cause for concern in Victorian fiction: in *Vanity Fair*, for instance, the gluttonous Jos Sedley's passion for Indian cuisine threatens to disfigure his body and undermine the security of his English identity. Anxieties regarding bodily distortion and the unstable distinction between 'civilized' and 'savage' consumption again arise in *Alice's Adventures in Wonderland* and *Through the Looking-Glass*, though here it is female alimentary desire that is primarily at stake. Indeed, the dangers of unregulated female appetite represent a recurrent theme in the works studied in this chapter. Christina Rossetti's 'Goblin Market' and George Eliot's 'Brother Jacob' both figure food as a source of temptation with the potential to damage not only bodily but also moral well-being; written at a time when the adulteration of food was common, they reflect contemporary fears regarding contaminated produce and the effects of imprudent ingestion on individual health and collective morality.

Chapter 6 examines the intersections between food and identity politics in twentieth- and twenty-first-century writing. In Joseph Conrad's fiction, the figure of the cannibal works ostensibly to secure the ontological ground between 'civilized' Self and 'primitive' Other; however, like the eighteenth-century colonial novels considered in Chapter 3, *Heart of Darkness* and 'Falk' in fact problematize simplistic assumptions regarding European civility and non-European savagery. Existential anxieties are further addressed in the modernist writings of James Joyce and Virginia Woolf, where food can be the fulcrum for pleasurable acts of communion (such as the meals at the centre of *To the Lighthouse* and *The Waves*), but can also elicit feelings of disgust and a consciousness of mortality, as shown by the reflections of Leopold Bloom in *Ulysses*. The proto-feminist interest in female relationships to food found in Woolf's fiction resurfaces in the novels of Angela Carter and Margaret Atwood in the 1960s, where representations of eating and non-eating are linked to questions of (self-)control and gendered (dis)empowerment. In the contemporary postcolonial writings of Salman Rushdie, Andrea Levy, Zadie Smith and Monica Ali, meanwhile, food functions as a complex signifier of national, racial and cultural identity. Repository of tradition, memory and heritage, food in *Midnight's Children*, *Fruit of the Lemon*, *White Teeth* and *Brick Lane* serves simultaneously as a marker of difference and as a symbol of hybridity and cultural fusion.

As these chapter summaries demonstrate, a number of key themes emerge across this volume. Excessive consumption of food and drink, for example, is prominent across the historical periods here considered. In Chapter 1 Gluttony is personified as a vomiting drunkard in Langland's *Piers Plowman* and in both this poem and Chaucer's *Canterbury Tales* gluttony is a sign of hypocrisy in religious figures who ought to share amongst the poor the provisions they overconsume; in this sense gluttony is repeatedly emphasized as a social sin as well as a moral failing. Shakespeare's Falstaff and Jonson's Epicure Mammon (Chapter 2) are obsessive in their pursuit of food, with Mammon (from *The Alchemist*) in particular viewing food not merely as an item of sustenance but as something with status value, an idea that will emerge also in later chapters. The physical effects of gluttony are condemned across all periods, from the dietary literature discussed in Chapters 1 and 2 to the figure of Jos Sedley in Thackeray's *Vanity Fair* (Chapter 5), where the nineteenth-century preoccupation with digestion harks back to a similar concern in the early modern dietaries. The early sense of moral abhorrence at the social consequences of the sin of gluttony is less overt in later works but still apparent, for example in Anne Brontë's Arthur Huntingdon from *The Tenant of Wildfell Hall* where, as in the earlier literature here considered, gustatory self-indulgence is coupled with alcoholic intemperance.

Of course enjoying food is not always condemned: feasting and commensality (the practice of eating in a group, often the same social group, as opposed to eating alone) are celebrated in a number of texts, for example *Sir Gawain and the Green Knight* (Chapter 1), a number of plays by Jonson and Shakespeare (Chapter 2), Dickens's *A Christmas Carol* (Chapter 5) and Woolf's *To the Lighthouse* and *The Waves* (Chapter 6), although the meals that tend to emerge without taint are those where there is a clear sense of food facilitating the strengthening of social bonds. Eating alone is often problematic: in Chapter 1 we see that those who dislike Margery Kempe refuse to eat with her and Heathcliff is not allowed to eat with the family in *Wuthering Heights* (Chapter 5). Food helps shape the identity of the Self and the Other: a recurring feature of the volume is that 'you are what you eat', a notion that emerges in early modern dietaries – where reducing the intake of a particular kind of food was said to affect one's dominant humour – and also in the sense of food as an indication of national and religious identity, where (for example) fish was regarded as distinctly Catholic (Chapter 2). Food is also a celebration of national identity: for example, Bartholomew Fair – in Jonson's play of the same name and where Ursula sells her pork and Joan her gingerbread – was an important English cultural event (Chapter 2). In other examples Smollett promotes plain but hearty English fare as preferable to over-refined and extravagant French cooking in *Humphry Clinker* (Chapter 4) and Rushdie utilizes the concept of 'chutnification' to describe the multiple religious and cultural identities of postcolonial India in *Midnight's Children* (Chapter 6).

At the other end of the gustatory spectrum, hunger, both literal and metaphorical, comes up repeatedly across the volume. It is a recurrent feature of Langland's poem in Chapter 1 (a consequence in part of the behaviour of the rich and powerful who overindulge) and is also evident in representations of the famished lower classes in Dickens's novels explored in Chapter 5. It is not clear if the hunger of Spenser's Maleger from *The Faerie Queene* is self-induced (Chapter 2) – certainly Spenser's Redcross Knight fasts to undergo a sort of moral cleansing – but dietary renunciation is usually a means of asserting control, deployed often (though not exclusively) by women, for example Margery Kempe (Chapter 1); a number of Shakespeare's characters (Chapter 2); Caroline Helstone in Charlotte Brontë's *Shirley* and Sarah Grand's eponymous heroine from *The Beth Book* (Chapter 5); Rhoda from *The Waves* and Marian from *The Edible Woman* (Chapter 6). Men who voluntarily limit what they eat include Jane Austen's Mr Woodhouse from *Emma* (Chapter 4) and James Joyce's Stephen Dedalus from *Ulysses* (Chapter 6). Extreme hunger, or famine, is a pervasive and threatening presence in Langland's *Piers Plowman* (Chapter 1) and an implicit feature of the Irish context of Spenser's *Faerie Queene* (Chapter 2). In Milton's *Paradise Lost* famine is part of a fallen humanity's future and Satan and his fellow fallen angels suffer from it, whilst Swift recounts a fear of famine amongst the Lilliputians to be a consequence of Gulliver's enormous appetite (Chapter 3). Literary representations of hunger are often inspired by historical events: in Chapter 4, the works of both Charlotte Smith and Hannah More respond to the food scarcities that plagued the revolutionary 1790s, while in the novels of the Brontës (Chapter 5) tacit references to the Irish Famine are displaced onto child characters and social outsiders, powerless figures who come to symbolize the hungry.

Where food comes from and how one gets it also emerge as repeated concerns across this volume. Milton describes how killing and death, including the killing and death of animals for food, is a consequence of the Fall (Chapter 3) and although hunting animals for food is more acceptable, admirable even, in the medieval period it is not an acceptable pastime for priests, for whom it is forbidden by Canon law. Throughout the volume the clergy are often presented as hypocritical: they are the targets of satire by Langland and Chaucer (Chapter 1) and are condemned as parasitic by Joyce's Bloom in *Ulysses* because they feed off others (Chapter 6). In later periods hunting is often portrayed as a brutal pursuit and one undertaken by boorish types; for example in Fielding's *Tom Jones* the brash drunkard Squire Western enjoys the sport (Chapter 3) and so too does the abusive alcoholic Huntingdon in Anne Brontë's *Tenant of Wildfell Hall* (Chapter 5). Further resistance to hunting can be found in early nineteenth-century vegetarianism, a movement that is about more than simply not eating meat, embracing as it does the Romantic aesthetics of humanity's relationship with nature and rebellion against increasing industrialization and consumerism. For Percy Shelley (Chapter 4), meat is a consequence of the Fall of humanity and yet for the early moderns it was considered ordained by God and more healthy than fish (Chapter 2). In later periods meat is also depicted in positive terms, for example the Boeuf en Daube in Woolf's *To the Lighthouse* (Chapter 6). Hunting is sometimes necessary – as discussed in Chapter 5, Sarah Grand's heroine Beth Caldwell engages in poaching in order to provide food for her family – but most often it is figured as self-indulgent and cruel. A recurrent motif in the texts here considered is that people, and especially women, are hunted as prey: Squire Western repeatedly refers to women, including his daughter Sophia, in these terms (Chapter 3); it is during the game season that Huntingdon undertakes his pursuit of Helen Lawrence (Chapter 5); and the attempted seduction of Gawain by Bertilak's wife is a clever inversion of the usual courtly hunt (Chapter 1).

Margaret Visser has remarked upon the violence of eating that the rituals of dining serve to obviate:

> Somewhere at the back of our minds, carefully walled off from ordinary consideration and discourse, lies the idea of cannibalism – that human beings might *become* food, and eaters of each other. Violence, after all, is necessary if any organism is to ingest another. Animals are murdered to produce meat; vegetables are torn up, peeled, and chopped; most of what we eat is treated with fire; and chewing is designed remorselessly to finish what killing and cooking began. People naturally prefer that none of this should happen to them. Behind every rule of table etiquette lurks the determination of each person present to be a diner, not a dish. It is one of the chief roles of etiquette to keep a lid on the violence which the meal being eaten presupposes.
>
> *Visser 2015, 3–4*

This distinction between what gets eaten and who or what does the eating crops up across the volume and is connected to the concept of cannibalism, correctly identified by Visser as the most feared of all consumption. In Spenser's *Faerie Queene* (Chapter 2) the cannibal is a savage figure, partly invoked by this Protestant poet to signal the Catholic practice of theophagy, a concept that also emerges in other Protestant writings (for example by Milton, Chapter 3) and in other writings involving Catholicism and/or Ireland, such as Joyce's *Ulysses* (Chapter 6). In later periods the cannibal is similarly invoked as savage Other but the cannibals that feature in Defoe's *Robinson Crusoe* (Chapter 3) and Conrad's 'Falk' (Chapter 6) reveal that the apparent dichotomy between 'savage' and 'civilized' is sometimes less than clear, a blurring of boundaries also explored in Swift's *Gulliver's Travels* (Chapter 3). Involuntary cannibalism, for example via the cook that leaks or flakes into his or her dish (Chaucer's Cook in Chapter 1 and Jonson's Ursula in Chapter 2), serves to convey – via the open and grotesque Rabelaisian body – the manner in which the diner is not always entirely in control of what gets consumed.

The biblical apple as a symbol for gluttony and disobedience is apparent throughout the medieval texts here considered and gets picked up again by Milton in *Paradise Lost* (Chapter 3). Adam and Eve enjoy a self-sufficient pastoral idyll before their consumption of the forbidden fruit and this connection between fruit, sweet things, appetite and its consequent harmful effects is explored also in later works: in Christina Rossetti's 'Goblin Market' (Chapter 5) Laura is an Eve-like figure who falls under the influence of the Satan-like goblin men; Lewis Carroll's Alice too must learn to control her curiosity and her appetite (Chapter 5); and Carter's Melanie from *The Magic Toyshop* develops a disorderly relationship with food after a night-time escapade in an apple tree (Chapter 6). Where honey is often mentioned in positive terms – it is, for example, a feature of the rural bliss enjoyed by Rossetti's Laura and Lizzie before they encounter the goblin men – sugar is a more problematic foodstuff. Although sugar was still considered medicinal by some in the early eighteenth century, there was increasing awareness of its negative effects, not just upon the body but as a sign of moral corruption. For the anti-saccharites of the 1790s, sugar was a product metaphorically stained by the iniquities of the transatlantic slave trade, a lucrative industry in which Defoe's Robinson Crusoe is engaged before his shipwreck (Chapter 3). Ambivalence towards sugar re-emerges in postcolonial fiction such as Levy's *Fruit of the Lemon* (Chapter 6), where the sugar in British tea-time treats is contextualized via the history of slavery and oppression. In George Eliot's short story 'Brother Jacob' (Chapter 5) sugar is implicated in the kind of food adulteration that was all too common in Victorian England, but that also features in texts as early as Langland's *Piers Plowman* where Rose the brewster adulterates her ale (Chapter 1).

There is a clear sense of degeneration when food enters the marketplace and simple items of sustenance turn into commodities that are advertised: Milton's Satan and Rossetti's goblin men (Chapters 3 and 5) both 'sell' fruit to their victims and expect something in return, signalling that there is something nefarious about the exchange of food for reward – the 'meed' explored via Langland in Chapter 1, where cooks make their pies for profit – an impulse contrary to that of the women who prepare food with love for others (Chapters 5 and 6). Milk (another key consumable) was historically a food for the poor: it is produced and consumed by Chaucer's Widow in 'The Nun's Priest's Tale' (Chapter 1) and lauded by Irish revivalists (a context for Joyce's work in Chapter 6) who saw it as native and egalitarian when compared to the foreign drink of tea. Milk is often associated with women and nourishment and human breast-milk provokes the joy of plenitude in Joyce's Molly Bloom (Chapter 6). Elsewhere in *Ulysses*, though, old and sterile breasts are an object of disgust, and so too Swift's Gulliver finds Lilliputian breasts and breastfeeding revolting (Chapter 3). In *The Book of Margery Kempe* (Chapter 1), by contrast, breast-milk is said to come from Christ himself, invoking the medieval belief that the fluid was derived from blood and suggesting that the blood of Christ will provide spiritual sustenance for humankind.

As this brief survey of key themes indicates, a wealth of meaning inheres in re-presentations of food, practices of consumption and non-consumption. When writing this volume we have been necessarily selective in our choice of texts, authors and contextual material used to signal the wider cultural impact of ideas about food and eating in specific periods. Nevertheless, since its inception, this project has grown significantly in scope. When we began the volume, we intended that it be shorter than its current length but as we investigated the presence and impact of food in literary and contextual writings across history, it soon became clear that more needed to be said. Some texts we knew ought to be included from the outset but others soon emerged as necessary for inclusion in order to allow the volume the breadth and depth we hope it now contains. As well as providing the reader with analyses of canonical texts, we wanted to ensure that we also included some works that have tended to fall out of favour in recent years, as well as those that we feel have not yet been given the attention they deserve. The texts and authors here considered all have something distinctive to say about culinary and alimentary culture, and that is one of the main reasons they have been chosen. Each historical period examined is also distinct but, as outlined above, fascinating connections emerge across them, some of which we expected and some of which came as a surprise. Despite our efforts to be comprehensive we realize that more remains to be said on this subject – not least because, as we suggest in the conclusion, new representations of consumption continue to emerge in contemporary writing – but we trust that the volume provides an important starting point for the complex and wonderful story of the history of food in literature across the centuries.

Notes

1 Richard Ligon noted: 'from the *Bermudoes*, some have been brought hither in their full ripenesse and perfection, where there has been a quick passage, and the fruites taken in the nick of time; but, that happens very seldome' (Ligon 1657, 84). For the history of the cultivation of the pineapple in Europe, see Beauman (2005) and O'Connor (2013).

2   Such cultural cachet would cleave to the pineapple long after hothouse cultivation made them a more regular sight in England: in Jane Austen's *Northanger Abbey*, for instance, General Tilney boasts about the number of fruits produced in his pinery in an effort to impress Catherine Morland (see Chapter 4).

References

Adams, Carol J. 2010. *The Sexual Politics of Meat: A Feminist-Vegetarian Critical Theory*. New York and London. Continuum.

Adamson, Melitta Weiss, ed. 1995. *Food in the Middle Ages: A Book of Essays*. Garland Medieval Casebooks. 11. New York. Garland.

Adolph, Andrea. 2009. *Food and Femininity in Twentieth-Century British Women's Fiction*. Farnham. Ashgate.

Anon. 1873. 'From the Coal Districts'. Cartoon. Attrib. George Du Maurier. *Punch* 25 October. 164.

Aoyama, Tomoko. 2008. *Reading Food in Modern Japanese Literature*. Honolulu. University of Hawai'i Press.

Appelbaum, Robert. 2006. *Aguecheek's Beef, Belch's Hiccup, and Other Gastronomic Interjections: Literature, Culture, and Food Among the Early Moderns*. Chicago, IL. University of Chicago Press.

Archer, Jayne Elisabeth, Richard Marggraf Turley and Howard Thomas. 2014. *Food and the Literary Imagination*. Basingstoke. Palgrave Macmillan.

Beauman, Fran. 2005. *The Pineapple: King of Fruits*. London. Chatto and Windus.

Bruce, John, ed. 1853. *Letters and Papers of the Verney Family Down to the End of the Year 1639*. London. Camden Society.

Carruth, Allison. 2013. *Global Appetites: American Power and the Literature of Food*. Cambridge. Cambridge University Press.

Cozzi, Annette. 2010. *The Discourses of Food in Nineteenth-Century British Fiction*. Nineteenth-Century Major Lives and Letters. New York. Palgrave Macmillan.

Daniel, Carolyn. 2006. *Voracious Children: Who Eats Whom in Children's Literature*. New York and London. Routledge.

Evelyn, John. 1995. *The Diary of John Evelyn*. Ed. Guy de la Bedoyere. Woodbridge. Boydell.

Fielding, Henry. 1996. *Tom Jones*. Eds. John Bender and Simon Stern. Oxford World's Classics. Oxford. Oxford University Press.

Fitzpatrick, Joan, ed. 2010. *Renaissance Food from Rabelais to Shakespeare: Culinary Readings and Culinary Histories*. Aldershot. Ashgate.

——. 2007. *Food in Shakespeare: Early Modern Dietaries and the Plays*. Aldershot. Ashgate.

Gilbert, Sandra M. 2014. *The Culinary Imagination: From Myth to Modernity*. New York. W. W. Norton.

Glenny, Allie. 1999. *Ravenous Identity: Eating and Eating Distress in the Life and Work of Virginia Woolf*. New York. St Martin's Press.

Guest, Kristen, ed. 2001. *Eating Their Words: Cannibalism and the Boundaries of Cultural Identity*. Albany. State University of New York Press.

Gutierrez, Nancy A. 2003. *'Shall She Famish Then'? Female Food Refusal in Early Modern England*. Women and Gender in the Early Modern World. Aldershot. Ashgate.

Houston, Gail Turley. 1994. *Consuming Fictions: Gender, Class, and Hunger in Dickens's Novels*. Carbondale and Edwardsville. Southern Illinois University Press.

Hyman, Gwen. 2009. *Making a Man: Gentlemanly Appetites in the Nineteenth-Century British Novel*. Athens. Ohio University Press.

Jerome, Jerome K. 1889. *Three Men in a Boat (to Say Nothing of the Dog)*. Illustr. A. Frederics. London. J. W. Arrowsmith.

Keeling, Kara K. and Scott T. Pollard, eds. 2009. *Critical Approaches to Food in Children's Literature*. Children's Literature and Culture. New York and London. Routledge.

Kilgour, Maggie. 1990. *From Communion to Cannibalism: An Anatomy of Metaphors of Incorporation*. Princeton, NJ. Princeton University Press.

Lamb, Charles. 2005. 'A Dissertation Upon Roast Pig'. *Gusto: Essential Writings in Nineteenth-Century Gastronomy*. Ed. Denise Gigante. New York and London. Routledge. 129–34.

Ligon, Richard. 1657. *A True and Exact History of the Island of Barbados*. London. Humphrey Moseley.

Mannur, Anita. 2010. *Culinary Fictions: Food in South Asian Diasporic Culture*. Philadelphia, PA. Temple University Press.

Mazzoni, Cristina. 2005. *The Women in God's Kitchen: Cooking, Eating, and Spiritual Writing*. New York. Continuum.

Morton, Timothy, ed. 2004. *Cultures of Taste / Theories of Appetite: Eating Romanticism*. Basingstoke. Palgrave Macmillan.

Moss, Sarah. 2009. *Spilling the Beans: Eating, Cooking, Reading and Writing in British Women's Fiction, 1770–1830*. Manchester. Manchester University Press.

O'Connor, Kaori. 2013. *Pineapple: A Global History*. London. Reaktion Books.

Opie, Amelia. 2010. *Adeline Mowbray, or The Mother and Daughter; a Tale*. Ed. Anne McWhir. Peterborough. Broadview.

Roy, Parama. 2010. *Alimentary Tracts: Appetites, Aversions, and the Postcolonial*. Durham, NC and London. Duke University Press.

Shulman, Nicola. 2015. 'Frames for Borders: Review of "Painting Paradise: The Art of the Garden", the Queen's Gallery, Buckingham Palace, until October 11'. *Times Literary Supplement* Number 5858 (10 July). 7–8.

Skubal, Susanne M. 2002. *Word of Mouth: Food and Fiction after Freud*. New York. Routledge.

Smollett, Tobias. 1964. *The Adventures of Peregrine Pickle*. Ed. James L. Clifford. London. Oxford University Press.

Visser, Margaret. 2015. *The Rituals of Dinner: The Origins, Evolution, Eccentricities, and Meaning of Table Manners*. New York. Penguin.

Winterson, Jeanette. 2001. *Sexing the Cherry*. London. Vintage.

Xu, Wenying. 2008. *Eating Identities: Reading Food in Asian American Literature*. Honolulu. University of Hawai'i Press.

1

PILGRIMS AND PARTRIDGES (1350–1550)

Joan Fitzpatrick

The pilgrims and partridges in this chapter's title signify opposites: the pilgrim as a religiously motivated traveller might be expected to be a man or woman with moderate habits, whilst the partridge suggests the kind of plenty ordinarily enjoyed by the nobility. Yet the medieval literary texts here considered – William Langland's *Piers Plowman*; the anonymous *Sir Gawain and the Green Knight*; Geoffrey Chaucer's *Canterbury Tales*; and *The Book of Margery Kempe* – reveal the manner in which such simple, dichotomizing categories slip: the man and woman who proclaim their godliness do not always behave as they ought when it comes to appetite and providing sustenance to others, and whilst the nobleman often demonstrates real hospitality his behaviour too is sometimes less than straightforward. It is not clear exactly when *Piers Plowman*, *Sir Gawain and the Green Knight* or *The Canterbury Tales* were written but all are late-fourteenth-century poems, and what emerges in these texts and in *The Book of Margery Kempe* also is a concern with religious authority and social rank, with these related concepts often explored via references to food. Across the texts a number of themes occur: gluttony; hunger; hunting; feasting; the motif of the apple, and even cannibalism. The contextual material that helps us make sense of the religiously inflected food references in these texts are: the Bible, often books from the Old Testament; the Rule of St Benedict, a list of precepts probably written early in the sixth century by Benedict for those living in monastic communities (Benedict 1952); and *The Golden Legend*, a collection of hagiographies compiled around the year 1260 by Jacobus De Voraigne (2012). Other contextual material includes cookery books, amongst them *The Forme of Cury*, a collection of fourteenth-century recipes reputedly gathered by the cooks of King Richard II. Rules for ecclesiastics were provided by Benedict and other rules applied to other social groups: the aristocratic hunter was provided with a guide in Gaston De Foix's *Livre de Chasse*, translated into English as *Master of Game*, and rules dictating what it takes to be a good knight were provided by Ramon Lull's *The Book of the*

Order of Chivalry (Lull 1926). Rules regarding dietary health – specifically what one ought to eat, when one ought to eat it, and why – are the focus of the hugely influential medieval regimen or dietary *Regimen sanitatis Salerni* (*The Salernitan Rule of Health*).[1]

William Langland, *Piers Plowman* (late 1300s)

In *Piers Plowman*, William Langland's dream-vision poem, we get an insight into fourteenth-century English society, with its strict hierarchical structure and the dominance of organized religion. The poem is an attack against corruption, specifically a corrupt clergy, and represents a call for the Catholic Church to return to its true spirit of faith and charity, justice and mercy, represented by the Christ-like ploughman Piers. In the prologue to the poem, Will – the narrator who represents the Christian everyman on his journey through the world – falls asleep one May morning on the Malvern Hills and dreams of a landscape featuring a tower (heaven), a dungeon (hell) and a field full of people who include ploughmen, hermits, tradesmen, jesters, beggars, pilgrims, friars and a pardoner. After discussion of a king and the rats and mice who are controlled by a cat, Will the Dreamer returns to the field full of people that includes noblemen, citizens and serfs.[2] Also present in the field are bakers, brewsters (female brewers), butchers and other tradesmen, as well as labourers. There are cooks, whose serving-men advertise their wares by crying 'hote pies, hote! / Gode gris and gees!' (pro.225–226) [hot pies, hot! / Good pork and geese!], and taverners who advertise their wines.[3] A. V. C. Schmidt rightly observes that the field functions as an important image for Langland since most of medieval England that was inhabited was cultivated field and the rest wilderness; all human life is here and, when dealing with the physical and spiritual struggles of humankind, the field with its labourers working to produce food is a dominant and recurring image (Schmidt 1980, 311). Will's comment upon those present in the field is sometimes laudatory: the ploughmen work hard planting and sowing the fields, even if they 'wonnen that wastours with glotonye destruyeth' (pro.22) [achieve that which wasters destroy with their gluttony], and the hermits devote their lives to prayer rather than lechery. However, most of the people present are morally lacking: the jesters have foul mouths, and the pilgrims are hypocrites. There is a sense also that those who advertise their wares, especially food and drink, are to be regarded with suspicion because they are selling sustenance, something that emerges also in later chapters of this book, for example in Satan's silver-tongued seduction of Eve (Chapter 3) and the sales patter of the goblin men in 'Goblin Market' (Chapter 5). The beggars and the friar, like those who benefit from the ploughmen's hard work, are motivated by greed: beggars who are full of bread fight over ale before slothfully going to bed and rising full of ribaldry; the friars also preach for their own benefit and the pardoner is described as a glutton and a lecher, supported by the people's gold.

The sin of gluttony is repeatedly invoked as a way of signalling moral corruption in *Piers Plowman*. In Passus 1 Will the Dreamer meets Holy Church – the true church rather than the earthly institution that is full of corruption – and she advises him how men ought to live. God has provided humankind with clothing, food and drink but these gifts are often abused. Gluttony included excessive drinking as well as eating too much and Holy Church specifically warns against the former: a man ought to drink when his throat is dry but not to the extent that he is incapacitated and unable to work. She offers the biblical example of Lot who allowed his two daughters to get him drunk on wine and then committed incest with them, resulting in evil offspring (Genesis 19:30–38).[4] Holy Church emphasizes the importance of moderation: 'Mesure is medcyne' (1.35) [moderation is medicine] because the devil uses man's fleshly appetites to gain access to his soul: 'þe fende and þi flesch folweth þe to-gidere' (1.40) [the devil and the flesh follow you together]. Gluttony was a familar allegorical figure in medieval culture, often making an appearance in morality plays; in the Latin emblems of Andreas Alciatus the sin is found in the guzzling pelican that feeds upon its own parent (Houle 1972; Daly *et al.* 1985, no. 91, 96).[5] The medieval dietary *Regimen sanitatis Salerni* urges the man who would be healthy and virtuous to drink only in moderation (De Mediolano and Harington 1607, A8v).

In Passus 2 Will describes the marriage of Meed the maid to False Fickle-Tongue; she is the enemy of Holy Church, her name signalling corrupt reward or bribery. G. R. Owst claims that her origins can be traced back to a story of the daughters of the devil and, as Margaret Kim notes, she 'is often associated with an emerging market economy in the later middle ages', making the desire for the consumption of worldly goods available to more of the people (Owst 1961, 93–97; Kim 2004, 357), something that will become more apparent in later chapters, when food and other necessities become fully implicated in the commercial economy. Guile presents Meed and False Fickle-Tongue with sins as wedding gifts, some in the form of land and property, for example the earldom of envy and wrath and the lordship of lechery. Gluttony is also presented to them:

> Glotonye he gaf hem eke and grete othes togydere,
> And alday to drynke at dyuerse tauernes,
> And there to iangle and to iape and iugge here euene cristene,
> And in fastyng-dayes to frete ar ful tyme were.
> And þanne to sitten and soupen til slepe hem assaille,
> And breden as burgh-swyn and bedden hem esily
> Tyl sleuth and slepe slyken his sides;
> And þanne wanhope to awake hym so with no wille to amend,
> For he leueth be lost – þis is here last ende.
> *(2.92–100)*

> [Gluttony he gave them also and great oaths together
> And all day to drink at diverse taverns
> There to jangle and jape and judge their fellow Christians
> And on fast days to feed before the full time

And then sit and sup till sleep them assail,
And to breed like town swine and rest at their ease
Till sloth and sleep make sleek their sides;
And then Despair to awaken them so with no will to amend;
They believe themselves lost: this is their last end.]

Only one meal was allowed on fast days and it was not permitted before noon ('the full time') but gluttony will make a man drink and eat all day. As William Ian Miller indicates, gluttony was considered one of many 'vices of the mouth' that included 'lying, backbiting, blaspheming, boasting, perjury, and grumbling' (Miller 1997, 99), so gluttony and his pal 'grete othes' are well suited 'to iangle and to iape and iugge' together.

Towards the end of Passus 2, when the marriage is disrupted, Liar, one of the guests, runs off and he is sought first by 'leeches' (2.223) [doctors] inspecting urine samples and then 'Spiceres spoke with hym to spien here ware, / For he couth of here craft and knewe many gommes' (2.225–226) [Spicers spoke with him to inspect their wares, / For he knew of their craft and knew many gums]. Both are lying to their customers: the doctors giving false diagnoses and the spicers selling inferior goods they pretend are of high quality (spices were expensive and it was a myth that they were used to disguise bad food because they would not have been wasted in this manner). In Passus 3 the debate between Meed and Conscience is attended by a range of social groups, including members of the victualling trade:

Brewesteres and bakesteres, bocheres and cokes;
For þise aren men on þis molde þat moste harme worcheth
To þe pore peple þat parcel-mele buggen.
For they poysoun þe peple priueliche and oft;
Thei rychen þorw regraterye and rentes hem buggen
With þat þe pore people shulde put in here wombe
(3.79–84)

[Brewsters and bakers, butchers and cooks,
For these are the men in this world that work the most harm
To the poor people that buy piece-meal.
For they poison the people secretly and oft,
They get rich through retailing and buy themselves rents
With what the poor people should put in their bellies]

As Paul Hammond points out, adulteration of food and drink was a real problem in the medieval period (and indeed beyond, reaching an apogee in the nineteenth century, as we see in Chapter 5) and he provides numerous examples of the practice in medieval London, including bread found to have contained sand, wine with pitch added to it, and attempts to pass off spices with false colouring (Hammond 1993, 80–90). It is the job of the mayors and those who enforce the law to stop such practices but they are in league with Meed.

In Passus 5 Langland personifies Gluttony, who is on his way to church to make a confession when he is distracted by a brewster called Betty who tells him 'I haue gode ale, gossib' (5.310) ['I have good ale, gossip'], the word 'gossib' suggesting they are familiar, and perhaps specifically drinking companions, as J. A. W. Bennett suggests (Langland 1976, 72n310). Women brewers, known as brewsters or alewives, produced most of the ale consumed in medieval England; ale-brewing was mainly small scale and domestic, so women could brew ale in small batches and sell it from home (Clark 1978, 51; Bennett 1996). Brewsters had a bad reputation in the period: suspected of adulterating their ale, frequently with water but also with salt and resin, they were also often accused of selling customers a short measure (Hammond 1993, 84–87). Avarice, the sin described just before we hear of Gluttony, tells how his wife, Rose, is 'a webbe and wollen cloth made' (5.215) [a weaver who makes woollen cloth], and she also is a brewster:

> I bouȝte hir barly malte; she brew it to selle,
> Peny ale and podyng ale she poured togideres
> For laboreres and for low folke; þat lay by hymselue.
> The best ale lay in my boure or in my bedchambre,
> And who-so bummed þer-of bouȝte it þer-after,
> A galoun for a grote, god wote, no lesse;
> And ȝit it cam in cupmel; þis crafte my wyf vsed.
> *(5.219–225)*

> [I bought her barley malt; she brewed it to sell.
> Penny-ale and pudding-ale she poured together
> For labourers and for low folk; that was kept by itself.
> The best ale lay in my bower or in my bedchamber
> And whoso tasted thereof bought it thereafter
> A gallon for a groat, God knows, no less;
> And yet it came in cupfuls; this craft my wife used.]

Penny ale was cheap and so drunk by the less well off; pudding ale was ale that had been brewed for only a few hours, without allowing the dregs to settle, and was thus thick and of inferior quality (Wilson 1976, 334). Rose the brewster allows her customers to taste the best ale but then sells them the ale that is a mixture of the cheap and inferior kind. Male brewers also come under Langland's fire: in Passus 19 a brewer complains about the teachings of Conscience, specifically regarding the spirit of justice, because he wants to sell the 'dregges & draffe' [the dregs and draff] of his ale and pass off mild ale for strong (19.397–398).

When Langland's Gluttony asks Betty the brewster if she has any hot spices, she replies: 'I haue peper and piones . . . and a pounde of garlike, / A ferthyngworth of fenel-seed for fastyngdayes' (5.311–313) ['I have pepper and peony seed . . . and a pound of garlic, / A farthing worth of fennel-seed for fastings']. Seeds and spices would have been available in the alehouse to use during brewing, as J. A. W.

Bennett notes, and the suggestion that seeds would not quite count as food and so could be nibbled on a fasting day is plausible (Langland 1976, 172n311–313). It is less clear that Gluttony wants the seeds for medicinal purposes, possibly as a remedy for excess wind, as Bennett suggests, but Langland presumably would have been aware of the virtues of certain spices. The *Regimen sanitatis Salerni* emphasizes the medicinal properties of pepper, which helps treat a windy stomach, coughs, phlegm and agues, and fennel seed was credited with expelling poison, correcting agues, settling the stomach and improving the sight (De Mediolano and Harington 1607, B8v, B4v). However, it is the brewster's reference to garlic that is most interesting: she would not have kept garlic in her alehouse to flavour the ale and although she might have used it to flavour pies or pasties, alehouses tended to provide fairly basic food such as bread, cheese, spiced buns and cake (Clark 1978, 54). She does not tell Gluttony that she has pies and pasties for him to eat, only that she has 'a pounde of garlike', so why might that particular foodstuff lure him into her establishment? The *Regimen sanitatis Salerni* states the following:

> Six things that heere in order shall insue,
> Against all poysons haue a secret poure,
> *Peares, Garlick, Reddish-roots, Nuts, Rape, & Rew,*
> But *Garlicke* cheefe, for they that it deuoure,
> May drink, and care not who their drink do brew
> May walke in ayres infected euery houre:
> Sith *Garlicke* then hath poure to saue from death,
> Beare with it though it make vnsauoury breath:
> And scorne not Garlicke like to some, that think
> It onely makes men winke, and drinke, and stink.
> *(De Mediolano and Harington 1607, A8r)*

> [Six things that here in order shall ensue,
> Against all poisons have a secret power,
> Pears, garlic, radish-roots, nuts, rape and rue,
> But garlic chief, for they that it devour,
> May drink, and care not who their drink do brew
> May walk in airs infected every hour.
> Since garlic then hath power to save from death,
> Bear with it, though it make unsavoury breath:
> And scorn not garlic like to some that think
> It only makes men wink, and drink, and stink.]

Although garlic was linked with moral corruption (as we shall see in the portrait of Chaucer's Summoner), it was also considered protective against suspicious beverages, providing a clear incentive for any drinker wavering as to whether or not to enter the alehouse and drink the alewife's brew.

When he reaches the alehouse, Gluttony drinks more than a gallon of ale before urinating and farting. He is incapacitated by his drunkenness: unable to walk properly without the support of his stick, he falls to the ground before vomiting and requiring the help of others to get home to bed. Here Langland anticipates the Rabelaisian grotesque body that influenced Jonathan Swift's description of bodily functions in *Gulliver's Travels* (discussed in Chapter 3). Elena Levy-Navarro rightly points out that Langland's Gluttony is not described as fat, merely 'great', which suggests he is strong and thus able to work (to support himself both economically and literally) and contribute to society. For Langland gluttony is characterized by its social consequences and it is only in later periods, Levy-Navarro claims, that gluttony is specifically focused on the horrors of the fat body, although she underplays the fact that the fat body is often a physical manifestation of the kind of behaviour that has social consequences (Levy-Navarro 2008, 42–43). Gluttony later repents this way of life: that he has gorged himself on food, lingered over his meals, and eaten before noon on fast days. He also laments the fact that what he has eaten might have fed the hungry, vowing to fast in future. Eating too much causes Langland's Gluttony physical harm but there is no mention of any physical disease. For Langland the main focus is on the moral and social harm done by overeating: harm to the soul but also to the poor who go hungry whilst others overeat in an era when, as Schmidt indicates, 'the general level of food production was low' (Schmidt 1980, 312). In the early modern writings discussed in the next chapter the focus is on the long-lasting physical effects upon the body as well as the moral consequences of excessive eating and drinking; the right of the poor to have access to food is a concern that emerges also in later periods.

Just as Gluttony feels guilty for eating the food he does not need, and that ought to feed the hungry, so too the hunger of others is invoked to highlight the hypocrisy of the wealthy. In Passus 10 Dame Study, the Wife of Wit, describes the gluttony at dinners where theology is discussed and they 'gnawen god with þe gorge whan her gutte is fulle' (10.57) [gorge on the body of God when their gut is full], while poor people starve outside the gates like dogs. As Margaret Kim puts it, this image of rich gluttons gorging on God while the poor starve 'identifies the socially uncharitable behaviour of wealthy people as the deepest offence against the divine', with the poor figured as 'Christ-like in their suffering' (Kim 2004, 351). Moreover, some of the rich prefer 'to eten bi hym-selue / In a pryue pa[r]loure' (10.96–97) [to eat by himself / In a private parlour], no longer eating in the main hall, 'al to spare to spille' (10.100) [all to spare to spill], to save money by preparing and consuming less food, with no scraps left over. Jill Mann observes how this new practice of eating privately denied 'the social importance of food, the benefit to the community from meals in hall which can be shared by travellers or beggars' (Mann 1979, 35); commensality (communal eating, as opposed to eating alone) is a key issue and one that emerges in the literature discussed throughout this volume.

The clergy also come under fire for their failure to provide the poor with food: in Passus 5 Sloth is a priest who would rather hunt hares than serve his parishioners and who has allowed good food to go bad rather than give it to the hungry (5.443–445).[6] As Anne Rooney observes, hunting was against canon law and yet 'the more worldly members of the clergy inevitably continued to engage in the sport', the hunting priest a symbol of worldly vanity since the activity distracted him from his spiritual duties (Rooney 1993, 41, 103). As we shall see, hunting clergy are also the target of Chaucer's satire in *The Canterbury Tales*.

In Passus 9 gluttony is considered a form of idolatry because 'þat be glotouns globbares her god is her wombe' (9.60) [those that be gluttons, their god is their belly], an allusion to the biblical Epistle of Paul the Apostle to the Philippians: 'they are the enemies of the cross of Christ: / Whose end is destruction, whose God is their belly, and whose glory is in their shame, who mind earthly things' (3:18–19). The Church is not fulfilling its duty: 'Shulde no crystene creature crien atte ȝate, / Ne faille payn ne potage, and prelates did as þei shulden' (9.79–80) [If prelates did as they ought then no Christian who cried at the gate (for alms) would go without pottage]. The corrupt and gluttonous clergy are compared to the self-denying saints:

> In *legenda sanctorum*, þe lyf of holy seyntes,
> What penaunce and pouerte and passioun þei suffred,
> In hunger, in hete, in al manere angres.
>
> *(15.264–266)*

> [In *The Golden Legend*, the life of holy saints,
> What penance and poverty and passion they suffered,
> In hunger, in heat, in all manner distress.]

Langland provides detail of the diet of some of the saints from *The Golden Legend*: Paul the Hermit who was fed by the birds of the air (De Voraigne 2012, chp. 15); Saint Giles who drank the milk of a female deer, and only rarely (chp. 130); the apostles Andrew and Paul who fished for food (chp. 2 and 28); Mary Magdalene (chp. 96) who 'by mores lyued and dewes' (15.289) [lived on roots and dew] but 'moste þorw deuocioun and mynde of god almiȝty' (15.290) [but mostly through devotion to and thinking on God almighty]. Those living the religious life who do not follow the example of the early saints are admonished:

> For had ȝe potage and payn ynough and peny-ale to drynke,
> And a messe þere-mydde of o manere kynde,
> Ȝe had riȝt ynough, ȝe Religious and so ȝowre reule me tolde.
>
> *(15.310–312)*

> [For had you pottage and bread enough, and penny-ale to drink,
> And a meal of only one kind,
> This would be enough for you religious men, and so your rule told me.]

The religious Rule of Saint Benedict dictated how much and what kind of food and drink ought to be consumed and when by monastic religious orders. The rule stipulated that a small number of dishes be present on each table (usually no more than three, one of which should be vegetables), insisting that 'Above all things, however, over-indulgence must be avoided' since 'there is nothing so opposed to the Christian character as over-indulgence' (Benedict 1952, chp. 39). Animal flesh was not usually allowed: 'Except the sick who are very weak, let all abstain entirely from eating the flesh of four-footed animals' (Benedict 1952, chp. 39). Pottage could contain meat, the expensive new cereal rice and spices but often contained mainly cheap grains and vegetables and the less well off might make a pottage based on oatmeal or barley (Wilson 1976, 182–190; Dyer 1998, 56–57). Perhaps unsurprisingly the recipes for pottages in medieval cookbooks (bought and used by the better off) tend to be fairly indulgent and contain expensive ingredients; even if they are vegetable-based, they will contain spices such as saffron (Anon. 1888, 8 xv, 10 xxiij, 11 xxvij, 16 lj, 33 cxlix; Anon. 1780, 12 iiii, v, 115 viii).[7] 'Penny ale' would have been low in alcohol and cheap; moreover, Benedict's Rule states that 'wine is by no means a drink for monastics', although it was allowed in moderation: 'let us at least agree to drink sparingly and not to satiety' (Benedict 1952, chp. 40).

In Passus 6 Piers the Ploughman tells the people he will provide food for them by ploughing his half-acre field, but they too are obliged to work: 'And alle manere of men þat þorw mete and drynke lybbeth / Helpith hym to worche wiȝtliche þat wynneth ȝowre fode' (6.20–21) [And all manner of men that by meat and drink live, / Help you them to work well that win you your food]. The knight offers to plough also but Piers tells him rather to protect Holy Church and himself from wasters, to hunt the animals that destroy his hedges and crops. Ramon Lull identifies hunting as one of the offices that pertain to a knight: 'Kniȝtes ouȝt to take coursers to juste & to go to tornoyes . . . to hūte at herts / at bores & other wyld bestes' [Knights ought to take coursers to joust and to go to tourneys . . . to hunt at harts / at boars and other wild beasts], just as it is the responsibility of the common people to 'laboure & cultyue the erthe' [labour and cultivate the land] (Lull 1926, 31, 32).

Piers and his fellow pilgrims set to ploughing the land but some are more interested in sitting around and singing over their ale. When Piers admonishes them, telling them they won't get any food if they do not work, they pretend to be disabled. He tells them that if they don't learn from Truth, then they will have to be content with the most basic sustenance: 'barly bred and of þe broke drynke' (6.137) [barley bread and water from the brook], since only the genuinely disabled, anchorites and hermits will get alms. When a waster and a Breton, who is a braggart, resist Piers, also ignoring the knight, Piers asks Hunger to take action and 'He bette hem so bothe he barste nere here guttes' (6.180) [He beat them so both that he near burst their guts] until Piers intervenes:

> Ne hadde Pieres with a pese-lof preyed Hunger to cesse,
> They hadde ben doluen bothe, ne deme þow non other.
> 'Suffre hem lyue,' he seyde, 'and lete hem ete with hogges,
> Or elles benes and bren ybaken togideres,
> Or elles melke and mene ale' þus preyed Pieres for hem.
>
> *(6.181–185)*

[Had not Piers with a pease-loaf prayed Hunger to cease,
They had been buried both, believe thou none other.
'Suffer them to live,' he said, 'and let them eat with the hogs,
Or else beans and bran baked up together,
Or else milk and mean ale': thus prayed Piers for them.]

Beans and bran were usually fed to animals, whilst bread made with beans would have been eaten by the poor in times of dearth and would not have tasted good (Wilson 1976, 220). Piers makes 'a potful of peses' (6.189) [a pot full of peas], presumably pease pottage, which keeps hunger at bay amongst the poor; those feigning disability are now willing to work for horses' food and the beggars for beans. Hunger advises Piers on how to avoid excess, that he should not drink before he has eaten nor sit too long over his food, advice consistent with the *Regimen sanitatis Salerni*: 'Drinke not much wine, sup light, and soone arise' (De Mediolano and Harington 1607, A6r). Hunger is also critical of rich doctors who benefit from people's lack of temperance (6.270–276), recalling the *Regimen's* advice that the best physicians are Doctor Quiet, Doctor Merryman and Doctor Diet (De Mediolano and Harington 1607, A6r).

Before he departs, Hunger asks Piers for a meal and Piers lists the basic foods he has:

'I haue no peny,' quod Peres 'poletes forto bigge,
Ne neyther gees ne grys, but two grene cheses,
A few cruddes and creem and an hauer cake,
And two loues of benes and bran ybake for my fauntis.
And ȝet I sey, by my soule, I haue no salt bacoun,
Ne no kokeney, bi cryst, coloppes forto maken.
Ac I haue percil and porettes and many kole-plantes
(6.282–288)

['I have no penny,' quoth Piers 'pullets for to buy,
Nor neither geese nor pigs but two green cheeses,
A few curds and cream and an oaten cake,
And two loaves of beans and bran baked for my children.
And yet I say, by my soul, I have no salt bacon;
Nor no hen's eggs, by Christ, collops for to make
But I have parsley and leeks with many cabbages]

That cheese was a common food amongst the less well-off is clear from the *Regimen sanitatis Salerni*: 'The poorer sort when other meat is scant, / For hunger eate it to releeue their want' (De Mediolano and Harington 1607, B2v); green cheese was unripe, the sense being that Piers cannot afford to keep his cheeses until they are mature (Langland 1976, 211n283). A collop was an egg fried on bacon, although it could refer to the bacon itself, which was a common meat for labourers because considered difficult to digest, but clearly, even though bacon was relatively cheap, Piers cannot afford any meat at all. He describes the usual diet of the poor: dairy produce, oats, cheap bread, herbs and vegetables. The people also bring Hunger some food – peascods, beans and baked apples, onions, chervil and ripe cherries – and they are so fearful of Hunger they try to poison him with green leeks and pease, presumably a reference to the belief that raw vegetables were especially harmful to health.

At harvest time the people feed Hunger with corn and put him to sleep with ale, 'as glotoun tauȝte' (6.303) [as Gluttony taught]. However, without fear of hunger the people become indolent again, refusing to eat simple foods – bread made with beans, cheap ale, old worts, a piece of bacon – and insisting upon receiving the best bread made from wheat, the finest ale, fresh flesh and fish that has been fried or baked (6.305–313). The consequence of this is that Hunger will return with a vengeance:

> Ar fyue ȝere be fulfilled suche famyn shal aryse,
> Thorwgh flodes and þourgh foul wederes frutes shul faille . . .
> Þanne shal deth withdrawe and derthe be iustice
> And dawe þe dyker deye for hunger
>
> *(6.325–326, 330–331)*

> [Ere five years be fulfilled such famine shall arise;
> Through floods and foul weather all fruits shall fail . . .
> Then shall Death withdraw him and Dearth be the judge,
> And Davy the ditcher shall die of hunger]

As Jill Mann observes, this society's human members 'depend on the power of hunger to drive them to work' and to that extent hunger is beneficial, yet although Hunger has a suitably moral effect, he 'cannot be summoned and dismissed as morally appropriate' (Mann 1979, 29). Langland's description of the constant threat of hunger is an accurate portrayal of the reality of life for many people in medieval England. Christopher Dyer argues that although the extent of starvation amongst the poor in the early modern period has been overstated (something that will be discussed further in Chapter 2), large numbers of English peasants did actually starve to death in the period *c.* 1290–1325 and periodically prior to 1375, when things generally improved as food became cheaper and more plentiful (Dyer 1998).

In Passus 13 Will is invited to a dinner by Conscience that is also attended by Clergy, Patience and a friar, a Doctor of Divinity, accompanied by his man. Will and his companions are served metaphorical dishes consisting of scripture and writings from the saints, whilst the Doctor and his man dine on literal food: 'mete of more cost mortrewes and potages' (13.41) [meat of more cost, mortrews and pottages], a mortrew being a thick soup usually made with fish or meat (Anon. 1888, 14 xliij, xliiij, 28 cxx; Anon. 1780, 28, 60). It is clear which food is most beneficial to humanity in the description of the sauce served to the Doctor and his man:

> her sauce was ouer sour & vnsauourely grounde
> In a morter, *post-mortem* of many bitter peyne,
> But if þei synge for þo soules and wepe salte teres
> *(13.43–45)*

> [Their sauce was over-sour and unsavourly ground
> In a mortar, after death, of many bitter pain,
> Unless they sing for those souls and weep salt tears]

The foods they enjoy satisfy a mortal appetite but this is not sufficient because if they do not pray and repent they will suffer in the next life. Will and Patience feed upon spiritual concepts – penance, perseverance, forgiveness and mercy – whilst the Doctor (in a clear violation of the Benedictine Rule) continues to gorge on lots of dishes: 'many sondry metes mortrewes and puddynges, / Wombe-cloutes and wylde braune & egges yfrved with grece' (13.62–63) [many sundry meats, mortrews and puddings / Tripes, and wild brawn, and eggs fried with grease]. Patience confirms that the Doctor preaches the virtues of hardship and hunger but is a hypocrite. As Anne Savage notes, allegorical food, the verbal truth of scripture, provides nourishment: 'the words are as simply life-giving as food', but the Doctor 'starves the illiterate poor by being unable to feed them with any of the truth of scripture to which he has access through his learning' and, of course, his behaviour serves to 'deprive others of real food as well as scriptural truth' (Savage 2008, 216–217). The people need both: spiritual sustenance is necessary but scripture alone isn't enough to fuel actual manual labour such as Piers's ploughing.

The Doctor asserts that some of the foods he eats – bacon, brawn, blancmanger, mortrews – are neither fish nor flesh, but food for a penitent, perhaps because the foods are processed or combined in a particular way.[8] Yet all the food consumed by the Doctor would have been considered indulgent and features in contemporary recipe books: puddings (dishes made from animal entrails or the neck), one using capon's neck and another porpoise guts (Anon. 1888, 41 xxxiiij, 42 xl); tripes made from mutton and fish (Anon. 1888, 7 ix, 18 lx); dishes made from brawn, which here means boar's flesh (Anon. 1888, 71); and blancmangers made from poultry and fish (Anon. 1888, 21 lxxxij, 23 lxxxxviij; Anon. 1780, 25 xxxvi). Eggs were often poached and so fried eggs would seem especially indulgent; certainly in the early modern period fried eggs were considered particularly unwholesome (Wilson 1976, 132). When Will challenges the Doctor on his hypocrisy and gluttony – typical characteristics of the clergy in the literature considered in this volume – a theological argument on how best to Do-well is concluded with Patience's advice that confirms the view of Piers Plowman: love – of one's own soul, God and one's enemy – is how to Do-well, Do-better and Do-best, a view the Doctor rejects outright. As Schmidt notes, for Langland gluttony was a huge social evil and through the Doctor 'he skillfully links literal gluttony with intellectual pride and cynical indifference', thus suggesting how these vices are all connected (Schmidt 1980, 312).

Conscience and Patience, like two pilgrims, leave with metaphorical provisions in their bag: 'Sobrete, and symple speche and sothfaste byleue' (13.217) [Sobriety and simple speech and truthful belief] in case they enter the hungry countries of unkindness and covetousness. Shortly after dinner, Will encounters Haukyn, a seller of wafers that represent the Holy sacrament. Haukyn's coat is stained with sin and, as Schmidt observes, both Haukyn and the Doctor 'play an important part in . . . [Will's] journey towards self-understanding, for they both contain elements of himself' (Schmidt 1980, 316). Yet unlike the Doctor at Conscience's diner, Haukyn shows remorse at the end of Passus 14 and thus 'represents an advance towards doing well from which Will can benefit', unlike the complacent Doctor whom Will 'must leave decisively behind, a negative example only' (Schmidt 1980, 316–317). Crucially, in the wafers 'made by Haukyn from the bread grown by Piers lies the one efficacious food for individual and society alike' (Schmidt 1980, 323).

The apple is a recurrent motif in Langland's poem. It is first mentioned in Passus 5 when Piers offers to show the way to the shrine of a saint called Truth, with directions given through a metaphorical landscape.[9] As James Snyder points out, the forbidden fruit was traditionally identified as an apple in the Latin West and this is the fruit 'in the vast majority of medieval and Renaissance representations of the Fall' (Snyder 1976, 511). Later, in Passus 12, Imagination complains about the kind of questions Will and other ignorant men ask the learned, questions such as: 'Why Adam ne hiled nouȝht firste his mouth þat eet þe apple, / Rather þan his lykam a-low?' (12.233) [Why didn't Adam first cover his mouth that ate the apple / Rather than his genitals?], responding that only God knows why. In Passus 16 Will meets Piers, who is responsible for tending the tree of Charity in a garden created by God. The devil does all he can to destroy the tree's fruit with sin but he is sometimes prevented by Piers's lieutenant Free Choice, who guards the tree with the help of the Holy Spirit. Piers describes the fruit in terms of marriage, virginity and widowhood, and when he tries to pick an apple for Will to taste, the fruit begins to cry out. The reason for this becomes clear when the fruit drops to the ground and the devil carries it off to Limbo: the fruit is described as Adam, Abraham, the prophet Isaiah and other just men who died before Christ could redeem them. There follows the story of the conception and birth of Christ who will save the world from sin and death, introduced to the world by the devil's deceit, which caused Adam to eat the apple. Christ's redemption and the devil's nihilism is figured by Christ in dietary terms:

> þe bitternesse þat þow hast browe brouke it þi-seluen,
> þat art doctour of deth, drynke þat þow madest!
> For I þat am lorde of lyf, loue is my drynke,
> And for þat drynke to-day, I deyde vpon erthe.
>
> *(18.361–364)*

[The bitterness that thou has brewed, now drink thyself;
That art doctor of death, drink that thou madest!
For I that am lord of life, love is my drink,
And for that drink today, I died upon earth.]

Moments later Christ declares that he still thirsts 'for mannes soule sake' (18.386), so that, as C. David Benson puts it, 'instead of mortals partaking of God's body and blood administered by the Church, human redemption is described as Christ's physical appetite for us' (Benson 2004, 152). Grace gives Piers the cardinal virtues in the form of seeds to plant, the poem ending as it begins, as Schmidt notes, in a field (Schmidt 1980, 311). The seed of temperance causes those who eat it to show moderation in all things, including the consumption of food and drink: 'Shulde neuere mete ne mochel drynke make hym to swelle . . . Ne no mete in his mouth þat maister Iohan spiced' (19.278, 283) [Should never meat or much drink make him swell . . . Nor no food come into his mouth that Master John has spiced].

The poem draws to its conclusion with Will dreaming that Antichrist tears up the crop of Truth, sowing instead the seeds of deception (20.52–56). In the face of old age and death, Nature tells Will that if he learns to love, he will never be short of food or anything else (20.198–210). The people have lost all fear of sinning and need Piers Plowman to return 'þat pryde may destruye' (20.380) [that pride may be defeated]. Conscience announces that he will search for Piers and it is at this point that Will the Dreamer awakes. On the one hand, the poem's message is a conservative one: work hard and you will eat, but its attacks upon gluttony and religious hypocrisy also carry a subversive message about the abuse of those in power. The radicalism of Langland's message was recognized by the Lollard priest John Ball, one of the leaders of the Peasants' Revolt of 1381, who invoked *Piers Plowman* in letters used to rally his fellow conspirators (Barr 1994, 10–13). Alongside its criticism of the undeserving poor, there is a real sense here that the undeserving rich are also part of the problem when it comes to adequate provision and moderate consumption of food and drink.

Anon., *Sir Gawain and the Green Knight* (late 1300s)

In the anonymous Arthurian chivalric romance *Sir Gawain and the Green Knight*, the focus shifts from gluttony and hunger to feasting and hunting. This is not to argue that feasting in the poem is unproblematic but that any negative connotations are more nuanced and subtle than in *Piers Plowman*. The absence of hunger is typical of medieval literature dealing with aristocratic subjects, and whilst hunting was unacceptable amongst the clergy, as is clear from Langland's poem, a hunting nobility is here broadly celebrated, although there are moments when a critique of its cruelty is arguably apparent.

Commensality (a common theme throughout this volume) is an important aspect of *Sir Gawain and the Green Knight*, which begins at Christmas time, with Arthur holding celebrations at Camelot; all his knights are present and there are joustings, dancing and plenty of food to enjoy. Arthur is seated at high table, ready to feast (those at high table are given double helpings); the ceremonial washing traditional before meals has taken place and, as befitting his courtesy, Arthur will not eat until everyone else has been served. He further delays feasting until he has been told of some strange tale, or marvellous adventure, a common opening to Arthurian stories (Anon. 1998, 92n6). The food served is briefly described: dainties, an abundance of the freshest, most expensive and delicious foods, with each pair of diners having twelve dishes between them as well as good beer and wine. It is at this point that the Green Knight comes into the hall. That he enters on horseback is significant: it would have been considered hostile or discourteous to ride one's horse into a dining hall where feasting is taking place but it might also indicate an entertainment or interlude between courses that was common during medieval banquets (Anon. 1998, 92–93n7). It is Gawain who responds to the Green Knight's challenge: that the strange knight receive a blow on his bare neck, without flinching, from the axe he carries by one of those present, providing he is allowed to return the blow in a year's time. After the Green Knight is beheaded and leaves, Arthur reassures Guinevere that the episode was indeed but an interlude and suggests that it was simply a trick (Anon. 1978, 225n472f). They proceed with their meal, Arthur and Gawain enjoying double helpings of the daintiest food, with all kinds of food served and entertainment provided by the minstrels present.

Feasting also forms a central part of life at the court of Sir Bertilak de Hautdesert, who will later reveal himself to be the Green Knight. When Gawain arrives at Bertilak's castle, he is treated hospitably: welcoming a stranger (and that is apparently what Gawain is at this point in the narrative) to one's house was considered Christian and courteous, indeed an essential part of courteous, knightly behaviour, as outlined by Ramon Lull in *The Book of the Order of Chivalry* when he states that one of the offices that pertain to a knight is to 'holde open table' (Lull 1926, 31). Sir Bertilak's servants bring Gawain to a sumptuous room, dress him in fine clothes, and a meal is prepared. They set up a trestle-table and lay a white cloth upon it, providing him also with a napkin, a salt cellar and silver spoons, all indicating that this is fine dining. After ceremonial washing, an important part of the dining ritual in high status households (Hammond 1993, 115–116), and which we are told took place in Arthur's court also, Gawain eats the food laid before him:

> . . . sere sewes and sete, sesounde of þe best,
> Doublefelde, as hit fallez, and fele kyn fischez –
> Summe baken in bred, summe brad on þe gledez,
> Summ soþen, summe in sewe sauered with spyces –
> And ay sawses so sleʒe þat þe segge lyked.
>
> *(889–893)*

[. . . various stews and fitting, seasoned of the best,
In double helpings, as it befits, and various kinds of fishes
Some baked in bread, some grilled on the red-hot embers
Some boiled, some in stews flavoured with spices
And all served with subtle sauces that he liked.][10]

Seasoning and sauces feature heavily in recipe books aimed at the wealthy, as do various ways of preparing and cooking fish (Anon. 1888, 77, 98–106; Anon. 1780, 52–57); contrary to popular belief, English food in this period was often highly spiced and flavoursome.

Gawain repeatedly praises the meal with which he is presented as a 'fest' [feast], although his companions call it a 'penaunce' [penance], Christmas Eve being a day of abstinence when meat was not allowed, and they promise to make amends, to serve him better food later, that is, on Christmas day (Anon. 1978, 241n897f). Of course this meal has not been sparse, despite having no meat, and wine is plentiful; indeed Gawain feels inebriated with the wine he has consumed (900). Later the ladies will call for more wine and spices (977–980), which were often served together at the end of banquets for medicinal reasons since spices were thought to warm the stomach and so help the digestion process, as C. Anne Wilson observes (Wilson 1991, 11). On Christmas day, as promised, lots more food is served: 'þurȝ dayntés mony: / Boþe at mes and at mele messes ful quaynt' (998–999) [throughout, many delicacies / Both at light meals and skilfully prepared dinners] but no further detail of the kind of food is provided. As at Arthur's court, there is a pattern of fasting (going without meat) and then feasting, although in Arthur's court the feast, interrupted by the Green Knight, is followed by a period of fasting during Lent – 'Þat fraystez flesch wyth þe fysche and fod more symple' (503) [which tests the body with fish and simple food] – before the feast on All Hallows' Day that precedes Gawain's departure. As in Arthur's court, Gawain sits in the seat of honour: just as he sat next to Guinevere at high table, here he is seated beside Sir Bertilak's lady 'Euen inmyddez' (1004) [right in the centre], where the food is served first.

During Gawain's journey to meet the Green Knight he faces many perils: he travels with only his horse for companionship through desolate parts of Wales and the wilderness of the Wirral, known in the fourteenth century as a refuge for outlaws (Anon. 1978, 234n701f). Here he encounters hostile creatures:

Sumwhyle wyth wormez he werrez and with wolues als,
Sumwhyle wyth wodwos þat woned in þe knarrez,
Boþe wyth bullez and berez, and borez oþerquyle.
And etaynez þat hym anelede of þe heȝe felle.

(720–723)

[Sometimes with dragons he fights and with wolves also,
Sometimes with wild wood-men, that lived in the crags
Both with bulls and bears, and sometimes boars
And giants that him pursued over the high fells.]

The winter weather is also hostile, with freezing rain, sleet and intense cold, so that 'Nade he ben duȝty and dryȝe and Dryȝtyn had serued, / Douteles he hade ben ded and dreped ful ofte' (724–725) [Had he not been brave and long-suffering, not served God, / Doubtless there were many times when he would have been killed]. Hunger is apparently not a feature of Gawain's suffering, and there is only a brief reference to food on his travels: 'Þer he fonde noȝt hym byfore þe fare þat he lyked' (694) [There he did not find before him the food that he liked]. The phrasing is ambiguous: does he find no food, or only basic food that he dislikes, and if he does find food that he dislikes, does he eat it anyway? As Susan E. Farrier points out, in medieval literature 'most fictional aristocrats simply do not experience hunger pangs' and although Gawain is given a fur cloak to warm him when he arrives at Bertilak's castle (which underlines how he has suffered from the cold weather), in romance 'hunger is in a different category from other physical ills', which Farrier suggests is partly due to 'its association with the lower classes' (Farrier 1995, 145–146).

Hunting was most definitely not associated with the lower classes since it was an aristocratic pursuit, and considered by Ramon Lull to be the proper office of a knight, as noted above in the discussion of *Piers Plowman* (Lull 1926, 31). Sir Bertilak goes hunting on three occasions: first hunting the deer, then the boar, then the fox. Bertilak and Gawain strike a bargain: 'Quatsowuer I wynne in þe wod hit worþez / And quat check so ȝe acheue chaunge me þerforne' (1106–1107) [Whatever I win in the wood becomes yours / And you give me in exchange whatever you achieve]. Gawain will give what he achieves or wins, as Jill Mann points out, the notion of exchange raising questions regarding commercial exchange and the relative price and value of what is earned and given (Mann 1986). Again, as we saw in Langland's poem and will see throughout this volume, the notion of exchange, specifically commercialism, taints simpler concepts such as providing sustenance and hospitality. On the morning of the hunt Bertilak 'Ete a sop hastyly, when he hade herde masse' (1135) [Ate a sop quickly, when he had heard mass]; a sop could be a piece of bread soaked in water or wine or a more extravagant dish, as enjoyed by Chaucer's Franklin and discussed below.

The hunting of the deer is described in detail and interspersed with the bedroom scenes of the lady's attempted seduction of Gawain, which is itself a kind of courtly hunt, as critics have noted (Rooney 1993, 159–165). After the attempted seduction, Gawain, like Bertilak, also has a meal after mass (1311–1312). The animals are described sympathetically, trembling (they 'quaked') at the sound of the hounds (1150); as Rooney observes, the repulsion felt by a modern reader may not have been shared by earlier readers yet the description provokes ambivalence about the hunt whereby we recognize both the savagery and joy involved (Rooney 1993, 169).[11] The poet also provides a detailed description of the cutting-up of one of the dead animals for food (what was termed the 'breaking' or 'undoing' or 'unlacing' of the prey), which is in keeping with the instructions laid out in medieval hunting manuals such as *Master of Game* (De Foix and Edward of Norwich 1909), and at this point the poem itself becomes a kind of hunting manual, celebrating the masculine skill of preparing the kill for consumption. The animal is then distributed as food, with each huntsman receiving a portion of meat, and their dogs being fed:

> Vpon a felle of þe fayre best fede þay þayr houndes
> Wyth þe lyure and þe ly3tez, þe leþer of þe paunchchez,
> And bred baþed in blod blende þeramongez.
>
> *(1359–1361)*

> [Upon a skin of the fair beasts they fed their hounds
> With the liver and the lungs, the lining of the stomachs,
> And bread bathed in blood that mingled with it.]

Feeding the dogs the offal of the animal on the skin of the dead beast is again as described in *Master of Game* and other hunting manuals (De Foix and Edward of Norwich 1909, 196). When Bertilak returns to his castle, he ceremoniously presents Gawain with the venison he has won that day and Gawain in turn gives Bertilak what he has received: a kiss from Bertilak's lady. The men then go to supper, eating 'dayntés nwe innowe' (1401) [delicacies new enough], although no mention is made of feasting on the venison caught that day, as might be expected. After their supper they sit before the fire drinking wine and agree to play their game again the following day, whilst, amid much mirth, more drinks are served: 'Þe beuerage watz bro3t forth in bourde at þat tyme' (1409) [The beverages were brought forth amidst jest at that time]; notably, in Middle English the word 'beverage' could mean not simply the drink used to seal a bargain but the bargain itself (Anon. 1978, 249n1112).[12]

The next day Bertilak repeats the ritual of hearing a mass, quickly eating and setting off to hunt, this time the boar. Again the hunting is described in detail, in line with hunting manuals of the time, and again the unlacing of the boar is described in detail, although the boar is described with less sympathy by the poet than the deer, with a greater focus on the animal's aggression, which corresponds to the nature of the boar as described in chapter 6 of *Master of Game* (De Foix and Edward of Norwich 1909, 46–53). The dogs are again fed in the same manner but this time the animal's entrails have been cooked since boar meat tastes better cooked and would help warm the hounds after a winter chase (Rooney 1993, 175). Upon his return home Bertilak presents the boar's head and flesh to Gawain – an apparent allusion to the beheading scene at the outset of the poem – and Gawain presents Bertilak with the two kisses he has received from his wife. The tables are set up on trestles and white cloths laid on top and again they feast and drink, although as before there is no specific mention of feasting on the day's kill. Next day – again after mass and a quick bite – Bertilak hunts the fox, the animal being described with some sympathy, with reference to the 'wo' (1717) [woe (fear)] the animal experiences, not mentioned in *Master of Game*, which focuses on the fox's cunning (De Foix and Edward of Norwich 1909, 64–67). When he returns from hunting Bertilak presents Gawain with the animal's pelt, receiving in return the three kisses

Gawain got from Bertilak's wife but with no mention made of the girdle Gawain also accepted. Again they feast and are entertained, although the description of the evening's events is somewhat briefer than before.

Hunting is praised in *Master of Game* for benefiting the body and the soul: it makes a man 'more just and more understanding, and more alert and more at ease and more undertaking, and better knowing of all countries and all passages', and being active keeps a man from being attracted to sin (De Foix and Edward of Norwich 1909, 4–5). The danger of inactivity is described:

> When a man is idle and reckless without work, and be not occupied in doing some thing, he abides in his bed or in his chamber, a thing which draweth men to imaginations of fleshly lust and pleasure. For such men have no wish but always to abide in one place, and think in pride, or in avarice, or in wrath, or in sloth, or in gluttony, or in lechery, or in envy. For the imagination of men rather turns to evil than to good, for the three enemies which mankind hath, are the devil, the world and the flesh, and this is proved enough.
>
> *De Foix and Edward of Norwich 1909, 5*

The hunter is described as better than other men:

> I say that hunters go into Paradise when they die, and live in this world more joyfully than any other men. Yet I will prove to you how hunters live longer than any other men, for as Hippocras the doctor telleth: 'full repletion of meat slayeth more men than any sword or knife.' They eat and drink less than any other men of this world, for in the morning at the assembly they eat a little, and if they eat well at supper, they will by the morning have corrected their nature, for then they have eaten but little, and their nature will not be prevented from doing her digestion, whereby no wicked humours or superfluities may be engendered.
>
> *De Foix and Edward of Norwich 1909, 11*

Moreover, the hunter sweats through physical exertion, which also causes the body to rid itself of any evil humours or superfluities, and so the author concludes that 'since hunters eat little and sweat always, they should live long and in health' (De Foix and Edward of Norwich 1909, 12). This is in keeping with the advice in the *Regimen sanitatis Salerni*: 'To shew you how to shun raw running Rhuemes / Exceed not much in meate, in drinke, and sleepe', which also recommends exercise 'that Vapours ill consumes' (De Mediolano and Harington 1607, C1v).

Gawain stays in his chamber while Bertilak goes to hunt and he is in bed each time the lady enters in an attempt to seduce him. Whilst Bertilak has a quick bite to eat after mass, Gawain apparently has a more leisurely breakfast: on the first morning 'he meued to his mete þat menskly hym keped, / And made myry al day til þe mone rysed, / With game' (1312–1314) [He went to eat his food that courteously awaited him / And made merry all day until the moon rose / With pleasure]. On the second morning, after hearing mass, Gawain's breakfast 'watz dyȝt and derely serued. / þe lede with þe ladyez layked alle day' (1559) [was prepared and courteously served. The knight with the ladies played all day], and on the third morning he speaks with the priest, makes his confession and receives absolution, again spending the day being merry among the ladies. There is no mention of Gawain's breakfast on the third morning or on the final morning of his stay with Bertilak, but on the first two mornings he has indulged his appetite and exposed himself to the dangers of lust. Gawain manages to resist the lady's advances, although by accepting her girdle and not revealing that he did so to Bertilak he has not been honest and thus breaks the code of hospitality by not honouring his obligations to his host. Gawain accepts the girdle because he thinks it will protect him in his battle with the Green Knight but instead it becomes a symbol of his shame.

When Gawain realizes he has been tricked by Bertilak, his wife and the sorcery of Morgan le Fay, he compares himself to male biblical figures who allegedly suffered at the hands of women: Adam (with Eve), Solomon (with his many wives), Samson (with Delilah) and David (with Bathsheba). During his travels in the wilderness, and just before spotting Bertilak's castle, Gawain prayed to the Virgin Mary (753–762) but after he has been tricked he seeks to blame women, forgetting his former reliance on female intercession. As Karen Cherewatuk observes, 'in equating himself with Adam, Gawain ignores the Virgin's reversal of the sin of Eve . . . and in comparing himself to David (in an interesting treatment of the victim Bathsheba as seducer), Gawain forgets the offspring that rises from the tree of Jesse through David – that is, the family of the Virgin Mary who produces the Christ' (Cherewatuk 2009, 19). According to Catherine S. Cox, 'Gawain aligns himself not with the biblical Adam per se, but with the texts and traditions that create and sustain "Adam" as a figure of the good man seduced' (Cox 2001, 379). Gawain 'has succumbed not to sexual temptation but to the fear of losing his life' and feeling shame for his cowardice, 'which is culturally marked as feminine', he now wants 'to reclaim his place in the masculine, homosocial world of Arthurian knightly codes' (Cox 2001, 381), which is partly achieved by identifying with Adam and the other men named, even if 'none of the catalogued men is actually seduced or deceived' (Cox 2001, 389n17). Gawain has not been honest with Bertilak and here he is not entirely honest with himself.

The common medieval comparison between the Virgin Mary and Eve is invoked when Gawain first meets Bertilak's lady and she is favourably compared to the old woman accompanying her (whom we later learn is the evil Morgan le Fay); as Cox notes, the description of the two women – one glowing pink in hue and the other rough and wrinkled – utilizes 'images of color and texture that call to mind fruit in general and apples in particular' (Cox 2001, 380). Later it will become clear that Bertilak's lady is not all that she appears to be and Gawain takes the girdle from her just as Adam took the apple from Eve. Of course the apple as symbol may be alluded to before Gawain ever meets Bertilak's lady, when he travels through the wilderness to reach Bertilak's castle. We are told then that in his battle with the 'wormez' (720) Gawain would have failed, had he not been brave and served God. The medieval word 'wormez' could signify dragons, worms or snakes (Anon. 1978, 361, 'worme'), which brings to mind Satan in the Garden of Eden. Gawain's successful battle with the 'wormez', where he firmly put his trust in God, serves as comparison to the later trials he will endure when, instead of putting his trust in the Holy Virgin, he trusts the girdle and is thus doomed to fail.

Geoffrey Chaucer, *The Canterbury Tales* (late 1300s)

Chaucer's *Canterbury Tales* begins at the Tabard Inn in Southwark, with the pilgrims present all making their way to Canterbury to visit the shrine of Saint Thomas à Becket. The story-telling competition is proposed by the Host of the Tabard Inn, whom we learn in the 'Prologue to the Cook's Tale' is called Harry Bailey (4358). The winner of the competition, he or she who is judged by Harry to have told the best tale, will be treated to supper at the expense of the others. So food is the object of the tales from the outset, providing the impetus for the stories told and the incentive to outdo other pilgrims with a suitably engaging narrative (recalling the link between narrative and food in *Sir Gawain and the Green Knight* when Arthur wants to hear a story before the feast can begin). Food also permeates the tales told by the pilgrims, indicating medieval attitudes to feasting, hospitality, gluttony, moderation, abstinence and hunting. The apple as a symbol of sin is evident here, as in *Piers Plowman*, but Chaucer elaborates upon the usual associations between fruit and sin in a rather ingenious and entertaining manner.

In 'The General Prologue' the portraits of the pilgrims often make reference to food and feeding as a way of suggesting something about their moral character. For example, we are told that the knight often 'hadde the bord bigonne' [had sat at the table in the place of honour] and that his Squire 'carf biforn his fader at the table' [carved before his father at the table] (52, 100).[13] The Prioress has exquisite manners when dining: allowing no morsel of food to fall from her lips, not putting her fingers into the sauce, and wiping her lips so there is no trace of grease upon them, behaviour more reminiscent of a fine lady than a nun. She loves her little dogs and feeds them roasted flesh, or milk, or 'wastel-breed' (147), that is, fine and expensive white bread, a parody of the alms-giving expected from those governed by the Rule of Saint Benedict according to John M. Steadman (1956, 5); the flesh she feeds her dogs also constitutes a violation of the rule that meat should not be eaten except by the sick, unless it is poultry, which was not explicitly banned (Steadman 1956, 2). The Monk enjoys hunting hare, which was against canon law (Rooney 1993, 39–42), and he does not follow the Rule of Saint Benedict or Saint Maurus (his follower in France): 'He yaf nat of that text a pulled hen' (177) [He gave not a plucked hen for that text]; similarly, another (unnamed) text – claiming that monks out of their cloister are like 'a fisshe that is waterlees' (180) [a fish out of water] – he regards as 'nat worth an oystre' (182) [not worth an oyster]. As critics have noted, the Monk's use of comparison reveals his preoccupation with food (Lumiansky 1966,

229–232; Grennen 1968, 573; Mann 1973, 20) and, as Kathryn Lynch observes, the Monk himself 'is imaged as a fish ready for the cooking pot' (Lynch 2007, 119). The Monk is especially partial to a fat, roasted swan, a bird associated with pride and sloth (Biebel 1998, 17), with the dish itself expensive and thus restricted to wealthy diners (Wilson 1976, 110–115). A recipe for roasted swan calls for the meat to be served with chawdron, a rich sauce made from offal or intestines, blood, bread and spices (Anon. 1888, 78, 76–77, 95). If the Monk is charged with providing food in the monastery, as suggested by the Host's reference to him as a 'celerer' in the prologue to his tale (1936), then, as Lynch points out, his appetites 'become especially threatening since he devours the resources of the community he ought to be protecting, both those of his fellow monks and of the outlying community on which they are dependent' (Lynch 2007, 120). This is the kind of behaviour we saw heavily criticized in *Piers Plowman*.

Like the Prioress and the Monk, the Friar behaves in a way not expected from a spiritual person: he frequents taverns and is more familiar with innkeepers and tapsters in any given town than its sick or poor. Whilst the Monk is 'a lord ful fat' (200), the Friar is described as 'strong', the Miller is 'stout' and the Host 'large'; indeed the only member of the company specifically described as thin is the Clerk (scholar) who is described as looking 'holwe' (289), that is, emaciated; Jill Mann notes the link between his appearance and 'the traditional poverty of his estate' (Mann 1973, 8). The Summoner enjoys garlic, onions, leeks and strong red wine, perhaps the cause of his pimply red face (indicating leprosy) and apparent alopecia, since these foods were thought by some authorities to provoke evil humours (Curry 1926, 45–46; Biggins 1964). Although leeks and garlic were considered unhealthy, as well as being biblical and satiric symbols of moral corruption (Mann 1973, 138), the *Regimen sanitatis Salerni* recommends garlic as an antidote to poison (as discussed in the section on Langland's poem above), noting that some physicians approve of leeks, although not the author of the *Regimen* (De Mediolano and Harington 1607, A8r, B8v). The *Regimen* also considers garlic, leeks and onions harmful to the sight, which perhaps explains why the Summoner has 'eyen narwe' (625) [swollen eyelids] (De Mediolano and Harington 1607, C1r).

The Cook too suffers from a skin disease, having a 'mormal' (an ulcer) on his shin. H. Braddy argues that the Cook's mormal is a running sore, not a dry one, but either condition is disgusting when mentioned in such close proximity to the cooking of his 'blankmanger', although the reader tends to get distracted by Chaucer's interesting focus on medieval cookery, as J. Swart points out (Braddy 1946; Swart 1954, 128). Blancmanger – a savoury dish usually combining minced poultry, or sometimes fish, with almond milk, rice, sugar and sometimes spices or salt (Anon. 1888, 21, 23, 85, 114) – was perhaps specifically mentioned by Chaucer because its creamy consistency adds to our revulsion if we imagine the Cook's sore either dripping or flaking into the dish, and it also suggests, albeit subtly, cannibalism since those who consume the Cook's blancmanger are also consuming bits of the Cook.

The figure whose relationship with food is considered in most detail in 'The General Prologue' is the Franklin. He is referred to as an Epicurean – 'Epicurus

owene sone' (336) [Epicure's own son] – enjoying good food and providing his
guests with a range of delectable dishes:

> His breed, his ale, was alweys after oon;
> A bettre envyned man was nowher noon.
> Withoute bake mete was nevere his hous,
> Of fissh and flessh, and that so plentevous
> It snewed in his hous of mete and drynke;
> Of alle deyntees that men koude thynke,
> After the sondry sesons of the yeer,
> So chaunged he his mete and his soper.
> Ful many a fat partrich hadde he in muwe,
> And many a breem and many a luce in stuwe.
>   *(341–350)*

> [His bread, his ale, was always of the same (good) quality;
> There was nowhere any man better stocked with wine.
> His house was never without baked pies
> Of fish and flesh, and that so plenteous
> That in his house it snowed with food and drink;
> Of all the dainties that men could imagine,
> According to the various seasons of the year,
> So he varied his dinner and his supper.
> Many a fat partridge had he in a pen,
> And many a bream and many a pike in his fish pond.]

Elizabeth M. Biebel argues against Jill Mann's view of the Franklin as a glutton,
although Mann's reading is more nuanced than Biebel suggests since she concluded
that the Franklin has a 'healthy and generous nature' unlike that of 'a diseased and
queasy glutton' (Biebel 1998, 19; see also Mann 1973, 156). Biebel concurs with
Joseph Bryant's view that the Franklin is a temperate man following a balanced and
seasonal diet (Biebel 1998, 19; see also Bryant 1948, 321). Critics are divided on the
image of it snowing food and drink in the Franklin's house, agreeing that it is an
allusion to manna from heaven – food sent by God to feed the Israelites in the desert,
Exodus 16:1–36) – but disagreeing as to whether it indicates the Franklin's spiritual
deficiency or the opposite. Biebel reads it as positive: 'Since the Old Testament's
manna is seen as the forerunner of the Eucharist in the New Testament, there is an
element of true communion and holy feast to be found within the Franklin's portrait',
and the 'sop in wyn' (334) [piece of bread in wine] that the Franklin eats for breakfast
'may also be seen as a Eucharistic image' (Biebel 1998, 20). His breakfast could be
indulgent since medieval recipes for the dish called for fine bread steeped in wine
and almond milk, laced with various spices and sugar, but Earle Birney argues that it
could have been fairly simple since it was recommended by dietary authors, including
the *Regimen sanitatis Salerni* (Anon. 1888, 11 xxvij, 90; Birney 1959, 346; see also De

Mediolano and Harington 1607, B5r). Birney suggests that a fairly basic dish, a bit of dry toast dunked in peppery wine, would suit a man given to excess the night before, like a sort of medieval seltzer, and it is something eaten also by January in 'The Merchant's Tale' after a night of excess (Birney 1959, 347).

The Franklin is clearly hospitable but is he hospitable to a fault? We are told that his table is not taken down between meals but 'stood redy covered al the longe day' to accommodate guests, not the usual medieval practice (Scully 1995, 169) and unlike the trestle table set up especially to accommodate a feast in *Sir Gawain and the Green Knight*. The Franklin is generous and who wouldn't want to be welcomed by such a host? But there is arguably a sense of pride in his display of wealth, especially if he entertains those who do not deserve it or need it, as Mann points out (Mann 1973, 157). D. W. Robertson suggests the reference to Epicureanism is negative, arguing that the Franklin is 'blind to anything beneath surface appearance', one possessing the 'superficial nobility of a wealthy man of the middle class' (Robertson 1963, 276). Certainly in a number of tales, as we shall see, the dangers attendant upon being hospitable are explored by Chaucer.

The portrait of the Doctor of Physic is similar to that of the Franklin in that Chaucer depicts his admirable qualities without overt criticism. Yet as Mann points out, the long list of medical authorities known to the Doctor might suggest that he 'is more familiar with medical names than with medical works' and although the Doctor's close relationship with the apothecaries is apparently admirable, it also suggests collusion between the two professions to extract money from their patients (Mann 1973, 93, 95–96). The Doctor's diet is a good one:

> Of his diet mesurable was he,
> For it was of no superfluitee,
> But of greet norissyng and digestible.
> *(435–437)*

> [Of his diet moderate he was,
> For it was of no excess,
> But greatly nourishing and digestible.]

This contrasts with the gluttony of other pilgrims and is in line with the view of the *Regimen sanitatis Salerni* that the best physicians are Doctor Quiet, Doctor Merryman and Doctor Diet (De Mediolano and Harington 1607, A6r). Yet it also suggests that if people followed the Doctor's diet, then he would be redundant (Mann 1973, 97); in *Piers Plowman* Hunger criticized the rich doctors who benefit financially from people's lack of temperance and thus avoid doing any real work (6.270–276).

The Reeve is attentive to the quality and welfare of his Lord's crops and animals:

> Ther nas baillif, ne hierde, nor oother hyne,
> That he ne knew his sleighte and his covyne;
> They were adrad of hym as of the deeth.
> *(603–605)*

[There was no farm manager, nor herdsman, nor other servant,
Whose trickery and treachery he did not know;
They were afraid of him as of the plague.]

He is a good employee and yet, as Mann notes, the fear felt by his fellow workers makes him unpleasant, although they are by no means victims (Mann 1973, 165). The Manciple is circumspect when purchasing food, which is no surprise given the dishonesty of the sort of people he would have had to deal with: the Miller, who steals grain, and the Shipman, who steals wine. However, it is suggested that the Manciple is also dishonest, that he has 'sette hir aller cappe' (586) [deceived them all], a claim developed in 'The Manciple's Prologue' when the Host warns him not to make the Cook too angry lest he claim the Manciple has fiddled his accounts (69–80). The Cook too is guilty of shoddy practices, accused by the Host in the prologue to his tale of draining the gravy from his pasties and selling food that has been heated up and allowed to go cold (4346–4434); again we see that commercialism in relation to food tends to warp social relations and obligations. The Plowman is the only pilgrim associated with food who is described in unequivocally positive terms: he works the land, preparing it for planting, 'For Christes sake, for every povre wight' (537), that is, in the name of Christ and to prevent the poor from starving. Here Chaucer is presumably indebted to Langland's Christ-like Piers.

The tales and their prologues further develop the relationship between food and moral status raised in 'The General Prologue': the hypocrisy of members of religious orders, the negative side of hospitality, the relationship between gluttony and lust, and the merits of moderation. A repeated theme during the telling of the tales and their prologues is the problem of gluttony and drunkenness. After the Knight has told his tale, the Miller, who is drunk on Southwark ale, insists on telling his tale before the Monk. The Reeve is offended with the Miller's story since it features a cuckolded carpenter (the Reeve is a carpenter by trade) and he gets his revenge by telling the story of a cuckolded miller in which the miller and his wife both get drunk. As Elizabeth M. Biebel notes, the miller in 'The Reeve's Tale' has to send his daughter to get ale and bread for his guests; although 'the Eucharistic symbol . . . is absent from this man's house', he does have a goose to hand that he will roast, part of a pattern Biebel detects in the tales of disreputable characters indulging in animal flesh (Biebel 1998, 22).

In 'The Wife of Bath's Prologue' the Wife recalls how, as a young woman, she was fond of 'a draughte of sweete wyn' (459) [a draught of sweet wine] and considers how wine makes her lecherous: 'A likerous mouth moste han a likeroud tayl' (466) [A gluttonous mouth must have a lecherous tail], a connection between eating and sex that emerges in a number of tales. Noting that 'In wommen vinolent is no defence – / This knowen lecchours by experience' (467–468) [In drunken women there is no defence – / This lechers know by experience], she is nonetheless amused by recalling the exploits of her youth: 'It tikleth me aboute myn herte roote' (471) [It tickles me to the bottom of my heart]. Other members of the company have also been drinking; after the Wife of Bath's lengthy prologue the Host tells the

Summoner and Friar that they must be drunk to argue so, urging them to be quiet so the Wife can tell her tale (850–853), and in 'The Prologue to the Manciple's Tale' the Cook is apparently so drunk that he falls off his horse (44–50).

'The Friar's Tale' features a corrupt summoner who will accept food in an alehouse as a bribe (1348–1349) and the Summoner retorts with his tale of a gluttonous friar. The friar in 'The Summoner's Tale' begs for money, apparently to build holy houses, and he also begs for food. He and his companion say they will accept whatever they can get: some grain, a bit of cheese, a 'Goddes kechyl' (1747) [an alms-cake], with the list extending to more substantial foodstuffs, namely brawn (boar's flesh), bacon and beef (1750–1753). The Summoner makes it clear that they are pretending to pray for those who have provided these gifts; the names of the faithful written down in a book, and owed a prayer, are later erased (1752–1760). In his visit to a sick man and his wife the friar proclaims that he does not want much to eat and then specifies his desire for the very finest foods:

> Have I nat of a capon but the lyvere,
> And of youre softe breed nat but a shyvere,
> And after that a rosted pigges heed –
> But that I nolde no beest for me were deed –
> Thanne hadd I with yow hoomly suffisaunce.
> *(1839–1843)*

> [I'll have of a capon only the liver,
> And of your soft bread nothing but a sliver,
> And after that a roasted pig's head –
> But that I would that no beast for me were dead –
> Then had I with you enough plain fare.]

The joke is, of course, that none of this is 'hoomly suffisaunce'. He further describes himself as a man lacking in appetite:

> I am a man of litel sustenaunce;
> My spirit hath his fostryng in the Bible.
> The body is ay so redy and penyble
> To wake, that my stomak is destroyed.
> *(1844–1847)*

> [I am a man who eats little;
> My spirit is nourished by the Bible.
> The body is so ready and so accustomed to suffering
> To spend the night in prayer and meditation, that my stomach is destroyed.]

The friar in 'The Summoner's Tale' claims that while the common people eat and drink much, friars condemn worldly appetite: 'we lyve in poverte and in abstinence'

(1873) [we live in poverty and in abstinence]. He cites the Bible in his lecture against gluttony, noting that 'Fro Paradys first, if I shal nat lye / Was man out chaced for his glotonye; / And chaast was man in Paradys, certeyn' (1915–1917) [From Paradise first, if I shall not lie / Was man chased out because of his gluttony / And chaste was man in Paradise, certainly]. This connection between gluttony and lust, mentioned also in 'The Wife of Bath's Prologue', was common in the period. In 'The Parson's Tale' gluttony and the other six deadly sins are described at length and here too the gluttony of Adam and Eve is described as the first sin and a conduit for other sins (819–821).[14] Like the friar in 'The Summoner's Tale', the Parson draws a link between gluttony and sexual sin – 'After Glotonye thanne comth Lecherie' (836) [After gluttony then comes lechery] – and in 'The Second Nun's Prologue' sloth, idleness and gluttony are related sins:

> . . . ydelnesse is roten slogardye,
> Of which ther nevere comth no good n'encrees;
> And . . . slouthe hire holdeth in a lees
> Oonly to sleep, and for to ete and drynke,
> And to devouren al that othere swynke
>
> *(17–21)*

> [. . . idleness is rotten laziness,
> Of which there never comes any good profit,
> And . . . sloth holds her on a leash
> Allowing her only to sleep, and to eat and drink
> And to devour all that others earn by working]

As in *Piers Plowman*, it is considered immoral to consume more than one's fair share of that which has been produced by the honest labour of others.

Gluttony in the form of drunkenness is denounced by the friar's story in 'The Summoner's Tale' of the drunkard Cambises (2043–2055) and in other tales also where biblical sources are invoked to illustrate its consequences, for example in 'The Tale of Melibee' when Melibius' wife Prudence, citing the biblical Book of Proverbs, warns her husband: 'For Salomon seith, "Ther is no privetee ther as regneth dronkenesse"' (1194; Proverbs 31:4) [For Solomon says, 'There is no secrecy where drunkenness reigns'], and in 'The Monk's Tale' when we are reminded that, in the deuterocanonical Book of Judith, Holofernes was drunk when decapitated by Judith (2567–2574). In 'The Man of Law's Tale' important messages that should protect the innocent Constance go undelivered due to drunkenness, which the teller of the tale laments:

> O messager, fulfild of dronkenesse,
> Strong is thy breeth, thy lymes faltren ay,
> And thou biwreyest alle secreenesse.
> Thy mynde is lorn, thou janglest as a jay,

Thy face is turned in a newe array.
Ther dronkenesse regneth in any route,
Ther is no conseil hyd, withouten doute.
(771–777)

[O messenger, filled with drunkenness,
Strong is thy breath, thy limbs are unsteady,
And you betray all secret information.
Your mind is lost, you chatter like a jay,
Your face is completely changed.
Where drunkenness reigns in any group,
There is no secret hidden, without doubt.]

The physical effects of drunkenness are apparently evident also in the description of the sleepy Cook, described in 'The Manciple's Prologue' as pale, with dazed eyes and bad breath (30–32). Indeed his breath is so bad that the Manciple tells him:

Hoold cloos thy mouth, man, by thy fader kyn!
The devel of helle sette his foot therin!
Thy cursed breeth infecte wole us alle.
(37–39)

[Keep thy mouth closed, man, by thy father's kin!
The devil of hell set his foot therein!
Thy cursed breath would infect us all.]

Again, there is fear of bodily contamination from the Cook, first via the sore that might weep or flake into his cooking and here from his very mouth. As noted in the discussion of *Piers Plowman*, gluttony was considered one of the sins of the mouth and, according to Roy Pearcy, there is a suggestion that the devil has entered Chaucer's Cook through his mouth (via his drink), which might also evoke the mouth of hell, a place often depicted as a sort of kitchen in the medieval period, with devils as cooks (Pearcy 1974, 167–168, 171–173). The Manciple calls the Cook a 'stynkyng swyn!' (40) [stinking swine!], adding: 'I trowe that ye dronken han wyn ape / And that is whan men pleyen with a straw' (44–45) [I believe that you are ape-drunk on wine / And that is when men play with a straw'], which makes the Cook angry. The reference here is to the medieval model of four stages of drunkenness, which corresponded to specific animal characteristics and also the four bodily humours: lamb- or mutton-drunk (meek and phlegmatic); lion-drunk (bold and choleric); ape-drunk (foolish and sanguine); sow- or swine-drunk (wallowing and melancholic) (Chaucer 1977, 524n494; Chaucer 1988, 953n44). Since the Manciple has called the Cook a swine, it is surprising that he would not characterize him as 'swine-drunk', especially since, as Nevill Coghill points out, the Cook has been described as pale and therefore cannot be sanguine. Coghill suggests that the

Manciple is referring to the surreptitious practice of drilling a hole in a cask of wine and sucking it out through a straw, behaviour known as 'sucking the monkey' in modern London Dock slang, which is perhaps a garbled form of the medieval notion of being 'ape-drunk' (Chaucer 1977, 524n494).

'The Pardoner's Tale' tells the story of three young revellers who frequent taverns and prostitutes and when drunk agree to seek out and challenge Death. Before the story itself, the Pardoner provides a long preamble about the horrors of excessive drinking, making the traditional connections between drunkenness and lust and describing gluttony as the original sin. In this preamble, paradise, before the Fall, is described by the Pardoner not as a place of pleasure but rather of denial:

> For whil that Adam fasted, as I rede,
> He was in Paradys; and whan that he
> Eet of the fruyt deffended on the tree,
> Anon he was out cast to wo and peyne.
> *(508–511)*

> [For while that Adam fasted, as I read,
> He was in Paradise, and when that he
> Ate of the forbidden fruit on the tree,
> Immediately he was cast out to woe and pain.]

As in 'The Second Nun's Prologue' and in *Piers Plowman*, the glutton is parasitical and it is considered wrong for 'men to swynke / To get a glotoun deyntee met and drynke!' (518–520) [men to work / To get a glutton dainty meat and drink!]. The language used by the Pardoner to describe the process of eating and drinking is scatological: the glutton 'of his throte he maketh his pryvee' (527) [makes his throat his toilet], his belly is stinking, full of 'dong and of corrupcioun' [dung and corruption], and at either end (mouth and anus) 'foul is the soun' (534–536) [the sound is foul]; as in Langland's *Piers Plowman*, the Rabelaisian grotesque body is here anticipated. Saint Paul is cited for denouncing the glutton as idolatrous, their 'wombe is hir god!' (533) [belly is their god], an allusion to the biblical Epistle of Saint Paul to the Romans (16:18). The glutton's reliance upon the labour of others is again denounced, with considerable attention given to the food that is produced for his pleasure:

> How greet labour and cost is thee to fynde!
> Thise cookes, how they stampe, and streyne, and grynde,
> And turnen substaunce into accident
> To fulfille al thy likerous talent!
> Out of the harde bones knokke they
> The mary, for they caste noght awey
> That may go thurgh the golet softe and swoote.
> Of spicerie of leef, and bark, and roote
> Shal been his sauce ymaked by delit,

To make hym yet a newer appetit.
But, certes, he that haunteth swiche delices
Is deed, whil that he lyveth in tho vices.

(537–548)

[How great labour and cost it is to provide food for you!
These cooks, how they pound, and strain, and grind,
And turn substance into outward appearance
To fulfil all thy gluttonous desire!
Out of the hard bones they knock
The marrow, for they throw nothing away
That may go through the gullet softly and sweetly.
Of spices of leaf, and bark, and root
Shall his sauce be made for delight,
To make him yet a newer appetite.
But, certainly, he who habitually seeks such delicacies
Is dead while he lives in those vices.]

Elizabeth M. Biebel perceives a link between this description of violent cooks and the Pardoner's earlier reference to tearing the body of Christ (474–475), suggesting 'the spiritual significance of Christ as passive victim, the sacrificial lamb' (Biebel 1998, 24), as well as the medieval tradition of a feminized Christ, something that similarly emerges in *The Book of Margery Kempe* discussed later in this chapter. Also evident is the notion of a gluttonous appetite being a kind of living death, a point reinforced by the notion of drunkenness as a 'verray sepulture / Of mannes wit and his discrecioun' (558–559) [a very sepulchre / Of man's wit and discretion], which also comes up in 'The Parson's Tale' (822). Men ought to avoid wine, especially 'the white wyn of Lepe' (563) [the white wine of Lepe], a cheap Spanish variety used to adulterate more expensive French wines (Hench 1937), and powerful men, especially those administering justice, ought not to get drunk. Ironically the Pardoner has a good appetite: it is only after he has had a cake and drunk a draught of 'corny ale' (315), a strong and malty drink, that he is ready to tell his tale. In the Pardoner's story of the three revellers drunkenness leads to murder: the gluttons who seek Death find him but not in the way they expected and, as a number of critics observe, the bread and wine that one of the rioters brings back to his companions becomes the means of their death rather than their salvation (Nichols Jr 1967; Leyerle 1976; Cooper 1989, 269; Biebel 1998, 20).

Hunger is not a recurring motif of *The Canterbury Tales* but moderation and abstinence do feature in a number of tales. In 'The Nun's Priest's Tale' the poor widow and her two daughters live a simple life, with a basic diet:

. . . she eet ful many a sklendre meel.
Of poynaunt sauce hir neded never a deel.

No deyntee morsel passed thurgh hir throte;
Hir diete was accordant to hir cote.
(2833–2836)

[. . . she ate many a slender meal.
Of spicy sauce she needed not a bit.
No dainty morsel passed through her throat;
Her diet was such as her farm produced.]

The widow does not apparently go hungry but nor is she gluttonous: 'Repleccioun ne made hire nevere sik; / Attempree diet was al hir phisik' (2837–2838) [Overeating never made her sick; / A temperate diet was all her medicine]. The food and drink she customarily consumes is described in detail:

No wyn ne drank she, neither whit ne reed;
Hir bord was served moost with whit and blak –
Milk and broun breed, in which she foond no lak,
Seynd bacoun, and somtyme an ey or tweye,
For she was, as it were a maner dye.
(2842–2846)

[No wine drank she, neither white nor red;
Her board was served most with white and black –
Milk and brown bread, in which she found no lack,
Broiled bacon, and sometimes an egg or two,
For she was, as it were, a sort of dairywoman.]

In other tales not drinking wine is a sign of virtue, often amongst women, for example the good daughter Virginius in 'The Physician's Tale' of whom we learn that 'Bacus hadde of hir mouth right no maistrie' (58) [Bacchus had no mastery of her mouth at all]; the patient Griselda in 'The Clerk's Tale' who 'Wel ofter of the welle than of the tonne / She drank' (215) [Much more often of the well than of the wine barrel / She drank]; and Canace, King Cambuskan's daughter, in 'The Squire's Tale' who eschews the wine that makes others sleep late because she is 'ful mesurable' (362) [very temperate]. In 'The Monk's Tale' Sampson is also described as abstinent: 'This Sampson nevere ciser drank ne wyn' (2055) [This Sampson never strong drink drank nor wine]. In 'The Nun's Priest's Tale' milk is provided by the widow's three cows; it was a common drink for the poor in medieval England, and Ireland also – and later praised by Irish revivalists as a drink of native purity (see Chapter 6) – although much of it would have been set aside for making butter and cheese (Wilson 1976, 141–147).

In 'The Nun's Priest's Tale' Chauntecleer dismisses Pertelote's advice that his dream was caused by excess choler provoked by overeating, an ailment that might be cured if he would eat the laxative herbs growing in the farmyard. As Patrick

Gallacher observes, 'The Nun's Priest's Tale' itself is a kind of purge coming after the 'surfeit of disasters' that is 'The Monk's Tale', the mock-epic story of a cock and his hens offering 'a catharsis of the sorrow built up through the Monk's Tale' (Gallacher 1976, 49, 50). Notably, the herbs recommended by Pertelote – spurge laurel, centaury, fumitory, hellebore, caper-spurge, rhamus, ground ivy (2963–2966) – were considered hot and dry and, as Corinne E. Kauffman points out, Pertelote's medical advice is not good. Based on an investigation of English herbals and the medieval encyclopedia *De Proprietatibus Rerum* (*On the Properties of Things*) by Bartholomaeus Anglicus, Kauffman notes that although Pertelote tells Chauntecleer to gather the herbs that grow in front of them in the yard, 'some of them would not have been ready for gathering in May' when the action of the story takes place; moreover, some of the herbs are apparently dangerous if taken internally, and taken together they would increase Chauntecleer's humoral imbalance to the extent that they could 'endanger his very life' (Kauffman 1970, 41). Even if some of these herbs were growing in the widow's yard, they would be wholly redundant, at least for their purgative qualities, because they are of no use to either Chauntecleer or the widow, whom we know does not overeat.

'The Summoner's Tale' tells of how a friar pretends to live an abstemious life whilst indulging his appetite; in other stories genuine fasting indicates genuine virtue. In 'The Franklin's Tale' Dorigen fasts in sorrow for her absent husband and 'The Second Nun's Prologue' describes the self-induced deprivations of Saint Cecilia – her story familiar from *The Golden Legend* – who fasted two days out of three for the love of Christ, voluntarily eschewing other bodily pleasures by wearing a hair shirt and refusing to have sex with her husband (De Voraigne 2012, chp. 169). The medieval practice of 'holy fasting' (or *anorexia mirabilis*) saw women starve themselves in order to reach what they regarded as an acceptable level of purity so as to commune with Christ or God (it is discussed further in the section on *The Book of Margery Kempe* below); it also gave them control over their bodies, which they may well have considered the only control available to them.[15] Fasting, especially (though not exclusively) by women, is a recurrent motif in the literature considered across this volume, and these women apparently share with their medieval forebears the desire to exert control, at least over their body.

Not all hunger is self-induced: 'The Monk's Tale' (that 'surfeit of disasters', as Gallacher characterizes it) features a story of involuntary hunger that is striking in its pathos, that of Count Ugolino of Pisa, which is based on the episode from canto 33 of Dante's *Inferno*. In 'The Monk's Tale' the number of children imprisoned with their father for his alleged treason is three (not four, as in Dante) but the story shares Dante's report that, with one child already dead from hunger, the remaining children urge their father to eat them. The children have interpreted their father gnawing his arm in grief as self-cannibalism:

> And seyde, 'Fader, do nat so, allas!
> But rather ete the flessh upon us two.

Oure flessh thou yaf us, take oure flessh us fro,
And ete ynogh' – right thus they to hym seyde
(2449–2452)

[And said, 'Father, do not so, alas!
But rather eat the flesh upon us two.
Our flesh thou gave us, take our flesh from us,
And eat enough' – right thus they to him said]

In 'The Monk's Tale' Chaucer omits the suggestion in Dante's poem that Count Ugolino did eventually resort to cannibalism. The wording in Dante's poem is ambiguous, 'Then fasting got / The mastery of grief' (Dante 1880, 156; 33.73–74), suggesting, although not unequivocally, that the count ate his own children. Chaucer's omission of any hint of cannibalism – the count dies from hunger after his children die – arguably increases our sympathy for the count but also lessens any sense that the power of hunger will drive men to terrible acts.

As in *Sir Gawain and the Green Knight,* the hospitality described in many of the tales is not all that it appears to be. Hospitality can backfire on the host as well as the guest, for example in 'The Reeve's Tale' when it exposes the miller to retribution from those he has cheated. Providing hospitality to strangers as well as friends is a Christian obligation but it has the potential to be sinful, something hinted at in the description of the Franklin in 'The General Prologue'. 'The Parson's Tale' describes the dangers of 'Pride of the table', which includes 'excess of diverse metes and drynkes' (444–445) [excess of diverse meats and drinks] as well as extravagant presentation, expensive receptacles and elaborate entertainment. It is this kind of ostentatious display that is described in 'The Franklin's Tale' by Aurelius' brother:

For ofte at feestes have I wel herd seye
That tregetours withinne an halle large
Have maad come in a water and a barge,
And in the halle rowen up and doun.
Somtyme hath semed come a grym leoun;
And somtyme floures sprynge as in a mede;
Somtyme a vyne, and grapes white and rede;
Somtyme a castel, al of lym and stoon;
And whan hem lyked, voyded it anon.
(1142–1150)

[For often at feasts have I well heard say
That illusionists within a large hall
Have made come in a water and a barge,
And in the hall row up and down.
Sometimes it seemed a grim lion has come;
And sometimes flowers spring as in a field;

Sometimes a vine, and grapes white and red;
Sometimes a castle, all of mortar and stone;
And when they pleased, caused it to disappear suddenly.]

Often feasting is celebratory but it can also be an occasion for subterfuge. In a number of tales a banquet turns bloody, for example the Franklin tells the story of Phido's daughters who are carried naked to a feast of tyrants and made to dance, but kill themselves by leaping into a well rather than be deflowered. In 'The Monk's Tale' Samson destroys his enemies by tearing down the supporting pillars of the building in which they are feasting and Belshazzar's idolatrous feasts – where he defiles the gold vessels from the temple of Jerusalem by drinking various wines out of them – end abruptly when he is slain by God. In 'The Man of Law's Tale' the feast celebrating the marriage between the Sultan and the good Constance is arranged by the Sultan's mother:

And to the feeste Cristen folk hem dresse
In general, ye, bothe yonge and olde.
Heere may men feeste and roialtee biholde,
And deyntees mo than I kan yow devyse
(416–419)

[And to the feast Christian folk go
All together, yes, both young and old.
Here may men behold feasting and royalty,
And dainties more than I can tell you]

The description sounds as though it might come from a romance such as *Sir Gawain and the Green Knight* but it soon becomes clear that this story is a tragedy:

For shortly for to tellen, at o word,
The Sowdan and the Cristen everichone
Been al tohewe and stiked at the bord,
But it were oonly dame Custance allone.
This olde Sowdanesse, cursed krone,
Hath with hir freendes doon this cursed dede,
For she hirself wolde al the contree lede.
(428–434)

[For shortly to tell, at one word,
The Sultan and the Christians each one
Are all hacked to pieces and stabbed at the table,
Except for only Lady Custance alone.
This old Sultaness, cursed crone,
Has with her friends done this cursed deed,
For she herself wanted to rule all the country.]

The Christians, including the newly converted Sultan, have been martyred in a barbaric fashion that is anathema to Christian notions of hospitality. What happens is part of a stereotypical concept of the non-Christian as duplicitous and savage but it also highlights the dangers of not being alert when indulging in 'dainties', especially those that have been provided by others.

Hunting is mentioned in a number of tales and usually briefly. 'The General Prologue' suggests that hunting is an inappropriate activity for a monk and in the tales it is usually the pursuit of aristocrats: Sir Topaz hunts and it is a favourite pastime of Walter, the Italian Marquis and husband of the patient Griselda in 'The Clerk's Tale'. Walter is of good lineage and described as fair, strong, young and 'ful of honour and curteisye' (74) [full of honour and courtesy] but we are also told that 'in somme thynges . . . he was to blame' (76), namely:

> that he considered noght
> In tyme comynge what myght hym bityde
> But on his lust present was al his thought,
> As for the hauke and hunte on every syde.
> Wel ny alle othere cures leet he slyde,
> And eek he nolde – and that was worst of alle –
> Weede no wyf, for noght that may bifalle.
> *(78–84)*

> [that he considered not
> In time coming what might happen to him
> But on his immediate desire was all his thought,
> Such as to hawk and hunt on every side.
> Well nigh all other cares he let slip,
> And also he would not – and that was worst of all –
> Marry a wife, for nought that might befall.]

The attitude here expressed towards hunting is not entirely approving, even for a young aristocrat. That Walter sees Griselda when he is out hunting invokes the classical notion, common in the medieval period, of love as a chase with the love object as its quarry (Thiébaux 1974), although the Clerk is quick to point out that 'He noght with wantown lookyng of folye / His eyen caste on hire, but in sad wyse' [He not with lecherous looking of folly / His eyes cast on her, but in serious manner] (236–237). Women as game, characterized specifically in terms of a father's proprietorial claim over his daughter, is also evident in Fielding's novel *Tom Jones*, considered in Chapter 3. Walter is attracted to Griselda for her virtue, and in her patience and obedience to her husband's unreasonable demands she is the opposite of Eve, the traditional figure of female disobedience whose gluttony acted as a conduit for lechery and caused the fall of humankind.

Another wife is the youthful May from 'The Merchant's Tale'. The story of the blind husband and the fruit tree is a common fabliau plot (Chaucer 1988, 884) but why does May's adulterous deception of January, her elderly husband, revolve around a pear tree? If May were to have sex with Damien, her young lover, in an apple tree, the cultural resonances for a medieval audience (who usually interpreted the paradisiacal fruit as a apple) would surely have been more palpable, so why might Chaucer have decided on this particular fruit? In her plan to arrange the tryst with Damien up the pear tree, May tells January that she has a craving 'To eten of the smale peres grene' (2333) [To eat some of the small green pears], adding 'I telle yow wel, a womman in my plit / May han to fryut so greet an appetit / That she may dyen but she of it have' (2335–2337) [I tell you well, a woman in my condition / May have for fruit so great an appetite / That she may die if she does not have some of it]. Milton Miller argues that this desire for pears causes January to believe that May is pregnant, something he desires, and she does indeed become pregnant after her encounter with Damien in the pear tree, although self-deception convinces January that she is innocent of adultery and that he has impregnated her (Miller 1950). Carol A. Everest points out that May's desire for the unripe fruit 'is a reference to the pica of pregnancy, the desire of pregnant women for odd or unpalatable food', and it is 'a condition recognized and well documented in the medical writings available to physicians of the Middle Ages' (Everest 1995, 165). May's desire for pears in particular is appropriate, claims Everest, because in medical formularies and herbals 'pears rank high in the foods suitable for pregnant women, probably because they are frequently prescribed as a stomachic to allay sensations of nausea' (Everest 1995, 166); one of the sources cited by Everest is the *Regimen sanitatis Salerni*, which claims pears are good for the stomach although it warns that pears must be cooked because raw pears are poisonous, in line with the customary view that uncooked fruit was harmful (De Mediolano and Harington 1607, B3r). Moreover, the pear was associated with male sexual organs (Olsen 1961, 207–208), which possibly 'owes something to the resemblance testicles bear to the shape of pears', something borne out by medical texts from the period, such as the *Trotula major*, which lists pears as one of the foods that will increase sexual potency (Everest 1995, 170).

May's adultery is facilitated by the pear tree that grows in January's garden; as Paul Olsen observes, January refers to his marriage to May as a paradise, and 'he builds an external paradise to complement the subjective paradise he found in May', adding that: 'If the first Eden was the Paradise of divine love, this is the paradise of earthly lust' (Olsen 1961, 207). There is thus an implicit connection between the paradisical garden, the tree-bearing fruit that grows in the garden, and the sin of lust, committed first by January in his physical desire for May and then by May in her adultery. As we have seen, elsewhere in *The Canterbury Tales* much is made of the sin of gluttony as a conduit for lust and how Adam and Eve were chaste before eating the fruit from the tree.

Before marrying May, January refers to his desire for a young wife in terms of food, specifically meat:

'I wol noon oold wyf han in no manere.
She shal nat passe twenty yeer, certayn;

Oold fissh and yong flessh wolde I have fayn.
Bet is,' quod he, 'a pyk than a pykerel,
And bet than old boef is the tendre veel
I wol no womman thritty yeer of age;
It is but bene-straw and greet forage.'
                                    (1416–1422)

['I will no old wife have in any way.
She shall not pass twenty years, certainly;
Old fish and young flesh would I gladly have.
Better is,' said he, 'a pike than a pickerel (young pike),
And better than old beef is the tender veal.
I want no woman thirty years of age;
It is but dry bean-stalks and coarse fodder.']

Biebel notes the connection between violent cooks, the breaking of Christ's body and Christ as sacrificial lamb in 'The Pardoner's Prologue' (discussed above) as part of a pattern throughout the poem of women as meat, lecherous men devouring them, and a feminized Christ (Biebel 1998, 24–25). January provides the most important example of the woman as meat motif but so too the Monk is said to love 'venerie', which Biebel argues implies that he preys upon women as well as animals (Biebel 1998, 24). The Wife of Bath figures herself in terms of food in her prologue, not meat but bread: where virginity is 'breed of pured whete-seed' (143) [bread of pure wheat-seed] and wives like her are 'barly-breed' (144) [barley bread], possibly a reference to Saint Jerome describing virginity as wheat and marriage as barley, a cheap grain that made less sought-after bread (Wilson 1985). It is men who are figured as meat when she recalls her old and rich husbands:

For wynnyng wolde I al his lust endure,
And make me a feyned appetit;
And yet in bacon hadde I nevere delit.
That made me that evere I wolde hem chide,
For thogh the pope hadde seten hem biside,
I wolde nat spare hem at hir owene bord,
For, by my trouthe, I quitte hem word for word.
                                    (416–422)

[For profit I would endure all his lust,
And make me a feigned appetite;
And yet in bacon I never had delight.
That made me so that I would always scold them,
For though the Pope had sat beside them,
I would not spare them at their own table,
For, by my troth, I repaid them word for word.]

F. N. Robinson suggests that 'bacon' may refer to 'old meat; and so here . . . old men' (Chaucer 1957, 700n418); the husband is difficult for the Wife to stomach in the same way that bacon was considered difficult to digest. In 'The Miller's Tale' another wife, called Alisoun, is characterized in terms of food: her apron is as white as milk and her breath as sweet as mead or apples (3236, 3261–3262). She is also wooed with food and drink by her lover Absoloun and, as Kathryn Lynch notes, the meed he offers her (which could be the honey-based drink or financial reward) suggests 'an equivalence between trade in food and other currency' (Lynch 2007, 123), reminding us also of Meed the Maid who signifies corrupt reward in *Piers Plowman*.

What emerges in *The Canterbury Tales* is a consistent pattern whereby attitudes towards food, as expressed by the poem's narrator and its pilgrims, reveal wider attitudes towards society. The desire for food is not a problem *per se* but it must correspond to one's professed beliefs and so the hypocrisy of the religious orders, claiming abstinence but enjoying a life of pleasure, is subtly condemned. So too food professionals, such as cooks and millers, are shown to fail in a way that compromises what their customers desire, which is basic hygiene and honest practices. Hospitality is to be applauded but, again, one should be wary of any tendency towards gluttony, showing off to one's guests or cheating them. The repeated connections drawn between food and sex suggest that it is not sexual desire itself that presents a problem but excess, cheating and corruption. With all the pilgrims, and the estates they represent, it is deception of others, and the self-deception, that manifests itself around food and eating that is roundly satirized.

Margery Kempe, *The Book of Margery Kempe* (early 1400s)

The manuscript of *The Book of Margery Kempe,* first discovered in 1934, is often termed an autobiography, apparently dictated by an illiterate woman to one or two scribes. The text is in third-person narration throughout, with Margery often referred to as 'this creature', although, as Lynn Staley observes, it is unclear if the scribe or scribes were constructed by Margery 'as an authorizing mediator between herself and the reader' (Kempe 2001, x). Where Langland's *Piers Plowman* and Chaucer's *Canterbury Tales* allow us some insight into the social reality of medieval England, we here get little sense of what life might have been like for an ordinary middle-aged mother because Margery is no ordinary woman, leaving her husband and fourteen children (who are mentioned only once, in chapter 48) to dedicate her life to God. Yet many of the places she visits and the people she encounters are historical figures and we do get a sense of the real world through which this exceptional figure travels. Like Chaucer's story-tellers, making their way to Canterbury, Margery is a pilgrim but she differs from Chaucer's pilgrims in her fundamentalism. As part of her spiritual journey Margery travels from her home in King's Lynn to Lincoln, Canterbury, Norwich, Rome, Jerusalem, Santiago de Compostela in Spain and later to Norway and Germany. In Norwich she meets the English anchoress and Christian mystic Julian of Norwich and although Margery's story 'is not officially produced' and 'includes no account of her girlhood or of her death' (Kempe 2001, ix), she bears a closer resemblance to Julian and the female saints from *The Golden Legend* – including Mary Magdalene and Cecilia, mentioned in the sections on Langland and Chaucer respectively – than the ordinary medieval wife. Indeed, she constitutes a kind of foil to the Wife of Bath: where Chaucer's Alisoun is pro-marriage and keen on sex, Margery refuses to have sex with her husband, dressing herself in virginal white and maintaining a life of celibacy.

Chaucer's company are on a pilgrimage so there is clearly a spiritual reason for their journey but there is also a distinct sense that their trip is a kind of holiday, with story-telling and drinking the sort of entertainment they expect. Margery is more serious. Her fellow pilgrims find her lengthy discussions of God and her bouts of crying irritating, as does the reader at times, as Staley observes (Kempe 2001, xiii), and her personal relationship with Christ, his mother and God is much more intimate and intense that that of Will the Dreamer in Langland's poem. *The Book of Margery Kempe* is, in many ways, distinct from the texts discussed above but like them it repeatedly figures food and eating in a social and religious context. As we saw earlier, some themes dominate in certain texts and figure less in others, for example whilst there is no specific reference to hunger in *Sir Gawain and the Green Knight* hunting is prominent. In *The Book of Margery Kempe* there is no hunting and less overt interest in gluttony than in earlier texts but there is a focus on fasting and hospitality (or the lack thereof); hunger and cannibalism also emerge, the latter not literally but in the figurative use of language. The relationship between food, virtue and sin is a thread that runs through these texts and, as in Chaucer's 'Merchant's Tale', the story of a pear tree is related by Margery as a means of illustrating the dangers of not doing God's will.

Before beginning her life of pilgrimage and devotion to God, Margery (like Rose and Betty in *Piers Plowman*, Passus 5) was a brewster. Having been told that Margery takes great pride in her dress and is envious of her neighbours if they also dress well, her brewing venture is described as another means by which she endeavours to be admired by others: 'And than, for pure coveytyse & for to maynten hir pride, sche gan to brewyn & was on of þe grettest brewers in þe town N.' (9, chp. 2) [And then, for pure covetousness and to maintain her pride, she began to brew and was one of the greatest brewers in the town N].[16] Despite having good servants and her own 'cunnyng' in brewing, the process itself always fails because the barm (the yeast formed on top of the brew) falls down and the ale is lost, which Margery interprets as a punishment from God for her pride and sin. Cristina Mazzoni observes that this experience 'left its mark on Margery's psyche and taste buds' since in the rest of the book 'she no longer refers to ale but prefers wine – the eucharistic drink – and on an occasion, even the still uncommon beer' (Mazzoni 2005, 106). After efforts at another food-related venture, a horse mill to grind corn, also fail, Margery hears a heavenly melody that prompts her to begin a regime of bodily penance: refusing to have sex with her husband, attending confession, fasting, keeping vigil and wearing a hair shirt, behaviour similar to the deprivations of Saint Cecilia in *The Golden Legend* and mentioned in Chaucer's 'Summoner's Tale' (discussed above). After several years of these privations Christ tells Margery to stop eating meat altogether and 'in-stede of þat flesch þow schalt etyn my flesch & my blod' [instead of that flesh thou shalt eat my flesh and my blood]; moreover, she should 'receyue my body euery Sonday' (17, chp. 4) [receive my body every Sunday], which was unusually often since medieval churchgoers were only required to celebrate Communion once a year (Kempe 2001, 14n8).

References to fasting, eating and hospitality recur throughout the text and Margery's trials are often figured in terms of food, sometimes invoking cannibalism, for example when Christ warns Margery that, for his sake, 'Þow xalt ben etyn & knawyn of þe pepul of þe world as any raton knawyth þe stokfysch' (17, chp. 4) [thou shalt be eaten and gnawed by the people of the world as any rat gnaws stockfish], stockfish being cured and dried cod, which was a commodity in medieval Lynn (Kempe 1985, 304n5), and here functioning as a kind of inverted transubstantiation whereby she is eaten instead of Christ and recalling Christ's thirst for humankind in *Piers Plowman*.[17] Another instance of cannibalistic food-inflected language is the recurring use of the rhetorical phrase of being 'chopped up as small meat for the pot' as a means of describing strength of feeling about something, which occurs three times in the text (15, 142, 204; chps. 4, 57 and 84). Similarly, when Margery visits a mad woman, she responds well to Margery but to other people 'sche cryid & gapyd as sche wolde an etyn hem' (178, chp. 75) [she cried and gaped as if she would have eaten them].

Devotion to Christ is figured in terms of nourishment: upon visiting an anchorite, as Christ has instructed, he tells Margery: 'Dowtyr, ȝe sowkyn euyn on Crystys brest' [Daughter, you suck even on Christ's breast] (18, chp. 5), a positive expression of breastfeeding, which contrasts with the negative depiction of the practice elsewhere in this volume (for example in *Gulliver's Travels*, see Chapter 3). Later, during one of her visions, Margery comforts the Virgin Mary in a maternal fashion (Mazzoni 2005, 108) with a hot drink of gruel and spiced wine but the Holy Virgin says she should take it away and 'ȝeue me no mete but myn owyn childe' (195, chp. 81) [give me no food but my own child]. As we saw in the discussion of Chaucer's 'Pardoner's Prologue', late medieval devotional literature often figured Christ using feminine or nutritive language (Bynum 1987, 270–276; Kempe 2001, 14n3). As Bynum notes:

> Both men and women . . . saw the body on the cross, which in dying fed the world, as in some sense female . . . To medieval natural philosophers, breast milk was transmuted blood, and a human mother – like the pelican that also symbolized Christ – fed her children from the fluid of life that coursed through her veins.
>
> *Bynum 1987, 270*

The sense that spiritual food is sufficient is evident throughout the text, although it is clear also that fasting is not ideal and God tells Margery that he is more pleased when she is silent and he can speak to her in her soul than when she wears her hair shirt or fasts on bread and water; God says that fasting and praying is good for 'ȝong be-gynnars' (89, chp. 36) [young beginners] but she will gain more merit in heaven by contemplation. As Mazzoni points out, there is little sense that Margery dislikes food; on the contrary, it gives her strength and comfort (Mazzoni 2005, 108–109), but she refrains from indulging when asked by Christ in order to demonstrate her spiritual devotion in physical terms.[18]

The other physical signs of Margery's devotion to God – her lengthy discussion of him, her bouts of crying and dressing in white – mark her out as odd and provoke harsh criticism from onlookers. The wearing of white clothes, something she claims is specifically requested by Christ, is associated with virginity but also carried other connotations in late medieval England. Sarah Salih argues that Margery's white clothing signals her liminality, suggesting specifically a holy virgin: one of the virgin martyrs or the member of a religious order (Salih 2001, 217–224). This mother of fourteen children, dressed in white and given to lengthy bouts of crying, presents a disturbing regression to childlike incontinence which is apparently at odds with her vociferous independence and intellectual abilities.

Margery's relationship with others, including her fellow pilgrims, is often described in terms of food, eating, hospitality and generosity or the lack thereof. A pattern emerges whereby those who love her invite her into their homes to dine, or provide her with food, and those who dislike her refuse to eat with her. For example, on her way to the Holy Land the pilgrims with whom she is travelling take against her because she does not wish to eat meat, and they also tire of her prolonged bouts of crying and her constant talk about God. They treat her with contempt, cutting her gown short and making her wear what looks like sackcloth, and 'Þei madyn hir to syttyn at þe tabelys ende be-nethyn all oþer þat sche durst ful euyl spekyn a word' (62, chp. 26) [they made her sit at the table's end, beneath all the others so that she dared hardly speak a word]. However, the man of the house where they are staying takes care of her before serving the others '& sent hir of hys owyn mees of swech seruyse as he had' (62, chp. 26) [and sent her of his own meal such service as he had]. She later promises not to talk of the Gospel but to sit and make merry at meals, like they do, but finds she cannot keep her promise and so goes to her chamber at mealtimes to eat alone, something she does for six weeks. Solitary eating was not usual in the medieval period and, as we saw in *Piers Plowman*, it was considered antisocial and uncharitable, although, unlike the rich in Langland's poem, Margery feels compelled to eat alone rather than choosing in any straightforward way to do so.

On one occasion, after God has told her to give away all her money, Margery meets the Italian Dame Margaret Florentine who seats her at a table above herself, lays her a meal with her own hands and gives her a hamper 'wyth oþer stuffe þat sche myght makyn hir potage þerwyth, as meche as wolde seruyn hir for a too days mete, & fille hir botel wyth good wyn' (93, chp. 38) ['with other stuff that she might make her pottage with, as much as would serve her for two days' food, and filled her bottle with good wine]. In the same chapter we are told how a man called Marcelle and his pregnant wife also feed her two days a week, and a holy maiden gives her food on Wednesdays, whilst the rest of the time Margery 'beggyd her mete fro dor to dore' (94, chp. 38) [begged her food from door to door]. When she is back in England, her loud crying is thought by some to come from the devil and the people who had given her food and drink now spurn her. Again we are told that God made some people love her and invite her home to eat and drink with them and hear her talk about God, one of whom is Thomas Marchale who 'ofte-tymes bad þis creatur to mete for to heryn hir dalyawns' (108, chp. 45) [often bade this creature to a meal in order to hear her dalliance] and who pays for her to get to Santiago. Again back in England, in Leicester, Margery is held on suspicion of being a Lollard; when no women's prison is available, the Jailer takes her back to his own home and, told by someone she is holy, he 'put hir in a fayr chawmbyr . . . lete hir gon to chirche . . . & dede hir etyn at his owyn tabyl' (112, chp. 46) [put her in a fair chamber . . . let her go to church . . . and eat at his own table].

Book 2 tells how when in London Margery is again taunted by people for not eating meat and at dinner a story is told about her alleged hypocrisy and gluttony, that, when dining at a good man's table and served with various fish, she chose a pike over a red herring, saying 'A, þu fals flesch, þu woldist now etyn reed heryng, but þu xalt no han þi wille' (244; Book 2, chp. 8) ['A, you false flesh, you would now eat red herring, but you shall not have your will'] – that is, she declined a humble fish to eat a better one (Kempe 1985, 329n9.2). The pike is praised by January in Chaucer's 'Merchant's Tale' and in 'The General Prologue' we are told it is one of the fish the Epicurean Franklin likes to serve to his guests (Chaucer 1988, lines 350, 1419). Great fun is had at Margery's expense until she rebukes them: 'I am þat same persone to whom þes wordys ben arectyd, whech oftyntyme suffir gret schame & repref & am not gylty in þis mater, God I take to record' [I am that same person to whom these words are imputed, who oftentimes suffers great shame and reproof and am not guilty in this matter, God I take to record] (244–245, chp. 9). Margery is offended by the lie being circulated about her but Mazzoni proposes that we readers take a different approach. In the story of Margery's alleged gluttony, 'Penance is eschewed in favor of pleasure' and so, 'rather than hastily reject the anecdote as false and even defamatory', we could instead perceive the situation as one where 'Margery identifies the excessive abstinence of red herrings as sinful, and enjoyment of the good pike as one of the gifts available in God's kitchen' (Mazzoni 2005, 113–114).

Margery is interrogated by the Archbishop of York on charges of Lollardy, which included illegal preaching, from which women were banned and which, it was often claimed, Lollards encouraged (Staley 1994, 7). She is also accused of defaming priests by a doctor who claims she 'told me þe werst talys of prestys þat euyr I herde' (126, chp. 52) [told me the worst tales of priests that ever I heard]. Margery tells the tale again to the Archbishop: a priest is wandering in a wood and when night falls he comes across a lovely garden, in the middle of which grows a pear tree that is covered with flowers, when an ugly bear shakes the tree, knocks down the flowers and devours them. The bear then turns his tail end towards the priest and voids out the flowers as excrement. The priest wonders what this means and a pilgrim or palmer, a messenger of God, explains that the priest himself is the pear tree, 'sumdel florischyng & floweryng thorw þi Seruyse seyyng & þe Sacramentys ministryng' [somewhat flourishing and flowering, through your service saying (i.e. of the mass) and administering of the sacrament], which he ruins by attending mass without devotion and receiving 'þe frute of euyrlestyng lyfe, þe Sacrament of þe Awter, in ful febyl disposicyon' (127, chp. 52) [the fruit of everlasting life, the sacrament of the altar, in full feeble disposition]. The priest also commits the sin of gluttony, drinking ale to excess, and is given to lechery, and he is thus like the bear, destroying the flowers of virtuous living.

Theresa Kemp observes that Margery's tale 'engages implicitly in several key theological debates of the time (including the effect of the priest's spiritual state on a communicant and the eucharist)' and it 'disturbs the authorities because it uses the material language of Lollard eucharistic discourse' (Kemp 1999, 243). Margery's tale is apparently orthodox, upholding the authority of the Church and the sacrament, despite the actions of one bad priest, yet Kemp detects 'an implicitly subversive meaning. The small fair white flowers of the pear tree, which the bear greedily eats and devours, visibly resemble the small white bit of bread consumed in the sacrament' (Kemp 1999, 244); as Lynn Staley observes, 'it is all too like Lollard attacks on the doctrine of transubstantiation' and their 'rebuttals of sacramental efficacy', which often 'focused on the physical process of defecation', that if the body of Christ is in the host and is consumed, then it is also digested and defecated (Staley 1994, 8). This would remain a concern for Protestant commentators: as discussed in Chapter 3, Milton too raises the question of what might happen to the body of Christ when consumed as the Communion bread in the context of the materiality of angels and their appetites in *Paradise Lost*. Notably, Margery's tale refers to the flowers of the pear tree, not its fruit, but she does make a reference to fruit in her tale. In the spirit of Lollard views on the sacrament of Communion, the bread might well be evoked by the little white flowers but it is also what Margery means when she refers to 'the fruit of everlasting life, the sacrament of the altar', by which she means the spiritual Eucharist not its physical presence. Margery's tale reworks the biblical story of gluttony and lechery. It is not a female sinner (our first mother, Eve) who is responsible for bringing ugliness to the beautiful garden by eating from the tree but a male sinner, the priest (our father), and the usual medieval notion of fruit suggesting gluttony and sexual sin is refigured in the flowers consumed by the bear and his excrement. This time fruit is something that the good Christian ought to consume; the 'fruit', that is, Christ's body, when received in a state of grace, is not forbidden but rather to be desired.

In the literary works considered in this chapter gluttony is repeatedly related to the original biblical transgression of Eve and connections are repeatedly drawn between gluttony and sex. Gluttony is a social sin as well as a personal one because taking more than one's fair share of food and drink means someone else will have to go without. Although in *Piers Plowman* Langland condemns wasters and shirkers, he especially condemns the hypocritical men of God, the wealthy, and professional men and women, such as spice merchants and brewsters, who cheat their customers, a view that also dominates in Chaucer's *Canterbury Tales*. Margery sublimates ordinary human desires – for sex with her husband, relationships with her children, and for food – but there is little sense that she is suffering deprivation as a result; rather, she apparently enjoys the abstinence she practises and the power it gives her. Self-induced hunger is one thing but hunger that is imposed by external factors quite another: it is a cruel enemy in Langland's poem and greatly feared by the ordinary people. An ideal state is one where humanity is neither hungry nor overfed, and the temperance of Chaucer's widow in 'The Nun's Priest's Tale' means she does not suffer the self-imposed ailments endured by the gluttonous. Whilst Margery cannot be sure to receive hospitality from those she encounters, the reader is warned against manipulative hosts in *Sir Gawain and the Green Knight* and *The Canterbury Tales*.

The motif of the biblical fruit, figured in medieval culture as an apple, runs throughout these texts but other phenomena can also represent indulgence: in Chaucer's 'Merchant's Tale' the pear stands for the paradisiacal fruit in much the same way that the girdle represents it in *Sir Gawain and the Green Knight*, with Chaucer's pear allowing for further signification, namely pregnancy and male genitalia, that the apple does not so readily evoke. The pear also appears in Margery's potentially subversive story about a gluttonous and hypocritical priest. In all these works of literature we see that food is never simply about what gets eaten but, rather, carries a range of complex and highly significant meanings that provide a way into the preoccupations and desires of our medieval ancestors.

Notes

1 In his translation of *Livre de Chasse* Edward of Norwich, Second Duke of York, omitted some of the detail about hunts and animals not found in England and added five new chapters which established the English tradition of hunting manuals. Lull's work was translated from Catalan into French and then into English by William Caxton who published it in 1484. The *Regimen sanitatis Salerni*, a Latin poem written in the twelfth or thirteenth century and attributed to Joannes De Mediolano (John of Milan), was first translated into verse by Sir John Harington in 1607, the first English translation to fully capture the spirit of the original text (De Mediolano and Harington 1607).

2 The cat controlling the mice is an allegory of John of Gaunt's control over Richard II's court.

3 All quotations of *Piers Plowman* are from Langland (1869), silently adopting square-bracketed readings (for variations between manuscripts) and italics used for expanded abbreviations.

4 Lot was often referred to as an example of how the sin of gluttony acted as a conduit to lust, both sins of the flesh, and excessive drinking was regularly condemned by the priest in medieval churches, with Noah also mentioned as an example of the dangers of drinking too much (*Genesis* 9:20). Throughout this volume the King James Bible is cited for the convenience of the modern reader; although medieval authors would have had access to the Latin Vulgate – and early modern authors to a number of English translations of this Latin text – no textual cruxes are considered in the book and it therefore seems unnecessary to cite a specific version of the Bible. Even if we could be sure which particular version of the Bible each of our authors used, they presumably would have recalled many of their biblical references and allusions from sermons and other religious and literary works they had encountered in written and verbal forms.

5 The pelican carried the dual signification of greedy young and generous parent, the latter sometimes used to signify Christ sacrificing his flesh and blood to feed humankind. See the section on *The Book of Margery Kempe* for more on this.

6 Hunting priests are also denounced by Conscience (3.309–312) and by Clergy (10. 306–316).

7 These are the earliest available printed volumes of these recipes; in citations the Arabic numeral indicates the page on which the recipe appears and (when available and unambiguous) the Roman numeral the specific recipe.

8 For more on blancmanger, see the section on *The Canterbury Tales* discussing Chaucer's Cook, below.

9 One must travel through meekness, or humility, until reaching Conscience, follow a brook called 'beth-buxum-of-speche' (5.575) [be gracious of speech], and other allegorical routes, until one reaches a gate kept by Grace: 'þe wiket þat þe womman shette / Tho Adam and Eue eten apples vnrosted' (5.611–612) [the wicket-gate that the woman shut / When Adam and Eve ate apples raw].

10 All quotations of *Sir Gawain and the Green Knight* are from Anon. (1978) and citations give line numbers from this edition.

11 The hunt is a deer-drive, the pursuit of barren female deer, which Rooney explains was less challenging for the hunter than pursuit of a solitary stag because most of the skill involved is that of the beaters driving the deer towards the hunters (Rooney 1993, 166–167).

12 James Heffernan points out that the word 'gome' / 'game', used several times in the poem, also carried multiple meanings: 'this richly polysemous word could signify a warrior, a person (as in 2161 . . .), a diversion (as in the "Crystemas gomme" proposed by the Green Knight, 284), an animal killed in a hunt, or sexual intercourse, the game of love' (Heffernan 2014, 101).

13 All quotations of *The Canterbury Tales* are from Chaucer (1988); citations give line numbers from this edition, and its notes inform the modernization given.

14 The connection between primal sin and lust is also apparent in 'The Cook's Tale' according to Olga Burakov who compares the disobedient Perkyn to the biblical Adam: Perkyn is described as the rotten apple that must be gotten rid of and, ousted from his master's shop, ends up keeping company with a fallen woman (Burakov 2002).

15 For a discussion of this phenomenon and how it relates to the modern condition of anorexia nervosa, see Bynum (1987, 194–207).

16 All quotations of *The Book of Margery Kempe* are from Kempe (1940) using page then chapter numbers and silently adopting its expansion of abbreviations.

17 The stockfish as metaphor also occurs later when God praises Margery's obedience, saying 'þu art so buxom to my wille & cleuyst as sore on-to me as þe skyn of stokfysche cleuyth to a mannys handys whan it is sothyn' (91, chp. 37) [thou art so kind to my will and cleave as fast onto me as the skin of the stockfish cleaves to a man's hand when it is boiled].

18 By fasting, even when not required to by God, Margery may also be asserting control over her own body, which seems to have been a common motive for the medieval practice by women of 'holy fasting' (or *anorexia mirabilis*), as noted in the discussion of Chaucer's reference to the fasting of Saint Cecilia in 'The Second Nun's Prologue' (above).

References

Anon. 1780. *The Forme of Cury, A Roll of Ancient English Cookery*. Ed. Samuel Pegge. London. J. Nichols.

——. 1888. *Two Fifteenth Century Cookery Books: Harleian MS. 279 (Ab 1430,) and Harl. MS. 4016 (Ab. 1450,) with Extracts from Ashmole MS. 1439, Laud MS. 553, and Douce MS. 55*. Ed. Thomas Austin. London. N. Trubner for the Early English Text Society.

——. 1978. *The Poems of the Pearl Manuscript: Pearl, Cleanness, Patience, Sir Gawain and the Green Knight*. Ed. Malcolm Andrew and Ronald Waldron. London. Edward Arnold.

——. 1998. *Sir Gawain and the Green Knight*. Trans. Keith Harrison. Intr. Helen Cooper. Oxford World's Classics. Oxford. Oxford University Press.

Barr, Helen. 1994. *Signes and Sothe: Language in the* Piers Plowman *Tradition*. Piers Plowman Studies. Vol. 10. Cambridge. D. S. Brewer.

Benedict, Saint. 1952. *The Rule of Saint Benedict: In Latin and English*. Trans. and ed. Justin McCann. Orchard Books. London. Burns Oates.

Bennett, Judith M. 1996. *Ale, Beer, and Brewsters in England: Women's Work in a Changing World, 1300–1600*. New York. Oxford University Press.

Benson, C. David. 2004. *Public* Piers Plowman: *Modern Scholarship and Late Medieval English Culture*. London (Eurospan). Pennsylvania State University Press.

Biebel, Elizabeth M. 1998. 'Pilgrims to Table: Food Consumption in Chaucer's *Canterbury Tales*'. *Food and Eating in Medieval Europe*. Eds. Martha Carlin and Joel T. Rosenthal. London. Hambledon. 15–26.

Biggins, D. 1964. 'Chaucer's Summoner: "Wel Loved he Garleek, Onyons, and Eek Lekes", C. T. I, 634'. *Notes and Queries*. n.s. 11. 48.

Birney, Earle. 1959. 'The Franklin's "Sop in Wyn"'. *Notes and Queries*. n.s. 6. 345–347.

Braddy, Haldeen. 1946. 'The Cook's Mormal and Its Cure'. *Modern Language Quarterly* 7. 265–267.

Bryant, Joseph. 1948. 'The Diet of Chaucer's Franklin'. *Modern Language Notes* 63. 318–325.

Burakov, Olga. 2002. 'Chaucer's the *Cook's Tale*'. *The Explicator* 61. 2–5.

Bynum, Caroline Walker. 1987. *Holy Feast and Holy Fast: The Religious Significance of Food to Medieval Women*. Berkeley. University of California Press.

Chaucer, Geoffrey. 1957. *The Works of Geoffrey Chaucer*. 2nd edn. Ed. F. N. Robinson. Boston, MA. Houghton Mifflin.

——. 1977. *The Canterbury Tales*. Trans. Nevill Coghill. Penguin Classics. London. Penguin.

——. 1988. *The Riverside Chaucer*. 3rd edn. Ed. Larry D. Benson based on the edition edited by F. N. Robinson. Oxford. Oxford University Press.

Cherewatuk, Karen. 2009. 'Becoming Male, Medieval Mothering, and Incarnational Theology in *Sir Gawain and the Green Knight* and *The Book of Margery Kempe*'. *Arthuriana* 19. 15–24.

Clark, Peter. 1978. 'The Alehouse and the Alternative Society'. *Puritans and Revolutionaries: Essays in Seventeenth-Century History Presented to Christopher Hill*. Eds. Donald Pennington and Keith Thomas. Oxford. Clarendon Press. 47–72.

Cooper, Helen. 1989. *The Canterbury Tales*. Oxford Guides to Chaucer. Oxford. Clarendon.

Cox, Catherine S. 2001. 'Genesis and Gender in *Sir Gawain and the Green Knight*'. *Chaucer Review* 35. 378–390.

Curry, Walter Clyde. 1926. *Chaucer and the Mediaeval Sciences*. London. Allen and Unwin.

Daly, Peter M., Virginia W. Callahan and Simon Cuttler, eds. 1985. *Andreas Alciatus*. Vol. 1: The Latin Emblems. Indexes and Lists. 2 vols. Index Emblematicus. Toronto. University of Toronto Press.

Dante, Alighieri. 1880. *Dante's Inferno*. Trans. Henry Francis Cary. New York. Cassell Publishing.

De Foix, Gaston and Second Duke of York Edward of Norwich. 1909. *The Master of Game*. Trans. and with additions by Edward of Norwich, Second Duke of York. Eds. William A. Baillie-Grohman and Florence Nickalls Baillie-Grohman. London. Chatto and Windus.

De Mediolano, Joannes and John Harington. 1607. *The Englishmans Docter or The Schoole of Salerne (Regimen sanitatis Salerni)*. Trans. Sir John Harington. STC 21605. London. Printed [by William Jaggard] for John Helme, and John Busby Junior.

De Voraigne, Jacobus. 2012. *The Golden Legend: Readings on the Saints*. Trans. William Granger Ryan. Intr. Eamon Duffy. Princeton, NJ. Princeton University Press.

Dyer, Christopher. 1998. 'Did the Peasants Really Starve in Medieval England?' *Food and Eating in Medieval Europe*. Eds. Martha Carlin and Joel T. Rosenthal. London. Hambledon Press. 53–71.

Everest, Carol A. 1995. 'Pears and Pregnancy in Chaucer's "Merchant's Tale"'. *Food in the Middle Ages: A Book of Essays*. Ed. Melitta Weiss Adamson. Garland Medieval Casebooks. 11. New York. Garland. 161–175.

Farrier, Susan E. 1995. 'Hungry Heroes in Medieval Literature'. *Food in the Middle Ages: A Book of Essays*. Ed. Melitta Weiss Adamson. Garland Medieval Casebooks. 12. New York. Garland. 145–159.

Gallacher, Patrick. 1976. 'Food, Laxatives, and Catharsis in Chaucer's *Nun's Priest's Tale*'. *Speculum* 51. 49–68.

Grennen, Joseph E. 1968. 'Chaucerian Portraiture: Medicine and the Monk'. *Neuphilologische Mitteilungen* 69. 569–574.

Hammond, P. W. 1993. *Food and Feast in Medieval England*. Stroud. Alan Sutton.

Heffernan, James A. W. 2014. *Hospitality and Treachery in Western Literature*. New Haven, CT. Yale University Press.

Hench, Atcheson L. 1937. 'On the Subtly Creeping Wine of Chaucer's Pardoner'. *Modern Language Notes* 52. 27–28.

Houle, Peter J. 1972. *The English Morality and Related Drama: A Bibliographical Survey*. Hamden, CT. Archon.

Kauffman, Corinne E. 1970. 'Dame Pertelote's Parlous Parle'. *Chaucer Review* 4. 41–48.

Kemp, Theresa D. 1999. 'The Lingua Materna and the Conflict over Vernacular Religious Discourse in Fifteenth-Century England'. *Philological Quarterly* 78. 233–257.

Kempe, Margery. 1940. *The Book of Margery Kempe*. Eds. Sanford Brown Meech and Hope Emily Allen. The Early English Text Society. London. Oxford University Press.

——. 1985. *The Book of Margery Kempe*. Trans. and intr. B. A. Windeatt. Penguin Classics. London. Penguin.

——. 2001. *The Book of Margery Kempe: A New Translation, Contexts, Criticism*. Ed. Lynn Staley. New York. Norton.

Kim, Margaret. 2004. 'The Politics of Consuming Worldly Goods: Negotiating Christian Discipline and Feudal Power in *Piers Plowman*'. *Traditio* 59. 339–368.

Langland, William. 1869. *The Vision of William Concerning Piers the Plowman*. Ed. Walter W. Skeat. The Early English Text Society. London. Oxford University Press.

——. 1976. *Piers Plowman: The Prologue and Passus I–VII of the B Text as Found in Bodleian MS. Laud 581*. Ed. J. A. W. Bennett. Clarendon Medieval and Tudor Series. Oxford. Oxford University Press.

Levy-Navarro, Elena. 2008. *The Culture of Obesity in Early and Late Modernity: Body Image in Shakespeare, Jonson, Middleton, and Skelton*. Basingstoke. Palgrave Macmillan.

Leyerle, John. 1976. 'Thematic Interlace in the *Canterbury Tales*'. *Essays and Studies* 29. 107–121.

Lull, Ramon. 1926. *The Book of the Ordre of Chyualry*. Trans. William Caxton. Ed. Alfred T. P. Byles. London. Oxford University Press.

Lumiansky, Robert Mayer. 1966. 'Two Notes on *The Canterbury Tales*'. *Studies in Language and Literature in Honour of Margaret Schlauch*. Eds. Mieczyslaw Brahmer, Stanislaw Helsztynski and Julian Kryzanowski. Warsaw. Polish Scientific Publishers. 227–232.

Lynch, Kathryn L. 2007. 'From Tavern to Pie Shop: The Raw, the Cooked, and the Rotten in Fragment 1 of Chaucer's *Canterbury Tales*'. *Exemplaria* 19. 117–138.

Mann, Jill. 1973. *Chaucer and Medieval Estates Satire: The Literature of Social Classes and the* General Prologue *to the* Canterbury Tales. Cambridge. Cambridge University Press.
——. 1979. 'Eating and Drinking in *Piers Plowman*'. *Essays and Studies* 32. 26–43.
——. 1986. 'Price and Value in *Sir Gawain and the Green Knight*'. *Essays in Criticism* 36.4. 294–318.
Mazzoni, Cristina. 2005. *The Women in God's Kitchen: Cooking, Eating, and Spiritual Writing.* New York. Continuum.
Miller, Milton. 1950. 'The Heir in the Merchant's Tale'. *Philological Quarterly* 29. 437–440.
Miller, William Ian. 1997. 'Gluttony'. *Representations* 60. 92–112.
Nichols Jr., Robert E. 1967. 'The Pardoner's Ale and Cake'. *Publications of the Modern Language Association* 82. 498–504.
Olsen, Paul. 1961. 'Chaucer's Merchant and January's "Hevene in Erthe Heere"'. *English Literary History* 28. 203–214.
Owst, G. R. 1961. *Literature and Pulpit in Medieval England: A Neglected Chapter in the History of English Letters and of the English People.* Oxford. Basil Blackwell.
Pearcy, Roy J. 1974. 'Does the Manciple's Prologue Contain a Reference to Hell's Mouth?' *English Language Notes* 11. 167–175.
Robertson, D. W. 1963. *A Preface to Chaucer: Studies in Medieval Perspectives.* Princeton, NJ. Princeton University Press.
Rooney, Anne. 1993. *Hunting in Middle English Literature.* Cambridge. D. S. Brewer.
Salih, Sarah. 2001. *Versions of Virginity in Late Medieval England.* Cambridge. D. S. Brewer.
Savage, Anne. 2008. '*Piers Plowman*: The Translation of Scripture and Food for the Soul'. *English Studies* 74. 209–221.
Schmidt, A. V. C. 1980. 'Langland's Structural Imagery'. *Essays in Criticism* 30. 311–325.
Scully, Terence. 1995. *The Art of Cookery in the Middle Ages.* Woodbridge. Boydell.
Snyder, James. 1976. 'Jan Van Eyck and Adam's Apple'. *Art Bulletin* 58. 511–515.
Staley, Lynn. 1994. *Margery Kempe's Dissenting Fictions.* Philadelphia, PA. Pennsylvania State University Press.
Steadman, John M. 1956. 'The Prioress' Dogs and Benedictine Discipline'. *Modern Philology* 54. 1–6.
Swart, J. 1954. 'The Construction of Chaucer's *General Prologue*'. *Neophilologus* 38. 127–136.
Thiébaux, Marcelle. 1974. *The Stag of Love: The Chase in Medieval Literature.* Ithaca, NY. Cornell University Press.
Wilson, C. Anne. 1976. *Food and Drink in Britain: From the Stone Age to Recent Times.* Harmondsworth. Penguin.
——. 1991. 'The Evolution of the Banquet Course: Some Medicinal, Culinary and Social Aspects'. *'Banquetting Stuff': The Fare and Social Background of the Tudor and Stuart Banquet.* Ed. C. Anne Wilson. Edinburgh. Edinburgh University Press. 9–35.
Wilson, Katharina M. 1985. 'Chaucer and St. Jerome: The Use of "Barley" in the Wife of Bath's Prologue'. *Chaucer Review* 19. 245–251.

2

BODILY HEALTH AND SPIRITUAL WEALTH (1550–1650)

Joan Fitzpatrick

This chapter begins with an early modern literary text that reveals a clear sense of continuity with the medieval past: Edmund Spenser's allegorical epic poem *The Faerie Queene*, the first three books of which were first published in 1590, with the next three complete books published in 1596. Spenser's poem is self-consciously archaic and while his debt to Chaucer and the classical world means he looks back to the past, his Faerie Land is rooted in early modern Protestant England under the governance of Queen Elizabeth. Also considered in this chapter are a number of plays by Shakespeare, with particular attention given to Shakespeare's depiction of Sir John Oldcastle (Falstaff), his engagement with ancient and early modern Catholic Italy, and the influence his writing had upon two of his contemporaries, Francis Beaumont and John Fletcher, in their play *The Woman Hater*, first published in 1607.[1] Analysis of three of the most important plays by another of Shakespeare's contemporaries, Ben Jonson, concludes the chapter: *Volpone*, *The Alchemist* and *Bartholomew Fair* (published in 1605, 1616 and 1631 respectively); all involve food to a remarkable degree, arguably revealing Jonson's debt to Langland as a prominent critic of England's social ills. In Chapter 1 we saw that medieval literature focused on religious authority and social rank, with these related concepts often explored via references to food, and some of the themes that emerged are also dominant in the early modern literature here discussed, namely gluttony, hunger, feasting and cannibalism. However, their treatment is often different, which is unsurprising given the important economic, political and social changes that took place in England during the late fifteenth and early sixteenth centuries, not least the end of feudalism and the emergence of a capitalist economy, England's shift from Catholicism to Protestantism, and the beginning also of European expansion abroad.

The contextual material that helps us to make sense of the food references in the literary texts here considered are religious and the Bible is still an important guide to moral behaviour, although much of its didacticism is now distilled through the Homilies, sermons on particular topics that were validated by the Church of England and delivered in churches across the country. The biblical story of Adam and Eve and the apple as a symbol of sin that appears so frequently in medieval literature is less dominant in the literature considered in this chapter. Hunting as a theme is also less dominant, with hunting knights relegated to the past: Spenser is more concerned with his knights' ability to defeat evil (often at some level a representative of Catholic sin) and Shakespeare's Sir John Oldcastle adheres to few of the chivalric codes outlined in Ramon Lull's medieval rules dictating what constitutes a good knight. More cookbooks were printed in the early modern period than before, amongst them Thomas Dawson's *The Good Housewife's Jewel* (1587) and Robert May's *The Accomplished Cook* (1650), the first English recipe book aimed at professional cooks, whilst the influence of ancient cookery books such as *De re coquinaria* (*The Art of Cooking*), attributed to the Roman Apicius, is also apparent, specifically in the works of Jonson. Dietary literature became an immensely popular genre, with the titles here considered including Thomas Elyot's *Castle of Health* (1541), Andrew Boorde's *Compendious Regiment of Health* (1547) and William Bullein's *Government of Health* (1558), all of which were reprinted several times and revised for subsequent editions. As the title of this chapter indicates, the texts here considered repeatedly draw connections between a healthy body and a healthy spirit, which is often figured in terms of moral and psychological well-being.

Edmund Spenser, *The Faerie Queene* (1590 and 1596)

In Edmund Spenser's epic poem *The Faerie Queene* food and feeding are presented allegorically and like Langland, and to some degree Chaucer also, Spenser tends to focus on the extremes of consumption, specifically gluttony and hunger. There is a repeated emphasis on how extremes ought to be tempered by moderation and continence: excess signals bodily and spiritual degeneration and the only way to remain free from sin is to behave moderately. The virtues extolled by Spenser in each of the six complete books of his poem reveal the importance of exerting physical, spiritual and social control upon impulses that would otherwise lead to sin and damnation. Holiness, Temperance, Chastity, Friendship, Justice and Courtesy are dependent upon one another, with each in turn relying upon a measured response to the passions and an ability to act with restraint. The connections drawn between gluttony and lust, apparent in the medieval literature considered in Chapter 1, are also evident in Spenser's poem, where an inclination to indulge in one kind of appetite exposes a good Christian to the dangers of the other. Not eating is more complex in Spenser, where the hungry are not simply victims of the gluttony of others. In *The Faerie Queene* hunger and signs of starvation often signal a lack of spiritual sustenance in both good Christian knights who have temporarily lost their way and the villain who is emaciated and beyond spiritual revival. Cannibalism as a perverse kind of consumption features prominently in Spenser's poem, where it is also aligned with lust and incest, the most extremely intemperate sexual behaviour. For this Protestant poet cannibalism also signals the Catholic sacrament of transubstantiation (a connection that similarly emerges in Joyce's *Ulysses* in Chapter 6) and, given that the poem was written whilst Spenser was living in colonial Ireland, cannibalism (like hunger) might also allude to the grim reality of desperate measures in times of war.

The Elizabethan *Homily Against Gluttony and Drunkenness* (1563) gave the Church line on appropriate consumption, which was comparable with medieval views on the harm done by gluttony considered in the previous chapter. According to the homily, excess offends God, and the abuse of food and drink, as well as other pleasures such as wearing sumptuous clothing, provokes disease and wrongdoing (Church of England 1563, Oo2r). Gluttony could extend to taking excessive pleasure in food as well as eating too much and it was akin to other crimes such as idolatry; indeed those who indulge in culinary pleasure are guilty of a kind of idolatry for they are 'belly gods' (Church of England 1563, Oo2r–Oo2v) and 'beastly belly-slaves' (Church of England 1563, Oo5r) who allow the body to take precedence over the spirit. The homily provides several biblical examples of the consequences of gluttony that were common also in medieval discussions of the sin: for example Adam and Eve's eating of the forbidden fruit, Noah's drunkenness and Lot's lust for his own daughters, with the faithful being warned that God might punish gluttony by sending famine (Church of England 1563, Oo3v, Oo4r–Oo4v). As well as making the body susceptible to all kinds of disease, gluttony makes the sinner intellectually feeble (Church of England 1563, Oo6v, Oo8v–Pp1r). Moreover, the glutton is potentially seditious: 'They are vnprofitable to the common wealth. For a dronkarde is neyther fyt to rule, nor to be ruled' (Church of England 1563, Pp1v).[2] Early modern dietaries also warn against gluttony, with Thomas Elyot denouncing the English habit of eating too much too often and consuming different sorts of food at one meal, a habit Andrew Boorde claims the English are especially prone to indulge (Boorde 1547, C4v). Elyot condemns 'the spirite of gluttony triumphynge amonge vs in his glorious chariotte . . . dryuynge [driving] vs afore hym, as his prisoners in to his dungeon of surfet' where the gluttons are tormented with many sicknesses before being 'cruelly put to dethe by them, oftentimes in youth or in the most pleasant tyme of our lyfe'; so too William Bullein warns against the diseases to which gluttons are prone (Elyot 1541, N1r; Bullein 1558, C2r).

When Spenser's knight of Holiness, Redcross, encounters Gluttony in the House of Pride he has already fallen into sin by allowing himself to be deceived by the evil magician Archimago, which has led him to abandon his lady Una and be seduced by Duessa, a witch and whore. The House of Pride is presided over by Lucifera and her six counsellors – Idleness, Gluttony, Lechery, Avarice, Envy and Wrath – who ride on the beasts that pull her chariot (recalling the chariot mentioned by Elyot above); each reveals the particular sin they represent through their attire, the beasts they ride and the diseases from which they suffer. The order in which they parade is important, suggesting that idleness leads to gluttony, gluttony to lechery and so on. Gluttony is described in terms of physical and moral degeneracy:

> Deformed creature, on a filthie swyne,
> His belly was vp-blowne with luxury,
> And eke with fatnesse swollen were his eyne,
> And like a Crane his necke was long and fyne,
> With which he swallowd vp excessiue feast,
> For want whereof poore people oft did pyne;
> And all the way, most like a brutish beast,
> He spued vp his gorge, that all did him deteast.
>
> *(1.4.21.2–9)*

With his over-large belly Gluttony clearly eats too much, yet it is not simply the volume of food consumed that presents a problem but the kind of food eaten: he is 'vp-blowne with luxury' (1.4.21.2) and takes enormous pleasure in food – the crane being an emblem of gluttony with its long neck facilitating extended pleasure in swallowing (Spenser 2001, 66n5) – thus conforming to Gregory the Great's definition of gluttony, whereby the sin might be committed not merely by eating too much but by eating too soon, too expensively, too eagerly and too daintily (Delany 1909). Like the gluttons in Langland's *Piers Plowman*, Gluttony's excessive consumption of food is sinful because it is selfish, depriving others of basic sustenance. Gluttony wears vine leaves because his hot and sweaty body is unable to bear any other clothes (1.4.22.3–4) and he eats and drinks constantly: 'Still as he rode, he somewhat still did eat, / And in his hand did beare a bouzing can' (1.4.22.6–7). Like Chaucer's Cook, who is apparently so drunk that he falls off his horse, Spenser's Gluttony drinks so often that 'His dronken corse he scarse vpholden can, / In shape and life more like a monster, then a man' (1.4.22.8–9).

The repeated references to Gluttony's unhuman nature – he is a 'creature', he rides on a filthy pig, he vomits like a beast – suggest degeneration from man to beast, something early modern dietary literature warns the glutton against. Andrew Boorde suggests that any man of leisure who eats more than two meals a day, or any labourer more than three, 'lyueth a beestly lyfe' [liveth a beastly life] and Thomas Elyot notes that excessive drinking 'transformeth a man or woman, makynge them beastly' (Boorde 1547, C4r; Elyot 1541, K3r–K3v). William Bullein warns against the 'gready [greedy] gluttons' who are responsible for deforming their bodies, listing the physical ailments likely to result from 'delight in plenty of bankettes [banquets]', amongst them stinking vomits and blindness (Bullein 1558, C2v). Spenser's glutton has harmed not only his body – with his distended stomach, swollen eyes, vomiting and diseases (1.4.23.6) – but also his moral character, whereby he is ' Vnfit . . . for any worldy thing' and 'Not meet to be of counsell to a king' (1.4.23.1–3).

Those staying in the House of Pride, and presumably Redcross also, enjoy an evening of pleasure:

That night they pas in ioy and iollity,
Feasting and courting both in bowre and hall;
For Steward was excessiue *Gluttonie*
That of his plenty poured forth to all;
Which doen, the Chamberlain *Slowth* did to rest them call.
(1.4.43.5–9)

After Redcross discovers a dungeon full of the damned, and realizes he is in real danger, he escapes from the House of Pride but is found by Duessa, his continued moral degeneration signalled by the fact that he is unarmed and 'feedes vpon the cooling shade' (1.7.3.1); later he will drink from a fountain, which exacerbates his idleness, before being captured by the giant Orgoglio, Duessa's lover. Excessive consumption, dietary and sexual, or the wrong kind of consumption indicates moral corruption and it is only when Redcross visits the House of Holiness that he will receive the spiritual sustenance he requires from the inhabitants of that house who include Cælia and her three daughters: Fidelia, Speranza and Charissa (Faith, Hope and Charity). Redcross repents for his sins and Charissa demonstrates selfless love:

Her necke and breasts were euer open bare,
That ay thereof her babes might sucke their fill;
The rest was all in yellow robes arayed still.
(1.10.30.7–9)

Unlike Gluttony and Redcross who feed themselves excessively or on the wrong sorts of things, Charissa provides wholesome sustenance to others; we are specifically told that her babies are fed 'whiles they were weake and young, / But thrust them forth still, as they wexed old' (1.10.3–4), the sense being that she will provide sustenance to the innocent until they can fend for themselves. Like the other inhabitants of the house, she instructs Redcross in virtue before he is led to a holy place where he meets seven Bead-men (men of prayer), the second of whom, the 'Almner of the place', is charged with providing relief to the needy:

His office was, the hungry for to feed,
And thristy giue to drinke, a worke of grace:
He feard not once him selfe to be in need,
Ne car'd to hoord for those, whom he did breede:
The grace of God he layd vp still in store,
Which as a stocke he left vnto his seede;
He had enough, what need him care for more?
And had he lesse, yet some he would giue to the pore.
(1.10.38.2.1–9)

When Redcross has been spiritually revived, he leaves the House of Holiness in preparation for his battle with the Dragon who holds Una's parents captive.

However, in the midst of this battle he will require further spiritual sustenance, a benefit that will come from the Well of Life, which is 'Full of great vertues, and for med'cine good', and the Tree of Life, which is 'Loaden with fruit and apples rosie red' (1.11.46.2).[3] Interestingly, Redcross does not drink from the well or eat from the tree but rather falls into the well and is restored by the balm of the tree. The water from the well clearly indicates baptism since it has the power to restore the dead to life: 'And guilt of sinfull crimes cleane wash away' (1.11.30.2). The balm from the tree is also restorative: 'Life and long health that gratious ointment gaue, / And deadly woundes could heale, and reare againe' (1.11.48.6), which John Erskine Hankins claims is the oil of 'Extreme Unction', also known as 'Anointing of the Sick', which is one of the 'Last Rites' administered in Catholic ritual to those close to death (Hankins 1971, 118–119). It is not clear why Spenser would avoid having Redcross eat the fruit from the Tree of Life, which the narrator claims will give 'happie life to all, which thereon fed, / And life eke euerlasting' (1.11.46.5–6), but he provides a clue in the narrator's reference to 'the crime of our first fathers fall' (1.11.46.9), that is Adam's sin in eating from the tree of knowledge which prevented his consumption of the Tree of Life. Spenser may have felt that there would be too great an association with Adam's sin if Redcross were to eat from the tree or that he requires receipt of the holy sacraments of baptism and extreme unction before he is ready to consume its fruit.

Abstinence from food is apparently part of Redcross's spiritual cleansing and can be contrasted with the degenerative feeding in which he earlier indulged, a feeding that was directly connected to his lustful relationship with Duessa. The good Christian knight is expected to regulate his appetites, dietary and sexual, and excess should be avoided at all cost. In Book Two of *The Faerie Queene* the reader encounters excess in two distinct forms: the seductive and pleasure-loving witch, Acrasia, and the ascetic and violent rebel, Maleger. The latter is the captain of a villainous mob who lay siege to Alma's House of Temperance; they are described as 'Vile caytiue wretches, ragged, rude, deformd, / All threatning death, all in straunge manner armd' (2.9.13.4–5). Their captain is described as follows:

> As pale and wan as ashes was his looke,
> His bodie leane and meagre as a rake,
> And skin all withered like a dryed rooke,
> Thereto as cold and drery as a Snake,
> That seem'd to tremble euermore, and quake:
> All in a canuas thin he was bedight,
> And girded with a belt of twisted brake,
> Vpon his head he wore an Helmet light,
> Made of a dead mans skull, that seem'd a ghastly sight.
> *(2.11.22.1–9)*

Although gluttony was considered a sin and roundly condemned from the pulpit, being ascetic could also be sinful; fasting was allowed, praised even, but it all depended upon the degree and purpose. The *Homily of Fastyng* (1563) outlines the three ways in which fasting was acceptable: it ought to chastise the flesh but not be too wanton (excessive, enjoyable), it should move the subject to be more keen to pray and more sincere in praying, and it should be a testimony to humility before God and an acknowledgement of human sin (Church of England 1563, Nn1v). In the early modern dietaries too fasting is recommended so long as it is in moderation, and certain humoral types are advised to proceed with caution: Thomas Elyot warns that 'fastyng in sommer drieth the bodye, maketh the colour salowe, ingendereth melancolye and hurteth the syght' (Elyot 1541, L3r) and Andrew Boorde that 'Cholorycke [choleric] men shulde nat be longe fastynge' (Boorde 1547, H3r). Similarly William Bullein observes that just as too much food is an enemy to the body and soul and provokes sudden death, 'euen so is emptinesse a shorter of time, a weaker of the braine, a hinderer of memorye, an increaser of winde, coller [choler] and melancholye', and Thomas Muffett warns against 'thin diets' and excessive fasting, which he terms 'self-pining' (Bullein 1558, G4v; Muffett 1655, B4v, Nn3v).

Does Maleger fast or is he thin and hungry for other reasons? M. M. Gray claims that in the depiction of the siege of Alma's castle Spenser was alluding to Irish rebellion, specifically the rebellion in Munster between 1579 and 1583, and the figure of Maleger is 'perhaps in some particulars like the starving rebel leaders' (Gray 1930, 416). Maleger is thin but he is also strong – we are told that 'Full large he was of limbe, and shoulders brode' (2.11.20.7) – so his emaciation apparently signals more than a lack of nutrition. He is accompanied by the wicked hags Impotence and Impatience, and critics concur that Maleger represents sickness, his name signifying 'badly' (*male*) and 'diseased' or 'sick' (*aeger*), with his sickness being both physical and spiritual and perhaps also mental (Osgood 1931, 504–506; Hankins 1971, 84–86; Rollinson 1990). Guyon, the hero of Book Two, and the Palmer who accompanies him have left Alma's house so it is up to the heroic Arthur (future King of the Britons) to do battle with Maleger. The fight between the two resembles that between Hercules and Antaeus in Greek myth. Like Antaeus, Maleger is revived by contact with the earth and when he is struck and falls 'groueling to the ground' he quickly revives:

> When suddein vp the villein ouerthrowne,
> Out of his swowne arose, fresh to contend,
> And gan himselfe to second battell bend,
> As hurt he had not bene.
>
> *(2.11.35.3–6)*

Like Hercules, who strangled Antaeus by holding him aloft, Arthur defeats Maleger by lifting him above the ground and squeezing him to death before carrying him to 'a standing lake' and hurling him into it (2.11.46.4–9). As I have noted elsewhere, it is arguably the case that the death of Maleger suggests Spenser's desire, as an English colonist living in Ireland, to present the Irish landscape as benevolent to those who would destroy the rebels, transforming it from a source of danger and a reviver of rebellion to a source of strength for those in authority who would suppress insurrection (Fitzpatrick 2000, 366–367). Whether or not Spenser had the starving Irish rebels in mind, it is clear that Maleger's lean, cold and dry body (the melancholic humoral type) is as undesirable as that which lies at the other end of the spectrum: the fat and sweaty body of Gluttony. Earlier in Book One Redcross meets a figure similar to Maleger, the melancholic and starving Despair, who is described as 'Musing full sadly in his sullein mind' and whose 'raw-bone cheekes through penurie and pine, / Were shronke into his iawes, as he did neuer dine' (1.9.35.8–9). Although Redcross resists Despair's temptations to commit suicide, the encounter is a prelude to his sojourn in the House of Holiness. Spenser thus makes it clear that the key to physical and spiritual health, and also to social order, is a temperate balance between the two extremes of gluttony and extreme hunger.

Like Redcross, revived by the inhabitants of the House of Holiness, Arthur too is nursed back to health in the House of Alma:

> Where many Groomes and Squiers readie were,
> To take him from his steed full tenderly,
> And eke the fairest *Alma* met him there
> With balme and wine and costly spicery,
> To comfort him in his infirmity;
> Eftsoones she causd him vp to be conuayd,
> And of his armes despoyled easily,
> In sumptuous bed she made him to be layd,
> And all the while his wounds were dressing, by him stayd.
> *(2.11.49.1–9)*

The 'balme' recalls the balm from the Tree of Life that restored Redcross in Book One and wine suggests the wine of Communion, thus being symbolic of the restorative powers of the blood of Christ. Spices were expensive, highly valued and often served with wine. As we saw in the discussion of *Sir Gawain and the Green Knight* in Chapter 1, spices were considered medicinal because they were thought to be warming to the stomach and thus good for digestion. Yet where Gawain is offered wine and spices after a fine meal, Spenser emphasizes their medicinal function, which, as Jean Louis Flandrin points out, was a quality originally prioritized over their use as a flavouring (Flandrin 1999, 315–317). Spices might also be used to perfume the air, which would suggest that Alma is promoting Guyon's recovery by stimulating all of his senses, which have been impaired by the baleful influence of Maleger.

The House (or Castle) of Alma represents the body and 'sober Alma' (2.9.argument.2) represents *anima*, its soul. The metaphor of the body as a castle that acts as a defence from illness and sin was a common metaphor in the period, for example used by Thomas Elyot in naming his dietary *The Castle of Health*. The narrator's description of temperance underlines the notion that moderation reinforces social order as well as keeping the body and mind in check:

> Of all Gods workes, which do this world adorne,
> There is no one more faire and excellent,
> Then is mans body both for powre and forme,
> Whiles it is kept in sober gouernment;
> But none then it, more fowle and indecent,
> Distempred through misrule and passions bace:
> It growes a Monster, and incontinent
> Doth loose his dignitie and natiue grace.
>
> *(2.9.1.1–9)*

Again the unhuman nature of one who gives into excess is underlined. Alma is described as a beautiful virgin, who 'had not yet felt Cupides wanton rage' (2.9.18.2), and before her castle is besieged by Maleger and his men she entertains Arthur and Guyon, showing them around her house/the body. The stomach is described as a cauldron, or large pot, into which food is received, boiled and thus digested, a concept that originated with Galen and was picked up by the early modern dietary authors (Elyot 1541, N4r; Boorde 1547, C3v). As Michael Schoenfeldt points out, Spenser's depiction of the stomach as a kind of kitchen 'filled with a baffling array of tasks and workers' would have been familiar to the early moderns, and the importance of proper digestion is stressed because 'if the stomach does not work well the entire being suffers and/or dies' (Schoenfeldt 1999, 59). 'Alma' means soul but, as Schoenfeldt notes, it also means 'nourishing'; for Spenser – prior to the Cartesian division of mind and body – the soul 'does not reside in a realm separate from the body but is in large part constituted by it' (Schoenfeldt 1999, 60) and if the body is diseased, then the soul too will be affected.

Alma's virginity is a physical and spiritual reality, with the suggestion that her hymen is literally intact: she 'had not yet *felt* Cupides wanton rage'. Yet for Spenser, a Protestant poet, chastity not virginity is the ideal state and so there is a sense in which she 'had not *yet* felt Cupides wanton rage' (my emphasis in both cases). Leaving aside the fact that chastity ought to be a temperate sexual desire (and not a 'wanton rage'), it seems that Alma is destined to experience sexual desire at some point in the future within a chaste married union. In Book One of the poem Duessa provokes wanton desire in Redcross and in Book Two it is Acrasia who presents an obstacle to temperance. She is a more subtle seductress than Duessa but presents a similar danger. In the story of Amavia the consequences of Acrasia's behaviour are evident. Amavia's husband, Mortdant, has been seduced and killed by Acrasia and Amavia herself commits suicide in desperation, leaving her baby patting its hands in a pool of her blood. Before taking her own life, Amavia describes Acrasia's manner of seduction in her Bower:

> Her blisse is all in pleasure and delight,
> Wherewith she makes her louers drunken mad,
> And then with words and weedes of wondrous might,
> On them she workes her will to vses bad
>
> *(2.1.52.1–4)*

Acrasia's attempts to drug her victims are similar to those of the witch Circe, the figure upon whom she is based, from Book 10 of Homer's *Odyssey*:

> She brought them in and made them sit on chairs and seats, and made for them a potion of cheese and barley meal and yellow honey with Pramnian wine; but in the food she mixed baneful drugs, that they might utterly forget their native land.
>
> *Homer 1919, 361, lines 232–236*

Acrasia's lovers are drunk with pleasure, their sexual excess signalled in gluttonous terms that contrast with the refreshing wine Alma gave to comfort Arthur after his encounter with Maleger. Similarly, where Alma proffered 'costly spicery', Acrasia proffers weeds (herbs or drugs) and 'drugs of foule intemperance' (2.1.54.8). Herbs were less valuable than spices so the distinction is a significant one: what Acrasia offers is less valuable (indeed of no value) compared to what Alma has to give. Unlike Circe, she does not even offer food. The metaphorical drink that makes Acrasia's lovers 'drunken mad' is made literal in the charmed cup of wine and water that kills Mortdant (2.1.55) and that recalls Duessa's golden cup (1.8.14.1) with its allusion to the biblical Book of Revelation and the whore of Babylon who carries 'a cup of golde in her hand, ful of abominations, and filthines of her fornication', from which 'all nations have dronken of the wine of the wrath of her fornication' (Revelation 17:4, 18:3). As Alastair Fowler points out, the dilution of wine with water is a traditional emblem of temperance (Fowler 1960, 147–148) but here the fluids will not combine, the suggestion being that the pure water will not be tainted with the wine, just as water will not cleanse the blood from the hands of Amavia's baby, Ruddymane (Spenser 2001, 168n55.6).

When he reaches Acrasia's Bower, Guyon must resist all the temptations it has to offer. He has earlier declined Mammon's invitation to rest on a silver stool and eat some 'fruit of gold' (2.7.63.7), an allusion to the fruit of ancient myth consumed by Proserpina that contrasts with the Tree of Life that revived Redcross (Prescott 1990, 452). He has gone without food or sleep for three days and so resisting sloth and gluttony is a real test of his ability to withstand sin. He only recovers upon receiving God's grace in the shape of Arthur who helps him defeat his enemies. He will defeat Acrasia with the help of the Palmer, a pilgrim returned from the Holy Land who represents reason linked to the Christian faith (Evans 1990, 526). On the journey to Acrasia's Bower Guyon must negotiate a hazardous landscape, one containing the Gulf of Greediness, the Rock of Reproach and the Wandering Islands, passing through the Quicksand of Unthriftyhead and the Whirlpool of Decay. He resists 'the wanton Phædria' (2.12.17.1) and the mermaids who kill their victims, negotiating heavy fog and an attack by birds, and upon reaching land Guyon and the Palmer are confronted by more challenges:

> Ere long they heard an hideous bellowing,
> Of many beasts, that roard outrageously,

As if that hungers point, or *Venus* sting
Had them enraged with fell surquedry;
Yet nought they feard, but past on hardily
                    (2.12.39.1–5)

The beasts behave as though they are either starving or consumed by lust because, for Spenser, both states signify moral degeneration. When Guyon and the Palmer arrive at a gate that leads into the garden containing the Bower of Bliss, Guyon refuses the bowl of wine offered by Genius (the god of generation who sits as porter at the gate), overturning the bowl and breaking Genius's staff (2.12.46–49). At another gate sits a woman wearing disordered garments and holding a cup of gold (recalling Duessa's 'golden cup' 1.8.14.1) and a cup of wine that, like Genius, she offers to every passing stranger. This is Excess, her apparent generosity a lure to commit sin, and again Guyon rejects the offer to drink, throwing the cup to the ground and breaking it (2.12.55–57). Both these servants of Acrasia would follow her in making lovers drunk with pleasure, further reinforcing the contrast drawn between this kind of wine and that offered by Alma in the House of Temperance. Just as the wine consumed in the garden is not life-giving, neither is its water: bathing in the fountain are two naked maidens who 'wrestle wantonly' (2.12.63.11) in an attempt to seduce Guyon, the water contrasting with the healing Well of Life in which Redcross immersed himself.

Guyon's destruction of Acrasia's Bower of Bliss is brutal:

But all those pleasant bowres and Pallace braue,
Guyon broke downe, with rigour pittilesse;
Ne ought their goodly workmanship might saue
Them from the tempest of his wrathfulnesse,
But that their blisse he turn'd to balefulnesse:
Their groues he feld, their gardins did deface,
Their arbers spoyle, their Cabinets suppresse,
Their banket houses burne, their buildings race,
And of the fairest late, now made the fowlest place.
                    (2.12.83.1–9)

Guyon destroys their ability to grow food as well as the banquet-houses within which they would dine, his act of violence resembling the biblical story of Samson tearing down the building in which his enemies offer a sacrifice to their god (Judges 16:23–30), a sacrifice which is specifically characterized as a feast in Chaucer's 'Monk's Tale', as noted in Chapter 1. The term 'banquet' carried several meanings in the early modern period: it could mean a feast in the modern sense but might also indicate a snack between meals (sometimes called a 'running banquet'), a course of sweetmeats and fruit (the origin of the modern dessert course) or a wine-drinking session or carousal. A banquet-house was often used for eating the course of sweetmeats and fruit after the main meal and so would have been considered a location especially associated with indulgence. Acrasia is caught in a net and bound in chains of adamant 'For nothing else might keepe her safe and sound' (2.12.82–87). Harriet Hawkins is typical of critics who wonder at the irony of the Knight of Temperance acting in such an intemperate manner: 'Why does Guyon go so far? The source of all the danger in the garden, the sorceress Acrasia, has already been captured' (Hawkins 1976, 72).[4] Yet if we recall the destruction of which Acrasia is capable – the death of Mortdant, the suicide of Amavia and the orphaning of Ruddymane described at the beginning of Book Two – we might better understand Guyon's ferocity. As Stephen Greenblatt puts it, 'Pitiless destruction is here not a stain but a virtue' (Greenblatt 1980, 187). Finally, the Palmer undoes Acrasia's magic by turning back into men those she had transformed into swine; her act of transformation is similar to that of Circe but whereas Odysseus' men look like swine and 'their minds remained unchanged even as before', Acrasia's victims are transformed in mind and body (Homer 1919, 363, lines 241–242). The power of Acrasia's influence is clear when one of the men, Grille, is unhappy to be made human again but, rather, 'Delights in filth and foule incontinence', preferring to retain 'his hoggish mind' (2.12.87.7, 8). The man who would choose a beastly body, gratifying only physical desires, will have a beastly mind and cannot be saved.

When Guyon and the Palmer discover Acrasia in her Bower, she is leaning over her new lover, the young knight Verdant:

> And all that while, right ouer him she hong,
> With her false eyes fast fixed in his sight,
> As seeking medicine, whence she was stong,
> Or greedily depasturing delight:
> And oft inclining downe with kisses light,
> For feare of waking him, his lips bedewd,
> And through his humid eyes did sucke his spright,
> Quite molten into lust and pleasure lewd;
> Wherewith she sighed soft, as if his case she rewd.
> *(2.12.73.1–9)*

The language is bestial (she depastures like cattle) and vampiric (she sucks forth his spirit) and her consumption of Verdant follows the obliteration of all his former glory: Verdant's 'warlike armes' are hung on a nearby tree and all signs of battle on his shield have been erased. Verdant no longer cares for honour 'But in lewd loues, and wastfull luxuree, / His dayes, his goods, his bodie he did spend' (2.1.2.80.7–8). Acrasia is not literally consuming Verdant, although witches were accused of killing and eating children, especially in mainland Europe (Guazzo 1970, 91, 136), but her feeding upon Verdant is a kind of inversion of maternal feeding, especially given Spenser's emphasis upon his youth: he is 'The young man sleeping by her', his 'sweet regard, and amiable grace' is said to be 'Mixed with manly sternnesse' and 'on his tender lips the downy heare / Did now but freshly spring' (2.12.79.1, 5–6, 8–9). The name 'Verdant' suggests green and abundant vegetation, the fresh new growth that emerges in spring, and whilst Acrasia remains bound, Verdant is released by Guyon 'And counsell sage in steed thereof to him applyde' (2.12.82.9); in other words, he is young enough to learn and mend his ways.

Acrasia's vampiric-like feeding upon Verdant is metaphorical but elsewhere in *The Faerie Queene* there is literal feeding upon blood and flesh. In Book One of the poem Redcross's first trial is with the monstrous serpent/woman Errour; when she is defeated by Redcross, strangled and then decapitated, her numerous young 'flocked all about her bleeding wound, / And sucked vp their dying mothers blood' (1.1.25.7–8). The unnatural act of devouring their mother is also an act of gluttony because they drink until their bellies swell and 'with fulnesse burst', the narrator emphasizing the appropriateness of their punishment: 'well worthy end / Of such as drunke her life, the which them nurst' (1.1.26.5, 6–7). Unnatural offspring also occur in Book Three, the Book of Chastity, in the shape of the giants Argante and Ollyphant, the children of Typhoeus 'who mad through merth, / And drunke with bloud of men, slaine by his might', committed incest with his own mother (3.7.47.6–7). The twins who are a product of this incest are also thought to have committed incest in their mother's womb, and continue their lustful life after birth:

> So liu'd they euer after in like sin,
> Gainst natures law, and good behauioure:
> But greatest shame was to that maiden twin,
> Who not content so fowly to deuoure
> Her natiue flesh, and staine her brothers bowre,
> Did wallow in all other fleshly myre,
> And suffred beasts her body to deflowre:
> So whot she burned in that lustfull fyre,
> Yet all that might not slake her sensuall desyre.
> *(3.7.49.1–9)*

Incest and bestiality, the most extreme manifestations of lust, are here figured in cannibalistic terms and it is a connection that Spenser will develop further in his characterization of Lust, the Wild Man who appears in Book Four of *The Faerie Queene*, the Book of Friendship. Lust is described as being shaped like a man but taller and covered with hair, with a wide mouth and 'huge great teeth, like to a tusked Bore', who seizes beasts and men and 'fed on fleshly gore, / The signe whereof yet stain'd his bloudy lips afore' (4.7.5.6, 8–9). That he feeds on raw flesh emphasizes his bestiality: as Claude Lévi-Strauss notes, the process of cooking flesh is an important indication of human culture (Lévi-Strauss 1983). The strangeness of Lust's appearance is stressed:

> His neather lip was not like man nor beast,
> But like a wide deepe poke, downe hanging low,
> In which he wont the relickes of his feast,
> And cruell spoyle, which he had spard, to stow:

And ouer it his huge great nose did grow,
Full dreadfully empurpled all with bloud;
And downe both sides two wide long eares did glow,
And raught downe to his waste, when vp he stood,
More great then th'eares of Elephants by *Indus* flood.
(4.7.6.1–9)

The description is clearly phallic, the ingenious use of his lower lip as a kind of larder reinforcing the link made between the lustful body and food. The description also suggests foreign practices: describing leftover food as relics was not unusual in the period but it also hints at Catholic ritual, and the ethnic Other is invoked by reference to the elephants of India. Although the narrator recounts how Lust feeds on 'men and beasts' (4.7.5.8), the captive Aemylia tells Amoret, his latest victim, that 'on the spoile of women he doth liue' (4.7.12.5); his victims are chaste and 'He with his shamefull lust doth first deflowre, / And afterwards themselues doth cruelly deuoure' (4.7.12.8–9). Aemylia has been imprisoned in Lust's cave for twenty days and has witnessed numerous acts of cannibalism:

During which space these sory eies haue seen
Seauen women by him slaine, and eaten clene.
And now no more for him but I alone,
And this old woman here remaining beene;
Till thou cam'st hither to augment our mone,
And of vs three to morrow he will sure eate one.
(4.7.13.4–9)

Lust's appetite for human flesh is disgusting but he does not eat to excess: just as he carefully plans his future meals by putting some flesh aside for later in his bottom lip, so he will eat only one of the unlucky women, not gorge on all three.[5] Yet Lust does resemble Gluttony from Lucifera's House of Pride (Book One): where Gluttony is clothed in green vine leaves (1.4.22.1), Lust wears a wreath of ivy about his waist (4.7.7.1), ivy being sacred to Bacchus as well as a symbol of lust when worn in this fashion (Spenser 2001, 66n22; 459n7.1–4). Amoret manages to escape from Lust's cave and Lust is killed by the virgin-warrior Belphoebe who puts an arrow through his 'greedy throat' (4.7.31.7), an interesting epithet to use given his tendency to moderation, even if he does dine on human flesh.

The Savage Nation who seize Serena in Book Six of the poem, the Book of Courtesy, are described as social parasites:

In these wylde deserts, where she now abode,
There dwelt a saluage nation, which did liue
Of stealth and spoile, and making nightly rode
Into their neighbours borders; ne did giue

> Them selues to any trade, as for to driue
> The painefull plough, or cattell for to breed,
> Or by aduentrous marchandize to thriue;
> But on the labours of poore men to feed,
> And serue their owne necessities with others need.
>
> *(6.8.35.1–9)*

Their slothful dependence on the labour of others – a social ill condemned in *Piers Plowman* (Chapter 1), in Jonson's *Volpone* (below) and said to characterize the priesthood in Joyce's *Ulysses* (Chapter 6) – is figured in cannibalistic terms and it is a small step from the metaphorical to the literal:

> Thereto they vsde one most accursed order,
> To eate the flesh of men, whom they mote fynde,
> And straungers to deuoure, which on their border
> Were brought by errour, or by wreckfull wynde.
> A monstrous cruelty gainst course of kynde.
>
> *(6.8.36.1–5)*

As well as being parasitic, the Savage Nation also break the laws of hospitality by eating those strangers to whom they should show generosity. They discuss amongst themselves what they ought to do with Serena:

> Whether to slay her there vpon the place,
> Or suffer her out of her sleepe to wake,
> And then her eate attonce; or many meales to make.
>
> *(6.8.37.7–9)*

Although we might expect animal instinct, and the desire for instant gratification, to prevail, the Savage Nation (like Lust in Book Four) take a more considered approach regarding what to do with their captive. They decide to let Serena sleep until she awakes naturally so as to fatten her for slaughter and thus maximize sustenance from her ('sleepe they sayd would make her battill better', 6.8.38.3) and then to sacrifice 'her guiltlesse bloud' to their god and 'of her dainty flesh . . . /To make a common feast, and feed with gurmandize' (6.8.38.7–9). Spenser describes the lustful and gluttonous gaze of the Savage Nation upon the various parts of Serena's body: 'Some with their eyes the daintest morsels chose; / Some praise her paps, some praise her lips and nose' (6.8.39.4–5) and after she is stripped naked, the itemizing of her body parts continues: 'Her yuorie necke, her alabaster brest, / Her paps, which like white silken pillowes were', and so on (6.8.42.1–2). Nancy Vickers explores the metaphorical dismemberment of the poetic blazon and the implied violence of the objectification involved and, as A. Leigh DeNeef points out, the Savage Nation take these latent desires to a literal extreme (Vickers 1981, 266; Vickers 1985, 97; DeNeef 1990, 637). Some members of the Savage Nation want 'by force to take their beastly pleasure' but are prevented by their priest who warns against polluting 'so sacred threasure, / Vow'd to the gods' (6.8.43.8–9).

Critics have identified the Savage Nation as Irish outlaws, with others claiming that the ritual of their ceremonies suggests the Catholic mass and transubstantiation (Fitzpatrick 1999, 99–101). Reports by English commentators suggest that survival cannibalism was practised by the Irish in times of war. In *A View of the Present State of Ireland* Spenser describes the starving Irish in Munster as 'Anotomies of deathe' that 'did eate the dead Carrions, happie wheare they Coulde finde them, Yea and one another sone after, in so muche as the verye carkasses they spared not to scrape out of theire graves' (Spenser 1949, 158). Yet it can sometimes be difficult to distinguish report from metaphor, fact from stereotype, for example when John Davies in *A Discovery of the True Causes Why Ireland Was Never Entirely Subdued* says of the Irish: 'they were little better then Canniballes, who doe hunt one another; and hee that hath most strength and swiftnes, doth eate and deuoure all his fellowes' (Davies 1612, Y2v–Y3r). Elsewhere in the *View* Spenser recounts how the Northern Irish will drink a bowl of blood when making solemn vows of friendship with former enemies (Spenser 1949, 108). Although accounts of cannibalism were also given by those returning from the New World, reference to the practice amongst the Catholic Irish allows for allusion to the Eucharist and transubstantiation as well as functioning as a convenient way to denounce the enemy as barbaric Other.[6] In *The Faerie Queene* Serena carries multiple significations: she is at the same time religious sacrifice, innocent victim of barbaric violence, sexual object and dinner. The description of her body parts in the traditional terms of the poetic blazon – 'the daintest morsels', 'tender sides, her bellie white and clere', 'daintie parts' – work also for her body parts as food. Like Amoret from Book Four, saved from Lust by the intervention of Belphoebe, so too Serena will be rescued from the Savage Nation by the noble Sir Calepine. Spenser's Ladies are salivated over, imagined as a delectable foodstuff by the hungry cannibals, but never actually carved up and consumed.

William Shakespeare, various works; Francis Beaumont and John Fletcher, *The Woman Hater* (1607)

Shakespeare warrants a rather different approach from that adopted towards the other canonical authors previously considered in this book, partly due to his influence, the volume of works he produced that are still performed and read today, and because the references to food and eating in his works are so numerous and diffuse (as in the works of Dickens, explored in Chapter 5); considering only two or three of Shakespeare's plays simply will not do. The first book on Shakespeare and food appeared in 2007 and considered a number of important plays, including *Henry V*, *As You Like It* and *Hamlet*, in the light of the hitherto neglected genre of dietary literature (Fitzpatrick 2007). This book also traced Shakespeare's engagement with several pertinent themes, including Celtic alterity, famine and rank, but more remains to be said about the topic. *Shakespeare and Food* featured Sir John Oldcastle, also known as Falstaff (and hereafter called merely Sir John), and here we will develop its analysis of Sir John's gluttony by considering the fat knight's impact upon Shakespeare's presentation of Italy, including ancient Rome, as a means of exploring Shakespeare's depiction of religious and national identity. We will also consider Sir John in relation to an important, but unfairly neglected, play by two of Shakespeare's contemporaries: Francis Beaumont and John Fletcher's *The Woman Hater*. Along the way other important questions about consumption in the plays emerge, including whether or not Shakespeare was generally negative about the enjoyment of food and his apparent attitude towards fasting, in particular female fasting, an important issue in the light of our consideration of Margery Kempe in Chapter 1 of this book and the discussion of female food refusal in Chapters 5 and 6.

In Shakespeare's plays, as with Spenser's *Faerie Queene*, the consumption of food and drink tends to fall into patterns of either excess or asceticism, although Shakespeare adopts a less clearly moralistic stance than Spenser. The dichotomizing of consumption is in line with classical, specifically Roman, philosophies regarding pleasure and self-control that informed early modern views on gluttony, moderation and fasting. Rome could also carry Catholic associations for early modern playgoers, and cannibalism, often categorized as gluttony, also suggested the Catholic sacrament of transubstantiation. Shakespeare's most notorious glutton, Sir John, is likely based on the proto-Protestant martyr Sir John Oldcastle (Wells *et al.* 1987, 330), and although this figure is clearly English, he often suggests, and alludes to, Catholic (and thus foreign) consumption. By tracing early modern views on eating too much and not eating enough we can trace the manner in which Shakespeare's plays, including his Roman plays, engage with early modern attitudes towards Catholic consumption, specifically the Catholic sacrament of Holy Communion and other dietary practices associated with Catholicism, notably fasting, and the eating of 'Catholic' foods such as fish. In Beaumont and Fletcher's *The Woman Hater* the Italian courtier Lazarello, whose only desire is to consume a fish-head, is apparently indebted to Shakespeare's Sir John, a connection that has hitherto gone unnoticed by critics but has much to tell us about the way in which consumption could signal religious practices.

As we saw in the discussion of Spenser's *Faerie Queene*, the glutton might take excessive pleasure in food as well as eating too much and in the *Homily Against Gluttony and Drunkenness* (1563), and early modern dietary literature also, there are warnings that gluttony is harmful to the body, soul and intellect. Sir John is Shakespeare's most notorious glutton and Shakespeare's focus is mainly on the excessive amounts Sir John consumes. In *1 Henry IV* numerous references are made by Prince Harry to Sir John's huge girth, for example he is described as a 'fat-kidneyed rascal' (2.2.6), a 'fat-guts' (2.2.31) and an 'obscene greasy tallow-catch' (2.5.232).[7] Sir John eats and drinks a huge amount; at one point Prince Harry, finding a receipt in Sir John's pockets for a capon, sauce, two gallons of sack, anchovies and bread, remarks: 'O monstrous! But one halfpennyworth of bread to this intolerable deal of sack' (2.5.543–544). Yet Sir John can be fussy about what he eats and drinks, and how it is prepared, for example in *The Merry Wives of Windsor* when he tells Bardolph: 'Go brew me a pottle of sack, finely'; when Bardolph asks 'With eggs, sir?', he replies, 'Simple of itself. I'll no pullet-sperms in my brewage' (2.5.27–30). In *2 Henry IV* Justice Shallow, entertaining Sir John in his orchard, tells his boy Davy to arrange 'Some pigeons, . . . a couple of short-legged hens, a joint of mutton, and any pretty little tiny kickshaws, tell William Cook' (5.1.22–24); he later invites Sir John to eat pippins and caraways in his orchard (5.3.1–4). Although we get the impression that there will be plenty, perhaps too much, to eat here, Shallow also seems keen to appeal to his friend's sense of taste, to appeal to Sir John the epicure as much as Sir John the glutton.

David B. Goldstein argues that Shakespeare is overwhelmingly negative about food, his argument made on the basis of just two plays: *Titus Andronicus* and *The Merchant of Venice* (Goldstein 2013, 21–93). Certainly in the last scene of *Titus Andronicus* the eating is not convivial but this is the exception rather than the rule with Shakespeare. In *The Merchant of Venice* Shylock's decision not to eat with the Christians only serves to heighten the sense in which eating, especially in the company of others, is a social act, which is specifically why Shylock will not participate. Notably, in *Titus Andronicus* Titus emphasizes Tamora's gluttony, in the sense that she eats too nicely, when he tells how Chiron and Demetrius are 'both baked in this pie, / Whereof their mother *daintily* hath fed, / Eating the flesh that she herself hath bred' (5.3.59–61, my emphasis). When Shakespeare refers to food elsewhere in his plays, he tends to emphasize that having plenty to eat is a good thing and that eating is convivial. There is a distinct view that commensality contributes to a strengthening of social bonds, something that comes up often in this volume, as in the works of Dickens (explored in Chapter 5) and in the works of Woolf and Carter (see Chapter 6). In *As You Like It* Orlando's brother, Oliver, is tyrannical, partly because he forces Orlando to 'feed with his hinds' (1.1.17). Later, when Orlando interrupts the meal being enjoyed by the banished nobles, announcing 'forbear, I say. / He dies that touches any of this fruit' (2.7.97–98), Duke Senior welcomes the unexpected guest, telling Orlando 'Sit down and feed, and welcome to our table' (2.7.105), later assuring him that Adam is welcome also: 'Go find him out, / And we will nothing waste till you return' (2.7.133–134).

In Shakespeare an argument is often resolved with an invitation to dine, for example in *Henry V* when Bardolph tells Nim that he and Pistol ought to be reconciled: 'I will bestow a breakfast to make you friends' (2.1.10). The excess apparent in *Antony and Cleopatra* – when we hear of 'Eight wild boars roasted whole at a breakfast and but twelve persons there' (2.2.186–187) – suggests admiration rather than moral admonition from Shakespeare. Boar was a delicacy and, as Ken Albala notes, it was 'usually only eaten by noblemen who had a right to hunt it' (Albala 2003, 62); in the first English recipe book aimed specifically at the professional cook, the French-trained chef Robert May provides a recipe for baking wild boar and one for wild boar 'that comes out of France' (May 1660, Q2r–Q2v). As we saw in Chapter 1, Bertilak presents a boar's head and flesh to Gawain and although boar's head would have been served at grand dinners, there is no mention of feasting upon boar in the poem. In Shakespeare normal eating is usually celebrated, for example in *Cymbeline* when Innogen prepares a meal for Belarius and her brothers (4.2.50–53), but perverse eating, specifically cannibalism, indicates a sick society. In *Titus Andronicus* and the *Rape of Lucrece*, as in Spenser's *Faerie Queene*, gluttony is proximate to lust and, in Shakespeare's narrative poem especially, lust is repeatedly figured in terms of appetite, surfeit and greed.

Drunkenness is another kind of excess warned against in the early modern homilies and dietaries and it is sometimes presented as a problem in Shakespeare, for example in *Othello* when a drunken Cassio becomes obstreperous, but Shakespeare is not condemnatory of alcohol *per se* and there are several instances when excessive consumption is a source of humour. For example in *Twelfth Night* Sir Toby is usually drunk but, like Sir John, remains witty and very much in control, although, as I have argued elsewhere, Sir John's excessive interest in food and drink contributes to his characterization as a figure of vice whom Prince Hal must reject when he gains power (Fitzpatrick 2007, 19). In *Othello* it is not so much Cassio's heavy drinking that is the problem, more the fact that he has allowed himself to be manipulated by Iago and given in to pressure from his peers and, arguably, we feel sympathy towards the drunk Lepidus in *Antony and Cleopatra* since, as David Bevington points out, he offers a toast in order to keep the peace amongst his companions who reward his charitable efforts by uncharitably plying him with more alcohol (Shakespeare 1990, 144n4). In most plays, to offer a companion wine or to drink it with them indicates civility and often friendship; in *Coriolanus* the affable Menenius describes himself as 'a humorous patrician, and one that loves a cup of hot wine with not a drop of allaying Tiber in't' (2.1.46–48) but, notably, we never see him drunk.

In *The Tempest*, the drunken butler Stephano and his companion Trinculo present a rather more sinister situation: Stephano's first thought upon seeing Caliban is how he might profit from him back home in Naples (2.2.68–70, 75–78) and he teaches Caliban to drink to excess as he does (2.2.82–86). Caliban is invoked in George Eliot's 'Brother Jacob' (discussed in Chapter 5) when describing Jacob's insatiable appetite for sugary lozenges, the addictive pleasure provoked by both substances (alcohol and sugar) facilitating control by their provider. Alcohol defines Stephano and it shapes the new environment in which he finds himself: having escaped the shipwreck upon a butt of sack, he makes a bottle from which to drink it from the bark of a tree and creates a cellar for it out of a rock (2.2.120–122, 133–134). His instruction that Caliban swear upon the bottle of sack – 'swear to that: kiss the book' (2.2.141) – fuses the traditional kissing of the Bible to make an oath and the proverbial 'kiss the cup' (Shakespeare 1987b, 149n124). As Andrew Gurr observes, the bottle carried on stage might well have been made of leather and thus it could have reminded the audience of a leather-clad book, either the kind of book used by Prospero or the Bible (Gurr 2012). The sack/Bible connection suggests Catholic idolatry (sack is a Spanish wine, after all), which the *Homily Against Gluttony and Drunkenness* claims is a consequence of excess.[8] More seriously,

Stephano agrees to help Caliban murder Prospero; that Stephano is too foolish to commit the act – getting distracted by the 'glistering apparel' (4.1.193.SD.1) left for them by Ariel and arguing over it – is rather beside the point since it is being willing to do it that matters.

At one point in *The Tempest* Caliban balks at Prospero's order to fetch more wood, replying to Prospero's abuse with the statement 'I must eat my dinner' (1.2.333). I have considered elsewhere what Caliban's dinner might consist of and what the dietary authors would have made of the food available to him on the island; although Caliban's desire to eat might suggest a creature driven by appetite, he is also (as critics have noted) shown to be capable of rational thought and wonderful poetry and thus is a more complex figure than his stated desire to feed suggests (Fitzpatrick 2010a). His curt statement and determination to eat constitutes an alternative strategy to that adopted by women such as Margery Kempe who assert power by refusing to eat. Another meal presented on the island is the banquet offered to the Italian nobles, detailed in the stage direction 'Enter several strange shapes bringing in a banquet, and dance about it with gentle actions of salutations; and inviting the King, etc., to eat, they depart' (3.3.19.SD.1–3). The reaction of the nobles to this is curious: Sebastian describes what he sees as 'A living drollery!' (3.3.21), Gonzalo refers to the 'monstrous shape' but 'gentle-kind' manners of the figures he sees before him (3.3.31, 32), and Alonso comments on their 'shapes', 'gesture' and 'excellent dumb discourse' (3.3.37, 39), before Sebastian, noting that they 'have left their viands behind', asks the others, 'Will't please you taste of what is here?' (3.3.41, 42). The focus is on those who serve the banquet and whilst this is understandable, given their 'strange shapes', it is surprising that more is not made of the food and drink laid out before them.

As will become clear in the discussion of his plays (below), Jonson often takes great pains to describe the food and drink that will be enjoyed whenever it is mentioned so we might wonder why that kind of detail is missing here. It may have something to do with staging the scene: Shakespeare is presenting an actual banquet, bringing food and drink on stage, whereas Jonson's characters tend to imagine their feasts and thus are free to conjure up with words copious amounts of ever more luxurious foods. It would make good practical sense for Shakespeare to draw the audience's attention away from the banquet, relieving pressure upon the theatre practitioners to present a stunning array of food and drink. Indeed Peter Holland suggests that 'the frequency of stage directions for banquets' in early modern drama 'suggests the theatre companies had a standard prop of a banquet which could be dressed as appropriate if needed by the demands of a particular play', and which could have been 'carried in as a table' (Holland 2009, 15). If the prop was repeatedly used, then playwrights would hardly wish to focus on the foodstuffs that formed part of the prop because that presumably would involve reference to the same foodstuffs time and time again.

Michael Dobson points to the difficulties of eating on stage, in particular how it can prove distracting to the audience (Dobson 2009), but of course the Italian nobles in *The Tempest* do not get to eat because soon after the banquet is presented to them, it is made to disappear: 'Enter Ariel, like a harpy, claps his wings upon the table, and with a quaint device the banquet vanishes' (3.3.52.SD.2–3). Similarly, in *Macbeth* the banquet is not eaten, in a scene amusingly described by Peter Holland as 'the world's worst dinner-party' (Holland 2009, 19). Stephen Orgel notes that 'with a quaint device' denotes 'by means of an ingenious mechanism (which probably whisked the banquet down through a hole in the table, perhaps with the assistance of a stagehand hidden beneath it)' and that 'the admiring vagueness of the wording' suggests it is a revision of Shakespeare's manuscript by the scrivener Ralph Crane (Shakespeare 1987b, 166n52.3). The episode is based on Virgil's *Aeneid* when Aeneas and his companions – taking shelter on the Strophades, islands inhabited by harpies – have their feast ruined by the creatures who swoop down upon their food, eating it and defecating upon it (Shakespeare 1987b, 166n52.2). Shakespeare's Ariel is less physically hostile than the harpies, again perhaps for reasons to do with staging (defecating especially would present difficulties), but he is morally censorious, calling the nobles 'men of sin' (3.3.53). There is an apparent connection drawn between their sin (usurpation of Prospero from his dukedom and plans to murder Alonso), the refusal to allow them to eat, and Ariel's statement about Destiny's motives, which is put in distinctly dietary terms: 'Destiny – / That hath to instrument this lower world / And what is in't, the never-surfeited sea / Hath caused to belch up you' (3.3.53–56). Ariel calls them 'unfit to live' (3.3.58) so they are, naturally, unfit to eat also.

As discussed in the section above on Spenser's *Faerie Queene*, the Elizabethan *Homily of Fastyng* (1563) found fasting acceptable but only if it were not too wanton (excessive, enjoyable), if it moved the subject to more enthusiastic and sincere prayer, and if one could demonstrate humility before God and acknowledge human sin (Church of England 1563, Nn1v); the early modern dietaries recommend fasting too, so long as it is done in moderation, warning certain humoral types to proceed with caution. In early modern drama fasting is often undertaken by women, for example in Thomas Heywood's *A Woman Killed with Kindness* and John Ford's *The Broken Heart*.[9] In these and other works where women refuse to eat, such as George Chapman's *The Widow's Tears*, fasting is undertaken as a means of control, at least over the body – something we saw with Margery Kempe in the previous chapter and evident also in Charlotte Brontë's *Shirley*, Sarah Grand's *The Beth Book* (Chapter 5) and a number of modern feminist novels (Chapter 6) – although the power of a woman's choice to refuse food is often undercut by her self-abnegation. In Shakespeare and Fletcher's *The Two Noble Kinsmen* the Jailer's daughter describes her suffering as a result of unrequited love for Palamon in terms of consumption:

> Food took I none these two days,
> Sipped some water. I have not closed mine eyes
> Save when my lids scoured off their brine. Alas,
> Dissolve, my life; let not my sense unsettle,
> Lest I should drown or stab or hang myself.
>
> *(3.2.26–30)*

It is not clear whether fasting accelerates her grief but in the next scene in which she appears the Jailer's daughter is clearly mad and singing a song containing Ophelia-like sexual innuendo:

> And I'll go seek him, through the world that is so wide,
> Hey nonny, nonny, nonny.
> O for a prick now, like a nightingale,
> To put my breast against. I shall sleep like a top else.
>
> *(3.4.23–26)*

As mentioned earlier, in the discussion of *The Faerie Queene*, the dietary author William Bullein warned that fasting was responsible for weakening the brain, increasing melancholy and bringing sudden death. Notably in 3.3 of *The Two Noble Kinsmen* – the scene that comes between the Jailer's daughter announcing that she has fasted and her subsequent madness – we witness Arcite and Palamon eating and drinking, their enmity temporarily forgotten as they recall their shared memories:

> ARCITE I am glad
> You have so good a stomach. PALAMON I am gladder
> I have so good meat to't. ARCITE Is't not mad, lodging
> Here in the wild woods, cousin? PALAMON Yes, for them
> That have wild consciences. ARCITE How tastes your victuals?
> Your hunger needs no sauce, I see. PALAMON Not much.
> But if it did, yours is too tart, sweet cousin.
> What is this? ARCITE Venison. PALAMON 'Tis a lusty meat –
> Give me more wine. Here, Arcite, to the wenches
> We have known in our days.
>
> *(3.3.20–29)*

There is some doubt that Shakespeare wrote 3.2 (where the Jailer's daughter talks of fasting), which might have been by Fletcher, but 3.4 (where the Jailer's daughter has gone mad) and 3.3 (where the two kinsmen eat) were certainly written by Fletcher (Wells *et al.* 1987, 625). So the focus on fasting and feeding in *The Two Noble Kinsmen* does not, apparently, come from Shakespeare who usually, though not always, refers to fasting being undertaken – voluntarily at least – by men (Fitzpatrick 2010b, 'fast/fasting').

Often Shakespeare reveals suspicion towards those who do not enjoy eating and drinking: in *Measure for Measure* the abstemious Angelo is a hypocrite and Malvolio's dislike of 'cakes and ale' in *Twelfth Night* (2.3.111) is in keeping with the negativity towards abstemious thin men in Shakespeare's comedies, amongst them the foolish Slender in *The Merry Wives of Windsor* who repeatedly refuses Master Ford's requests to eat (Fitzpatrick 2007, 23–24). In *Julius Caesar* this same negativity towards thin men is apparent, for example when Caesar proclaims:

Let me have men about me that are fat,
Sleek-headed men, and such as sleep a-nights.
Yon Cassius has a lean and hungry look.
He thinks too much. Such men are dangerous.

(1.2.193–196)

Later in the play Cassius refers to his belief in Epicurus (5.1.77–79), but this specifically refers to the Epicurean belief that there was no supernatural intervention in human affairs rather than that of pleasure as the greatest good. Often in the Roman plays fasting indicates strength of purpose, as when Titus plans revenge against his enemies, telling the Andronici to 'eat no more / Than will preserve just so much strength in us' (3.2.1–2). In *Antony and Cleopatra* Caesar urges Antony to abandon the 'lascivious wassails' (1.4.56) he enjoys in Egypt, reminding him of the time when, faced with famine, he behaved as a stoic Roman ought to and drank horse urine (1.4.60–63). Yet the Egyptians are also capable of stoicism when necessary: Cleopatra tells her Roman captor, 'Sir, I will eat no meat. I'll not drink, sir' (3.2.48), a proclamation similar to that made by the Roman matron Volumnia in *Coriolanus*: 'Anger's my meat, I sup upon myself, / And so shall starve with feeding' (4.2.53–54). Again, it seems that food refusal is a distinctly feminine form of protest. Menenius is more given to pleasure than asceticism and R. B. Parker perceives connections between him and Sir John:

> Both father-figures are ageing *bons vivants*, vulgarly at ease with commoners they intend to exploit, with an attractive verbal wit that can become bitterly destructive, as Menenius' does in 5.4. Without being cowards, each tries to avoid direct involvement in fighting, and there is a striking resemblance between the curt rebuffs they both receive at the end of each play after too possessive demands in public – to which the audience responds ambivalently in either case.
>
> *Shakespeare 1994, 13–14*

Menenius enjoys eating and entertaining: the tribune Brutus tells him 'you are well understood to be a perfecter giber for the table than a necessary bencher in the Capitol' (2.1.79–81), which Parker glosses as a better 'wit at the dinner-table [than] indispensable member of the Senate' (Shakespeare 1994, 210n79–80); it is his invitation to dinner that Volumnia rejects (4.2.52–54); he favours wine undiluted with water (2.1.46–48); and he considers Coriolanus, like all men, more amenable to reason 'with wine and feeding' (5.1.50–56). On the other hand, Coriolanus draws a parallel between self-induced starvation and honour (Fitzpatrick 2007, 96–99), although he too apparently enjoys alcohol since, following his defeat of Aufidius, he asks 'Have we no wine here?' (1.10.91).

The main reason for the caveats around fasting during the early modern period was the perception that fasting was part of the Catholic tradition. After the Reformation people were still expected to refrain from eating animal flesh during fast days, which were also termed 'fish days', but for Protestant authorities 'fish days' were primarily economic: to encourage the fishing industry, and the navy, and reduce the high price of meat. The policy of promoting fish over meat for economic reasons was endorsed by the *Homily of Fastyng*: 'If the Prince requested our obedience to forbeare one daye from flesh more then we do, and to be contented with one meale in the same daye, should not our owne commoditie thereby perswade vs to subjection?' (Church of England 1563, Nn4r). Since the subject was duty-bound to obey the monarch, the eating of fish thus became a moral obligation. But fish days were unpopular amongst Protestants because they were associated with England's Catholic past, specifically the practice of abstaining from animal flesh on Fridays. Fish was also generally considered less substantial than animal flesh, and the dietary authors thought fish less healthy than meat. The dietary author Thomas Elyot observes that 'al kyndes of fyshe maketh more thinner bloud than fleshe, so that it dothe not moche nouryshe, and it doth soner passe out by vapors'; similarly Andrew Boorde notes that 'All maner of fysshe is colde of nature, and doth ingender fleume [phlegm], it doth lytle nurysshe'; and William Bullein, citing Galen, claims 'the nourishments of flesh is better than the nourishme[n]ts of fish' (Elyot 1541, G3r; Boorde 1547, F1r; Bullein 1558, P1r). In Shakespeare's *2 Henry IV* Sir John complains about Prince John's diet, specifically that he does not drink wine and eats too much fish, a criticism that is in keeping with the historical figure upon whom Sir John was apparently based, the proto-Protestant martyr Sir John Oldcastle (Wells *et al.* 1987, 330).[10] Fish was not merely a foodstuff but carried important socio-political and religious significance in the early modern period. Of course Sir John also enjoys the Spanish wine sack, conveniently ignoring its foreign origins and lying about the unhealthy effects of drinking it to excess because it suits him, that is, he enjoys it. So it is fish, rather than sack, that carries the full weight of Sir John's contempt.

For Sir John, eating fish is synonymous with a sober diet; it was not a foodstuff normally associated with gluttony and, indeed, Sir John himself prefers capon. However, fish is specifically sought after by one particular glutton: Lazarello, the 'hungry courier', from Beaumont and Fletcher's *The Woman Hater,* first performed in 1606 and first published in 1607. Lazarello is introduced to the audience by a fellow courtier who tells the Duke of Milan that he is 'one that I wonder your grace knowes not: for he hath followed your Court, and your last predecessors, from place to place, any time this seaven yeare, as faithfully as your Spits and your Dripping-pans have done, and almost as greasely', to which the Duke replies: 'O we knowe him: as we have heard, he keepes a kallender of all the famous dishes of meate, that have bin in the Court, ever since our great Graundfathers time; and when he can thrust in at no Table, hee makes his meate of that' (1.1.49–57).[11] Lazarello sounds rather like Shakespeare's Sir John, another follower of royalty who is described in *1 Henry IV* as a 'whoreson obscene greasy tallow-catch' (2.5.231–232) and in *The Merry Wives of Windsor* as 'this greasy knight' (2.1.63–103) but Lazarello is a different type of glutton. Although Sir John can be particular about what he eats – 'I'll no pullet-sperms in my brewage' (2.5.27–30) – he is mainly gluttonous in terms of the volume of food and drink he consumes, but this is not the case with Lazarello who, incidentally, does not drink sack.

In *The Woman Hater* Lazarello spends the entire play trying to taste the head of an umbrana, a rare fish, that is sent from one location to the other with him in hot pursuit. We might wonder at Lazarello's desire for such a dish but an early eighteenth-century English cookery book and guide to household management by Richard Bradley says of another fish, the carp, that 'The Head is accounted much the best part of the Fish, and is therefore presented as a Compliment to the greatest Stranger at the Table' (Bradley 1728, 132). Lazarello is apparently based on the figure Tamisius from a Latin treatise on Roman fishes (*De Romanis piscibus*, 1524) by the early modern Italian physician and historian Paulus Jovius (1483–1582) or on 'some intermediate source' (Gayley 1914, 78). Lazarello praises the Prince's tables full of 'nourishing foode' and his 'cupbords heavie laden with rich wines' (1.2.13–14) but his focus is on variety and choice foods and he appeals to the Goddess of Plenty: 'Fill me this day with some rare delicates, / And I will every yeare most constantly, / As this day celebrate a sumptuous feast' (1.2.18–20). When his Boy relates what food will be served that day at Court, Lazarello balks at the three shins of beef and two rolls of sturgeon planned for the Captain of the guards' table: 'A portly service, but grosse, grosse' (54–55). It is at this point that Lazarello is first informed about the fish-head destined for the Duke's table: 'Is't posible! / Can Heaven bee so propitious to the Duke?' (1.3.57–58) and he thinks possession of the fish-head better than any land or palace the Duke might possess. His Boy describes the fish-head he desires as 'fresh and sweet' and 'a rare noveltie' (1.3. 66–67) and it is clear that Lazarello's gluttony is not one of eating too much but of taking too much pleasure in the food he consumes, which conforms to Gregory the Great's definition of gluttony and the sin as characterized in the *Homily Against Gluttony and Drunkenness* and the dietaries.

Lazarello is also guilty of a kind of idolatry – something the *Homily Against Gluttony and Drunkenness* specifically warns against – when he proclaims:

> If poore unworthy I may come to eat
> Of this most sacred dish, I here do vow
> (If that blind huswife Fortune will bestow
> But meanes on me) to keepe a sumptuous house
> *(1.2.69–72)*

He is besotted with the idea of tasting the fish-head and part of the humour of the scenes in which he appears is that the fish-head is repeatedly figured in romantic terms ('Thither must I / To see my loves face, the chast virgin head / Of a deere Fish, yet pure and undeflowered', 1.3.216–218). Earlier, he imagines eating this longed-for dish as the ultimate act of consumption:

> When I have tasted of this sacred dish,
> Then shall my bones rest in my father's tombe

In peace, then shall I dye most willingly,
And as a dish be serv'd to satisfie
Deaths hunger, and I will be buried thus:
My Beere shalbe a charger borne by foure,
The coffin where I lye, a powdring tubbe,
Bestrew'd with Lettice, and coole sallet hearbes;
My winding sheet of Tanseyes, the blacke guard
Shalbe my solemne mourners, and in stead
Of ceremonies, wholesome buriall prayers,
A printed dirge in ryme shall burie me:
In stead of teares let them poure Capon sauce
Upon my hearse, and salt in stead of dust,
Manchets for stones, for other glorious shields
Give me a Voyder, and above my hearse
For a Trutch sword, my naked knife stucke up.
(1.3.99–115)

The bawdy humour of his 'naked knife stucke up' is part of the bathos of romance figured in terms of food and connects also with the general sense of fish being associated with sex, specifically female flesh and genitalia, that was common in the period. The cannibalistic dimension is disconcerting; there is a possible allusion here not only to *Titus Andronicus*, with human flesh baked in a pie, but also Shakespeare's Sir John who figures himself in cannibalistic terms in *The Merry Wives of Windsor* when he refers to himself as 'a mountain of mummy!' (3.5.14–17), to being 'half stewed in grease like a Dutch dish', and to having his 'brains ta'en out and buttered, and [given] . . . to a dog' (3.5.110, 3.5.4–8). Since *The Woman Hater* is set in Catholic Italy, this play may also hint at the disturbing proximity between Eucharistic theophagy (the literal eating of God) and cannibalism. Lazarello's overwhelming desire to consume fish also takes a swipe at the Catholic practice of fasting on Fridays, as is clear in the following exchange between Lazarello and the whore at the brothel where the fish-head is finally sent:

LAZARELLO.   I have not eate to day.
JULIA.   You will have the better stomacke to your supper; in the meane time, Ile feed ye with delight.
LAZARELLO.   'Tis not so good upon an emptie stomacke: if it might be without the trouble of your house, I would eate?
JULIA: Sir, we can have a Capon ready.
LAZARELLO.   The day?
JULIA.   'Tis Friday Sir.
LAZARELLO.   I doe eat little flesh upon these daies.
(4.2.205–213)

The humour lies in the idea that anyone would refuse capon for fish, coupled with the idea that Catholics present themselves as pious, their outward show of fasting masking their real motives. The cost of tasting the fish-head is high, for Lazarello must promise to marry Julia, the brothel-whore, before he may enjoy it and his Boy tells him he will 'repent, upon a full stomacke' (5.3.81–82).

Lazarello is presumably based on the hungry servant in the Spanish novella *Lazarillo de Tormes*, which appeared in a sixteenth-century English translation (Hurtado de Mendoza 1586), and there are Lazarillos in plays that appeared before and after *The Woman Hater*, some of whom make a similar connection between this character and food. As Christian Biet points out, the hungry servant or slave was a traditional stereotype from Greek and Roman comedy and suggests covert criticism of either master or servant; in such drama 'we find that hunger is caused by the master's rapacity and by the poverty he imposes on his servant, or, conversely, by the servant's reckless passion for food, his infinite desire which threatens the prevailing order and stability' (Biet 2008, 57). In Thomas Dekker's *Blurt, Master Constable*, first performed in 1601 or 1602 and first published in 1602, five years before *The Woman Hater*, Lazarillo is primarily lustful rather than gluttonous and he pines for female flesh: '*Cupid* hath got me a stomacke, and I long for lac'd mutton'; it is Lazarillo's hungry servant Pilcher who desires food: 'Plaine mutton without a lace would serue me' (Dekker 1602, B1r). The play is set in Venice but Lazarillo and Pilcher are both Spaniards, and Dandyprat, a citizen of Venice, repeatedly refers to Pilcher's thin body, calling him a 'leane stripling' (Dekker 1602, B1v), 'Sirra thin-gut' and 'a most pittifull dryed one' (Dekker 1602, B3v). There is also the inevitable connection between Spanish Catholics and fish (and cannibalism also) when Dandyprat observes: 'I wonder thy master does not slice thee, and swallow thee for an *Anchoues* [anchovie]' (Dekker 1602, B3v); in a song about Spaniards eating fish, Pilcher longs for a change in his diet:

> Doyt. Wouldst thou not leape at a piece of meate?
> Pilcher. O how my teeth doe water, I could eate
> For the heauens; my flesh is almost gone
> With eating of *Pilcher* and poore *Iohn*
> (Dekker 1602, B4r)

The name Lazarillo next appears in Beaumont and Fletcher's *Love's Cure*, which was first performed around 1606 and apparently revised by Philip Massinger in 1625; the play was first published in the 1647 Beaumont and Fletcher Folio. E. H. C. Oliphant argued that the character of Lazarillo in *Love's Cure* is a preliminary sketch of the character that appears in *The Woman Hater*, which represents a 'more complete and finished creation' (Beaumont and Fletcher 1966, 5). As in Dekker's *Blurt, Master Constable*, Lazarillo in *Love's Cure* is a hungry servant and repeated jokes emerge from the fact that his master, a cobbler called Panchieco, is apparently ascetic. The play is set in Spain and when we first meet Lazarillo he tells his master: '*Signior*, I am very hungry, they tell me in *Civill* here, I looke like an Eele, with a mans head', to which his master replies: 'oppresse not thy stomach too much: grosse feeders, great sleepers: great sleepers, fat bodies; fat bodies, lean braines'

(Beaumont and Fletcher 1976, 2.1.3–5, 9–11). When Lazarillo requests 'but a red herring a day', his master asks: 'woulds't thou be gluttonous in thy delicacies?', urging him to 'let contemplation be thy food' (2.1.39). Poor Lazarillo is so hungry that when one of the tradesmen friends of his master appears, he says: '[he] looks as if he were dowgh-bak'd; a little butter now, and I could eate him like an oaten-Cake' (2.1.63–64), so again we have references to Spanish eating and cannibalism. It later emerges that the ascetic Panchieco is not as high-minded as he pretends when he and his tradesmen friends are shown to be thieves. As in *The Woman Hater*, there are humorous connections drawn between Catholic Spaniards and fish, including when Lazarillo is sent to the galleys for his part in the robbery and observes: 'Well, though herrings want, I shall have rowes' (5.3.247); 'rowes' being a pun on fish-roe and rowing a boat. Here, too, a character is 'punished' by marrying a whore, though this time it is not Lazarillo who suffers this fate. The name Lazarillo appears in two other plays that emerged later than *The Woman Hater*: Dekker's *Match Me in London* (1631) and William Rowley's *All's Lost in Lust* (1633), where it is spelt 'Lazarello', but neither figure is especially interested in food.

A number of critics recognize Beaumont and Fletcher's debt to Shakespeare in *The Woman Hater* but none have spotted the strong parallels between Lazarello and Shakespeare's Sir John.[12] Andrew Gurr observes an allusion to Sir John's joke in *1 Henry IV* about Prince Harry as 'heir apparent' (1.2.57) in a speech from *The Woman Hater* condemning social climbers at court (1.3.13–21) but not that Beaumont and Fletcher's glutton is indebted to Shakespeare. Lazarello's bathetic reference to heraldry in the speech quoted above when he imagines being consumed by death and proclaims 'for other glorious shields / Give me a Voyder' (1.3.113–114) is also perhaps mockery of Shakespeare's social pretensions, with specific allusion to Jonson's take on *Non Sanz Droict* (the motto that accompanied Shakespeare's new coat of arms) in *Every Man Out of His Humour*: 'Not Without Mustard'. As Ruth Vanita observes, 'Lazarello's devotion to the fish head [which] lands him in a brothel (which is compared to hell) . . . follows the morality play tradition of punishing the deadly sin of gluttony with hell' (1995, 71). Vanita also notes the connections between the fish and eating in *Hamlet* and *The Woman Hater*, specifically 'Hamlet's account of how a king may go on a progress through the guts of a beggar [which] both resounds and expands in the frequent references to Lazarello's "guts" as having a greedy life of their own' and a 'play with the word "stomach" [which] mocks pretensions to valour by reducing them to self-serving greed' (1995, 71). Of course Shakespeare's Sir John is also repeatedly figured in terms of his guts (see *1 Henry IV* 2.2.31, 2.5.231, 2.5.457, 3.3.156 and *Merry Wives* 2.1.30) and Lazarello's declaration that 'Hunger commaunds, my valour must obey' (3.3.133) recalls Sir John's consideration of 'honour' as irrelevant, higher values having no place when it comes to physical, bodily needs: 'What is that "honour"? Air. A trim reckoning! . . . Therefore I'll none of it' (5.1.135–139).

Beaumont and Fletcher's Lazarello is a different type of glutton from Shakespeare's Sir John (as noted above, Lazarello does not consume sack) but both men are overly interested in food and this interest is a source of humour. Both are also of a high social rank (Sir John a knight and Lazarello a courtier), and both mooch around their social betters from the court trying to get something for nothing. Crucially, both men are described in terms of their greasiness and both imagine their flesh consumed as food by others. Although at the end of *2 Henry IV* Sir John cuts a more pathetic figure than Lazarello, who is content to marry a whore, there is a sense in both plays of the inevitably undignified end to a gluttonous life. King Harry's rejection of Sir John – 'I know thee not, old man. Fall to thy prayers' (5.5.47) – is more cutting than the Boy's smug 'you'l begin to repent, upon a full stomacke' (5.3.81–82) directed at Lazarello, but in both cases the conclusion is a moral one, that of prayer and repentance as the logical consequence of a life devoted to gluttony. Shakespeare's Sir John is rooted firmly in early modern England, in the taverns of Eastcheap and the houses of Windsor, yet his appetite, wit, questionable sense of honour and familiarity with subordinates are transcultural, again picked up by Shakespeare in his creation of the Roman patrician Menenius and influencing Beaumont and Fletcher in their delineation of the 'hungry courtier' Lazarello. Sir John's pronouncements on fish and flesh (in particular the consumption of his own flesh) clearly triggered Catholic associations that were fully exploited by Beaumont and Fletcher in their delineation of the fish-obsessed Italian glutton who imagines himself served as a dish for death.

Ben Jonson, *Volpone* (1605), *The Alchemist* (1616) and *Bartholomew Fair* (1631)

Critics have hitherto tended to overlook the focus on food and eating in Jonson's plays. E. Pearlman remarks upon the ubiquity of eating in Jonson's work but her analysis of the man and his work – via Edmund Wilson's view that Jonson conformed to the psychological type Freud termed anal erotic, characterized by, amongst other traits, a fixation with excrement and its substitutes – is predominantly focused on the body, including Jonson's own body (Wilson 1952, 203–220; Pearlman 1979). Jonson was a large man and he was also a heavy drinker, both of which he commented on himself, referring disparagingly to his huge girth and claiming to have written several of his plays whilst drunk (Jonson 1999, 9–10, 51–52n25; Levy-Navarro 2008, 147–191). The detailed description of a banquet in Jonson's poem 'Inviting a Friend to Supper' led Bruce Boehrer to conclude that Jonson was a glutton, a point dismissed by Gary Schmidgall, who argues that Boehrer missed the humour of the piece, and by Elena Levy-Navarro who claims that Jonson was not yet fat when he wrote the poem but that critics need to think of him as obese and thus make judgements about his personality (Boehrer 1990; Schmidgall and Boehrer 1991, 317–18; Levy-Navarro 2008, 149). Elsewhere Boehrer, like others, tends to focus on how Jonson's writing engages with the body and bodily functions, both also of particular interest to Gail Kern Paster (1993, 23–24, 34–49, 143–162) and Levy-Navarro (2008, 147–191). So, critical comment on Jonson and his work has tended to circle around the periphery of food, while the food and drink that features in the plays have largely been sidelined.

Jonson's treatment of food is exotic, visceral, fecund, and yet it can also be everyday and mundane, all for specific effect: the ubiquitous references to food in Jonson's drama often reveal the hypocrisy and foolishness of the society at which he aimed his satire. For Volpone and for Epicure Mammon in *The Alchemist* food is a means by which they can indulge their appetite for money and power; their desire for worldly commodities, including food, is perverse, acquisitive and ultimately doomed to failure. Yet food also signals the prosaic, repeatedly acting as a means by which to undermine the pompous, delusional and superficial, as is evident in scenes featuring Sir Politic Would-Be in *Volpone* and Dapper in *The Alchemist*. In *Bartholomew Fair* the Puritan preacher Zeale of the Land Busy espouses views about food that he does not really hold, his attitude to consumption epitomizing the hypocrisy at the heart of religion that Jonson found so repulsive. Ursula, the pig-woman, evokes the cannibalistic, dripping her own sweat into the pork she prepares for others, but even with her gluttony and cheating she is less morally offensive than the seemingly upstanding members of society who frequent her booth.

In the discussion of *The Faerie Queene* (above) we saw that Lust's leftover food, the human flesh that he stores in his bottom lip, is described as 'the relickes of his feast' (4.7.6.3), a hint at Catholic ritual: the worship of relics and transubstantiation. The other cannibals in the poem, the Savage Nation, do not work for their food but, rather, depend upon the labour of others, stealing what they need, a social ill condemned also in Langland's *Piers Plowman*. With Volpone's opening speech Jonson situates his anti-hero within this context of religious difference and social ills: 'Good morning to the day; and, next, my gold! / Open the shrine, that I may see my saint' (1.1.1–2).[13] When Mosca reveals his treasure, Volpone continues his encomium to wealth: 'Hail the world's soul, and mine!' (1.1.3), and he makes explicit connections between the natural world and the treasure he worships:

> O, thou sun of Sol,
> But brighter than thy father, let me kiss,
> With adoration, thee, and every relic
> Of sacred treasure in this blessèd room.
> *(1.1.10–13)*

Volpone values his treasure above family, children, friends 'Or any other waking dream on earth' (1.1.18) and celebrates the means by which he gets it:

> Yet, I glory
> More in the cunning purchase of my wealth
> Than in the glad possession, since I gain
> No common way: I use no trade, no venture;
> I wound no earth with ploughshares; fat no beasts
> To feed the shambles; have no mills for iron,
> Oil, corn, or men, to grind 'em into powder;
> I blow no subtle glass; expose no ships

To threat'nings of the furrow-facèd sea;
I turn no monies in the public bank
Nor usure private –

(1.1.30–40)

Volpone presents not 'wounding' the earth or providing animals for the slaughter-house as a virtue but it makes him a parasite, like Mosca, feeding upon the industry of others rather than being a producer of food for himself and the wider community. Arguably the legacy hunters upon whom Volpone feeds deserve all they get but the innocent too get caught up in their machinations, with Celia in particular suffering as a result of Volpone's greed and lust. Mosca adds to Volpone's self-congratulations when he tells him that, unlike some rich men, he is not a miserly hoarder:

You are not like the thresher, that doth stand
With a huge flail, watching a heap of corn,
And, hungry, dares not taste the smallest grain,
But feeds on mallows, and such bitter herbs;
Not like the merchant, who hath filled his vaults
With *Romagnia*, and rich Candian wines
Yet drinks the lees of Lombard's vinegar.
You will not lie in straw, whilst moths, and worms
Feed on your sumptuous hangings and soft beds.
You know the use of riches

(1.1.53–62)

In a society where the threat of hunger was real it is significant that the first examples that spring to Mosca's mind when it comes to abundance are dietary. Mosca suggests that Volpone's munificence is self-directed, noting that his master merely 'allows maintenance' to himself and the other inhabitants of the house, not that he is generous with them. Just before this, Mosca compares Volpone to those who will exploit softer targets than his legacy hunters: 'You shall ha' some will swallow / A melting heir, as glibly as your Dutch / Will pills of butter, and ne'er purge for't' (1.1.41–43). The Dutch were commonly thought to be great eaters of butter (the term 'butterbox' was often used as a nickname for them) and they were criticized by English dietary authors for their habit of eating too much butter and eating it after rather than with other foods (Boorde 1547, E2v; Cogan 1588, U3r; Munday 1990, 84n1–2).

   The food-related comparisons drawn by Mosca suggest that food and drink have potent metaphorical significance for him, that he craves the butter, wine and corn imagined but not afforded by mere 'maintenance'. As we saw in the discussion of Lazarello from *The Woman Hater*, the hungry servant or slave was a traditional stereotype from Greek and Roman comedy, suggesting covert criticism of either master or servant. Productions of *Volpone* that cast a lean actor in the part of Mosca – and most do, for example the Royal Shakespeare Company's production which featured a lanky Guy Henry in the part (Jonson 1999–2000) – conform to the notion that his latent bitterness towards Volpone, a bitterness that will emerge as the business progresses, may be in no small part due to his master's tendency to keep him hungry; cast a fatter actor in the part of Mosca and the motive for bitterness seems less obvious. A similar situation arises in Shakespeare's *Merchant of Venice* when Lancelot Gobbo complains that Shylock keeps him 'famished' (2.2.100–101); if Gobbo is fat, then he is clearly not telling the truth about his hunger and we might doubt everything else he has to say.

In his efforts to woo Celia, Volpone uses two of the most valuable commodities at his disposal: jewels and food. He begins by combining the two when he says: 'See, here, a rope of pearl, and each more orient / Than that the brave Egyptian queen caroused; / Dissolve and drink 'em' (3.7.190–192), here alluding to a story from Pliny's *Natural History* telling how Cleopatra responded to a challenge from Mark Antony, to spend a lot of money at one meal, by drinking a priceless pearl dissolved in vinegar (Jonson 1968, 87n192). Volpone offers other jewels of great worth to Celia, including a diamond that would have impressed Lollia Paulina (the consort of Emperor Caligula), but claims that they are 'nothing' compared to what they will consume 'at a meal', presumably at one sitting:

> The heads of parrots, tongues of nightingales,
> The brains of peacocks, and of ostriches
> Shall be our food, and, could we get the phoenix,
> Though nature lost her kind, she were our dish.
> *(3.7.201–204)*

As Brian Parker points out, this is indebted to Lampridius's account of the feasts of Roman Emperor Heliogabalus (Jonson 1999, 200n201). In Bullein's dietary *The Government of Health* the moderate Humphrey warns the profligate John against the example of this notorious Roman glutton who 'was daily fedde with many hundred fishes and foules, and was acco[m]panied with manye brothels, baudes [bawds], harlottes, and glottons' (Bullein 1558, C1v). Peacocks would have been served at elaborate banquets in the medieval period and into the beginning of the early modern era, with diners consuming their flesh rather than their brains. Thomas Dawson includes peacock amongst the meats that could be served for the second course at dinner on flesh days (when meat was allowed to be consumed) and although he does not give any instructions for cooking peacock, there is a recipe for roasted peacock in *Two Fifteenth Century Cookery Books* that stipulates how the bird should be served 'as [if] he were a-live', including the feathers carefully arranged on the carcass of the bird (Dawson 1587, A2v; Anon. 1888, 79). Yet by the seventeenth century peacock was generally replaced by turkey, in part because the flesh of the turkey was less tough (Wilson 1976, 118–119; Albala 2003, 68). So the peacock invoked by Volpone is rare and its brain even more unusual as a dish.

Neither parrots nor ostriches appear to feature in descriptions of early modern feasts but they add to the sense that Volpone offers Celia rare and extravagant delicacies. There is also a distinct perversion in the notion of consuming the heads and brains of such beautiful birds, and eating the tongue of the nightingale seems especially cruel since it is the means by which she sings, perhaps also prefiguring the near-rape of Celia by Volpone by evoking Ovid's Philomela (Ovid 1965, chp. 6). Small garden birds were eaten in the early modern period: dietaries refer to larks, sparrows, blackbirds and robins (Elyot 1541, F4v–G1r; Boorde 1547, F1v; Bullein 1558, O7r–O7v) and recipes featuring such birds appear in cookery books by John Murrell (1617, E1r–E1v) and Thomas Dawson (1587, A3v) but they make no mention of the nightingale so again the sense is that of Volpone boasting about providing an exotic dish. There is also the sense of Volpone getting overexcited, overreaching himself, by suggesting they could eat the phoenix, a food that he quickly admits does not exist; effectively he promises what he cannot deliver and the sense of anti-climax, the illusory nature of this fantastic feast, mirrors the other acts of illusion and deception in the play. As Parker notes, the extravagancies promised by Volpone are ironic because all ended badly: Antony was ultimately defeated, Lollia Paulina committed suicide, and Heliogabalus died violently (Jonson 1999, 200n192–201).

Volpone continues to tempt Celia with sensual pleasures:

> Thy baths shall be the juice of July-flowers,
> Spirit of roses, and of violets,
> The milk of unicorns, and panthers' breath
> Gathered in bags, and mixed with Cretan wines.
> Our drink shall be prepared gold and amber,
> Which we will take, until my roof whirl round
> With the vertigo
>
> *(3.7.212–218)*

With the scented baths and gold the extravagancies of Heliogabalus are again invoked: extracting juice from the flowers is labour intensive and wasteful – since presumably the flower will get discarded, like the nightingale and the bodies of the other birds that are required only for specific body parts – and again fantasy is a feature of his proposed indulgence, his desire to impress becoming increasingly desperate with talk of the impossible task of gathering breath in bags. Yet for the chaste Celia, the only thing that will satisfy her sense of morality is the consumption of her beauty:

> for seducing
> Your blood to this rebellion.—Rub these hands,
> With what may cause an eating leprosy,
> E'en to my bones and marrow—anything
> That may disfavour me, save in my honour
>
> *(3.7.252–256)*

She imagines a kind of autocannibalism, a disintegration of her own flesh, rather than consumption of the birds proposed by Volpone. However, violence is redirected towards Volpone when she is saved by Bonario, who threatens her would-be seducer:

> Forbear, foul ravisher, libidinous swine!
> Free the forced lady, or thou di'st, imposter.
> But that I am loath to snatch thy punishment
> Out of the hand of justice, thou shouldst yet,
> Be made the timely sacrifice of vengeance,
> Before this altar, and this dross, thy idol.
>
> *(3.7.266–271)*

Volpone is like Spenser's Savage Nation, who worship false gods, and is himself almost sacrificed (like the animal to which he is compared) before Bonario who, like a good Christian, refrains from violence and leaves Volpone's punishment to God.

Jonson seems to shift from one extreme to the other when discussing food and drink: it is exotic and indulgent but it can also be prosaic and thus deflationary. When Peregrine tells the foolish Sir Politic Would-Be that Stone the Fool is dead, Sir Politic insists that Stone was no fool but a secret spy:

> He has received weekly intelligence,
> Upon my knowledge, out of the Low Countries,
> For all parts of the world, in cabbages;
> And those dispensed, again, t'ambassadors
> In oranges, musk melons, apricots,
> Lemons, pome-citrons, and such-like; sometimes
> In Colchester oysters, and your Selsey cockles.
>
> *(2.1.68–74)*

As John Creaser points out, for the ambassadors the information is carried in more expensive and aristocratic produce than the cabbages received by Stone: the 'musk-melon' was an oriental melon with a distinctive musky taste, 'pome-citron' was a term generally used for citron, lemon and probably also lime, and the shellfish named were expensive delicacies (Jonson 1978, 229n70, 72–74). Yet the main point of the reference to food is to make ridiculous and deflate Sir Politic's grand talk, which is achieved via reference to the common food of cabbages. A similar effect is achieved when Sir Politic claims that Stone, dining in 'a public ordinary' (a tavern or inn serving food at a fixed price), received secret messages 'in a trencher of meat' and would 'Convey an answer in a toothpick' (2.1.76, 78–80); tooth-picks were fashionable in this period (Jonson 1999, 220n139) and come up again in Sir Politic's list of the things he has bought during a shopping trip (see below). Again the humour, at Politic's expense, results in a shift from the sublime to the ridiculous; the everyday matter that punctures Sir Politic's pomposity is almost always food-related. Peregrine acts as a prompt by which to elicit humour from Sir Politic, humour that emerges from the bathetic nature of the material involved: we move from government spies and intelligence to cabbages, meat and toothpicks. Sir Politic offers Peregrine advice on appropriate ways of behaving whilst abroad, but his advice is facile and includes what to wear, to 'never speak a truth' (4.1.17), and how to dine:

> Then must you learn the use,
> And handling of your silver fork at meals,
> The metal of your glass – these are main matters,
> With your Italian – and to know the hour
> When you must eat your melons and your figs.
> *(4.1.27–31)*

Sir Politic also shares with Peregrine the various projects, or schemes, he has in mind that he believes will make him a fortune:

> One is (and that
> I care not greatly, who knows) to serve the state
> Of Venice with red herrings, for three years,
> And at a certain rate, from Rotterdam,
> Where I have a correspondence.
> *(4.1.49–53)*

The letter he shows Peregrine comes from 'a cheesemonger' (4.1.56), whilst another project involves detecting the presence of plague in newly arrived ships:

> First, I bring in your ship, 'twixt two brick walls—
> But those the state shall venture; on the one
> I strain me a fair tarpaulin, and, in that
> I stick my onions, cut in halves; the other
> Is full of loopholes, out at which I thrust
> The noses of my bellows; and those bellows
> I keep, with water-works, in perpetual motion,
> (Which is the easiest matter of a hundred).
> Now, sir, your onion, which doth naturally
> Attract th' infection, and your bellows blowing
> The air upon him, will show instantly,
> By his changed colour, if there be contagion,
> Or else remain as fair as at the first.
> *(4.1.113–125)*

It is the precision of his planning, the convoluted nature of it and the visual image of sticking onions in a tarpaulin (as well as the use of the word 'stick') that make the speech effective as a source of humour. Sir Politic's schemes are similar to Merecraft's project of forks in Jonson's *The Devil Is an Ass* where Merecraft proposes to promote the use of forks in England to save on napkins, forks being rare in England at this time but fashionable in Italy (Jonson 1994, 5.4.18–32).

Sir Politic's diary 'Wherein I note my actions of the day' (4.1.134) contains references to shopping for toothpicks and sprats as well as other insignificant matters and at one point Peregrine wonders if the 'grave affair of state' Sir Politic claims to be preoccupied with is 'how to make / Bolognian sausages here in Venice, sparing / One o'th'ingredients' (5.4.20–22). Claiming to be saving Sir Politic from the authorities who think he has hatched a plot to sell Venice to the Turk, Peregrine advises Sir Politic to 'Convey yourself into a sugar chest, / Or, if you could lie round, a frail were rare' (5.4.44–45) – a frail being a rush basket to hold figs and raisins – or he could 'leap into' a 'currant-butt' (5.4.49) – a cask used to hold currants or currant-wine (Jonson 1999, 264n45, n49) – so that Peregrine might bring him aboard a ship and thus escape. Eventually Politic hides in a tortoise-shell and tells his wife's women to burn his papers. When he learns that he has been made a fool he says:

> O, I shall be the fable of all feasts,
> The freight of the *gazetti*, ship-boys' tale;
> And, which is worst, even talk for ordinaries.
> *(5.4.82–84)*

With its shift from 'feasts' to 'ordinaries' even Sir Politic's sense of humiliation is expressed using deflationary and food-related language, as though being spoken of amongst the rabble when they dine is worse than being mocked by those from the higher ranks.

A similar sense of extremes – the exotic and indulgent, the prosaic and deflationary – is evident in *The Alchemist* with Epicure Mammon's fantasy of the sensual pleasures he will enjoy once possessed of the Philosopher's Stone and Dapper's experience in his desire to meet with the Queen of the Fairies. Mammon invokes the same kinds of physical pleasure as Volpone (jewels, perfumes, exotic foodstuffs and so forth) but where Volpone did so in an effort to seduce Celia, Mammon imagines multiple 'wives, and concubines', with multiple beds upon which to perform sexual acts (2.2.35, 41).[14] His seduction is less focused, more self-obsessed and in one sense more perverse as he imagines walking 'Naked between my *succubae*' and using 'fathers and mothers' as bawds (2.2.48, 58), but it is also perhaps less dangerous since he does not target any specific victim with rape as Volpone does Celia. The imaginary feast is also similar to the one Volpone invokes to seduce Celia:

> My meat shall all come in, in Indian shells,
> Dishes of agate, set in gold, and studded,
> With emeralds, sapphires, hyacinths, and rubies.
> The tongues of carps, dormice, and camels' heels,
> Boil'd i' the spirit of Sol, and dissolv'd pearl,

(Apicius' diet, 'gainst the epilepsy)
And I will eat these broths with spoons of amber,
Headed with diamond, and carbuncle.
My foot-boy shall eat pheasants, calver'd salmons,
Knots, godwits, lampreys: I myself will have
The beards of barbels, serv'd, instead of salads;
Oil'd mushrooms; and the swelling unctuous paps
Of a fat pregnant sow, newly cut off,
Dress'd with an exquisite, and poignant sauce;
For which, I'll say unto my cook, 'There's gold,
Go forth, and be a knight'.

(2.2.72–87)

Again the Roman world suggests the exotic and indulgent, as well as cruelty and wastefulness, with a focus on taste and conspicuous display over sustenance. Pliny recommends consumption of sow paps and claims they 'are the best, provided it has not yet suckled the litter', and the Roman cookery book attributed to Apicius, *De re coquinaria* (*The Art of Cooking*), provides a recipe for udder stuffed with sea urchin and seasoned with spices, as well as dormice stuffed with pork and the minced meat of dormice, also seasoned with spices (Pliny 1940, XI.lxxxiv; Apicius 1958, 159, 205; Jonson 1967, 56n75, 57n83–84). In *Bartholomew Fair* Ursula accuses Knockem of spreading a rumour that she has died 'of a surfeit of bottle-ale and tripes', which he corrects: 'No, 'twas better meat, Urs: cow's udders, cow's udders' (2.3.14–16). The dietary author Thomas Muffett thought udders superior to tripe and various recipes for cooking udders, containing expensive ingredients such as spices and wine, feature in Robert May's cookery book (Muffett 1655, Q3r; May 1660, I8r–I8v).[15] Heliogabalus, the Roman emperor, also alluded to by Volpone, was reputed to have eaten camels' heels and the beards of another kind of fish, the mullet (Anon. 1924, 147, chapter 20; Jonson 1991, 43n75). Broth, a dish that could be fairly humble, is here made indulgent by its ingredients and the notion that serving it in precious dishes and eating it with precious spoons in some way suggests that the expensive metals and stones are also being consumed by the diner, just as he will consume gold (via the 'spirit of sol') and 'dissolved pearl'.

As in *Piers Plowman*, where the rich and powerful do not fulfil their social obligations by feeding the poor, so too in Mammon's fantasy social obligations are warped in that a footboy ought not to eat expensive and extravagant dishes such as calvered salmon, which was prepared whilst the fish was very fresh and usually still alive; a recipe for the dish in Robert May's cookery book requires lots of spices and other expensive ingredients (May 1660, Y7r–Y7v). Similarly, a cook ought not to be made a knight, not least because cooks had a poor reputation, as witnessed by Chaucer's Cook (discussed in Chapter 1), and the negativity with which the profession was regarded in medieval times continued into the early modern period when cooks had a reputation for getting drunk, having poor hygiene, ruining ingredients and even poisoning their customers (Fitzpatrick 2010b, 'cooks/

cookery'). There is perhaps also a hint that this subversion of social hierarchies will not end well since the consumption of a surfeit of lampreys was reputed to have killed King John (Jonson 1967, 57n81). The perversity of feeding servants with fine foods extends also to the unnaturalness of consuming the 'swelling unctuous paps' of the pregnant animal, full of milk intended for its young. Mushrooms were regarded with suspicion by the early moderns and specifically associated with social ambition – in Marlowe's *Edward II* the lowly Gaveston is referred to as 'a night grown mushroom' (Marlowe 1994, 1.4.284) – which fits with Mammon's fantasy of lording it over everyone once he has possession of the Philosopher's Stone (Fitzpatrick 2010b, 'mushrooms'). Robert May's recipe for dressing mushrooms 'in the Italian fashion' is to fry them in sweet salad oil and serve them in a dish with oil (May 1660, Cc7v) and if playgoers were alert to this fashion of serving mushrooms, they might also recall that Marlowe's Gaveston is fond of Italian fashion and masques. Like Volpone's fantasy of eating the phoenix, Mammon's plans will come to nothing because he will not get the Philosopher's Stone; Jonson does not engage with whether or not it is possible to create the Stone but he does make it clear that Subtle, Face and Doll will not create it because they are fraudsters.

Where Mammon's fantasy revolves around sex and food, which he thinks he will achieve with the help of the Philosopher's Stone, Dapper wants to win at gambling with the help of a familiar or spirit. Like Mammon, Dapper is gullible; he is also prone to flattery and social climbing, believing Face when he tells him that Dapper was born under 'a rare star' and is allied to the Queen of Fairy, who is his aunt (1.2.122,126, 149). Dapper is told that he must perform certain rituals before he can meet with the Queen (Doll, disguised):

> prepare yourself.
> Till when you must be fasting; only, take
> Three drops of vinegar in, at your nose;
> Two at your mouth; and one, at either ear;
> Then, bathe your fingers' ends; and wash your eyes;
> To sharpen your five senses; and cry hum,
> Thrice; and then buzz, as often; and then, come.
> *(1.2.164–170)*

This is self-induced and pointless fasting, arguably a parody of medieval fasting and unlike the genuine hunger experienced by Subtle that we are told of at the outset of the play, when Face reminds him that he first found him 'Taking your meal of steam in, from cooks' stalls, / Where, like the father of hunger, you did walk / Piteously costive' (1.1.26–28). In order to keep Dapper out of the way while they deal with another visit from Epicure Mammon, Subtle tells him that he has to wait a little longer before he can meet the Queen:

> She, now, is set
> At dinner, in her bed; and she has sent you,

From her own private trencher, a dead mouse,
And a piece of gingerbread, to be merry withal,
And stay your stomach, lest you faint with fasting:
Yet, if you could hold out, till she saw you (she says),
It would be better for you.

(3.5.63–69)

Already bound with a rag, they gag him with the gingerbread and put him in the privy, making jokes to each other about its perfume (3.5.79–81). An earlier joke about Dapper being ready for the roasting spit (3.5.56) emphasizes his status as victim and carries with it a hint of cannibalism: in keeping with the emphasis on food and feeding throughout the play Dapper is here presented as a kind of foodstuff, as innocent and as prone to attack as the dumb animal hoist on the spit.

With Dapper safely confined in the privy, Doll is free to meet with Mammon who thinks she is 'a most rare scholar' who is 'mad' from studying the puritanical religious writings of Hugh Broughton (2.3.237–238). In a scene echoing Volpone's wooing of Celia, Mammon woos Doll with the promise of public admiration:

I am pleas'd the glory of her sex should know,
This nook, here, of the Friars, is no climate
For her, to live obscurely in, to learn
Physic, and surgery, for the Constable's wife
Of some odd hundred in Essex; but come forth,
And taste the air of palaces; eat, drink
The toils of emp'rics, and their boasted practice;
Tincture of pearl, and coral, gold, and amber;
Be seen at feasts, and triumphs

(4.1.130–138)

Mammon here prefigures Milton's serpent tempting Eve in *Paradise Lost* (considered in Chapter 3) when he tells her that she should reside not 'In this enclosure wild, these beasts among' but ' should be seen / A goddess among gods, adored and served / By angels numberless' (Milton 1993, 349; 9.543, 546–548).[16] When Doll warns Mammon that the Prince might seize the Philosopher's Stone, 'being a wealth unfit / For any private subject' (4.1.148–149), he tells her they will live in a republic:

where we will eat our mullets,
Sous'd in high-country wines, sup pheasants' eggs,
And have our cockles, boil'd in silver shells,
Our shrimps to swim again, as when they liv'd,
In a rare butter, made of dolphins' milk,
Whose cream does look like opals; and, with these
Delicate meats, set ourselves high for pleasure,

> And take us down again, and then renew
> Our youth, and strength, with drinking the elixir,
> And so enjoy a perpetuity
> Of life, and lust

> *(4.1.156–166)*

This fantastical feast is a curious mixture of the grand and the ordinary, with relatively simple foodstuffs presented in an elaborate fashion and containing exotic ingredients. When they eventually remember Dapper and release him from the privy, he has eaten the gingerbread gag in order to 'stay my stomach', affected by the bad smell from the privy (5.4.1–6); the gag might be expected to have left a darkish-coloured mess around his mouth, thus allowing Jonson to make a crude visual joke aligning the gingerbread with excrement. Doll, pretending to be the Queen of Fairy, claims to present Dapper with a familiar spirit, telling him that he must feed it for a week with his own blood (5.4.36–37), again highlighting Dapper's victimhood and Dapper as a source of nutrition. She and Subtle also order him to make sure he is worthy of the blood from which he comes (his fictional relation to this pretend queen) by eating 'no more Woolsack pies, / Nor Dagger furmety. / Nor break his fast, / In Heaven and Hell' (5.4.41–43) – the Woolsack, Dagger and Heaven and Hell being inns and taverns in London (Jonson 1967, 178 n41–43) – which is ironic given Subtle's fondness for hanging around pie-corner referred to at the beginning of the play.[17]

In *Bartholomew Fair* food is again used as a means to highlight the foolishness and hypocrisy at the heart of Jonson's society and prick the pomposity of the arrogant who proclaim loudly about the moral responsibility of others. There are those who attend the fair in order to see its entertainment and consume its food and drink and there are others who wish to police the behaviour and appetite of those present: Wasp would prevent his master Cokes from going to the fair because Cokes lacks discrimination in what he would purchase, Zeal-of-the-land Busy would prevent any activity he condemns as idolatrous, and Justice Overdo would prevent what he terms 'enormities' (wrongdoings) from occurring at the fair.

Wasp has a low opinion of his young master, Bartholomew Cokes: 'His foolish schoolmasters have done nothing but run up and down the county with him, to beg puddings, and cake-bread, of his tenants, and almost spoiled him; he has learn'd nothing, but to sing catches . . . He has a head full of bees!' (1.4.69–78). Wasp despairs at the idea of Cokes attending the fair:

> If he go to the Fair, he will buy of every thing to a baby there; and household-stuff for that too. If a leg or an arm on him did not grow on, he would lose it i' the press. Pray heaven I bring him off with one stone! And then he is such a ravener after fruit! You will not believe what a coil I had, t'other day, to compound a business between a Cather'ne-pear-woman, and him, about snatching! 'Tis intolerable, gentlemen!

> *1.5.110–117*

Why would the foolish Cokes be said to love fruit? An early modern audience would have been familiar with warnings in dietary literature against consuming too much fruit, and uncooked fruit was thought to be especially harmful since it was thought likely to cause bad humours and thus bring about disease (Elyot 1541, G4r; Boorde 1547, G3v–H1v; Bullein 1558, M6v–N3v). As Ken Albala points out, pears were thought to be cold and moist and difficult to digest and were not generally recommended by physicians; he cites Thomas Cogan's advice 'That peares may not hurt thee, take out the coares: pare them, and salte them, & cast them out of doores' (Cogan 1588, M2r; Albala 2003, 50). The Catherine pear was a small and early variety and John Parkinson describes it as 'a yellow red sided peare, of a full waterish sweete taste, and ripe with the foremost' (Parkinson 1629, 3D2v; Jonson 1960, 35n116). Thomas Muffett remarks that it is 'simply best and best relished' but still warns against eating pears raw (Muffett 1655, Ee1v, Ee2r). So, eating an excess of fruit would indicate that Cokes is a man driven by his appetite (a comic mirror to Win's putative pregnancy cravings) and perhaps also that he is not very bright, eating lots of a foodstuff the authorities warn ought not to be overconsumed.[18]

Cokes also buys Joan Trash's gingerbread to provide the banquet at his forthcoming wedding and then has another bright idea: 'And my wedding gloves too! (That I never thought on afore.) All my wedding gloves, gingerbread! O me! what a device will there be, to make 'em eat their fingers' ends! And delicate brooches for the bridemen!' (3.4.154–158). Giving gifts to guests at a wedding was common in the early modern period, and it was customary for the better off to give their guests gloves or jewellery (Cressy 1997, 362–363), but not made from gingerbread. Cokes' idea is bathetic and the hint of cannibalism in his suggestion that guests would be eating their fingers is mildly disturbing. Similarly it is not clear if Coke intends to serve just gingerbread at his wedding banquet or to serve it as the course of sweetmeats or fruit that was the precursor to the modern dessert course and was also termed a banquet; Gervase Markham provides two recipes for gingerbread under the heading 'Banquetting Stuffe' consisting of cakes and other sweet dishes (Markham 1615, Cc2). E. A. Horsman suggests Coke means dessert but Coke thinks gingerbread gloves are an acceptable wedding gift so a wedding banquet consisting entirely of gingerbread is not out of the question, and a modern audience would in any case assume that he meant banquet in the sense of a feast (Jonson 1960, 83n141). Gingerbread served at banquets was gilded with gold leaf and flavoured with expensive spices (Brears 1991, 100); Sir Hugh Platt provides a recipe for gingerbread containing spices and wine that he claims was used at courts and the houses of gentlewomen and Robert May concludes his recipe, containing spices and rose water, by observing 'and gild it if you please' (Platt 1602, B11r; May 1660, T2v). Yet if Leatherhead is to be believed about the poor quality of Joan Trash's wares, then her gingerbread would not be an acceptable food for Coke to give to his wedding guests. For Jonson gingerbread seems to signal gullibility – as when Dapper gets put in the privy wearing a gingerbread gag – perhaps because it was sweet and would appeal to the childlike, as would Joan Trash's doll-like 'gingerbread progeny'.

It is only by subterfuge that John Littlewit and his wife Win manage to persuade Win's mother, Dame Purecraft, to let them go to the fair by pretending that the pregnant Win has a longing for pork; it is not for the fair's pork that John wishes to go but to see the puppet show he has devised.[19] Dame Purecraft is under the influence of her suitor Busy, who objects not to pork, which he considers 'a meat that is nourishing', but to Bartholomew pork sold at the fair, which he condemns as idolatrous because the fair and the pig/pork is named after a saint (1.6.50, 54). We hear about Busy before we meet him. Littlewit and Quarlous, his companion, discuss how Busy used to be a baker but he objected that 'those cakes he made were serv'd to bridales, maypoles, morrises, and such profane feasts and meetings' (1.3.121–123) – Puritans objected to wedding feasts, maypoles and dancing – and he is characterized by Quarlous as a 'notable hypocritical vermin' and 'a fellow of a most arrogant and invincible dullness' (1.3.133, 145–146).[20] Busy gives Purecraft permission for the family to attend the fair, announcing 'we may be religious in the midst of the profane, so it be eaten with a reformed mouth, with sobriety, and humbleness; not gorg'd in with gluttony, or greediness' (1.6.71–74). He will go with them and 'will eat exceedingly, and prophesy . . . [and] by the public eating of swine's flesh . . . profess our hate and loathing of Judaism, whereof the brethren stand taxed' (1.6.92–95). Jonson's timing is great: just before this pompous speech, when it is clear that Busy will have his pork and eat it, Littlewit tells his wife and mother-in-law that Busy is just coming 'Presently, mother, as soon as he has cleans'd his beard. I found him, fast by the teeth i' the cold turkey-pie, i' the cupboard, with a great white loaf on his left hand, and a glass of malmsey on his right' (1.6.32–35). As Tracy Thong points out, this is 'a kind of inhospitality' since Busy 'takes it upon himself to distribute the food and drink in the Littlewit household, which involves withholding it from even the hosts themselves, and exploits his authority by selecting the best of it for his own secret indulgence' (Thong 2008, 6). An additional, more subtle, criticism of Busy would have been available to an early modern audience familiar with dietary literature, which generally considered pork good for consumption by younger men and those who were physically active and could therefore properly digest it.[21] Busy's gluttony would suggest a corpulent man so if an elderly and overweight actor were to be cast in the part of Busy, his overeating of pork would appear even more unseemly.

Justice Overdo wants to root out the kind of enormities of which Leatherhead claims Joan Trash is guilty. Leatherhead ridicules what he terms her 'gingerbread progeny', complaining that she is putting off his customers, and he threatens to 'ha' it proclaim'd i' the Fair, what stuff they are made on' if she doesn't move away from his stall (2.2.3–4, 5–6). Leatherhead is a bully but Joan proudly defends herself:

> TRASH. Why, what stuff are they made on, Brother Leatherhead? Nothing but what's wholesome, I assure you.
> LEA. Yes, stale bread, rotten eggs, musty ginger, and dead honey, you know.
> (2.2.7–10)

He accuses her of using arsedine, which was imitation gold leaf made of copper and zinc and used in the production of toys (Jonson 1960, 44n19), but Joan continues in her spirited self-defence: 'I pay for my ground, as well as thou dost: an' thou wrong'st me', declaring 'though I be a little crooked o' my body, I'll be found as upright in my dealing as any woman in Smithfield' (2.2.14–16, 24–26). We do not know if Leatherhead speaks the truth but Joan's reference to the other upright women of Smithfield is unfortunate given the nefarious practices we know Ursula, the pig-woman, to be guilty of, for example adulterating tobacco with the herb coltsfoot, a practice we saw also in Langland's *Piers Plowman* where Rose the Brewster adulterates her ale (Chapter 1) and that we will encounter again in Chapter 5 with the widespread adulteration of foodstuffs in nineteenth-century England. Ursula also sells her customers frothy beer that is quickly taken from them before they have finished and sold back to them again, and she overcharges pregnant customers craving pork (2.2.90–113).

As I have argued elsewhere, Ursula resembles Shakespeare's Sir John in the repeated references to her huge body, its sweating and comparisons to butter, and there is a suggestion that the sweat from her body bastes the pork she is cooking, making for a kind of cannibalism whereby this pig-woman is dishing up part of herself in the pork consumed by her customers (Fitzpatrick 2011). Ursula also evokes the traditional association between hell and kitchens – discussed in Chapter 1 in the description of Chaucer's Cook – when she complains about the hot work of roasting pig (2.2.42–45). Yet Jonson suggests that Ursula is no worse than Busy – who Knockem proclaims 'eats with his eyes, as well as his teeth' (3.6.49) – because although she cheats her customers, she lacks his pomposity, hypocrisy and desire to control the morals of those around her. As Elena Levy-Navarro rightly observes, the 'civilized elite' who attend the fair are far worse than the fair-folk, although Levy rather over-sentimentalizes the fair-folk's camaraderie in her focus on Ursula, failing to mention Leatherhead's bullying of old Joan (Levy-Navarro 2008, 176–191). Yet at the play's conclusion Busy, one of the elite, announces himself 'changed' after having lost an argument with a puppet over idolatry (5.5.109), and Overdo too, embarrassed into silence by his drunken wife, realizes that he is not perfect; as Quarlous tells Overdo, 'you are but Adam, flesh and blood! You have your frailty' (5.6.100–101), and the chastened Justice invites everyone home to supper.

It is fitting that *Bartholomew Fair*, a play so preoccupied with food and eating, should end with an invitation to supper. A reference to feasting also concludes *The Alchemist* when Face tells the audience:

> My part a little fell in this last scene,
> Yet 'twas decorum. And though I am clean
> Got off, from Subtle, Surly, Mammon, Doll,
> Hot Ananias, Dapper, Drugger, all
> With whom I traded, yet I put my self
> On you, that are my country: and this pelf,

> Which I have got, if you do quit me, rests
> To feast you often, and invite new guests.
> *(5.5.158–165)*

The metadramatic reference to the money paid by the audience to see the play (their 'pelf') refers also to the pelf the tricksters have gained throughout the action of the play, just as the 'feast' refers not only to food, the concept of elaborately feeding the audience members, but to performing for them, to entertaining them. *Volpone* also concludes with a reference to feeding when the 1st Advocatore states:

> Let all that see these vices thus rewarded
> Take heart, and love to study 'em! Mischiefs feed
> Like beasts till they be fat, and then they bleed.
> *(5.12.149–151)*

This reference to the fattening of animals for slaughter (which will, of course, provide meat) is followed by Volpone's epilogue where he observes that 'The seasoning of a play is the applause' (5.epilogue.1). For Jonson food is the most convenient motif by which to have his protagonists draw a moral, and he repeatedly frames his narratives around food so that, in his plays, food and entertainment are effectively synonymous.

Although we must avoid simplistic assertions about a particular author's attitude to food and drink, it does seem that Spenser is more censorious than Shakespeare and that Jonson is more interested than either Spenser or Shakespeare in presenting detailed descriptions of food. Genre has an important part to play in these authors' depictions of food and the process of consuming it: Shakespeare seems more concerned than Jonson with the practical considerations of writing for performance, with Jonson presenting more lengthy, poetical and fantastical encomiums to exotic foodstuffs that require no on-stage preparation or presentation, with some exceptions, mainly when one particular foodstuff is involved, for example gingerbread or pork. Writing in the medium of poetry allows Spenser to encourage the reader to use their imagination to conjure elaborate feasts and monstrous skeletal or cannibalistic figures. Location also has an important part to play in how these authors engage with food in their writing. Spenser's Faerie Land invokes the classical past as well as Elizabethan England and, at times, gives a thinly veiled nod towards the colony of Ireland. Shakespeare's plays, including his Roman plays, tend to dichotomize feeding as either excess or asceticism, with Rome carrying a Catholic signification and the fish-hating English Sir John betraying his origins as a Protestant martyr, his influence extending to Beaumont and Fletcher's fish-loving Lazarello. Like Spenser, Jonson invokes the classical past yet at the same time his plays are firmly rooted in England – even the Venice of *Volpone* seems familiarly English – so that indulgent Roman dishes co-exist with English sweetmeats and Bartholomew pig. Shakespeare's tendency to dichotomize feeding as either excess or asceticism does not mean that he offers the strict moral admonitions we find in Spenser but Shakespeare is alert to the dangers of excess, particularly drunkenness, and although Jonson's reputation for being obsessive about food is well-deserved, he is no mere glutton; although Jonson clearly enjoys describing food and drink – and we get the sense he is anticipating its deliciousness – it is also a vehicle by which he delivers his razor-sharp satire of contemporary society.

Notes

1 All performance and publication dates for plays are from the electronic resource 'Database of Early English Playbooks', or 'DEEP', created by Alan B. Farmer and Zachary Lesser and hosted by the University of Pennsylvania.

2 Quotations from early modern texts, such as the Homilies, dietaries and Spenser's poem, have not been modernized here because they seem close enough to modern English, although individual words are sometimes followed by their modern equivalents in square brackets. A fully modernized critical edition of three of the dietaries here cited, by Elyot, Boorde and Bullein, will be published shortly (Fitzpatrick forthcoming 2017).

3 The Well of Life and the Tree of Life are both biblical in origin: 'The water that I shall give him, shall be in him a well of water, springing up into everlasting life' (John 4:14); 'And out of the ground made the LORD God to grow every tree that is pleasant to the sight, and good for food; the tree of life also in the midst of the garden, and the tree of knowledge of good and evil' (Genesis 2:9); 'And the LORD God said, Behold, the man is become as one of us, to know good and evil: and now, lest he put forth his hand, and take also of the tree of life, and eat, and live for ever: Therefore the LORD God sent him forth from the garden of Eden, to till the ground from whence he was taken' (Genesis 3:22–23); 'To him that overcometh wil I give to eat of the tree of life which is in the middes of the Paradise of God' (Revelation 2:7); 'The tree of life, which bare twelve maner of frutes' (Revelation 22:2).

4 A useful synopsis of critical responses to the Bower of Bliss episode can be found in Alpers (1990).

5 In keeping some food aside for later, Lust perhaps influenced Shakespeare in Hamlet's description of Claudius' attitude to flatterers like Rosencrantz and Guildenstern: 'He keeps them, like an ape an apple in the corner of his jaw, first mouthed, to be last swallowed' (4.2.16–17); the First Quarto (Q1) edition of the play has 'as an Ape doth nuttes' but this is thought to be a memorial reconstruction and thus is an unreliable text (Shakespeare 1987a, 291n16). Like Spenser's Lust, Shakespeare's ape is like a man but not quite; both creatures are bestial yet thoughtful enough to store food for later.

6 For a discussion of the conflicting interpretations of the Host that emerged between Catholics and Protestants in the early modern period and how this relates to the issue of consumption and cannibalism, see Kilgour (1990, 79–85).

7 All quotations of Shakespeare are from Shakespeare (1989).

8 For early modern views regarding the dangers of English addiction to foreign wines, see Raber (2016).

9 The role of female fasting in these plays is considered in Gutierrez (2003) and Garwood (2009).

10 For a more detailed discussion of Sir John's criticisms of the prince, see Fitzpatrick (2007, 26–29).

11 All quotations of *The Woman Hater* are from Beaumont and Fletcher (1966).

12 Richard Levin cites an early work by Charles Mills Gayley, who detects allusion to *Antony and Cleopatra* in the following passage where Lazarello contemplates having lost the fish-head: 'If it be eaten, here stands, that is the most dejected, most unfortunate, miserable, accursed, forsaken slave, this Province yeelds: I will not sure outlive it, no I will die bravely, and like a Roman; and after death, amidst the Elizian shades, Ile meete my love again'

(3.2.110–114). The allusion is apparently to the passage from *Antony and Cleopatra* where Antony hopes to meet Cleopatra in Elysium 'Where souls do couch on flowers' (4.14.50–54) and where Cleopatra states she will emulate him by committing suicide 'after the high Roman fashion' (4.15.86–87) (Gayley 1914, 75–79; Levin 2005). Katherine Duncan-Jones finds the argument for a debt to *Antony and Cleopatra* unconvincing, noting that, 'despite an allusion to a posthumous encounter in the "Elizian shades", the passage quoted shares no precise words or phrases' with its alleged source. She detects, rather, specific allusion to King Lear's 'I will die bravely, like a smug bridegroom' (4.6.194) and 'perhaps more broadly to *Julius Caesar* and the suicides of Cassius and Brutus' (Duncan-Jones 2007, 321). Duncan-Jones also detects allusions to Shakespeare's *Measure for Measure* in the play's spying Duke and the busybody Lucio (Duncan-Jones 2007, 321). Levin similarly follows Charles Gayley by briefly pointing out the debt to *Hamlet* in *The Woman Hater*, a debt considered in more detail by Ruth Vanita (1995, 64). Critics have also noted a link between the incompetent informers in *The Woman Hater* and Dogberry and Verges in *Much Ado About Nothing*. For this and other echoes of Shakespeare in *The Woman Hater* detected by early critics, see McKeithan (1938, 19–23). The debt to *All's Well That Ends Well*, noted by early critics, is considered in further detail by C. Bryan Love, who focuses on the main plot of *The Woman Hater* and the motif of the 'exceptional woman' in each play (Love 2012).

13 All quotations of *Volpone* are from Jonson (1999).
14 All quotations of *The Alchemist* are from Jonson (1967).
15 Udders still feature as a dish in traditional German beer halls. Quotations of *Bartholomew Fair* are from Jonson (1960).
16 I here quote from the 1967 Revels edition of *The Alchemist*. The 1991 New Mermaids second edition of the play has 'places' at line 135 without explanation, which is clearly an error since the 1966 New Mermaids edition of the play has 'palaces', which makes better sense than 'places'; 'palaces' is also present in the quarto of 1612 and the folio *Works* of 1616, upon which the New Mermaids edition is based (Jonson 1966, 4.1.135; Jonson 1991, 4.1.135).
17 Furmety, or frumenty, was a dish made from hulled wheat boiled in milk and seasoned with spices; Robert May provides a recipe for it in his cookery book (May 1660, Ee2r).
18 In the US comedy show *Seinfeld* the likeably eccentric and often idiotic character Kramer loves fruit.
19 For a detailed discussion of the implications of Win's desire to eat pork, see Thong (2008, 288).
20 Busy is from Banbury, a town famous for its cakes; Gervase Markham provides a recipe for 'a very good banbury cake' amongst his 'Banquetting Stuffe' (Markham 1615, CC2r–CC2v).
21 Contrary to Thong's assertion that early modern dietaries advised against the consumption of pork, they generally approved of the meat (recommended by Galen) with qualifications depending on the consumer's age, complexion, occupation and moderate consumption, and with young pig (not over a month old) being considered nutritious (Thong 2008, 2–4; see also Elyot 1541, F3r; Boorde 1547, F2v–F3r; Bullein 1558, N5v–N7v).

References

Albala, Ken. 2003. *Food in Early Modern Europe*. Food Through History. Westport, CT. Greenwood.

Alpers, Paul J. 1990. 'Bower of Bliss'. *The Spenser Encyclopedia*. Ed. A. C. Hamilton. Toronto. University of Toronto Press. 104–107.

Anon. 1888. *Two Fifteenth Century Cookery Books: Harleian MS. 279 (Ab 1430,) and Harl. MS. 4016 (Ab. 1450,) with Extracts from Ashmole MS. 1439, Laud MS. 553, and Douce MS. 55*. Ed. Thomas Austin. London. N. Trubner for the Early English Text Society.

——. 1924. *Historia Augusta*. Trans. David Magie. Vol. 2. 2 vols. Loeb Classical Library. Cambridge, MA. Harvard University Press.

Apicius. 1958. *The Roman Cookery Book: A Critical Translation of* The Art of Cooking *by Apicius for Use in the Study and the Kitchen*. Trans. Barbara Flower and Elisabeth Rosenbaum. London. Harrap.

Beaumont, Francis and John Fletcher. 1966. *The Dramatic Works in the Beaumont and Fletcher Canon*. Eds. Cyrus Hoy, Fredson Bowers, George Walton Williams, Irby B. Cauthen, Jr., Robert K. Turner, L. A. Beaurline. Vol. 1: *The Knight of the Burning Pestle*; *The Masque of the Inner Temple and Gray's Inn*; *The Woman Hater*; *The Coxcomb*; *Philaster*; *The Captain*. 10 vols. Cambridge. Cambridge University Press.

——. 1976. *The Dramatic Works in the Beaumont and Fletcher Canon*. Eds. George Walton Williams, L. A. Beaurline, Fredson Bowers, Robert K. Turner, Jnr., Cyrus Hoy. Vol. 3: *Love's Cure*; *The Noble Gentleman*; *Beggar's Bush*; *The Tragedy of Thierry and Theodoret*; *The Faithful Shepherdess*. 10 vols. Cambridge. Cambridge University Press.

Biet, Christian. 2008. 'Child Pasties and Devoured Hearts: Anthropophagous Feasts and Theatrical Cruelty in England and France (Late 16th – Early 17th Centuries)'. *Hunger on the Stage*. Eds. Elisabeth Angel-Perez and Alexandra Poulain. Newcastle. Cambridge Scholars Publishing. 56–77.

Boehrer, Bruce. 1990. 'Renaissance Overeating: The Sad Case of Ben Jonson'. *Publications of the Modern Language Association of America* 105. 1071–82.

Boorde, Andrew. 1547. *[Compendious Regiment] A Compendyous Regyment or a Dyetary of Healthe Newly Corrected with Dyuers Addycyons*. STC 3380. London. William Powell.

Bradley, R. 1728. *The Country Housewife and Lady's Director*. London. Woodman and Lyon.

Brears, Peter. 1991. 'Rare Conceites and Strange Delightes: The Practical Aspects of Culinary Sculpture'. *'Banquetting Stuffe': The Fare and Social Background of the Tudor and Stuart Banquet*. Ed. Anne C. Wilson. Edinburgh. Edinburgh University Press. 60–114.

Bullein, William. 1558. *[The Government of Health] A Newe Boke of Phisicke Called the Government of Health*. STC 4040. London. John Day.

Church of England. 1563. *The Seconde Tome of Homelyes of Such Matters as Were Promised and Intituled in the Former Part of Homelyes, Set Out by the Aucthoritie of the Quenes Maiestie: and to Be Read in Every Paryshe Churche Agreablye*. STC 13664. London. Richard Jugge and John Cawood.

Cogan, Thomas. 1588. *[The Haven of Health] The Hauen of Health Chiefly Made for the Comfort of Students, and Consequently for All Those That Haue a Care of Their Health . . . Now of Late Corrected and Augmented*. STC 5479. London. Thomas Orwin for William Norton.

Cressy, David. 1997. *Birth, Marriage, and Death: Ritual, Religion, and the Life-Cycle in Tudor and Stuart England*. Oxford. Oxford University Press.

Davies, John. 1612. *A Discoverie of the True Causes Why Ireland Was Never Entirely Subdued, Untill His Majesties Raigne*. STC 6348. London. W. Jaggard for J. Jaggard.

Dawson, Thomas. 1587. *[Good Huswifes Jewell. Part 1] The Good Huswifes Jewell. Wherein Is to Be Found Most Excellent and Rare Devises for Conceits in Cookerie . . .* Part 1. STC 6391. London. John Wolfe for Edward White.

Dekker, Thomas. 1602. *Blurt, Master Constable Or the Spaniards Night-Walk*. STC 17876. London. Printed [by Edward Allde] for Henry Rockytt.

Delany, Joseph F. 1909. 'Gluttony'. *The Catholic Encyclopedia: An International Work of Reference on the Constitution, Doctrine, Discipline, and History of the Catholic Church*. Vol. 6. 17 vols. Eds. Charles G. Herbermann, Edward A. Pace, Conde B. Pallen, Thomas J. Shahan and John J. Wynne. London. Caxton Publishing. 590.

DeNeef, A. Leigh. 1990. 'Serena'. *The Spenser Encyclopedia*. Ed. A. C. Hamilton. Toronto. University of Toronto Press. 733.

Dobson, Michael. 2009. '"His Banquet is Prepared": Onstage Food and the Permeability of Time in Shakespearean Performance'. *Shakespeare Jahrbuch* 145. 62–73.

Duncan-Jones, Katherine. 2007. 'Francis Beaumont's Allusions to Shakespeare in *The Woman Hater*'. *Notes and Queries*. n.s. 54. 320–321.

Elyot, Thomas. 1541. *The Castell of Helthe*. STC 7644. London. Thomas Berthelet.

Evans, Maurice. 1990. 'Palmer'. *The Spenser Encyclopedia*. Ed. A. C. Hamilton. Toronto. University of Toronto Press. 526–527.

Fitzpatrick, Joan. 1999. 'Pastoral Idylls and Lawless Rebels: Sexual Politics in Books 5 and 6 of Spenser's *Faerie Queene*'. *Explorations in Renaissance Culture* 25. 87–111.

——. 2000. 'Spenser and Land: Political Conflict Resolved in Physical Topography'. *Ben Jonson Journal* 7. 365–377.

——. 2007. *Food in Shakespeare: Early Modern Dietaries and the Plays*. Aldershot. Ashgate.

——. 2010a. '"I Must Eat My Dinner": Shakespeare's Foods from Apples to Walrus'. *Renaissance Food from Rabelais to Shakespeare: Culinary Readings and Culinary Histories*. Ed. Joan Fitzpatrick. Aldershot. Ashgate. 127–143.

——. 2010b. *Shakespeare and the Language of Food: A Dictionary*. Arden Shakespeare Dictionaries. London. Bloomsbury.

——. 2011. 'Shakespeare's Sir John Oldcastle and Jonson's Ursula the Pig Woman'. *Cahiers Elisabethains* 79. 45–46.

——. Forthcoming 2017. *Three Sixteenth-Century Dietaries: A Critical Edition*. The Revels Companion Library. Manchester. Manchester University Press.

Flandrin, Jean-Louis. 1999. 'Seasoning, Cooking, and Dietetics in the Late Middle Ages'. Trans. Clarissa Botsford, Arthur Goldhammer, Charles Lambert, Frances M. Lopez-Morillas, Sylvia Stevens. *Food: A Culinary History from Antiquity to the Present*. Eds. Jean-Louis Flandrin, Massimo Montanari and Albert Sonnenfeld. European Perspectives: A Series in Social Thought and Cultural Criticism. New York. Columbia University Press. 313–327.

Fowler, A. D. S. 1960. 'Emblems of Temperance in *The Faerie Queene* Book II'. *Review of English Studies* 42. 143–149.

Garwood, Sasha. 2009. '"The Skull Beneath the Skin": Women and Self-Starvation on the Renaissance Stage'. *Shakespeare Jahrbuch* 145. 106–123.

Gayley, Charles Mills. 1914. *Francis Beaumont: Dramatist, with Some Account of His Circle, Elizabethan and Jacobean, and of His Association with John Fletcher*. London. Duckworth.

Goldstein, David B. 2013. *Eating and Ethics in Shakespeare's England*. Cambridge. Cambridge University Press.

Gray, M. M. 1930. 'The Influence of Spenser's Irish Experiences on *The Faerie Queene*'. *Review of English Studies* 6.21–24. 413–428.

Greenblatt, Stephen. 1980. *Renaissance Self-Fashioning: From More to Shakespeare*. Chicago, IL, and London. University of Chicago Press.

Guazzo, Francesco Maria. 1970. *Compendium Maleficarum: Collected in 3 Books from Many Sources, Showing the Iniquitous and Execrable Operations of Witches Against the Human Race, and the Divine Remedies by Which They May Be Frustrated*. Ed. Montague Summers. Trans. E. A. Ashwin. London. Frederick Muller.

Gurr, Andrew. 2012. 'Stephano's Leather Bottle'. *Notes and Queries*. n.s. 59. 549–550.

Gutierrez, Nancy A. 2003. *'Shall She Famish Then'? Female Food Refusal in Early Modern England*. Women and Gender in the Early Modern World. Aldershot. Ashgate.

Hankins, John Erskine. 1971. *Source and Meaning in Spenser's Allegory: A Study of* The Faerie Queene. Oxford. Clarendon Press.

Hawkins, Harriett. 1976. *Poetic Freedom and Poetic Truth: Chaucer, Shakespeare, Marlowe, Milton*. Oxford. Clarendon Press.

Holland, Peter. 2009. 'Feasting and Starving: Staging Food in Shakespeare'. *Shakespeare Jahrbuch* 145. 11–28.

Homer. 1919. *The Odyssey*. Trans. A. T. Murray. Vol. 1. 2 vols. The Loeb Classical Library. London. William Heinemann.

Hurtado de Mendoza, Diego. 1586. *The Pleasant History of Lazarillo de Tormes a Spaniard Wherein Is Contained His Marvellous Deeds and Life . . . Drawn Out of Spanish by David Rowland of Anglesey*. STC 15336. London. Abell Jeffes.

Jonson, Ben. 1960. *Bartholomew Fair*. Ed. E. A. Horsman. The Revels Plays. London. Methuen.

——. 1966. *The Alchemist*. Ed. Douglas Brown. New Mermaids. London. Ernest Benn.

——. 1967. *The Alchemist*. Ed. F. H. Mares. The Revels Plays. London. Methuen.

——. 1968. *Volpone*. Ed. Philip Brockbank. New Mermaids. London. A & C Black.

——. 1978. *Volpone, or the Fox*. Ed. John W. Creaser. The London and Medieval Series. London. Hodder and Stoughton.

——. 1991. *The Alchemist*. 2nd edn. Ed. Elizabeth Cook. New Mermaids. London. A & C Black.

——. 1994. *The Devil Is an Ass*. Ed. Peter Happe. The Revels Plays. Manchester. Manchester University Press.

——. 1999. *Volpone, or The Fox*. Ed. Brian Parker. Rev. edn. The Revels Plays. Manchester. Manchester University Press.

——. 1999–2000. *The Royal Shakespeare Company Production of* Volpone *Directed by Lindsay Posner*. Swan; Pit; Newcastle Playhouse.

Kilgour, Maggie. 1990. *From Communion to Cannibalism: An Anatomy of Metaphors of Incorporation*. Princeton, NJ. Princeton University Press.

Lévi-Strauss, Claude. 1983. *The Raw and the Cooked: Introduction to a Science of Mythology*. Trans. John and Doreen Weightman. Vol. 1. Chicago, IL. University of Chicago Press.

Levin, Richard. 2005. 'More Jibes at Shakespeare in 1606 and the Date of *Antony and Cleopatra*'. *Notes and Queries*. n.s. 52. 207–208.

Levy-Navarro, Elena. 2008. *The Culture of Obesity in Early and Late Modernity: Body Image in Shakespeare, Jonson, Middleton, and Skelton*. Basingstoke. Palgrave Macmillan.

Love, C. Bryan. 2012. 'Ending Well: Mixed Genres and Audience Response, 1604–06'. *Renaissance Papers 2011*. Eds. Andrew Shifflett and Edward Gieskes. Rochester. Camden House. 53–64.

McKeithan, Daniel Morley. 1938. *The Debt to Shakespeare in the Beaumont and Fletcher Plays*. Austin. University of Texas Press.

Markham, Gervase. 1615. *Countrey Contentments, in Two Bookes . . . The Second Intituled, The English Huswife: Containing the Inward and Outward Vertues Which Ought to Be in a Compleate Woman: as Her Phisicke, Cookery, Banqueting-stuffe, Distillation, Perfumes, Wooll, Hemp, Flaxe, Dairies, Brewing, Baking, and All Other Things Belonging to an Houshold*. STC 17342. London. By J[ohn] B[eale] for R. Jackson.

Marlowe, Christopher. 1994. *Edward the Second*. Ed. Charles R. Forker. The Revels Plays. Manchester. Manchester University Press.

May, Robert. 1660. *The Accomplisht Cook, or The Art and Mystery of Cookery*. Wing M1391. London. R.W. for Nath. Brooke.

Milton, John. 1993. *Complete English Poems, Of Education, Areopagitica*. Ed. Gordon Campbell. London. J. M. Dent.

Muffett, Thomas. 1655. *[Health's Improvement] Healths Improvement, or Rules Comprizing and Discovering the Nature, Method, and Manner of Preparing All Sorts of Food Used in This Nation*. 1st edn. Wing M2382. London. Tho[mas] Newcomb for Samuel Thomson.

Munday, Anthony. 1990. *Sir Thomas More*. (Rev. by Henry Chettle, Thomas Dekker, Thomas Heywood and William Shakespeare.) Eds. Vittorio Gabrieli and Giorgio Melchiori. The Revels Plays. Manchester. Manchester University Press.

Murrell, John. 1617. *A New Booke of Cookerie*. STC 18300. London. Printed [by T. Snodham] for John Browne.

Osgood, Charles G. 1931. 'Comments on the Moral Allegory of *The Faerie Queene*'. *Modern Language Notes* 46. 502–507.

Ovid. 1965. *Metamorphoses, 1567*. Trans. Arthur Golding. Ed. John Frederick Nims. New York. Macmillan.

Parkinson, John. 1629. *Paradisi in Sole Paradisus Terrestris. Or A Garden of All Sorts of Pleasant Flowers Which Our English Ayre Will Permitt to be Noursed Up: with a Kitchen Garden of All Manner of Herbes, Rootes, and Fruites, for Meate or Sause Used with Us, and an Orchard of All Sorte of Fruitbearing Trees and Shrubbes Fit for Our Land Together with the Right Ordering Planting and Preserving of Them and Their Uses and Vertues*. STC 19300. London. Humfrey Lownes and Robert Young.

Paster, Gail Kern. 1993. *The Body Embarrassed: Drama and the Disciplines of Shame in Early Modern England*. Ithaca, NY. Cornell University Press.

Pearlman, E. 1979. 'Ben Jonson: An Anatomy'. *English Literary Renaissance* 9. 364–394.

Platt, Hugh. 1602. *Delightes for Ladies, to Adorne Their Persons, Tables, Closets, and Distillatories*. STC 19978. London. Peter Short.

Pliny. 1940. *Natural History*. Trans. H. Rackham. Vol. 3. 10 vols. Loeb Classical Library. London. Heinemann.

Prescott, Anne Lake. 1990. 'Mammon'. *The Spenser Encyclopedia*. Ed. A. C. Hamilton. Toronto. University of Toronto Press. 451–452.

Raber, Karen. 2016. 'Fluid Mechanics: Shakespeare's Subversive Liquors'. *Culinary Shakespeare: Staging Food and Drink in Early Modern England*. Eds. David B. Goldstein and Amy L. Tigner. Pittsburgh, PA. Duquesne University Press. 75–96.

Rollinson, Philip B. 1990. 'Maleger'. *The Spenser Encyclopedia*. Ed. A. C. Hamilton. Toronto. University of Toronto Press. 449–450.

Schmidgall, Gary and Bruce Thomas Boehrer. 1991. 'Ben Jonson at Table'. *Publications of the Modern Language Association of America* 106. 317–319.

Schoenfeldt, Michael C. 1999. *Bodies and Selves in Early Modern England: Physiology and Inwardness in Spenser, Shakespeare, Herbert, and Milton*. Cambridge. Cambridge University Press.

Shakespeare, William. 1987a. *Hamlet*. Ed. G. R. Hibbard. The Oxford Shakespeare. Oxford. Oxford University Press.

——. 1987b. *The Tempest*. Ed. Stephen Orgel. The Oxford Shakespeare. Oxford. Oxford University Press.

——. 1989. *The Complete Works*. Eds. Stanley Wells, Gary Taylor, John Jowett, William Montgomery. Prepared by William Montgomery and Lou Burnard. Oxford. Oxford Electronic Publishing, Oxford University Press.

——. 1990. *Antony and Cleopatra*. Ed. David Bevington. The New Cambridge Shakespeare. Cambridge. Cambridge University Press.

——. 1994. *The Tragedy of Coriolanus*. Ed. R. B. Parker. The Oxford Shakespeare. Oxford. Clarendon Press.

Spenser, Edmund. 1949. *Prose Works*. Ed. Rudolf Gottfried. The Works of Edmund Spenser: A Variorum Edition. Vol. 10. 11 vols. Baltimore, MD. Johns Hopkins University Press.

——. 2001. *The Faerie Queene*. Eds. A. C. Hamilton, Shohachi Fukuda, Hiroshi Yamashita and Toshiyuki Suzuki. Longman Annotated English Poets. London. Longman.

Thong, Tracy. 2008. '"Quality Food, Honestly Priced": Traders and Tricksters in Ben Jonson's *Bartholomew Fair'*. *Food and Morality: Proceedings of the Oxford Symposium on Food and Cookery 2007*. Ed. Susan R. Friedland. Totnes. Prospect. 288–297.

Vanita, Ruth. 1995. '*The Woman Hater* as Beaumont and Fletcher's Reading of *Hamlet'*. *Hamlet Studies* 17. 63–77.

Vickers, Nancy J. 1981. 'Diana Described: Scattered Woman and Scattered Rhyme'. *Critical Inquiry* 8.2. 265–279.

——. 1985. 'The Blazon of Sweet Beauty's Best: Shakespeare's Lucrece'. *Shakespeare and the Question of Theory*. Ed. Patricia Parker and Geoffrey Hartman. New York. Methuen. 95–115.

Wells, Stanley, Gary Taylor, John Jowett and William Montgomery. 1987. *William Shakespeare: A Textual Companion*. Oxford. Clarendon Press.

Wilson, C. Anne. 1976. *Food and Drink in Britain: From the Stone Age to Recent Times*. Harmondsworth. Penguin.

Wilson, Edmund. 1952. *The Triple Thinkers: Twelve Essays on Literary Subjects*. London. John Lehmann.

3

ADVENTURES IN ENGLAND AND BEYOND ITS SHORES (1650–1750)

Joan Fitzpatrick

This chapter opens by considering *Paradise Lost*, a poem that dramatizes the first act of gluttony in human history according to the Christian tradition: Eve's consumption of the Edenic fruit, as related in the biblical Book of Genesis. The poem builds up to this important act, which is not dramatized until Book Nine, exploring along the way key theological and philosophical issues regarding the nature of paradise, hell, virtue, sin and angelic appetite. The motif of the apple, that dominates the medieval texts hitherto explored in this volume but features less in the early modern literature considered, is again a means to explore the nature of human identity, our relationship with each other, and the divine. *Paradise Regained*, also here considered, is an unjustly neglected poem. Focusing on Christ's hunger and temptation at the hands of Satan in the wilderness – temptations that will involve a grand banquet as well as more modest bread – Milton again develops the sparse biblical details available to him in an attempt to 'justify the ways of God to men' (1.26).[1] Christ's hunger is a consequence of the gluttony of human-kind, a gluttony all the more inexcusable because in paradise God provides Adam and Eve with nature's plenty; he gives them all they could possibly need, save knowledge. Another thing lacking in paradise is animal flesh, since it is only after the Fall of humankind, when sin has been committed, that death, hunting and even cannibalism will emerge. As we shall see in later chapters, *Paradise Lost* was enormously influential in subsequent literary representations of food (for example in writings by Percy Shelley, John Keats and Christina Rossetti) and the view that meat-eating was a direct result of the Fall was endorsed by Romantic vegeta-rians. As with the literary texts considered in Chapter 1, the Bible is a prominent context for Milton's poem, with other contextual material revealing why the biblical fruit that features in *Paradise Lost* might be specifically an apple, and how the general hostility, in dietary literature and elsewhere, towards fruit as unhealthy was beginning to diminish.

Where cannibalism is briefly mentioned in *Paradise Lost* as a consequence of Eve's sin (in the cannibalistic children that are the offspring of Sin and Death), it is an important mark of savagery in Daniel Defoe's novel *Robinson Crusoe,* just as it was for the figure of Lust and the Savage Nation in Spenser's *Faerie Queene* discussed in Chapter 2. Yet before Crusoe is aware of the cannibals who live on the island on which he is stranded, there are lengthy descriptions of his own efforts to find, grow and hunt for food, which reveals much about early eighteenth-century attitudes and fashions, for example the use of turtle and also sugar, an increasingly available and popular foodstuff, which was still considered by many to be medicinal. Colonial expansion provides an important historical context for the prose texts considered in this chapter, with real-life journeys beyond England informing the exotic locations that feature in the literature. Another feigned travel narrative here explored is Jonathan Swift's *Gulliver's Travels* where again gluttony, hunger and cannibalism feature and the concept of meat-eating raises important questions about the nature of civility. The chapter concludes with an exploration of two novels by Henry Fielding: *Joseph Andrews* and *Tom Jones,* where the appetite for food and drink is repeatedly figured in terms of sexual appetite and, as in Swift's *Gulliver's Travels,* food and drink provide a means by which virtue and vice are explored. Sugar and coffee – both important commodities emerging from England's expansion abroad and from English involvement in the slave trade – feature in the literature here considered, providing insight into the socio-political context of food and drink as well as the literary development which saw the rise of the novel. Sugar features in Defoe's novel, providing sustenance for Crusoe, and it is listed amongst the foods he manages to gather together from the shipwreck, but is also implicated in his hubris. Coffee, specifically the important social space of the coffee-house, comes up in Fielding's writing, with Samuel Pepys providing a context for both colonial commodities (coffee and sugar), and thus revealing that food and drink are about more than simply sustenance. What gets eaten and drunk allows us to get to the heart of a society's social, moral and political preoccupations.

John Milton, *Paradise Lost* (1667)

In Book Four of his epic poem *Paradise Lost* Milton provides the reader with a detailed description of the world God has provided for Adam and Eve. It is first seen through the eyes of Satan and the description emphasizes that the 'pleasant soil' and 'fertile ground' of the garden (4.214, 215) are a sensual delight: 'rich trees wept odorous gums and balm / . . . fruit, burnished with golden rind / Hung amiable . . . / and of delicious taste' (4.248–251). The climate is temperate and the labour undertaken by Adam and Eve in the garden is not arduous:

> Under a tuft of shade that on a green
> Stood whispering soft, by a fresh fountain-side,
> They sat them down, and, after no more toil
> Of their sweet gardening labour than sufficed

> To recommend cool Zephyr, and made ease
> More easy, wholesome thirst and appetite
> More grateful, to their supper-fruits they fell –
> Nectarine fruits, which the compliant boughs
> Yielded them, sidelong as they sat recline
> On the soft downy bank damasked with flowers:
> The savoury pulp they chew, and in the rind,
> Still as they thirsted, scoop the brimming stream
>
> *(4.325–336)*

Since paradise is a place where death is unknown, the animals in the garden are not hunted or eaten by Adam and Eve, and nor do the animals hunt or eat each other:

> About them frisking played
> All beasts of the earth, since wild, and of all chase
> In wood or wilderness, forest or den;
> Sporting the lion ramped, and in his paw
> Dandled the kid; bears, tigers, ounces, pards,
> Gambolled before them
>
> *(4.340–345)*

The prelapsarian environment is pleasurable and kind – the gentleness with which the lion regards the kid is picked up on by Shelley in his poem *Queen Mab* (see Chapter 4) – with the work that Adam and Eve experience tending the garden described as a 'delightful task' and 'pleasant labour' (4.437, 625). Yet they are both aware that the garden's 'wanton growth' renders it unmanageable (4.629) and they tell God that although they are happy in their 'mutual help, / And mutual love', the garden he has given them is 'too large', reminding him of his promise to provide a race of humans to help them contain it (4.727–728, 730). It is having too much work to do in the garden that encourages Eve to persuade Adam that they ought to go about their work separately, so they will not distract each other, and thus get more work done. Adam reminds her that God does not expect them to work so hard that they cannot enjoy the refreshment that they need, 'whether food or talk between, / Food of the mind' (9.237–238), and that they are more vulnerable to temptation apart, and yet he allows her to go, to exercise her free will.

Milton usually refers to the diet enjoyed by Adam and Eve in the garden using the generic term 'fruit' and the produce from the Tree of Knowledge they have been forbidden to touch is also described as 'fruit'. It is only Satan in the form of a serpent who refers to the forbidden fruit specifically as an apple. When tempting Eve to eat from the tree, he describes how it appealed to his senses, being 'Loaden with fruit of fairest colours mixed, / Ruddy and gold' and exuding 'a savoury odour' more pleasing than 'sweetest fennel, or the teats / Of ewe or goat dropping with milk at even' (9.577–578, 579, 581–582). Fennel was symbolic of flattery and serpents were thought to suck the milk from lactating animals, which is in keeping with their reputation for guile, stealing what should provide nourishment for the animal's young (Topsell 1608, L3r; Fitzpatrick 2010, 'Fennel'). Satan's consumption of the apples is described in terms of gluttony and ambition: he tells of 'the sharp desire I had / Of tasting those fair apples' (9.584–585) and how, with his appetite provoked, 'I resolved / Not to defer; hunger and thirst at once, / Powerful persuaders' (9.585–587). The serpent informs Eve that before eating from the tree he was just like other animals, eating the lowly herb with 'abject thoughts and low' (thoughts only of food and sex), but that the fruit, a 'godlike food', has given him reason and speech and will allow her to know both good and evil, as the gods do (9.572, 717). Eve herself reasons that she and Adam ought not to be denied 'this intellectual food' that the serpent has enjoyed and her consumption of the fruit is described in terms of gluttony:

> such delight till then, as seemed,
> In fruit she never tasted, whether true,
> Or fancied so through expectation high
> Of knowledge; nor was godhead from her thought.
> Greedily she engorged without restraint
>
> *(9.787–791)*

Eve eats only one apple but the manner in which she eats and the pleasure she takes from eating are in keeping with the early modern definition of gluttony as an excessive *interest* in food as well as the consumption of an excessive *amount* of food (see Chapter 2). A similar greedy devouring of fruit and a concomitant lack of control are picked up on in later writings such as Keats's *The Fall of Hyperion* and Rossetti's 'Goblin Market' (discussed in Chapters 4 and 5). When Adam eats the fruit, he 'took no thought, / Eating his fill' (9.1004–1005). As in early modern warnings against gluttony, one sin leads to another: 'Carnal desire inflaming; he on Eve / Began to cast lascivious eyes; she him / As wantonly repaid; in lust they burn' (9.1013–1015). Thomas Arvind argues that Eve's gorging of the apple in silence, and Adam's silent consumption of the fruit, violate the earlier scenes of mannerly eating between the two, noting that although critics have spotted here Milton's critique of Royalist hedonism and Restoration Epicureanism, they have not observed his engagement with humanist views on manners and civility (Arvind 2006). As Arvind notes, their silent gluttony appears to invoke humanist principles of civil eating, whilst their excited libido, indigestion and sense of shame that is consequent to their acts of gluttony appear to violate humanist standards of social decorum.

The second time the word 'apple' is used to describe the fruit from the Tree of Knowledge it is again Satan who speaks. In Book Ten, having achieved his aim of persuading humankind to commit sin, Satan returns to hell and informs his companions there of his success:

> him by fraud I have seduced
> From his creator, and the more to increase

> Your wonder, with an apple; he, thereat
> Offended – worth your laughter – hath given up
> Both his beloved man and all his world
> To Sin and Death a prey
>
> *(10.485–490)*

Expecting to hear the applause of his audience Satan instead hears them hiss and realizes that they, and he, have been turned into serpents: 'punished in the shape he sinned, / According to his doom' (10.516–517). It is not clear why Milton allows only Satan-as-serpent to call the fruit an apple and we might wonder why he does this at all since the biblical Book of Genesis does not specify what kind of fruit grows on the Tree of Knowledge.

In *Pseudodoxia Epidemica* (1646) Thomas Browne traces the association between the Edenic fruit and the apple: 'That the Forbidden Fruit of Paradise was an Apple, is commonly believed, confirmed by Tradition, perpetuated by Writings, Verses, Pictures; and some have been so bad Prosodians, as from thence to derive the Latine word *malum*, because that fruit was the first occasion of evil' (Browne 1646, Vv2). So the connection made between the fruit consumed by Eve and the apple did not originate with Milton but he is tapping into an already established tradition, possibly making a connection between the Latin word for apple and Satan, the only figure to specify the fruit, and also wanting to retain the generic nature of the Edenic fruit. Robert Appelbaum considers what he terms the 'double nature' of Milton's fruit, whereby it starts out by resembling an apple ('ruddy and gold') but, after Eve has eaten it, the noun 'nectar' and the adjectives 'ambrosial' and 'downy' are used to describe the fruit, which sounds more like a peach (Appelbaum 2006, 196–198). The words 'nectar' and 'ambrosial' also suggest the food and drink of the gods of course, and Milton often invokes the classical in his religious epic, but clearly an apple would carry most resonance with an English audience. This common English fruit allows Milton's Satan to mock Adam and Eve who have relinquished paradise for a mere apple, not a rare and exotic fruit. As we saw in Chapter 1, the apple was a recurrent motif in medieval English literature, where it repeatedly functions as a symbol of sin, and although this signification is less apparent in the literature from 1550–1650, considered in Chapter 2, it is picked up by Milton who again makes the apple–sin relationship a prominent literary motif.

Although, as Appelbaum indicates, fruit was increasingly recommended for health by scientists and experts such as the gardening writer Ralph Austen, who considered the fruits of an orchard 'good and healthfull to the body, as well as pleas-ant to the taste' (Austen 1657, E3r), Milton's readers would have been familiar with the commonly held view, espoused by the sixteenth-century dietary authors, that the consumption of fruit should be approached with caution. In his dietary *Health's Improvement*, Thomas Muffett warns that the nature of man's relationship with fruit had changed since Adam and Eve: 'for as before the floud men were of stronger constitution, and vegitable fruit grew void of superfluous moisture: so by the floud these were endued with weaker nourishment, and men made more subject to violent diseases and infirmities' (Muffett 1655, E4r). Where Austen advocates consumption of 'all sorts of ripe and raw fruits', noting that 'some Apples are accounted Cordials', Muffett advises that apples 'are worst raw, and best baked or preserved' (Muffett 1655, Cc3r; Austen 1657, E2v–E3r). Muffett's dietary was first published in 1655 but written earlier (he died in 1604); another early modern dietary author, Thomas Cogan, is perhaps thinking of Eve when he advises against the consumption of raw apples, observing that 'unruly people through wanton appetite will not refraine them, and chieflie in youth when (as it were) by a naturall affection they greedily covet them' (Cogan 1584, L4v–M1r). Still current in the seventeenth century was a general association between the apple and lust: in his work on the medicinal value of herbs and plants the herbalist and physician Nicholas Culpepper lists the apple tree under the dominion of the planet Venus, and Kenelm Digby's cookery book provides a recipe for a drink made from apples that treats venereal disease (Culpepper 1652, B3v; Digby 1669, I3r).

As a consequence of the Fall the diet of Adam and Eve and their descendants is changed forever:

> Cursed is the ground for thy sake; thou in sorrow
> Shalt eat thereof all the days of thy life;
> Thorns also and thistles it shall bring thee forth
> Unbid, and thou shalt eat the herb of the field;
> In the sweat of thy face shalt thou eat bread,
> Till thou return unto the ground; for thou
> Out of the ground wast taken: know thy birth,
> For dust thou art, and shalt to dust return.
> *(10.201–208)*

Sin and Death, 'the hellish pair', arrive in paradise (10.585–595) and the animals that once lived in harmony with man and with each other 'to graze the herb all leaving / Devoured each other; nor stood much in awe / Of man, but fled him' (10.711–712). Earlier in the poem Sin tells how she has been raped by Death, the child she has conceived with Satan, and how the offspring that are a product of that rape consume her: 'when they list, into the womb / That bred them they return, and howl and gnaw / My bowels, their repast' (2.798–800). Death too would have devoured his own mother, were it not for Eve's transgression, for he suffers famine before the Fall of humankind (2.805, 847). Describing Sin and Death as 'unmannerly and repulsive diners', Michael Schoenfeldt compares the incestuous cannibalism of Sin's children with Milton's conception of the Catholic Eucharist in his theological treatise *Christian Doctrine*, where he describes the Catholic Mass as 'a banquet of cannibals' (Schoenfeldt 1999, 136), a connection also drawn in other literary works discussed in this volume: in Spenser's *Faerie Queene* (Chapter 2), in Byron's *Don Juan* (Chapter 4) and Joyce's *Ulysses* (Chapter 6). Eve advocates suicide to avoid resigning their offspring to death's 'ravenous maw' (10.991) but Adam counsels against despair and, full of repentance for their sin, they pray to God. They are banished from paradise but first the archangel Michael is sent to reveal the future to Adam (in Books Eleven and Twelve), a future full of famine and intemperance, feasting and luxury, before God punishes humankind again by sending a Flood, and Michael traces the subsequent degeneration of humankind until the arrival of Christ who will redeem their sins.

Of course the Fall of Adam and Eve is preceded by another Fall, that of Lucifer and his fellow-angels who are flung from heaven for rebelling against God's authority. Where the world God has created for Adam and Eve is a green and luscious paradise with a temperate climate, hell is described as a place 'Of fierce extremes, extremes by change more fierce', in which the fallen angels can move only 'From beds of raging fire to starve in ice' (2.599–600). This is a place where it seems that nothing can grow because, unlike the 'pleasant soil' of paradise (4.214) and the 'celestial light' and 'happy fields' of heaven, here is only 'mournful gloom' where the soil is 'burnt' (1.245, 249, 244, 562); hell is a 'desert', a place of 'Rocks, caves, lakes, fens, bogs, dens, and shades of death – / A universe of death' (2.270, 621–622). When the fallen angels try to drink from the River Lethe and 'with one small drop to lose / In sweet forgetfulness all pain and woe', they are prevented by Medusa who guards against any such attempt. After the temptation of Eve and the Fall of humankind, Satan and his companions, already condemned to take the shape of serpents, are also tricked by God into eating from a tree 'laden with fair fruit, like that which grew in Paradise' (10.550–551), and which they consume with great appetite, but as additional punishment from God 'instead of fruit / [they] Chewed bitter ashes', which provide no sustenance and instead they are 'plagued, / And worn with famine long' (10.565–566, 572–573). As Schoenfeldt points out, this is the only time we see Satan and his companions eat and their 'distastefully unsatisfying meal . . . entails an unsavory disgust appropriate to celebrating the alimentary cramming of Adam and Eve, and Death' (Schoenfeldt 1999, 158). We might consider the fallen angels' appetite and hunger to be part of their punishment for sinning against God, were it not for the fact that elsewhere in *Paradise Lost* angels who have not sinned also eat and digest food, but it is a very different kind of appetite and eating experienced by those angels who have remained obedient.

In Book Five of *Paradise Lost* the archangel Raphael is sent by God to warn Adam against Satan's plan and is invited by Adam to dine with him and Eve. The scene is based on a similar scene in the Book of Genesis in which Abraham and Sarah are visited by three angels (one of them Raphael) who eat the bread, milk, butter and calf's flesh given to them by Abraham (18:1–8), and Milton's meal informs the eating scene in Part 1 of Keats' *The Fall of Hyperion* (as discussed in Chapter 4). Adam and Eve have been tending the garden all morning and they are ready for their midday meal, apparently not having eaten since waking, although Eve later refers to their habit of stopping work to snack and chat when persuading Adam that they would be more industrious if they worked separately. Adam is refreshed and ready for the day ahead 'for his sleep / Was airy light, from pure digestion bred, / And temperate vapours bland' (5.3–5), although Milton does not go into detail about the final act of digestion since, as William Kerrigan observes, 'evacuation is the one everyday function of the body whose Edenic exercise Milton has not seen fit to tell us about directly' (Kerrigan 1983, 210). This is in contrast to Joyce's modern epic *Ulysses,* considered in Chapter 6, which reveals a distinct interest in urination and defecation. Schoenfeldt discusses Kerrigan's point, and the whole issue of bodily functions in paradise, in the context of Milton's mockery of transubstantiation in *Christian Doctrine,* where he proclaimed: 'Whereas if we eat his flesh it will not remain in us, but, to speake candidly, after being digested in the stomach, it will be at length exuded . . . Then, when it has been driven through all the stomach's filthy channels, it shoots it out – one shudders even to mention it – into the latrine' (qtd. in Schoenfeldt 1999, 141). Milton does not tell us whether Adam is hungry when he wakes up but he does not seem to be because he delays eating in order to converse with Raphael, having no fear that their lunch of fruits will go cold (5.395–396). The fruit is raw (uncooked) because it is only after the Fall that fruit would become less nourishing, and especially harmful when raw, because full of water, which Muffett believed to be a consequence of the biblical Flood (Muffett 1655, E4r).

Whilst Adam sits in the heat from the sun that serves to 'warm / Earth's inmost womb', Eve is already preparing a meal for them both, one of 'savoury fruits' and 'nectarous draughts . . . from milky stream, / Berry or grape' (5. 302–303, 304, 306–307). Seeing the angel Raphael approaching, Adam instructs Eve to 'go with speed, / And what thy stores contain bring forth', but she corrects his assumption that most of their food is in storage, noting that rather it 'All seasons, ripe for use hangs on the stalk' (5.313–314, 323), a feature also of Shelley's utopian vision in *Queen Mab* (Chapter 4). Doing as Adam asks, she goes 'on hospitable thoughts intent' to get more food:

> Whatever Earth all-bearing mother yields
> In India east or west, or middle shore
> In Pontus or the Punic coast, or where
> Alcinöus reigned, fruit of all kinds, in coat
> Rough or smooth rined, or bearded husk, or shell,
> She gathers, tribute large, and on the board
> Heaps with unsparing hand; for drink the grape
> She crushes, inoffensive must, and meaths
> From many a berry, and from sweet kernels pressed
> She tempers dulcet creams – nor these to hold
> Wants her fit vessels pure
>
> *(5.338–348)*

As Susannah B. Mintz observes, this episode reveals Eve's connection to the landscape and food of Eden, which is figured in maternal terms – the sun warms 'Earth's inmost womb' and their drink comes from a 'milky stream' – and Eve nourishes her guest at the centre of the Edenic body (Mintz 2002, 160–161). It is this connection with landscape that serves to explain its reaction to the moment Eve consumes the forbidden fruit: 'Earth felt the wound; and nature from her seat, / Sighing through all her works, gave signs of woe, / That all was lost' (9.782–783). When Adam eats the forbidden fruit, the earth trembles, suffers pangs and groans, but the first wound is arguably more visceral. Yet Eve's collection of all the edible commodities the earth can yield suggests colonial pillage (something that also emerges in Satan's banquet in *Paradise Regained* considered below) and it is perhaps not too fanciful to detect in Milton's language hints of overseas travel in references to the 'shore', the 'coast' and 'vessels'.

The meal prepared by Eve includes both nuts and fruits ('nuts' were also termed 'fruit' in this period) and their drinks are non-alcoholic ('inoffensive'); it is only after the Fall that wine is invoked in terms of the senses of Adam and Eve being 'heightened' (9.793). The bucolic idyll is further emphasized when we learn that they are served by a naked Eve, described as 'Undecked, save with herself', and that their table is made from 'grassy turf' with seats of moss (5.380, 391). Responding to Adam's concern that Raphael might find the food and drink presented to him 'unsavoury' – that it might be neither pleasing to the senses nor spiritually edifying (Milton 1993, 252n84) – the angel tells Adam that 'food alike those pure / Intelligential substances require, / As doth your rational', and that angels as well as men possess the five senses and can 'digest, assimilate, / And corporeal to incorporeal turn' (5.407–409, 412–413). Engaging with theological debates regarding the nature of angelic diet, Milton is unequivocal that Raphael actually eats:

> So down they sat,
> And to their viands fell, nor seemingly
> The angel, nor in mist – the common gloss
> Of theologians – but with keen dispatch
> Of real hunger, and concoctive heat
> To transubstantiate: what redounds transpires
> Through Spirits with ease
>
> *(5.433–439)*

Milton here alludes to the biblical Book of Tobit where Raphael claims that his eating in the Book of Genesis was illusory: 'I did appear unto you; but I did neither eat nor drink, but ye did see a vision' (12:19).[2]

In *A Preface to Paradise Lost* (first published in 1942) C. S. Lewis points out that Milton was not alone in his view of angels as corporeal since it was one held by Platonic theologians, challenging that of Thomas Aquinas who believed angels were immaterial, and discussed by contemporaries of Milton such as Henry More and Robert Burton (Lewis 1960, 109–11). Michael Schoenfeldt and Denise Gigante see a link between Raphael eating with pleasure and enthusiasm and Milton's views on transubstantiation in his *Christian Doctrine*. As Schoenfeldt puts it, Milton here establishes the legitimacy of hunger and 'reveals angelic digestion to be a far greater miracle than the transubstantiation at the center of the Catholic Mass' (Schoenfeldt

1999, 140). Gigante compares Milton's pleasure in describing the eating and digestion of angels in *Paradise Lost* with the 'negative pleasure' apparent in his description of 'the digestive reality of the sacrament of transubstantiation' in *Christian Doctrine*, for in *Paradise Lost* the corporeal will be transformed into the incorporeal and 'sublimated upward as spirit' rather than being purged (Gigante 2000, 98).

Just as the whole process of digestion is different for angels, so Raphael tells Adam that food in heaven is different from that available in paradise, being 'more refined, more spirituous and pure' (5.426–428, 475), although in both regions the food is described using the noun 'nectar' and the adjective 'ambrosial' (9.838, 852; 5.426–428, 475), and in paradise God has 'Varied his bounty so with new delights' (5.431). Prompted further by Adam to reveal the details of life in heaven, Raphael describes the moment God declared Christ his only son and vice-regent, with authority over the angels, and of the dancing and feasting that followed this declaration:

> Forthwith from dance to sweet repast they turn
> Desirous: all in circles as they stood,
> Tables are set, and on a sudden piled
> With angels' food; and rubied nectar flows
> In pearl, in diamond, and massy gold,
> Fruit of delicious vines, the growth of heaven.
> On flowers reposed, and with fresh flowerets crowned,
> They eat, they drink, and in communion sweet
> Quaff immortality and joy, secure
> Of surfeit where full measure only bounds
> Excess, before the all-bounteous king, who showered
> With copious hand, rejoicing in their joy.
>
> *(5.630–641)*

For Schoenfeldt the description of this heavenly banquet is a deliberate contrast to the incestuous cannibalism indulged in by the children of Sin (Schoenfeldt 1999, 136). Raphael does not specify what he means by 'angels' food' – presumably manna, which was often linked with honey (Sullivan 2015, 250) – but nectar is generally accepted as the drink of the gods (the drinks Eve prepares are 'nectarous'), and the fruit of the vines is presumably non-alcoholic (as in paradise) so they cannot get drunk. Although they eat their fill, it is made clear that heaven is no place for gluttony. Raphael tells Adam that it was after this angelic banquet that Lucifer, envious of Christ's authority, plotted rebellion in heaven. Milton also seems to be suggesting that not all desire is negative: where Eve eats alone, greedily and selfishly satisfying an individual desire, and both Adam and Eve eat silently, the angels' feast is commensal in that it involves 'communion sweet'. It is this notion of food as social, and how it relates to Christ's hunger as a demonstration of his love for humankind, that Milton will elaborate upon in *Paradise Regained*.

John Milton, *Paradise Regained* (1671)

In *Paradise Regained* Milton describes how, after his baptism, Christ is led by a spirit into the wilderness where he fasts for forty days and nights and undergoes temptation by the devil. In the Bible the story appears in the gospels of Mark, Matthew and Luke, with Mark providing only a basic outline of the story. In Matthew and Luke the devil tempts Christ three times: to relieve his hunger by making bread out of stones; to jump from the pinnacle of a temple to see if angels will break his fall; and to achieve dominion over all worldly kingdoms in return for worshipping Satan. In Matthew the first temptation is over relatively quickly: 'And when the tempter came to him, he said, If thou be the Son of God, command that these stones be made bread. But he answered and said, It is written, Man shall not live by bread alone, but by every word that proceedeth out of the mouth of God' (4.3–4). The text of Luke is similar: 'And the devil said unto him, If thou be the Son of God, command this stone that it be made bread. And Jesus answered him, saying, It is written, That man shall not live by bread alone, but by every word of God' (4.3–4). Milton elaborates upon this first temptation of Christ by the devil, who appears in Book One of *Paradise Regained* as a swain, telling Christ that a miracle may lead him out of the desert, but yet:

> What other way I see not; for we here
> Live on tough roots and stubs, to thirst inured
> More than the camel, and to drink go far –
> Men to much misery and hardship born
> > *(1.338–341)*

The devil suggests that Christ may relieve his own hunger by commanding 'that out of these hard stones be made thee bread' but where the biblical temptation is for Christ to save only himself, Milton makes this proposed act of transformation social: 'So shalt thou save thyself, and us relieve / With food, whereof we wretched seldom taste' (1.344–345). Milton's temptation is harder and the rejection firmer. In the Bible the devil swiftly moves on to his next temptation after Christ proclaims that man lives not only by bread but by the word of God, but again Milton elaborates upon the biblical text and Christ invokes God's treatment of the hungry faithful: the feeding of the Israelites with manna and how Moses and Elijah both survived without food for forty days (1.350–354).[3]

Earlier in the poem Milton expands upon the biblical description of the hunger Christ experiences during his ordeal. Matthew states only that 'when he had fasted forty days and forty nights, he was afterward an hungred' (4:2) and Luke is similarly brief: 'And in those days he did eat nothing: and when they were ended, he afterward hungered' (4:2). Milton comments upon the sparse details given in the Bible of how Christ spent his time in the wilderness and imagines possible scenarios:

Full forty days he passed – whether on hill
Sometimes, anon in shady vale, each night
Under the covert of some ancient oak
Or cedar, to defend him from the dew,
Or harboured in one cave, is not revealed;
Nor tasted human food, nor hunger felt,
Till those days ended, hungered then at last
Among wild beasts; they at his sight grew mild,
Nor sleeping him nor waking harmed; his walk
The fiery serpent fled and noxious worm;
The lion and fierce tiger glared aloof.

(1.303–313)

The Bible leaves us wondering if any food was eaten during that time and Milton does not clarify, although he does assert (as the Bible does not) that after the forty days have ended Christ and the wild animals that might have been a food source for him enjoy a prelapsarian co-existence.

The hunger felt by Christ is also considered in Book Two of *Paradise Regained* when Satan discusses with his fellow devils how best to succeed in his temptation of Christ. Rejecting Beliah's suggestion that Christ might be vulnerable to lust, Satan proclaims:

Therefore with manlier objects we must try
His constancy – with such as have more show
Of worth, of honour, glory, and popular praise
(Rocks whereon greatest men have oftest wrecked);
Or that which only seems to satisfy
Lawful desires of nature, not beyond;
And now I know he hungers, where no food
Is to be found, in the wide wilderness;
The rest commit to me; I shall let pass
No advantage, and his strength as oft assay.

(2.225–234)

In Matthew the reader is told: 'Then was Jesus led up of the spirit into the wilderness to be tempted of the devil' (4:1); Luke states: 'And Jesus being full of the Holy Ghost returned from Jordan, and was led by the Spirit into the wilderness' (4:1). Milton makes it clear (where the Bible does not) that God is testing Christ by sending him into the desert as preparation for his ultimate battle with Satan: 'But first I mean / To exercise him in the wilderness' (1.155–156). Milton perhaps here invokes the medieval theme of Christ as knight (as described in Woolf 1962) but where the medieval knight prepares for battle by jousting and tournaments, God intends for Christ to prepare to 'conquer Sin and Death, the two grand foes, / By humiliation and strong sufferance' (1.159–160).

Milton's Christ seems very human in his sense of bemusement at the situation in which he finds himself:

> Where will this end? Four times ten days I have passed
> Wandering this woody maze, and human food
> Nor tasted, nor had appetite;
>
> *(2.245–247)*

Again Milton refers to 'human food' (as he did in Book 1, line 308), possibly alluding to Christ's dual nature (human and divine) whereby Christ might be expected to consume heavenly food, or he might mean food that is cooked since it is cooking that signals the main difference between the human and animal diet. As noted in the discussion of Spenser's depiction of Lust in Chapter 2, Claude Lévi-Strauss considered the process of cooking to be an important indication of human culture (Lévi-Strauss 1983). Of course cooked food would not have been available to Christ in the desert that the devil characterizes as full of 'roots and stubs'. Christ modestly observes that it is not virtue that has allowed him to exist in the desert for so long without the burden of appetite but either God or Nature, and so 'what praise is it to endure?' (2.251). However, the real test has just begun:

> But now I feel I hunger; which declares
> Nature hath need of what she asks; yet God
> Can satisfy that need some other way,
> Though hunger still remain: so it remain
> Without this body's wasting, I content me,
> And from the sting of famine fear no harm,
> Nor mind it, fed with better thoughts, that feed
> Me hungering more to do my Father's will.
>
> *(2.252–259)*

In Book 1 of *Paradise Regained* Christ condemns Satan's deceit: 'For lying is thy sustenance, thy food. / Yet thou pretend'st to truth' (1.429–430). As Lee Sheridan Cox observes, the dialogue between Christ and Satan reveals that 'the image of Christ, the true food from Heaven . . . offers life to man as opposed to the image of Satan, the false food', with Milton distinguishing between 'the Word, Christ's food, and the lie, Satan's food' (Cox 1961, 226). Unlike Eve, who believes Satan's lies when he tells her that the fruit from the Tree of Knowledge is 'godlike food', what she terms 'intellectual food' (9.717, 768), Christ understands that he receives sustenance from the word of God and that the sensation of hunger (the 'sting of famine') he experiences is harmless even though it is painful. The hunger to do God's will is insatiable and Christ can only be satisfied by feeding the spirit.

Throughout Christ's trial in the wilderness food is illusory: he dreams of eating with virtuous men from the Bible – supper with the prophet Elijah and pulses with Daniel – but awakes still physically hungry.[4] The banquet presented to Christ by Satan is also illusory, appearing suddenly in the middle of the desert:

> Our Saviour, lifting up his eyes, beheld,
> In ample space under the broadest shade,
> A table richly spread in regal mode,
> With dishes piled and meats of noblest sort
> And savour – beasts of chase, or fowl of game,
> In pastry built, or from the spit, or boiled,
> Grisamber-steamed; all fish, from sea or shore,
> Freshet or purling brook, of shell or fin,
> And exquisitest name, for which was drained
> Pontus, and Lucrine bay, and Afric coast,
> Alas how simple, to these cates compared,
> Was that crude Apple that diverted Eve!
> And at a stately sideboard, by the wine
> That fragrant smell diffused, in order stood
> Tall stripling youths rich-clad, of fairer hue
> Than Ganymede or Hylas
>
> *(2.338–353)*

As Cox notes, Satan cannot distinguish between Christ's 'dream hunger' and his 'real hunger' to do his father's will, and thus 'caters to the dream appetite' (Cox 1961, 231–232). The geographical reach of this feast recalls the description of Eve's ingredients for the meal served to Raphael in *Paradise Lost* (5.338–348) and although Eve's meal is vegetarian rather than meat-based, both seem to involve plundering the globe. Satan's banquet contains the kind of dishes typically served on grand occasions and, as in the serpent's temptation of Eve, what is presented appeals to all of the senses: aside from the spectacle of 'dishes piled' there is the 'savour' of meats and the expensive and exotic ingredient of ambergris ('Grisamber') – secretion from a sperm whale's intestines – used to provide aroma. Ambergris was often used in sweetmeats and Hannah Woolley provides a recipe for 'A pretty Sweet-meat with Roses and Almonds' that calls for 'a grain of Musk or Ambergreece' (Woolley 1670, F2r). Curiously there is no mention of fruit being served at this banquet (it would have been a feature of most banquets), but its absence allows Milton to compare the fabulous array of foods on offer to Christ with the simple food that successfully seduced Eve.

Leigh Hunt regarded the biblical temptation of stones being transformed into bread 'quite sufficient', regretting Milton's decision to present 'with more poetry than propriety . . . a great feast, containing every delicacy in and out of season' (qtd. in Gigante 2000, 88). Yet Hunt rather misses the point because, as in the moment when Satan-as-Swain suggests turning stones into bread, the aim of this visionary banquet is not simply to invoke gluttony, suggested by its plenitude, but also the social aspect of consumption. A banquet is a meal prepared to be enjoyed by many (like the heavenly banquet in *Paradise Lost*, 5.630–641) yet Satan presents it for the benefit of only one. Satan thus misjudges Christ's nature by failing to realize that this temptation of what Christ calls 'pompous delicacies' is actually easier for him to reject than the turning of stones into bread because only Christ and not others will suffer by his rejection of it, although Christ is aware that any pleasure to be had from it is transitory because Satan offers 'no gifts, but guiles' (2.390, 391). Charles Lamb's observation about the banquet is more astute: 'The mighty artillery of sauces, which the cook-fiend conjures up, is out of proportion to the simple wants and plain hunger of the guest' (qtd. in Gigante 2000, 107).[5] Satan (though not Milton) gets the degree of temptation wrong and having his banquet served by 'stripling youths' – hinting that homosexual liaisons will form part of the entertainment – suggests he has also forgotten his earlier dismissal of Beliah's suggestion that they use lust to defeat Christ.

Christ replies to Satan's invitation that he 'Sit down and eat' by 'temperately' reminding the devil of the power he has at his command, should he choose to use it:

> Said'st thou not that to all things I had right?
> And who withholds my power that right to use?
> Shall I receive by gift what of my own,
> When and where likes me best, I can command?
> I can at will, doubt not, as soon as thou,
> Command a table in this wilderness,
> And call swift flights of angels ministrant,
> Arrayed in glory, on my cup to attend
>
> *(2.379–386)*

Ironically there is an element of pride in Christ's competing with Satan, and in both cases the banquets convey a sense of dramatic spectacle. Annoyed that Christ does not appreciate his efforts, Satan tells him that others will enjoy it, 'Whose pains have earned the far-fet spoil', and takes the banquet away: 'Both table and provision vanished quite, / With sound of harpies' wings and talons heard' (2.401–403).

Satan's banquet and its disappearance recall the banquet in Shakespeare's *Tempest* and the moment when Ariel, 'like a harpy, claps his wings upon the table, and with a quaint device the banquet vanishes' (3.3.52.SD.2–3), considered in Chapter 2. Unlike Shakespeare, who describes the food that actually appears on stage, Milton, like Ben Jonson, provides poetical imaginings, which arguably allow for greater elaboration than the practical necessity of having to show the food would allow.[6] Like Shakespeare, Milton bases this banquet episode on the moment from Virgil's *Aeneid* when Aeneas and his companions – taking shelter on the Strophades, islands inhabited by harpies – have their feast ruined by the creatures who swoop down upon their food, eating it and defecating upon it. In neither Shakespeare nor Milton is there any defecation, but in both cases the figure responsible for making the banquet disappear is morally censorious and punishment involves withdrawing food: Ariel calls the Italian nobles 'men of sin' (3.3.53) and Satan complains that his decision to respond to Christ's needs has been met with unreasonable suspicion.

His ordeal over, Christ is rewarded in heaven:

> So Satan fell; and straight a fiery globe
> Of angels on full sail of wing flew nigh,
> Who on their plumy vans received him soft
> From his uneasy station, and upbore,
> As on a floating couch, through the blithe air;
> Then, in a flowery valley, set him down
> On a green bank, and set before him spread
> A table of celestial food, divine
> Ambrosial fruits fetched from the tree of life,
> And from the fount of life ambrosial drink,
> That soon refreshed him wearied, and repaired
> What hunger, if aught hunger, had impaired,
> Or thirst; and, as he fed, angelic choirs
> Sung heavenly anthems of his victory
> Over temptation and the tempter proud
> *(4.581–595)*

Like the banquet presented to Christ by the devil, this 'table of celestial food' has no biblical source. The Tree of Life does feature in Genesis, which describes it growing next to the Tree of Knowledge; how man is banished from the garden so he cannot eat from the Tree of Life 'and live forever' (3:22); and how God sets angels and 'a flaming sword' to guard the tree (2:9; 3:22–24).[7] In *Paradise Lost* Satan sits upon the Tree of Life, described as the highest tree in the garden, 'like a cormorant . . . / devising death / To them who lived' (4.196–198); Milton describes the Tree of Life as 'High eminent, blooming ambrosial fruit / Of vegetable gold' and adds to his biblical source by claiming that after humanity's transgression the Tree of Life will be 'removed where first it grew' and transported to heaven (4.196–198, 219–220; 3.356), allowing him to make a connection between the spiritual sustenance provided to Christ and that denied to humanity until his Second Coming. In *Paradise Regained* Milton again dramatizes Satan's fall and Christ's victory over him is rewarded by comforts and feasting in an environment remarkably similar to the green and luscious garden provided for Adam and Eve, which they lost in return for the taste of an apple.

Daniel Defoe, *Robinson Crusoe* (1719)

When Robinson Crusoe finds himself shipwrecked on the Caribbean island that will become his home for twenty-eight years, he realizes that money and gold are useless to him in his current circumstances and it is food and shelter that count. Making eleven trips to his stricken vessel, he retrieves what he can, taking biscuits, rum, bread, rice, cheese, goat meat, cordials, some grain, sugar and flour. All these foods would have been considered healthy, even sugar, which, as Sidney Mintz points out, was still thought to be medicinal by many in the early eighteenth century (Mintz 1985, 103–108). In a diary entry for 26 July 1664 Samuel Pepys tells how some women at dinner advised him to drink mum (beer made from wheat malt and aromatic herbs) and sugar in order to conceive children, suggesting that sugar was still being consumed for its curative powers (Pepys 1971b, 222). As well as taking food from his wrecked ship, Crusoe also takes tools, which he regards as more valuable than gold, and ammunition, necessary for hunting wild animals and for protection against these and the other enemies he might encounter on the island. It is on his final trip to the wrecked ship that he finds money, proclaiming: 'O Drug! . . . Thou art not worth to me, no not the taking off of the Ground, one of those Knives is worth all this Heap, I have no Manner of use for thee, e'en remain where thou art, and go to the Bottom as a Creature whose Life is not worth saving' (50).[8] Yet he takes it anyway, without informing the reader of his reasons for doing so, but presumably in anticipation of using the money to bargain for his life or safe passage. Later in the novel when he boards a Spanish ship that has wrecked and finds money, he similarly observes: 'I had no manner of occasion for it; 'Twas to me as the Dirt under my Feet', but again he takes it back to his cave and is annoyed he could not get hold of more and come back for it if he did manage to escape the island (163). He also takes food, including brandy, sugar and biscuits, for which he has more immediate needs.

The act of taking the money from the wrecked ship reminds the reader how Crusoe has come to be shipwrecked on the island in the first place. Not satisfied with the flourishing plantation he has established for himself in Brazil, Crusoe is encouraged by other plantation-owners to undertake an expedition to Guinea, in West Africa, to capture Negro slaves as workers on their tobacco and sugar plantations. African slaves were the main source of labour on these plantations, which were, as Sidney Mintz puts it, 'a synthesis of field and factory' with extremely harsh working conditions: those forced to produce sugar for Western tables – the demand for sugar increasing as its price began to fall – were often exhausted and starving and the process of manufacture was hot and dangerous (Mintz 1985, 46–53, 166–170). Looking back upon his decision to leave his plantation to seize slaves, Crusoe acknowledges his failings: 'I was born to be my own Destroyer, could no more resist the Offer than I could restrain my first rambling Designs, when my Father's good Counsel was lost upon me' (35). An eighteenth-century reader would not necessarily have felt the same disgust that a modern reader finds in the concept of slavery, although many did, particularly from the 1770s onwards (see the discussion of the anti-saccharite movement in Chapter 4). Yet Defoe does not focus on the misery of slavery but rather on Crusoe's sense of shame at giving into his desire for adventure and profit. Crusoe repeatedly recalls his father's advice and warnings against travelling abroad and makes his first journey by sea 'without asking

God's Blessing, or my Father's' (9). During this first journey, in the midst of a terrible storm, Crusoe resolves never to sail again, but a calmer sea and the encouragement of a fellow sailor see his resolution falter, and he recalls the moment when he and his fellow sailors get drunk on punch: 'in that one Night's Wickedness I drowned all my Repentance, all my Reflections upon my past Conduct, and all my Resolutions for my future' (10). Like Milton's Eve, Crusoe is curious about the world around him, he is seduced by the arguments of others to go against paternal advice, and it is an act of gluttony that seals his fate.

Much of the novel consists of detailed descriptions of Crusoe's efforts to build shelter and to find and grow food, the kind of narrative realism – what Ian Watt terms 'the novel's air of total authenticity' – that developed with the emergence of this literary form in the eighteenth century (Watt 1957, 32, 9–34). Making a list of the negative and positive aspects of the condition in which he finds himself, Crusoe notes amongst the latter 'I am not starv'd and perishing on a barren Place, affording no Sustenance' (57); unlike the fallen angels in *Paradise Lost* he is not consigned to live in a place of darkness where nothing will grow. Having built his dwelling, Crusoe observes that the island is inhabited by goats and he hunts them for food. When he kills a she-goat, her kid follows him to his enclosure but his plan to tame it fails when it will not eat and 'so I was forc'd to kill it and eat it my self' (54). Crusoe is not heartless and, upon discovering that he has killed the mother of the kid, it 'griev'd me heartily', but he must be practical – 'these two supply'd me with Flesh a great while' (54) – even if the modern reader balks at the cruelty of the episode. There are several other moments in the novel where animals are treated thoughtlessly, for example when Crusoe forgets about the goat he has captured and the animal nearly starves to death (95) and in the pointless deaths of numerous animals, including a hawk and a wild cat, whose flesh he finds inedible (46, 62), although this is not clear to him before killing the creatures.

The killing and eating of animals in Defoe's novel blur the category between human and savage, as Alex Mackintosh observes, with any sympathy shown by Crusoe for his animals (and later his servants) being 'an intrinsic part of his strategy of domination, which is based on a combination of brute force and disciplinary power' (Mackintosh 2011, 40). Human mistreatment of animals was a concern for the Romantic vegetarians who thought meat-eating the source of human cruelty and violence (as discussed in Chapter 4). Friday's torture of a bear towards the end of the novel, as Crusoe makes his way home to England, is especially problematic because the bear is no threat to the humans around it; indeed the animal is retreating when Friday teases it mercilessly before shooting it in the head in order to amuse his master and their company. Crusoe regards Friday's joke as 'indeed a good Diversion to us' (249), a sentiment which jars with the repeated references to the hunger experienced by the bears and the wolves around them.

Besides goat meat, and the butter and cheese he gets from goats, Crusoe mainly eats the flesh of birds and their eggs, fish and the flesh of turtles and their eggs, with the rest of his diet made up of grains and fruit. Goat meat was less popular in Britain in the eighteenth century than in earlier periods, although it was still a favourite in

Wales, and milk and cheese had been mainly sourced from cows from the sixteenth century (Dohner 2001, 33). Although the unfashionable goat does not tend to feature in cookery books from the period, turtle was a new and exciting ingredient. As Ken Albala points out, 'in the eighteenth century, and especially in England, turtle soup became all the rage. Turtles could also be roasted or baked, but the difficulty of preparing them meant that only the best equipped kitchens could deal with them' (Albala 2003, 76); little wonder turtle dinners signify luxury in some of the literary texts considered in Chapter 4. Albala cites Hannah Glasse on 'How to Dress a Turtle the West India Way', the recipe being included as an appendix in the revised and expanded fifth edition of her *Art of Cookery Made Plain and Easy*, published in 1755 (Glasse 1755, Uu1r–Uu1v). As Albala notes, following Glasse's instructions 'yielded several different courses: a soup, a fricasee, fins and the *calapee* or flipper meat and *calapash* which is the meat from the upper shell that is greenish and gelatinous' (Albala 2003, 76), so the luxury is counterbalanced somewhat by the economical use of every conceivable part of the animal.

Crusoe also manages to make himself bread. Having thrown away some husks and dust present in the bottom of a bag that once held grain, he is astonished when, after a long period of rain, some ears of barley (which he calls 'corn') and rice have emerged from the soil.[9] This he considers a miracle, the result of divine providence, until he recalls his act of shaking the detritus from the bag and so his religious fervour at the thought of God's intervention in his trials is tempered (67). He will go on to make loaves, or cakes, of barley bread from the grains he grows (117), a bread inferior to that made from grains of wheat but the best he can manage in his current situation. Despite the hardships initially faced by Crusoe, the Edenic nature of the island is emphasized, especially those parts of the island he has not hitherto explored where he finds fruit in 'great Abundance', namely melons, grapes and raisins (85) but no apples, which do not grow in the Caribbean (Houston 2005, xxxi).

It is when Crusoe descends to the west of the island that it reveals its plenty: 'the Country appear'd so fresh, so green, so flourishing, every thing being in a constant Verdure, or Flourish of Spring, that it looked like a planted Garden' (85). Crusoe celebrates his autonomy: 'to think that this was all my own, that I was King and Lord of all this Country indefeasibly, and had a Right of Possession; and if I could convey it, I might have it in Inheritance, as compleatly as any Lord of a Mannor in *England*' (85). Notably Crusoe does not think of the land as belonging to God or nature but, rather, feels the impulse of the colonizer to acquire land and profit from it. As Brett McInelly observes, Crusoe's self-image, his development as a character with a growing sense of confidence and self-importance, is contingent on the colonial setting of the novel, an environment in which 'Crusoe gradually learns how to assert himself over land and people', which reflects a growing sense of confidence and pride amongst eighteenth-century British people in Britain's colonial activities (McInelly 2003, 2). In the west of the island Crusoe finds cocoa trees as well as orange, lemon and citron trees, and although few of the trees bear fruit, he does get some limes, later mixing their juice with water to make a refreshing drink (85–86).[10] Having gathered together what he can, Crusoe carries the fruit back to his dwelling but finds it has spoiled on the journey: 'the Richness of the Fruits, and the Weight of the Juice having broken them, and bruis'd them, they were good for little or nothing' (86). The Edenic nature of this part of the island is thus compromised and later it will become clear that, like the biblical Eden that harbours the serpent, there are dangers lurking here too in the shape of cannibals.

As the novel progresses, any fear of going hungry dissipates. Indeed Crusoe feasts like a rich man: 'I had no Want of Food . . . [I had] Goats, Pidgeons, and Turtle or Tortoise; which, added to my Grapes, *Leaden-hall* Market could not have furnish'd a Table better than I' (93), and earlier in the novel Crusoe catches a dolphin to eat (73). From the outset of his plight Crusoe reads the Bible daily, regarding the words 'I will never, never leave thee, nor forsake thee' to be a message addressed to him personally; yet despite repeated references to God's will and providence there is an increasing focus on Crusoe's autonomy and he again compares himself to a king, one dining alone and attended only by the animals he keeps for companionship, whom he terms his 'servants' (126). This sense of having plenty will be disrupted by the arrival of Friday for, having more than one human mouth to feed, Crusoe must grow more grain to make bread and teach Friday to hunt for food. The potential for hunger will emerge again later when there is concern about how Crusoe will provide for the people now living with him: Friday, Friday's father and the shipwrecked Spanish sailors who have reached the island (207). Before allowing more sailors to join the one Spanish Captain who resides with them, Crusoe and the Captain agree that they need to grow sufficient food for these men because otherwise 'Want might be a Temptation to them to disagree' and they would react like the Children of Israel, who rejoiced when first delivered out of Egypt, 'yet rebell'd even against God himself that deliver'd them, when they came to want Bread in the Wilderness' (207). Earlier Crusoe has observed that the three men living with him on the island are his subjects: 'I was absolute Lord and Law-giver; they all owed their Lives to me, and were ready to lay down their Lives . . . for me' (203), the sense being that any rebellion from the Spanish sailors would be directed against Crusoe, the 'King' and God of the island.

When it comes to the subject of food in *Robinson Crusoe,* critics focus not on Crusoe's diet but that of Friday and the other cannibals that populate the island.[11] It is shortly after reflecting upon the plenty he enjoys alone that Crusoe discovers the first sign that he is not the only human on the island: 'I was exceedingly surpriz'd with the Print of a Man's naked Foot on the Shore' (130). Crusoe's uneasiness at the sight of the footprint is justified when he finds evidence of cannibalism in the south-west part of the island:

> I was perfectly confounded and amaz'd; nor is it possible for me to express the Horror of my Mind, at seeing the Shore spread with Skulls, Hands, Feet, and other Bones of humane Bodies; and particularly I observ'd a Place where there had been a Fire made, and a Circle dug in the Earth, like a

> Cockpit, where it is suppos'd the Savage Wretches had sat down to their inhumane Feastings upon the Bodies of their Fellow-Creatures.
>
> *139*

Crusoe's incredulity means that for a moment he does not consider the potential danger he is in but focuses rather on 'the Thoughts of such a Pitch of inhuman, hellish Brutality, and the Horror of the Degeneracy of Humane Nature; which though I had heard of often, yet I never had so near a View of it before', and his psychological trauma soon becomes physical: 'my Stomach grew sick, and I was just at the Point of Fainting, when Nature discharg'd the Disorder from my Stomach; and having vomited with an uncommon Violence, I was a little reliev'd; but cou'd not bear to stay in the Place a Moment' (139–140). He is terrified by the thought of encountering the cannibals, 'who would have seiz'd on me with the same View, as I did of a Goat, or a Turtle' (166), noting the distinction between himself and the cannibals but at the same time imagining himself in their place and implicitly equating himself with his own prey, thus undermining the boundary between animal and human as well as that between savage and civilized. Crusoe's vomiting signals his disgust at the cannibalism but may also signal an unconscious attempt to reinstate the boundary between himself and the savages and thus prevent the emergence of an unconscious desire to eat human flesh, an aspect of human psychology described by William Ian Miller in his study of disgust (Miller 1997, 109–116).

Earlier in the novel Crusoe expresses fears of degenerating into a savage – a preoccupation also of Joseph Conrad's *Heart of Darkness* and 'Falk' (Chapter 6) – when he wonders how he would have fared without tools and weapons, whereby if he had killed an animal, 'I had no way to flea or open them . . . or to cut it up; but must gnaw it with my Teeth, and pull it with my Claws like a Beast' (111). When he comes across a cannibalistic feast, noticing one man out of three fleeing his captors faster than the others, his first instinct is in line with his general desire to rule over others: 'now was my Time to get me a servant'; it is only after this that he observes: 'I was call'd plainly by Providence to save this poor Creature's life' (171). Having saved Friday from the cannibals, he feeds him with bread and raisins, and gives him water, later providing him with milk and bread, apparently not yet wanting to give him flesh of any kind to eat. Returning the next day to the place where Friday has buried the two cannibals he killed earlier, Friday makes signs 'that we should dig them up again, and eat them' (174), Crusoe indicating that the thought of such an act makes him want to vomit. When they reach the place of the cannibals' feast, they find it 'cover'd with humane Bones, the Ground dy'd with their Blood, great pieces of Flesh left here and there, half eaten, mangl'd and scorch'd' (175) and, perceiving that '*Friday* had still a hankering Stomach after some of the Flesh, and was still a Cannibal in his Nature' (175), Crusoe again indicates his horror at Friday's desire for human flesh. He is initially afraid that Friday will make a meal of him, barricading his dwelling against Friday, but this fear does not last and he quickly finds that 'never Man had a more faithful, loving, sincere Servant, than Friday was to me . . . his very Affections were ty'd to me, like those of a Child to a Father' (176). After tasting the kid that Crusoe has roasted for him, Friday tells his master how much he likes it and that he will never again eat human flesh (179).

Some cannibals are apparently capable of reform, thus disrupting contemporary assumptions about racial characteristics being inherent and the notion of the white race as superior to others, as propagated by David Hume in his essay 'Of National Characters' (Hume 1963, 213n1).[12] Yet how far Friday proclaims his distaste for human flesh to please his new master (what Hume considered the ability of the racially inferior to mimic their superiors 'like a parrot', Hume 1963, 213n1) is less than clear, and his 'reformation' is perhaps a nod towards England's own reformed Catholics who at one time consumed the flesh of Christ. It is ironic that Crusoe should figure the relationship with Friday in paternal terms, given his repeated references to disobeying his own father. Crusoe's idyll resembles Milton's prelapsarian Eden but only sometimes and only briefly, for from the very outset the memory, threat or realization of sin, against the mortal father and the divine, is never far away.

Jonathan Swift, *Gulliver's Travels* (1726)

Where Crusoe survives on his island for more than twenty years alone, with only animals for company before meeting Friday, Lemuel Gulliver quickly encounters the inhabitants of the island upon which he is shipwrecked. The narrative realism that dominates Defoe's novel is less evident in *Gulliver's Travels*, for although it is ostensibly a travel narrative, the situations encountered by Gulliver are more fantastical than those described by Crusoe. The focus is on the strangeness of the various places Gulliver visits and less on the verisimilitude provided by the sometimes deliberately mundane detail with which Crusoe describes his day-to-day existence. Gulliver has much to say about the culinary habits of the exotic lands in which he finds himself and how the inhabitants cope with the demands his appetite places upon them. Depending upon where Gulliver is, of course, appetite is relative: he is considered a giant by the tiny population of Lilliput and so they regard his appetite as prodigious; a curiosity by the giants of Brobdingnag who feed him titbits from their massive dishes; and a savage by the Houyhnhnms who exist on a wholly vegetarian diet. Yet, despite the strangeness of the places and people Gulliver encounters, cannibalism (that most unnatural act of consumption) features only metaphorically, with both the conscious impulse towards and the fear of eating human flesh coming from Gulliver himself rather than an exotic and savage external source.

Upon being shipwrecked on the island of Lilliput, Gulliver drinks half a pint of brandy when leaving his ship and it is this, along with exhaustion and heat, that makes him fall asleep, whereby he is tied up by the Lilliputians and attacked with bows and arrows. Gulliver is 'almost famished with Hunger' and signals to his captors that he needs to eat by putting his finger to his mouth, an act he observes is 'perhaps against the strict Rules of Decency' (19).[13] (The tension between the urgency for action and manners is something that recurs in the novel when Gulliver, again having drunk to excess, urinates on a fire that threatens to engulf the apartment of the Empress of Blefuscu, a nearby island, who is visiting Lilliput.) Understanding by his actions that Gulliver is hungry and thirsty, the Lilliputians bring him food and drink: 'There were Shoulders, Legs and Loins shaped like those of Mutton, and very well dressed, but smaller than the Wings of a Lark. I eat them by two or three at a Mouthful; and took three Loaves at a time, about the bigness of Musket Bullets' (19). They also provide two large barrels of what appears to be wine, each holding about half a pint of liquid.

Gulliver's prodigious appetite, drinking and bodily functions allude to the antics of Gargantua in François Rabelais' sixteenth-century stories of two giants *Gargantua and Pantagruel*, which critics have long recognized as a source for Swift's novel (Eddy 1922; Swift 2005, 289n19). The prospect of cannibalism is raised when Gulliver relates how, after picking up six Lilliputians who have attacked him and putting five in his coat-pocket, he terrifies the one he holds in his hand: 'I made a Countenance as if I would eat him alive' (26). Gulliver soon learns that the court is concerned that he might break loose and 'that my Diet would be very expensive, and might cause a Famine' (27). The fear of famine is not unreasonable since the king promises to provide 'the *Man-Mountain*', as Gulliver is termed, with 'a daily Allowance of Meat and Drink, sufficient for the Support of 1728 of our Subjects' (38); Gulliver is, moreover, provided with 'three hundred Cooks' who 'prepared me two Dishes a-piece', telling the reader that 'A Dish of their Meat was a good Mouthful, and a Barrel of their Liquor a reasonable Draught' and that he eats their geese and turkey in one mouthful (57). It is not surprising that starvation is proposed, although subsequently rejected, as a suitable punishment for Gulliver's act of urinating on the Empress of Blefuscu's apartment (64). In eighteenth-century England the threat of famine was less pervasive than it had been in previous centuries (see Chapters 1 and 2) but hunger was still an everyday reality for the poor: Ireland would see a severe famine in 1740–1741, followed by the so-called Great Famine of 1845–1852, whilst a severe food scarcity affected the whole of the British Isles in the mid-1790s (discussed in Chapter 4).

In Brobdingnag it is the inhabitants who appear monstrous to Gulliver and again the prospect of cannibalism is raised when, realizing that to these people he resembles a Lilliputian, Gulliver observes: 'what could I expect but to be a Morsel in the Mouth of the first among these enormous Barbarians that could happen to seize me?' (78). Here the wing of a lark appears to Gulliver nine times as large as a turkey and a bit of bread as big as two loaves is eaten by the queen in one mouthful (95–96). It is somewhat ironic that when a whale is served to the king, Gulliver notes that he does not appear to be fond of it, adding 'I think, indeed, the Bigness disgusted him' (101). Gulliver repeatedly reports how repulsive he finds the female Brobdingnagians' large naked breasts and breastfeeding; upon witnessing a nurse feeding her baby, he remarks: 'I must confess no Object ever disgusted me so much as the Sight of her monstrous Breast', noting that 'the Nipple was about half the Bigness of my head, and the Hue both of that and the Dug so varified with Spots,

Pimples and Freckles, that nothing could appear more nauseous' (82–83).[14] Gulliver's disgust is in part to do with seeing the skin and breast up close; as William Ian Miller notes: 'The beauty of skin and hair . . . depends on imprecise vision. Too close a look can render what was enticing disgusting or horrifying' (Miller 1997, 56). As with Crusoe's vomiting at the sight of cannibalism, Gulliver's disgust, which similarly manifests itself in nausea, may also signal an attempt to prevent the emergence of unconscious desires, this time those of a sexual nature.

Gulliver is again threatened with starvation, this time by the thoughtlessness of a farmer who overworks him when showing him as a prodigy in various towns, so that 'I had quite lost my Stomach, and was almost reduced to a Skelton. The Farmer . . . conclud[ed] I soon must die' (91). When he escapes starvation by being sold to the queen of Brobdingnag, he is again threatened, this time by the harsh treatment of her dwarf. It is during these episodes at court that food is used as a weapon by the dwarf against Gulliver: he is dropped into a bowl of cream and nearly drowns (97), wedged into a marrow bone (98) and hit on the head by apples when the dwarf shakes a tree over his head (105). Earlier in the novel, during his tour of various towns as the farmer's prodigy, he is nearly hit in the head by a hazelnut a boy has thrown directly at him, which 'would have infallibly knocked out my Brains; for it was almost as large as a small Pumpion' (89). As Ian Higgins points out, A. C. L Brown suggests that Swift's debt here is to the sixteenth-century Irish story *Aidedh Ferghusa* (*The Death of Fergus*) where Esirt almost drowns when dropped into a wine goblet by the king's cupbearer and gets stuck up to his waist in a porridge bowl into which he has slipped (Brown 1904; Swift 2005, 308n97). Animals also threaten to injure Gulliver by either feeding him or treating him as food: he is carried off by a monkey that forces food into his mouth, whereby he is 'almost choaked with the filthy stuff . . . crammed down my Throat', and is abducted by an eagle which, he presumes, wants to break open his travelling-box 'and then pick out my Body and devour it' but accidentally drops the box into the sea (111, 129).

The island of Laputa, where mathematics and music dominate to the exclusion of everything else, sees Gulliver served meat, puddings and bread in the shape of various mathematical figures and musical instruments: 'a shoulder of mutton, cut into an Equilateral Triangle' and 'a Breast of Veal in the Shape of a Harp' (148). The focus on form clearly takes precedence over taste, which is not mentioned, and Gulliver tires of the people's narrowness of focus and introspection. Visiting the nearby island of Balnibarbi, Gulliver discovers that each town has an Academy of Projectors given to various inventions or schemes, such as making fruit come to maturity out of season. However, the numerous projects in hand have not yet been successful so that, 'in the mean time, the whole Country lies miserably waste, the Houses in Ruins, and the People without Food or Cloaths' (165). At the grand Academy of Lagado, the capital of Balnibarbi, Gulliver witnesses several projects, some of which involve food, such as the one for 'extracting Sun-Beams out of Cucumbers' so as to 'warm the Air in raw inclement Summers' and another involving 'an Operation to reduce human Excrement to its original Food, by separating the several Parts, removing the Tincture which it receives from the Gall, making the Odour exhale, and scumming off the Saliva' (167–168). Critics have identified the institutions being satirized by Swift as the Royal Society in London, the University of Leiden and the Dublin Philosophical Society, as Ian Higgins points out; the scientific experiments witnessed by Gulliver were based on contemporary experiments, specifically those reported in the *Philosophical Transactions of the Royal Society*, which also published accounts of travel, as shown by Marjorie Nicolson and Nora M. Mohler (Nicolson 1956, 110–154; Swift 2005, 327n167).

When Gulliver hears about the group of people known as Struldbrugs or immortals he is at first excited by the prospect of eternal life, proclaiming what he would do were he to be so fortunate, but his enthusiasm wanes when he learns that they remain alive but grow old, possessing 'not only all the Follies and Infirmities of other old Men, but many more which arose from the dreadful Prospect of never dying' (197). Their physical degeneration is described in detail: 'At Ninety they lose their Teeth and Hair; they have at that Age no Distinction of Taste, but eat and drink whatever they can get, without Relish or Appetite' (198); they also suffer life-long diseases and severe memory loss. There is a sense that their lack of discernment when it comes to eating makes them worse than animals, who at least possess an appetite to eat and enjoy their food. On the island of Glubbdubdrib, which lies to the south-west of Laputa, Gulliver takes advantage of the inhabitants' ability to summon the dead by reviving the cooks of the gluttonous Roman Emperor Heliogabalus (a figure also discussed in Chapter 2 in the context of Jonson's *Volpone*), although there seems little point in doing this since 'they could not shew us much of their Skill for want of materials' (185). A recurring phenomenon in Gulliver's experience of Laputa and its neighbouring islands is that of deflation and disappointment.

The Houyhnhnms behave with more rationality and civility than the inhabitants of any other land visited by Gulliver and with more humanity than the Yahoos who live amongst them. Both Gulliver and Crusoe express anxiety at the thought of degeneration into savagery and at the threat of cannibalism – an anxiety evident also in Conrad's writings (discussed in Chapter 6) – and some of Gulliver's negative feelings towards the Yahoos stem from their proximity to him: he despises the Yahoos but is conscious that, to the Houyhnhnms, he is one of these revolting creatures (they refer to him as a Yahoo), albeit a well-behaved one, wearing clothes, with less body hair and without claws. The Yahoos are degenerate (although not cannibals), representing a sort of missing link between the animal and human. Presumably the Yahoos are not cannibals because the only food resource available would be other Yahoos and a diet of Yahoo flesh would soon render them extinct.

Where the Houyhnhnms survive on a wholly vegetarian (one might say Edenic) diet of hay, oats and milk (but curiously, given that they are horses, no apples), the Yahoos feed on roots and the flesh of asses, dogs, diseased beef and carrion as well as weasels, a kind of wild rat, and they are also said to devour the Houyhnhnms' cats. Where the Houyhnhnms dine in an orderly fashion 'with much Decency and Regularity' (216), the Yahoos eat without discernment or manners: they 'devour every thing that came in their Way, whether Herbs, Roots, Berries, the corrupted Flesh of Animals, or all mingled together' (243). The Yahoos resemble Shakespeare's Caliban in that they dig with their nails for food (Caliban tells Trinculo: 'And I with my long nails will dig thee pig-nuts', *The Tempest,* 2.2.167). Sharing the diet of the Houyhnhnms, making their oats into a kind of bread to eat warm with milk, is not entirely satisfactory to Gulliver: 'It was at first a very insipid Diet . . . but grew tolerable by Time' (217). Significantly, given his resemblance to the Yahoos, he misses meat: 'I sometimes made a shift to catch a rabbet or Bird', and although he initially also misses salt, 'Custom soon reconciled the Want of it' (217). In his *Natural History* Pliny observed that 'a civilized life is impossible without salt' and indeed the Yahoos do not seem to use it, but neither do the civilized Houyhnhnms and so Gulliver concludes that salt is merely 'an Effect of Luxury, and was first introduced only as a Provocative to Drink', serving little purpose aside from preserving meat on long journeys (217; Pliny 1963, XXXI.xli; Swift 2005, 344n217). The effect of luxury is also a prevailing concern in the second half of the eighteenth century, as we shall see in Chapter 4.

Describing the practices that are common in England to his Houyhnhnm master, Gulliver explains how money affords the Yahoos living there (the English Yahoos) to buy fine clothing, houses, land and costly food and drink. The Houyhnhnm expresses dismay upon hearing that many of these foods are imported: 'That must needs be a miserable Country which cannot furnish Food for its own Inhabitants' (234), a point also made in *The Tryal of the Lady Allurea Luxury* (Chapter 4). Gulliver explains that the English Yahoos are given to luxury, intemperance and vanity and that wine (an unnecessary beverage since they have water) causes temporary merriness but ultimately poor spirits and disease. These English Yahoos are not as rational and civil as the Houyhnhnms, but nor have they degenerated to the level of the savage Yahoos who live amongst the Houyhnhnms. Gulliver makes ridiculous the religious controversy that is current amongst the English Yahoos, with specific reference to the Catholic belief in transubstantiation – the wars that can begin over a difference of opinion: 'For instance, whether *Flesh* be *Bread*, or *Bread* be *Flesh*: Whether the juice of a certain *Berry* be *Blood* or *Wine*' (229) – but this intolerance of difference is not the same as outright degeneracy.

Critics have long identified the savage Yahoos with the colonized Irish and the Houyhnhnms with their English colonizers, but some argue that the Yahoos represent the first wave of English colonizers into Ireland who went native.[15] As far back as Edmund Spenser's *View of the Present State of Ireland* English commentators complained that English colonizers from the twelfth century (termed the Old English) became degenerate via miscegenation with the natives. Spenser was especially critical of the Old English practice of using native Irish nurses to breastfeed their children since it was believed that the child would absorb undesirable character traits through the nurse's milk (Spenser 1949, 119), a pertinent context for Gulliver's disgust towards the breastfeeding he sees amongst the Brobdingnagians, and a striking contrast to the positive breastfeeding of Christ invoked in *The Book of Margery Kempe* (Chapter 1).

In his subsequent prose tract *A Modest Proposal* Swift would invoke cannibalism as a rhetorical device in order to highlight the savagery of the rich in their treatment of Ireland's poor. His ironic proposal – that the ruling class should eat the children of the Irish poor – works because Swift builds up to it with an air of serious reasonableness. The reader is simply not expecting the proposal that 'a young healthy child, well nursed, is at a year old a most delicious, nourishing, and wholesome food, whether *stewed*, *roasted*, *baked*, or *boiled*, and I make no doubt that it will equally serve in a *fricassee*, or a ragout' (Swift 2003, 493–494). The first-time reader (if unaware of the tract's reputation) cannot quite take in the word 'delicious', nor the word 'food', in relation to human flesh and the detail on the various means of preparing it only serves to increase the reader's incredulity. Anyone expressing concern at this proposal, suggests Swift, should consider that the ruling classes 'have already devoured most of the parents' (494). Proposals for sorting out Ireland and the Irish were nothing new (witness Spenser's *View*) and, as shocking as Swift's proposal is, it should perhaps be considered in the light of Irenius' suggestion in the *View* that England consider a scorched-earth policy causing mass starvation in order to deal with Irish rebels.

In Swift's novel Gulliver settles happily into life amongst the Houyhnhnms, eating honey out of hollow trees and generally enjoying an Edenic existence when, hearing of a decree from the Houyhnhnms' general assembly that he must leave the house of his master and the land of the Houyhnhmns, he is 'struck with the utmost Grief and Despair at my Master's Discourse; and being unable to support the Agonies I was under, I fell into a Swoon at his Feet' (262). His banishment, and the pain he incurs as a result, mirrors that of Adam and Eve's exile from the Garden of Eden. When he returns to the English Yahoos, his overwhelming feeling is one of disgust: 'During the first year, I could not endure my Wife or Children in my Presence, the very Smell of them was intolerable; much less could I suffer them to eat in the same Room. To this Hour they dare not presume to touch my Bread, or drink out of the same Cup, neither was I ever able to let one of them take me by the Hand' (271). Although gradually becoming more familiar with his surroundings – 'I began last Week to permit my Wife to sit at Dinner with me, at the farthest End of a long Table; and to answer (but with the utmost Brevity) the few Questions I asked her' (276) – he is still offended by their smell ('I always keep my Nose well stopt with Rue, Lavender, or Tobacco-Leaves', 276) and worried about what a fellow Yahoo might do with his teeth and claws. Like the colonists criticized by Edmund Spenser for going native, Gulliver has effectively been transformed by his encounter with foreign inhabitants and customs rather than imposing a colonial sense of superiority upon them.

Henry Fielding, *Joseph Andrews* (1742) and *Tom Jones* (1749)

Samuel Richardson's epistolary novel *Pamela: Or Virtue Rewarded*, published in 1740, tells the story of the virtuous servant Pamela Andrews who is repeatedly subjected to the sexual advances of her master, the wealthy landowner Mr B., but whose persistence in maintaining her chastity is rewarded by marriage to her master and the social advancement this union brings. In *Joseph Andrews* Fielding presents a parody of Richardson's novel whereby Joseph, the chaste seventeen-year-old brother of Pamela, undergoes similar attempted seduction at the hands of Lady Booby, Mr B.'s sister, by whom he is employed as a footman. Fielding's later novel *Tom Jones* also features an eponymous young hero who attracts the attention of women, although where Joseph is chaste, Tom most certainly is not. Yet in both novels there is an emphasis on the good nature of the young protagonist and each conforms to the traditional *Bildungsroman*, with a conclusion that sees our hero marry the young lady with whom he has long been in love. Crucially, in both works we see how food and eating are repeatedly figured in terms of sexual appetite and feature heavily in the attempted seductions of Joseph and the sexual exploits of Tom.

In *Joseph Andrews* Fielding parodies Richardson by inverting the gender of the pursued and pursuer, and also by presenting Mrs Slipslop, Lady Booby's maid, as another admirer of Joseph. The women attempt to seduce Joseph under the cover of domestic chores and via domestic favours: Lady Booby makes advances having summoned Joseph to bring a tea-kettle up to her bedroom, whilst Mrs Slipslop has, for a while, been trying to seduce him with food: 'Tea, Sweetmeats, Wine, and many other Delicacies, of which by keeping the Keys, she had the absolute Command' (27).[16] Joseph has apparently accepted these culinary bribes and thus seems less aware of the implications of accepting gifts than the heroines of sentimental fiction, such as Richardson's eponymous heroine Clarissa who starves herself in what Maud Ellmann considers an act of protest akin to political hunger strikes (Ellmann 1993, 70–89). Where Lady Booby reveals her feelings to Joseph – he writes to his sister Pamela describing how she 'talked exactly as a Lady does to her Sweetheart in a Stage-Play . . . while she wanted him to be no better than he should be' (26) – Mrs Slipslop's tendency to speak in malapropisms means Joseph does not understand what she wants from him. Realizing that her bribes with food and drink and her words have had little effect, Mrs Slipslop prepares to take action:

> As when a hungry Tygress, who long had traversed the Woods in fruitless search, sees within the Reach of her Claws a Lamb, she prepares to leap on her Prey; or as a voracious Pike, of immense Size, surveys through the liquid Element a Roach or Gudgeon which cannot escape her Jaws, opens them wide to swallow the little Fish: so did Mrs. *Slipslop* prepare to lay her violent amorous Hands on the poor *Joseph*, when luckily her Mistress's Bell rung, and delivered the intended Martyr from her Clutches.
>
> *29*

The predatory woman who (figuratively) devours her victim features also in Spenser's *Faerie Queene*, with Acrasia's consumption of Verdant, and in Thackeray's *Vanity Fair*, where Becky Sharp preys on the hapless Jos Sedley (discussed in Chapter 2 and 5 respectively). The comedy is darker in Thackeray's novel than in Fielding's because it is implied Becky eventually kills Jos, but even in Fielding's comedic novel the amusing hyperbole has a serious underlying point since here and throughout the story the virtue of Joseph is favourably compared to the vice of those he encounters. Compelled to leave the London house of Lady Booby, where the attempted seduction has taken place, Joseph travels towards his home in the country and his true-love, the virtuous Fanny. On the way, Joseph is robbed and, whilst recovering at an inn, meets his old friend and mentor from home, the charitable Parson Abraham Adams.

Much of the action of *Joseph Andrews* takes place in or around inns and alehouses, demonstrating the historical shift in the source of hospitality, both food and rest, from the private home (as witnessed in *Sir Gawain and the Green Knight*, Chapter 1) to commercial establishments (Heffernan 2014, 117–119). Of course inns and alehouses were nothing new – Chaucer's pilgrims meet at the Tabard Inn after all – but as the sense of obligation upon house-holders to provide hospitality to strangers diminished, so establishments providing drink, food and rest became more common. In *Tom Jones* food forms part of the successful seduction of Tom by Mrs Waters when she presents him with dinner in her room at Upton Inn. Having rescued Mrs Waters from an attack – and run the gauntlet of the landlady of the inn who disapproves of the half-naked Mrs Waters before discovering who she is – Tom is exceedingly hungry. The narrator compares him to a classical hero for the enthusiasm with which he goes about tackling the meal, suggesting a masculine, animalistic virility in his consumption of the meat: 'it may be doubted whether Ulysses, who by the way seems to have had the best stomach of all the heroes in that eating poem of the *Odyssey*, ever made a better meal. Three pounds at least of that flesh which formerly had contributed to the composition of an ox was now honoured with becoming part of the individual Mr Jones' (440).[17] The narrator suggests that Mrs Waters' passion for Tom is part of a continuum: 'she was in love, according to the present universally received sense of that phrase, by which love is applied indiscriminately to the desirable objects of all our passions, appetites, and senses, and is understood to be that preference which we give to one kind of food rather than to another' (441). A distinction is drawn between the appetite for love and that for food since it is usually when the latter is absent that one pines for it and it is in the presence of Tom that Mrs Waters finds her appetite increased.

Mrs Waters attempts to use her charms to attract Tom but bathetic humour sees the lovely look from her eyes, 'whose bright orbs flashed lightning at their discharge', fall instead upon 'a vast piece of beef', and the sigh that comes forth from her bosom, 'which was sufficient at once to have swept off a dozen beaux', goes unheard by Tom, who instead hears 'the coarse bubbling of some bottle ale, which at that time he was pouring forth' (442–443). The narrator claims that the other 'weapons' she uses are, in a similar fashion, deflected by 'the god of eating (if there be any such deity, for I do not confidently assert it)' who protects Tom, 'his votary' from her advances whilst he enjoys his meal (443). After he has finished his meal, and Mrs Waters again utilizes her charms, figured by the narrator in terms of military attack, Tom 'delivered up the garrison' (444). As James Heffernan indicates, Tom's Samaritan kindness to the lady in distress is rewarded 'in a manner hardly authorized by scripture' (Heffernan 2014, 207). Later in the novel, when Tom is hungry, the narrator relates how he has enjoyed 'all the delicacies which love had set before him' but cannot withstand his desire for 'some food of a grosser kind' (621), the suggestion being that romantic love is all very well but men must eat, an idea also apparent in Byron's *Don Juan* (Chapter 4).

In both novels food and drink are often the means by which the tension between virtue and vice is explored and the uncharitable religious man is a target for satire, a feature also of medieval and early modern literature, as we saw in Chapters 1 and 2. After Joseph Andrews is robbed and feared to be so sick that he will die, Mr Barnabas the clergyman is sent for. Before going to see Joseph, the clergyman has 'a Dish of Tea with the Landlady, and afterwards a Bowl of Punch with the Landlord'; upon finding Joseph asleep, he returns to 'take the other sneaker', or large vessel of drink (Fielding 1999, 383n50), and leaves without speaking to the sick man (50). Prevailed upon to return, Barnabas says a prayer as quickly as he can because the company downstairs are preparing more punch.

Later in the novel Adams has an unpleasant encounter with Parson Trulliber, who is also a farmer and owns a considerable amount of land. Whilst Trulliber's wife takes care of his cows, managing his dairy and taking the butter and eggs to market (as in the early modern period, women were often responsible for dairy produce), he takes care of his hogs and when Adams comes to visit, he has just come from feeding them. The narrator describes how a large intake of ale has rendered Trulliver as big as his pigs: 'He was indeed one of the largest Men you should see, and could have acted the part of *Sir John Falstaff* without stuffing' (141). Realizing that Adams has not come to buy some of his pigs, Trulliber begrudges Adams any hospitality, telling his wife 'to draw a little of the worst Ale' and offer that to their guest while he drinks the good ale (143), a practice criticized by Langland in *Piers Plowman* (Chapter 1). When Mrs Trulliber offers Adams something to eat, her husband 'bid her "hold her impertient Tongue"' (143) and it is only after making a long speech 'On the Dignity of the Cloth' that he offers Adams some porridge that his wife has made, with Trulliber eating it as enthusiastically as he criticizes his wife's cookery. When Mrs Trulliber gives Adams a cup of ale, Trulliber snatches it from him, proclaiming that he must drink first in his own house. When Adams raises the prospect of borrowing seven shillings, to pay the bill he has incurred at a nearby inn, Trulliber reacts with astonishment, pretending he thinks Adams means to rob him and threatening to have him punished as a vagabond. Adams responds by telling Trulliber that he is devoid of charity and therefore no Christian, leaving Trulliber ready to strike him, which he would have done, were it not for his wife's intervention.

In *Tom Jones* the parson Mr Thwackum is another hypocritical religious figure. Tutor to young Tom, Thwackum hates the child and beats him regularly so as to gain favour with Mrs Blifil, the sister of Tom's guardian Mr Allworthy, who it ultimately transpires is Tom's real mother and who affects dislike of Tom to cover for her former indiscretion. Thwackum's pugilistic nature and gluttony – he fights with the adult Tom and there are repeated references to his heavy drinking – are clearly at odds with his professed Christianity. Similarly, Parson Supple, although shocked by the swearing of the wealthy Mr Western, is willing to compromise his principles and act with duplicity in order to satisfy his appetite: 'the parson submitted to please his palate at the squire's table, at the expense of suffering now and then this violence to his ears' (264). As Jocelyne Kolb notes: 'Supple's appetite at table is implicitly connected to sexual appetite when we learn in the final pages of the novel that he has married Mrs. Waters, an ironic sequel to her culinary seduction of Tom', although Kolb's characterization of Supple's appetites as 'comic and harmless' seems overly generous (Kolb 1995, 48, 49). Rather, the description of Supple and Thwackum, albeit humorous, is in the spirit of Langland's denunciation of the clergy in *Piers Plowman* because here too gluttony and lack of charity from men of God are indicative of the moral corruption at the heart of an ostensibly Christian society.

An apparent digression in *Joseph Andrews*, but one that is pertinent to the novel's main plot, involves the story of Wilson and the dissolute life he leads before meeting his wife and settling down to a quiet existence in the country. Wilson's former life in London consists of visits to St James's Coffee-House where he gossips about the character of a young lady and ignores the challenge of an Officer of the Guards. The coffee-house often comes up in Fielding's writings as a place for gossip, which was certainly true of the coffee-houses of the day, although the establishments also facilitated serious political discussions as well as intellectual debate and business deals. Customers came from a wide range of social classes and would generally have been expected to behave in a mannerly fashion (there should be none of the drunkenness likely in an alehouse), which would explain why Wilson is challenged for defaming a lady. The anonymous poem 'The Character of a Coffee-House', first published in 1655, describes the establishment's typical inhabitants in its early days as well as the medicinal virtues of coffee: 'I affirm there's no disease / Men have that drink it but find ease' (Anon. 1655, A3r). Samuel Pepys frequently records visiting the coffee-house in his *Diary*, saying of one such visit on 23 January 1663: 'to a Coffee-house and there drunk more, till I was almost sick. And here much discourse, but little to be learned – but of a design in the North of a riseing which is discovered among some men of condition, and they sent for up' (Pepys 1971a, 22–23).[18] In the eighteenth century philosophical learning and political discussion came to dominate the coffee-house environment (where, presumably, Pepys would have found much to learn), as is clear from Addison's essays in *The Spectator* entitled 'Coffee-House Politicians' and 'Coffee-House Opinon' (Addison 1909, 182–185, 201–204).

When Wilson goes into the law, he meets men of poor character: 'smart Fellows who drank with Lords they did not know, and intrigued with Women they never saw' (179). He becomes sick and falls in with companions who sleep all day and drink all night; at one point he is nearly starving and his sedentary life as a poet and playwright is making him ill. Wilson spends the last money he has on a lottery ticket but is forced to exchange it for bread. When in jail for debt he learns that the ticket he sold has won the lottery; the daughter of the winner hears about his situation, pays his debts, and they fall in love and marry. Wilson takes over his father-in-law's business, becoming a wine merchant, but he does not do well because he is too honest, refusing to dilute the wines that are therefore too expensive to make a decent profit. Realizing that 'the Pleasures of the World are chiefly Folly, and the Business of it mostly Knavery; and both, nothing better then Vanity', he and his wife retire from business (194). Wilson tells Adams that the local squire thinks he is mad and the local parson thinks he is a Presbyterian because he will not hunt with the former nor drink with the latter. Their happiness is marred only by the theft of their son many years before by gypsies, whom Wilson is hopeful to meet again one day and would know by the mark on his left breast in the shape of a strawberry, 'which his mother had given him by longing for that Fruit' (196), the belief that a mother's cravings in pregnancy could give the unborn child a birthmark being fairly common. (It will transpire towards the end of the novel that their son is none other than our hero, Joseph Andrews.)

The narrator describes the pastoral idyll in which Wilson now lives:

> No Parterres, no Fountains, no Statues embellished this little Garden. Its only ornament was a short Walk, shaded on each side by a Filbert Hedge, with a small Alcove at one end, whither in hot Weather the Gentleman and his Wife used to retire and divert themselves with their Children, who played in the Walk before them: But tho' Vanity had no Votary in this little Spot, here was variety of Fruit, and every thing useful for the Kitchin, which was abundantly sufficient to catch the Admiration of *Adams*, who told the Gentleman he had certainly a good Gardener. Sir, answered he, that Gardener is now before you; whatever you see here, is the Work solely of my own Hands. Whilst I am providing Necessaries for my Table, I likewise procure myself an Appetite for them.
>
> *196*

The focus is on the garden's natural beauty rather than artifice (fountains and statues) and the plants that grow are not merely decorative but are put to use for food. The eighteenth-century manual *Adam's Luxury and Eve's Cookery; or the Kitchen-Garden Display'd* is a pertinent context here, providing the reader with advice on growing, storing and cooking vegetables, and with an emphasis on simplicity and seasonality (Anon. 1744). This life of rural bliss, following a life of vice, is a kind of inversion of the biblical paradise: the work in the garden is clearly pleasurable, as was the work of Adam and Eve in Milton's paradise before the Fall, and the hunger Wilson feels has been earned by his labour. Moreover, this pleasurable physical labour, a contrast to his former sedentary life as a writer, allows Wilson to remain healthy 'without Assistance from Physick' (196) and, like Adam and Eve before the Fall, Wilson and his wife spend the day together, either in the garden or in their house. Wilson's wife, Harriet, resembles Milton's Eve before the Fall in her knowledge of their store of foods and her hospitality. Wilson tells Adams:

> the House-keepers of few Gentlemen understand Cookery or Confectionary better; but these are Arts which she hath no great Occasion for now:

however, the Wine you commended so much last Night at Supper, was of her own making, as is indeed all the Liquor in my House, except my Beer, which falls to my Province.

197

Again, as in the garden, the artifice of the cook or the confectioner is not needed, it seems, but there is a focus on more practical skills; similar to Milton's Eve who collects raw materials from the garden for the meal with the angel Raphael, Harriet reveals both her expertise and her hospitality in welcoming Adams and the others. Later we learn that Harriet assists a sick neighbour with some cordials she has made for the public and so conforms to the Christian ideal of charity, attending not only to those she loves and her guests but also to those who are in need.

Adams proclaims that they live as in the Golden Age, but the cruelty of the post-lapsarian world is present when the idyllic existence witnessed by Adams and his companions is interrupted by the shooting of a dog belonging to Wilson's eldest daughter:

> the Son of the Lord of the Manor, had shot him as he past by, swearing at the same time he would prosecute the Master of him for keeping a Spaniel; for that he had given Notice he would not suffer one in the Parish. The Dog, whom his Mistress had taken into her Lap, died in a few Minutes, licking her Hand. She exprest great Agony at his Loss, and the other Children begin to cry for their Sister's Misfortune, nor could *Fanny* herself refrain.

198

Later the hunting of a hare by the Lord of the Manor, or Squire, is described with similar sympathy for the animal's plight: it is 'their poor reeling, staggering Prey . . . fainting almost at every Step', before being 'overtaken by its Enemies . . . caught, and instantly tore to pieces' (206). As in Milton's *Paradise Lost*, enmity between humanity and animals interrupts the idyll that has existed and hunting is primarily an act of savagery that disrupts a peaceful co-existence between the species, a point also made in the works of Shelley discussed in Chapter 4.

The same hounds that have killed the hare, described above, attack Adams, who is asleep near the bloody hare they devour, and the Lord of the Manor encourages his dogs to chase the Pastor for fun. Pretending to be sorry for teasing Adams, the Squire invites the party to his house for dinner, his main aim being the seduction of Fanny. It is whilst at the Squire's house that Adams is subjected to more derision – which the chapter title describes as '*A Scene of Roasting*', meaning severe or merciless ridicule – with soup emptied into his breeches and gin put into his ale as well as other tricks that are played upon him (211–218). The narrator describes the Squire as one who from youth has 'addicted himself entirely to Hunting' and who had 'a very early relish' for drink (211–212). The Squire, who serves as a foil to Wilson, is told by Adams that he violates the laws of hospitality in ridiculing a guest but this makes less impact than the revenge Adams has upon the Squire by ducking him into a tub of water into which Adams himself has been dropped (218). The company escape the Squire's house and eat at an inn where the bread and cheese they are given provides 'a very comfortable Meal; for Hunger is better than a *French* cook' (219). Adams thanks God for this modest food, which he enjoys more than the 'splendid Dinner' provided by the Squire, and he expresses contempt for the foolish who prefer wealth over salvation (219), prefiguring the attacks on luxury evident also in the late eighteenth and early nineteenth-century literature discussed in Chapter 4.

In *Tom Jones* too hunting is enjoyed by boorish men. Mr Western, father to Sophia Western with whom Tom is in love, is a keen hunter and a heavy drinker, his love of hunting and immoderate drinking indicative of his reckless nature and hot temper. Tom accompanies Western on his hunts and Sophia asks him to help curb her father's excesses: 'She therefore begged him, for her sake, to be more cautious; and as he well knew Mr Western would follow him, not to ride so madly, nor to take those dangerous leaps for the future' (146). Sophia hunts with her father to please him but dislikes the sport, which is 'too rough and masculine' for her (172). Just as Adams is hunted in *Joseph Andrews*, so too in *Tom Jones* humans are referred to as game, although it is primarily women who are spoken about in these terms and usually by Mr Western. Timothy D. O'Brien reads food imagery in the novel in terms of how its characters use food or the language of food to relate to those around them: they are 'either false or true epicures, either hoarders and spoilers of food and appetite' or 'friendly providers with hearty, uncloyed appetites' (O'Brien 1985, 620). For O'Brien, Squire Western, unlike the generous Allworthy, is one of the novel's hoarders and spoilers: he greedily preserves game just so he can slaughter it himself and repeatedly threatens to withdraw food from Sophia – invoking Richardson's starving heroine Clarissa – at one point threatening to allow her 'to beg and starve and rot in the Streets' whereby 'She shall be no better than carrion' (265); as O'Brien puts it: 'A fine game and a promising dish, Sophia will spoil, rot, become an unwholesome object to any man's appetite if Western cannot have her will as his own' (O'Brien 1985, 621). When a resolution is finally reached between father and daughter, Western reacts by getting drunk, another act of greed and selfishness.

Aside from the references to food and drink that permeate both *Joseph Andrews* and *Tom Jones* in scenes of seduction, religious hypocrisy, pastoral idyll and hunting, Fielding also uses food as a means to explore the process of writing itself, namely the production and reception of literary texts. In *Joseph Andrews* the narrator compares the author's act of dividing a work into books and chapters to a butcher jointing a piece of meat (78), and later compares plays to mushrooms grown in a rich soil since both shoot up quickly when encouraged and nourished (226). In the opening chapter of *Tom Jones* the narrator compares the author to a host who keeps a public ordinary (a tavern): unlike the gentleman providing a private dinner, the host must satisfy the palates of men who are paying for their food and so too the author must satisfy the reader who has paid for his book. The author, like the host of an ordinary, will provide his reader with 'a general bill of fare to our whole entertainment' (29). The reader will be presented with human nature, which is not simply one article but, like the tortoise or turtle, with its calipash and calipee (edible parts near the upper and lower shells, also spelt 'calapash' and 'capapee'), contains many different kinds of food, as the alderman of Bristol, 'well learned in eating, knows by much experience' (30). Turtle was traditionally served at banquets of the aldermen of Bristol and thus became associated with politics and satire (Kolb 1995, 45; Fielding 1996, 874n30).[19] Human nature offers the author 'prodigious variety' and the author has an advantage over the cook who 'will have sooner gone through all the several species of animal and vegetable food in the world than an author will be able to exhaust so extensive a subject' (30). Although some will object that the dish of human nature – found in many romances, novels, plays and poems sold to the general public – is too 'vulgar', Fielding contends that it is 'the cookery of the author' that will impress, and he will demonstrate his skill by 'the seasoning, the dressing, the garnishing, and the setting forth' (30). As in *Gulliver's Travels* (considered above) and Jonson's *Volpone* (considered in Chapter 2), so too here the cook of the gluttonous Roman Emperor Heliogabalus is invoked, with our author promising the reader different sorts of human nature in order to whet their appetite and sustain their interest.

Whilst Fielding's novels are firmly rooted in a recognizable England, with its taverns and coffee-shops – ironically, the English coffee-shop sells a beverage which is a colonial import – Defoe and Swift present what are ostensibly travel narratives of distant lands full of strange inhabitants and stranger customs. Swift's narrative is the more outlandish of the two but both novels present the reader with food that would have been familiar to contemporary readers (for example bread, meat, brandy) as well as that which would have been unfamiliar to most (for example goat, lark, vegetarianism) and in both novels the most extreme and unusual dish is that of human flesh. Where Crusoe distinguishes himself from the uncivilized natives who indulge in cannibalism, a dichotomizing the narrative resists, Gulliver initially constructs himself as a cannibal in Lilliput (making as if to eat the Lilliputians who have attacked him) only to realize that he might well himself be a morsel consumed by the giants in Brobdingnag. Stranded on his island and struggling to survive, Crusoe cannot afford to be gluttonous, at least initially, but he does feast like a rich man when he finds himself with a plentiful supply of food, whilst Gulliver's drinking as well as his prodigious appetite are emphasized, especially in Lilliput. In both narratives the Englishman abroad fears hunger and both experience an Edenic idyll before returning home, Crusoe willingly and Gulliver having been banished by his beloved Houyhnhnms. In the exploration of gluttony and an Edenic idyll that does not last, both authors arguably gesture towards Milton's epic poem *Paradise Lost* and its biblical source, a feature also of Fielding's *Joseph Andrews*, where the first act of human disobedience and all its consequences were the result of an inordinate desire to consume that most English of fruits.

Notes

1 All quotations of Milton's poems are from Milton (1993).
2 As Gordon Campbell notes, this explanation was accepted by Catholics who considered the Book of Tobit to be canonical but rejected by Protestants like Milton who did not (Milton 1993, 261n434–438). For analysis of ancient Jewish and early Christian commentaries on moments from scripture where angels have apparently eaten food, see Goodman (1986).
3 The story of the Israelites is told in the biblical Book of Exodus 16:1–36, Moses in Exodus 24:12–18 and Elijah in 1 Kings 19:8.
4 Daniel will not consume the fine foods offered him that are forbidden by God according to the Laws of Moses and instead asks for pulses (Book of Daniel 1:1–16).
5 Denise Gigante considers these Romantic readers of *Paradise Regained* (Hunt and Lamb, in their "Eating Songs" and "Grace Before Meat" respectively) in the context of taste and the sublime, which figured taste in terms of aesthetics as well as diet. Gigante's essay on Milton's poems, here cited, is reprinted with minor alterations as a chapter in her later book *Taste: A Literary History* (Gigante 2000, 88, 107; Gigante 2005).
6 Denise Gigante observes the links between Satan's banquet and that which appears in Shakespeare's *Tempest* but appears to confuse the meat-filled pies served at Renaissance banquets (and here presented by Satan) with ornate subtleties constructed from sugar that would take pride of place at the banquet table but do not feature in Satan's feast (Gigante 2000, 107). For a discussion of the subtleties presented at medieval and Renaissance banquets, see Mintz (1985, 87–96).
7 Genesis is rather ambiguous about the number of trees actually growing in the garden when it states: 'And out of the ground made the LORD God to grow every tree that is pleasant to the sight, and good for food; the tree of life also in the midst of the garden, and the tree of knowledge of good and evil' (2:9), which suggests that the Tree of Knowledge and the Tree of Life might be the same tree, although subsequent references to the Tree of Life in Genesis make it clear that two trees are intended. The Tree of Life and the Fountain of Life both appear in the biblical Book of Revelation (tree: 2:7, 22:2, 22:14; fountain: 7:17, 21:6).
8 All quotations of *Robinson Crusoe* are from Defoe (2007).
9 The term 'corn' was often used generically to refer to any kind of grain; what modern consumers usually refer to as corn is maize, which was imported to Europe from the Americas.
10 Albala describes citrons as 'the oldest of the citrus fruits'; known to Europeans as candied peel, they look like lemons when fresh but 'contain little juice' (Albala 2003, 52).
11 For example see Gliserman (1990); Armstrong (1992); Jooma (1997).
12 Hume initially wrote in his footnote: 'I am apt to suspect the negroes, and in general all the other species of men (for there are four or five different kinds) to be naturally inferior to the whites. There never was a civilized nation of any other complexion than white, nor even any individual eminent either in action or speculation.' He revised this footnote in a later edition to: 'I am apt to suspect the negroes to be naturally inferior to the whites. There scarcely ever was a civilized nation of that complexion, nor even any individual eminent either in action or speculation' (qtd. in Palter 1995, 4). Palter rightly notes that most editions of Hume's *Essays*, including the one cited here, do not signal Hume's revision and he considers the possible reasons for the revision.
13 All quotations of *Gulliver's Travels* are from Swift (2005).
14 See also pages 101, 107, 108.
15 For a useful discussion of critical views on the Yahoos as Irish (either native Irish or degenerated Old English), see Hodgkins (2002, 162–166).
16 All quotations of *Joseph Andrews* are from Fielding (1999).
17 All quotations of *Tom Jones* are from Fielding (1996).
18 Pepys' references to visiting the coffee-house cease from 1666 to 1669, which was presumably due to the severe outbreak of plague in London in 1665. For the cultural

significance of the coffee-house in seventeenth- and eighteenth-century society, see Ellis (2004).

19 As noted in the discussion of *Robinson Crusoe*, Ken Albala explains how the turtle 'yielded several different courses: a soup, a fricasee, fins and the *calapee* or flipper meat and *calapash* which is the meat from the upper shell that is greenish and gelatinous' (Albala 2003, 76).

References

Addison, Joseph. 1909. *Selections from* The Spectator. Ed. J. H. Lobban. Cambridge. Cambridge University Press.

Albala, Ken. 2003. *Food in Early Modern Europe*. Food Through History. Westport, CT. Greenwood.

Anon. 1655. *The Character of a Coffee-House*. Wing C1967. London. N. pub.

——. 1744. *Adam's Luxury and Eve's Cookery; Or, the Kitchen-Garden Display'd*. ESTC T020339. London. Printed for R. Dodsley . . . and sold by M. Cooper.

Appelbaum, Robert. 2006. *Aguecheek's Beef, Belch's Hiccup, and Other Gastronomic Interjections: Literature, Culture, and Food Among the Early Moderns*. Chicago, IL. University of Chicago Press.

Armstrong, Diane. 1992. 'The Myth of Cronus: Cannibal and Sign in *Robinson Crusoe*'. *Eighteenth-Century Fiction* 4. 207–220.

Arvind, Thomas. 2006. 'Milton and Table Manners'. *Milton Quarterly* 40.1. 37–47.

Austen, Ralph. 1657. *A Treatise of Fruit Trees . . . to Which May Be Annexed the Second Part, Viz. The Spiritual Use of an Orchard*. Wing A4329 (v. 1, A treatise); A4326 (v. 2, The spiritual use). Oxford. Printed by Henry Hall for Thomas Robinson.

Brown, A. C. L. 1904. '*Gulliver's Travels* and an Irish Folktale'. *Modern Language Notes* 19. 45–46.

Browne, Thomas. 1646. *Pseudodoxia Epidemica: Or, Enquiries into Very Many Received Tenents, and Commonly Presumed Truths*. Wing B5159. London. T[homas] H[arper] for Edward Dod.

Cogan, Thomas. 1584. *The Haven of Health*. 2nd edn. STC 5478. London. Henrie Midleton for William Norton.

Cox, Lee Sheridan. 1961. 'Food-Word Imagery in *Paradise Regained*'. *English Literary History* 28. 225–243.

Culpepper, Nicholas. 1652. *The English Physician: Or An Astrologo-physical Discourse of the Vulgar Herbs of This Nation*. Wing C7501. London. Peter Cole.

Defoe, Daniel. 2007. *Robinson Crusoe*. Eds. Thomas Keymer and James Kelly. Oxford World's Classics. Oxford. Oxford University Press.

Digby, Kenelm. 1669. *The Closet of the Eminently Learned Sir Kenelme Digbie K[nigh]t Opened*. Wing D1427. London. Printed by E[llen] C[otes] for H. Brome.

Dohner, Janet Vorwald. 2001. *The Encyclopedia of Historic and Endangered Livestock and Poultry Breeds*. Yale Agrarian Studies. New Haven, CT. Yale University Press.

Eddy, William A. 1922. 'Rabelais – a Source for *Gulliver's Travels*'. *Modern Language Notes* 37. 416–418.

Ellis, Markman. 2004. *The Coffee-House: A Cultural History*. London. Weidenfeld and Nicolson.

Ellmann, Maud. 1993. *The Hunger Artists: Starving, Writing, and Imprisonment*. London. Virago.

Fielding, Henry. 1996. *Tom Jones*. Eds. John Bender and Simon Stern. Oxford World's Classics. Oxford. Oxford University Press.

——. 1999. *The History of the Adventures of Joseph Andrews and of His Friend Mr Abraham Adams and An Apology for the Life of Mrs. Shamela Andrews*. Ed. Douglas Brooks-Davies. Rev. Thomas Keymer. Oxford World's Classics. Oxford. Oxford University Press.

Fitzpatrick, Joan. 2010. *Shakespeare and the Language of Food: A Dictionary*. Arden Shakespeare Dictionaries. London. Bloomsbury.

Gigante, Denise. 2000. 'Milton's Aesthetics of Eating'. *Diacritics* 30. 88–112.

——. 2005. *Taste: A Literary History*. New Haven, CT. Yale University Press.

Glasse, Hannah. 1755. *The Art of Cookery Made Plain and Easy (Fifth Edition, with Additions)*. ESTC N014610. London. Printed and sold at Mrs. Ashburn's China-Shop.

Gliserman, Martin. 1990. '*Robinson Crusoe*: The Vicissitudes of Greed: Cannibalism and Capitalism'. *The American Imago: A Psychoanalytic Journal for the Arts and Sciences* 47. 197–231.

Goodman, David. 1986. 'Do Angels Eat?' *Journal of Jewish Studies* 37. 160–175.

Heffernan, James A. W. 2014. *Hospitality and Treachery in Western Literature*. New Haven, CT. Yale University Press.

Hodgkins, Christopher. 2002. *Reforming Empire: Protestant Colonialism and Conscience in British Literature*. Columbia. University of Missouri Press.

Houston, Lynn Marie. 2005. *Food Culture in the Caribbean*. Food Culture around the World. Westport, CT. Greenwood.

Hume, David. 1963. *Essays: Moral, Political and Literary*. Oxford. Oxford University Press.

Jooma, Minaz. 1997. 'Robinson Crusoe Inc(corporates): Domestic Economy, Incest, and the Trope of Cannibalism'. *LIT: Literature Interpretation Theory* 8. 61–81.

Kerrigan, William. 1983. *The Sacred Complex: On the Psychogenesis of* Paradise Lost. Harvard, MA. Harvard University Press.

Kolb, Jocelyne. 1995. *The Ambiguity of Taste: Freedom and Food in European Romanticism*. Ann Arbor. University of Michigan Press.

Lévi-Strauss, Claude. 1983. *The Raw and the Cooked: Introduction to a Science of Mythology*. Trans. John and Doreen Weightman. Vol. 1. Chicago, IL. University of Chicago Press.

Lewis, C. S. 1960. *A Preface to* Paradise Lost. Oxford University Press Paperback. London. Oxford University Press.

McInelly, Brett C. 2003. 'Expanding Empires, Expanding Selves: Colonialism, the Novel, and *Robinson Crusoe*'. *Studies in the Novel* 35. 1–21.

Mackintosh, Alex. 2011. 'Crusoe's Abattoir: Cannibalism and Animal Slaughter in *Robinson Crusoe*'. *Critical Quarterly* 53. 24–43.

Miller, William Ian. 1997. *The Anatomy of Disgust*. Cambridge, MA. Harvard University Press.

Milton, John. 1993. *Complete English Poems, Of Education, Areopagitica*. Ed. Gordon Campbell. London. J. M. Dent.

Mintz, Sidney W. 1985. *Sweetness and Power: The Place of Sugar in Modern History*. London. Viking.

Mintz, Susannah B. 2002. 'On an Empty Stomach: Milton's Food Imagery and Disordered Eating'. *Reassembling Truth: Twenty-First Century Milton*. Eds. Charles W. Durham and Kristin A. Pruitt. Selinsgrove, PA. Susquehanna University Press. 145–172.

Muffett, Thomas. 1655. *[Health's Improvement] Healths Improvement, or Rules Comprizing and Discovering the Nature, Method, and Manner of Preparing All Sorts of Food Used in This Nation*. 1st edn. Wing M2382. London. Tho[mas] Newcomb for Samuel Thomson.

Nicolson, Marjorie. 1956. *Science and Imagination*. Ithaca, NY. Cornell University Press.

O'Brien, Timothy D. 1985. 'The Hungry Author and Narrative Performance in *Tom Jones*'. *Studies in English Literature, 1500–1900* 25. 615–632.

Palter, Robert. 1995. 'Hume and Prejudice'. *Hume Studies* 21. 3–24.

Pepys, Samuel. 1971a. *The Diary of Samuel Pepys: A New and Complete Transcription*. Eds. Robert Latham and William Matthews. Vol. 4: 1663. 11 vols. London. G. Bell and Sons.

——. 1971b. *The Diary of Samuel Pepys: A New and Complete Transcription*. Eds. Robert Latham and William Matthews. Vol. 5: 1664. 11 vols. London. G. Bell and Sons.

Pliny. 1963. *Natural History*. Trans. W. H. S. Jones. Vol. 8. 10 vols. Loeb Classical Library. London. Heinemann.

Schoenfeldt, Michael C. 1999. *Bodies and Selves in Early Modern England: Physiology and Inwardness in Spenser, Shakespeare, Herbert, and Milton*. Cambridge. Cambridge University Press.

Spenser, Edmund. 1949. *Prose Works*. Ed. Rudolf Gottfried. The Works of Edmund Spenser: A Variorum Edition. Vol. 10. 11 vols. Baltimore, MD. Johns Hopkins University Press.

Sullivan, Kevin. 2015. 'Jesus, Angels, and the Honeycomb in Luke 24.42'. *The Open Mind: Essays in Honour of Christopher Rowland*. Eds. Jonathan Knight and Kevin Sullivan. London. Bloomsbury. 240–255.

Swift, Jonathan. 2003. *Major Works*. Eds. Angus Ross and David Woolley. Oxford World's Classics. Oxford. Oxford University Press.

——. 2005. *Gulliver's Travels*. Ed. and intr. Claude Rawson and Ian Higgins. Oxford World's Classics. Oxford. Oxford University Press.

Topsell, Edward. 1608. *The Historie of Serpents*. STC 24124. London. William Jaggard.

Watt, Ian. 1957. *The Rise of the Novel: Studies in Defoe, Richardson, and Fielding*. London. Chatto and Windus.

Woolf, Rosemary. 1962. 'The Theme of Christ the Lover-Knight in Medieval English Literature'. *Review of English Studies* 13. 1–16.

Woolley, Hannah. 1670. *The Queen-Like Closet; Or, Rich Cabinet: Stored with All Manner of Rare Receipts for Preserving, Candying and Cookery*. Wing W3282. London. Printed for R. Lowndes.

4

LUXURY, GLUTTONY, DOMESTIC ECONOMY AND ETHICAL EATING (1750–1830)

Charlotte Boyce

Owing to their enduring association with sensory indulgence, moral corruption and national decline, luxury and gluttony have long been the target of literary critique, as the previous chapters in this book have demonstrated. However, with the advance of what has been called the eighteenth-century 'consumer revolution' (McKendrick *et al.* 1983, 1), debates about the social, ethical and economic implications of excessive eating and luxurious living took on a new intensity. For some, conspicuous consumption retained the negative valence traditionally assigned to it in classical and Christian thought – a negativity that predominated in the medieval and early modern periods discussed in Chapters 1 and 2. Others, such as the eighteenth-century political economists Adam Smith and David Hume, reconceived luxury as a socially beneficial force – one that enhanced national prosperity by 'nourish[ing] commerce and industry' (Hume 1752, 35).

Within the literature considered in this chapter, food is central to such debates. As comestibles that had once been the exclusive preserve of the rich (for instance, tea, sugar and white bread) were brought more and more within the compass of the poor, texts such as *The Tryal of the Lady Allurea Luxury* and *The Expedition of Humphry Clinker* fretted about the erosion of traditional class boundaries by emulative consumption. The consumer society's taste for exotic culinary imports and foreign standards of fashionability were further recurrent literary concerns, as dietary transculturation was perceived as a threat to British national identity. Yet, while advocating native nutriment and denigrating the culinary culture of the French in particular, poets such as Robert Burns and Robert Fergusson also explored the acculturating impact of *English* eating habits on Scottish foodways following the political union of these nations in 1707, demonstrating that eighteenth-century alimentary anxieties were not only directed towards an international 'Other'.

The issue of gluttonous consumption (so often a feature of the writings on food considered in this book) took on a new moral urgency in this period as successive shortages engendered widespread hunger and posed vital questions regarding access to food. Through its representations of aristocratic and mercantile voraciousness, Charlotte Smith's *Desmond* critiques the social and alimentary inequalities that characterized the revolutionary 1790s. The Cheap Repository Tracts of Smith's contemporary Hannah More, by contrast, adopt a more conservative politics, positioning domestic economy as an effective remedy to social deprivation. Later, in the nineteenth century, Jane Austen's fiction implies that benevolent paternalism can mitigate lower-class poverty, a political issue that is less pressing in her novels than the metaphorical hungers experienced by female characters, which are often sublimated into food refusal.

Abstemious appetites feature, too, in Romantic writing. In Byron's poetry, for instance, asceticism is associated with male heroism, and gluttony with the debauched tastes of the Regency aristocracy. Elsewhere, abstinence is linked with consumer morality: vested with new cultural and economic powers, progressively minded eighteenth- and nineteenth-century consumers pursued ethical agendas through the boycotting of foods, such as sugar (the target of abolitionist Mary Birkett's *Poem on the African Slave Trade*) and meat (source of immorality, cruelty and violence in the vegetarian works of Percy and Mary Shelley). Alimentary distaste also appears in the poetry of John Keats; however, his verse more often luxuriates in gustatory experience, savouring the sensory gratification to be derived from 'natural' produce. If Romantic writers were frequently involved in a critique of the emergent consumer culture, they were also highly alert to the aesthetic pleasures of consumption, as we shall see.

Anon., *The Tryal of the Lady Allurea Luxury* (1757)

The satirical play *The Tryal of the Lady Allurea Luxury* dramatizes the competing discursive positions around eighteenth-century luxury in terms that are 'relentlessly gastronomic', as Sarah Moss points out (2009, 33). The eponymous Lady Allurea – who, significantly, is labelled 'a Foreigner' (Anon. 1757, 1) – is brought before an English jury, including 'Sir Oliver Roastbeef' and 'William Strongbeer', on charges of having 'conspired the Destruction of this Land' by inculcating a love of luxury in the people (5–6). Her machinations are alleged to have had particularly damaging effects on the nation's dining habits: one aristocratic witness testifies that, only a few days after the defendant befriended his wife,

> my old *English* hospitable Table was covered with nothing but Frenchified disguised Dishes . . . my strong Beer and roast Beef were sent to the Dog-Boy . . . All my old faithful Servants discharged, to make Room for *French* Cooks . . . and nothing produced in our own Climate bearable.
>
> *13–14*

The dichotomy established here between fashionable French cuisine and simple English fare is continued in the evidence of the Lord Mayor, who attests that, owing to Lady Allurea's influence at city feasts, 'of late . . . we have had nothing to eat, fit for an *Englishman* to put in his Stomach. High-seasoned Ragouts and masqueraded Poisons have been substituted in the place of honest roast Beef and Plumb-Pudding' (19). In both of these depositions, articles of food are freighted with transferable moral attributes. Whereas English cookery is represented as plain and 'honest' (in common, we are invited to presume, with its consumers), luxurious foreign dishes, elaborately garnished and cloaked in rich sauces, are associated with extravagance and artifice (an association that also emerges in the definition of 'kickshaw' presented in Samuel Johnson's *Dictionary*: 'a dish so changed by the cookery that it can scarcely be known' [1785, n.p.]). The corollary to this dietary logic is that, by eating 'Frenchified' foods, English consumers endanger the integrity of their national identity. Ingestion, then, is implicitly invested here with the worrying potential to collapse distinctions between self and Other.

To defend against such Anglo-Gallic transculturation, the Lord Mayor suggests that the British should return to the food of 'their Ancestors' (19), although, as Moss points out, a number of the foodstuffs he characterizes as essentially British are not in fact indigenous but 'merely well-naturalized' (2009, 35). Nevertheless, his appeal to culinary patriotism would have resonated in the mid-eighteenth century, when anti-French sentiment, spurred by military conflict and colonial competition, was commonplace. The entrenched cultural affection for traditional British fare typically found in Georgian literature, periodicals and cookery books was not simply nation-alistic, however. As Roy Porter suggests, the 'Englishman's cultic roast beef' – a foodstuff widely celebrated in mid-century texts, including Fielding's *Tom Jones* (Chapter 3) – was also imagined as 'positively therapeutic' in the period (1993, 59). By contrast, refined but insubstantial delicacies of the type denounced in *Lady Allurea Luxury* were thought to endanger not only individual bodily economies but also, synecdochically, the health of the nation. As Elizabeth Kowaleski-Wallace points out, in eighteenth-century culture 'consumption' could signify in multiple ways, denoting both healthy ingestion and bodily depletion (1997, 7). In light of this semantic mobility, it is notable that *Lady Allurea Luxury* shows a recurrent concern for the enervating effects of luxurious consumption and, in particular, its consequences for British martial power. Among the consumers purportedly affected by Lady Allurea's charms are sailors in the merchant and Royal navies, whose new-found taste for luxury causes them to refuse to eat their basic 'salt Provisions' (18), and officers in the army, who now spend their time 'lolling' around 'drinking Tea' instead of marshalling their troops (23).

Tea-drinking is also blamed for the putative indolence of the lower classes. One witness reports that Lady Allurea is often seen 'in the Kitchen with the meanest Servants and Apprentices, advising them to lie in Bed long in the Morning, and to drink Tea for their Breakfasts' (18). Formerly an activity restricted to the wealthy, tea-drinking underwent a gradual process of democratization during the eighteenth century, much to the chagrin of campaigners such as Jonas Hanway, whose 'Essay on Tea' (1756) ascribes a variety of social, moral and economic ills to this 'prejudicial article of commerce' (2010, 65). Not only is tea 'very injurious to health', it also has 'a most pernicious tendency with regard to domestic industry and labor', according to Hanway, who calculates that tea-drinking costs the nation £583,333 annually in lost productivity (2010, 65, 100). He also deplores the effeminating effects of this vitiating beverage on the British character, asking, in typically hyperbolic language: 'Were they the sons of TEA-SIPPERS, who won the fields of CRESSY and AGINCOURT[?]' (87). As Matthew Mauger notes, tea, for Hanway, 'damages Britain's presence as an imperial power, humbling it to a commodity that cannot be produced in the native land' (2010, 60). Similarly, in *Lady Allurea Luxury*, exotic goods such as tea represent a double threat to British liberty and authority, simultaneously sapping the nation's masculine vigour *and* activating a perturbing dependency on foreign markets.

The eighteenth-century trend for tea-drinking was bolstered by the culture of politeness with which it was contemporaneous. Integral to that culture was the idea that refined consumption might elevate the manners of the nation and advance the progress of civilization – a notion that forms a key component of Lady Allurea's defence. One witness affirms that Britons 'had not known' culinary delicacies such as 'Callipash or Callipee' (turtle meat) until she 'taught us how to eat . . . how to enjoy this Life in Perfection' (48), while another thanks Lady Allurea for having shown his wife 'the true Elegance of Living, which has done Honour to my Table . . . ever since' (36).[1] The association, here, of gourmandism with cultivation echoes Hume's claims that 'the ages of refinement and luxury are both the happiest and most virtuous' (1752, 24), and that only a mind 'frenzie[d]' by 'fanatical enthusiasm' would consider indulgence 'in meats [or] drinks' to be, 'of itself, a vice' (1752, 23). Lady Allurea's representatives also deploy well-rehearsed economic arguments to contest the notion that luxury is necessarily deleterious in its effects. Harriet Guest points out that 'the witnesses for the defense are mostly tradesmen and shopkeepers' who imply that 'luxurious commerce' is advantageous because it 'maintains circulation, both social and monetary' (2000, 80). Figuring money as 'the Blood, the Life of every state' (67), Lady Allurea's lead advocate challenges the prosecution's link between luxury and debilitation, submitting that his client instead invigorates the body politic by increasing revenues and stimulating trade.

Yet, this position is, in turn, subject to dispute. The Attorney General counters that the culture of luxury, funded by paper credit, causes the provisioners of ordinary necessities ('Butchers . . . Bakers . . . Brewers, &c.') to go unpaid (45). He also claims, in an argument reminiscent of the critique of culinary importation found in *Gulliver's Travels* (Chapter 3), that luxurious tastes sustain Britain's commercial rivals at the expense of domestic markets, for, 'whereas the Materials of *French* Prodigality, are, in a great measure, the Produce of their own Climate', British 'Profuseness' is dependent 'chiefly on the Delicacies of Foreign Countries' (80).[2] Ultimately, the prosecution's case wins out: Lady Allurea is found 'Guilty of every Charge' (91), although she escapes from custody before sentence can be passed. Her symbolic defeat nevertheless provides an important caveat to the idea that luxury debates underwent significant 'de-moralization' in the eighteenth century (see Berry 1994, 126). Although Enlightenment economic discourse repeatedly emphasized fiscal benefits over moral arguments, in much literary representation the pejorative con-notations of luxurious consumption found in earlier works, such as *Piers Plowman* (Chapter 1), *The Faerie Queene* (Chapter 2) and *Paradise Lost* (Chapter 3), not only endured but intensified, as a protean set of social and cultural anxieties came to be focalized through representations of epicurean indulgence.

Tobias Smollett, *The Expedition of Humphry Clinker* (1771)

One of the most notorious critics of luxurious living in eighteenth-century literature is Matthew Bramble, the paternalistic country squire of Smollett's epistolary satire *The Expedition of Humphry Clinker*. During the course of his family's journey around Britain, Bramble rails against the lavish but degraded food he finds in fashionable cities such as London and Bath, yearning instead for the wholesome produce of his Welsh estate, Brambleton-hall. This domestically nurtured fare is endorsed consistently in the text as the epitome of health-giving nutriment. In one lengthy encomium, loaded with the language of purity and plenitude, Bramble proudly explains that, at home,

> my bread is sweet and nourishing, made from my own wheat, ground in my own mill, and baked in my own oven; my table is, in a great measure, furnished from my own ground; my five-year old mutton, fed on the fra-grant herbage of the mountains, that might vie with venison in juice and flavour; my delicious veal, fattened with nothing but the mother's milk, that fills the dish with gravy; my poultry from the barn-door, that never knew confinement, but when they were at roost; my rabbits panting from the warren; my game fresh from the moors; my trout and salmon struggling from the stream . . . My sallads, roots, and pot-herbs, my own garden yields in plenty and perfection; the produce of the natural soil, prepared by moderate cultivation. The same soil affords all the different fruits which England may call her own, so that my desert [*sic*] is every day fresh-gathered from the tree; my dairy flows with nectarious tides of milk and cream, from whence we derive abundance of excellent butter, curds, and cheese; and the refuse fattens my pigs, that are destined for hams and bacon.
>
> *Smollett 1984, 118–119*

This paean to dietary self-sufficiency constructs Brambleton-hall as a salutary natural economy, reminiscent of Milton's Eden (Chapter 3), in which human, animal and vegetable life exist in cooperative symbiosis. References to labour and husbandry are minimal: the fecund land 'yields' its produce in abundance, with only 'moderate cultivation'; free-range animals and fish appear to offer themselves up willingly for consumption, in tacit mitigation of this new Eden's non-vegetarian status; and the dairy 'flows' quasi-spontaneously with 'tides of milk and cream'. The sense that the estate represents a self-contained, organic order is heightened by what Nicholas Smith calls Bramble's '(almost obsessive) anaphoric use of personal and possessive pronouns' (2004, 410); syntactically, as well as semantically, Brambleton-hall is configured here as an autonomous dietary space, insulated from a potentially corrupting external world.

In particular, the estate provides an imaginative 'refuge from the contaminated and contaminating food of London', as Charlotte Sussman suggests (1994, 613). Whereas, in Monmouthshire, Bramble can map precisely his food's journey from field to table, in the metropolis the link between producers and consumers is severed, as ostensibly 'fresh' fish, fruit and eggs are imported from geographically distant locations. Furthermore, Bramble complains, Londoners' bread – a mixture of 'chalk, alum, and bone-ashes' – is 'insipid to the taste and destructive to the constitution' (120); their vegetables, 'produced in an artificial soil', taste of 'nothing but the dunghills from whence they spring' (121); and their butter, 'manufactured with candle-grease and kitchen-stuff', constitutes a 'tallowy rancid mass' (122). Luxurious tastes and aspirational behaviours are blamed for the prevalence of these alimentary abominations; Bramble notes with bemusement that Londoners know their food to be adulterated but are prepared to sacrifice their health to 'a most absurd gratification of a mis-judging eye' (120). Such concerns about market-place frauds echo those found in earlier literary texts, such as *The Canterbury Tales* (Chapter 1) and *Bartholomew Fair* (Chapter 2), as well as the raft of polemics on consumer culture that appeared in the mid-eighteenth century. One anonymous pamphleteer expressed astonishment 'that People who boast of *Taste*, should merely for the sake of a Colour, exchange the Sweetness, Elasticity and Consistence, of a pure home-made Loaf, for a harsh, dry, and crumbling Composition of, *they really know not what*' (Anon. 1758, 26), while another despaired that, owing to the spread of 'malignant luxury', ordinary folk who had once subsisted happily on brown bread now felt 'compelled' to eat fashionable '*White Bread*' adulterated with 'lime', 'chalk' and 'allum [*sic*]' (Anon. 1777, 10, 11).

Embedded in such warnings against emulative consumption are apprehensions regarding social mobility. In 1767, the political economist Nathaniel Forster observed that 'in England the several ranks of men slide into each other almost imperceptibly', giving rise to 'a perpetual restless ambition in each of the inferior ranks to raise themselves to the level of those immediately above them' (1767, 41). In *Humphry Clinker*, this social climbing manifests itself most forcefully in gastro-nomic terms: Bramble complains that, 'at present, every trader in any degree of credit' hosts 'sumptuous entertainments' at his home, whereas, a generation ago, the tables of even 'the most opulent citizens of London . . . produced nothing but plain boiled and roasted, with a bottle of port and a tankard of beer' (87–88). If food, here, demonstrates the erosion of customary hierarchies and sumptuary distinctions (an erosion also seen earlier in the tea-drinking habits of servants in *Lady Allurea Luxury*), then promiscuous cross-class interaction is reciprocally conceptualized in *Humphry Clinker* as 'a problem of ingestion', as Sussman suggests (1994, 607). After watching 'a dirty barrow-bunter . . . cleaning her dusty fruit with her own spittle', Bramble anxiously speculates that 'some fine lady of St. James's parish' might subsequently 'admit into her delicate mouth those very cherries, which had been rolled and moistened between the filthy, and, perhaps, ulcerated chops of a St. Giles's huckster' (122). He similarly fears that the capital's respectable purchasers of milk might inadvertently be exposed to 'the vermin that drops from the rags of the nasty drab that vends this precious mixture' in the streets (122), his anxiety echoing the concerns about cross-contamination that arise in relation to the wares of Roger the Cook in *The Canterbury Tales* (Chapter 1) and Ursula the pig-woman in *Bartholomew Fair* (Chapter 2).

As Bramble's fixation on impurity and miscibility indicates, for him the city represents a disorderly space – a 'farrago', Smith suggests (2004, 409), in an appropriately culinary metaphor – where the classes mingle indiscriminately and food facilitates the collapse of traditional social distinctions. This loss of proper subordination is not restricted to urban communities, however; as a cautionary subplot reveals, the rural order is by no means immune from the damaging effects of ostentation and emulative consumption. While travelling back to Monmouthshire, Bramble is horrified to discover that the once-productive country estate of his friend Baynard has been sacrificed to his wife's social pretensions. In order to display her 'taste in laying out ground', Mrs Baynard has appropriated 200 acres of previously fruitful farmland, with the result that the estate no longer supports itself; every item of food, from milk to 'hot rolls for breakfast', must be purchased from a town five miles away (292). Mrs Baynard has also hired a French cook so that her entertainments might exceed in 'variety, delicacy and expence' those hosted by her wealthy neighbours (294). The ensuing fare is ill-adapted to an 'English appetite', Bramble complains, in language reminiscent of *Lady Allurea Luxury*: 'the pottage was little better than bread soaked in dishwashings'; 'the ragouts looked as if they had been once eaten and half digested'; and 'the desert [*sic*] consisted of faded fruit and iced froth, a good emblem of our landlady's character' (295). The novel's recommended corrective to this ruinously extravagant household regime is a thoroughgoing system of domestic economy. Following Mrs Baynard's expedient demise, Bramble quickly 'disband[s] that legion of supernumerary domestics, who had preyed so long upon the vitals of [his] friend' (342), instigates a policy of general retrenchment, and orders that Mrs Baynard's 'pleasure-ground' be restored 'to its original use of corn-field and pasture' (343). He also places Baynard under the mentorship of Charles Dennison, another old friend, whose dedication to the principles of husbandry and agricultural improvement has enabled him to attain the 'pitch of rural felicity' (320).

Despite this apparent endorsement of domestic economy, however, *Humphry Clinker* can also be disparaging about frugal household management, particularly when it is deemed to be excessive or overzealous. The target of the novel's critique in this respect is specifically gendered: as Gilly Lehmann notes, 'by the 1770s the country lady fussing over her preserves or her dairy had become a stock figure of fun' (2003, 71), ridiculed in periodicals such as the *Rambler* and the *Connoisseur*. In Smollett's novel, it is Matthew Bramble's unmarried sister, Tabitha – a woman derided by her nephew, Jery, as a 'maiden of forty-five' (60) who has doubled her income 'by living free of all expence, in her brother's house; and dealing in cheese and Welsh flannel, the produce of his flocks and dairy' (61) – who fulfils this denigrated role of notable housewife. Her comical missives to the housekeeper at Brambleton-hall, packed with minute enquiries about the readiness of her dairy produce and directions to monitor the servants' consumption of butter, caricature her as 'domestic dæmon' (77), whose petty economizing contrasts with the liberal munificence of her brother (in his very first letter home, Matthew Bramble instructs his correspondent, Dr Lewis, to give away his Alderney cow and sell his corn below market price for the benefit of the poor [5]). Yet, for all that we are encouraged to mock Tabitha's frugality, we might also take her seriously when she suggests that she has 'toiled and moyled' for the advantage of her family (78), and that, without the income supplied by her unstinting labour and commercial nous, her brother's charities would deplete the resources of the Brambleton estate. As Michael McKeon suggests: 'Smollett's epistolary novel is an experiment in the multiplicity and relativity of perspective . . . the truth of things lies in a composite and mixed view of reality' (2003, 59). Certainly, as Sussman points out, Tabitha's interactions with the 'contaminating world of trade' undercut her brother's fantasy vision of Brambleton-hall as a hermetically 'self-contained nutritional system' (1994, 614, 613).

In light of this challenge to Matthew Bramble's idyllic vision, it is significant that the novel ends *before* the family arrives back at Brambleton-hall; as Susan L. Jacobsen notes, 'it is almost as if Bramble's home is too perfect' for representation, too evocative 'of a time and place that can no longer exist, except in fairy tales' (1996, 88). Bramble's narrative position is further undermined by the reader's realization that he is not totally disconnected from the world of luxury and commerce which he outwardly disdains: he takes ginseng (an imported medicinal preparation) for his gout (an illness associated with gluttony) and engages enthusiastically in sociable male dining: at one point, Jery is confident of persuading him to give a turtle dinner, the definitive symbol of eighteenth-century exotic luxury (see Chapter 3). What is more, Bramble does not greet the revelation that his friend Dennison has learnt to cook foreign delicacies, 'such as *ollas*, *pepper-pots*, *pillaws*, *corys*, *chabobs*, and *stufatas*', with the kind of excoriating moral judgement he earlier applied to Mrs Baynard's French kickshaws and ragouts (326). Fittingly, it seems, for a multi-vocal satire (etymologically, a 'mixed dish'), *Humphry Clinker* offers not only miscellaneous perspectives on culinary matters, but also internally inconsistent accounts that highlight the complexity of responses to food, luxury and consumerism in eighteenth-century society.

Robert Fergusson, 'The Farmer's Ingle' and 'To the Principal and Professors of the University of St Andrews, on Their Superb Treat to Dr Samuel Johnson' (1773); Robert Burns, 'Address to a Haggis' and 'The Cotter's Saturday Night' (1786)

Halfway through his mock-heroic 'Address to a Haggis', Burns's speaker invites the reader to compare the merits of his native dish with those of continental-style cuisine, enquiring:

Is there that owre his French *ragout*,	[over]
Or *olio* that wad staw a sow,	[would bloat]
Or *fricassee* wad mak her spew	[would make her vomit]
Wi' perfect sconner,	[disgust]
Looks down wi' sneering, scornfu' view	
On sic a dinner?	[such]

(2001a, ll. 25–30)

At first glance, this spirited denigration of foreign 'trash' (l. 31) in favour of indigenous fare appears continuous with the discourse of culinary patriotism evident in earlier literary texts like *Lady Allurea Luxury* and *Humphry Clinker*, and cookery books such as Ann Peckham's *The Complete English Cook*, which deploys a vocabulary of revulsion similar to Burns's in its assurance that 'the following collection of receipts . . . is not stuffed with a nauseous hodge-podge of French kickshaws' (1771, 3). Significantly, though, in place of the 'skinking ware' (l. 45) associated with foreign countries and modish British dinner tables, Burns endorses not the conventional 'Roast Beef of Old England' but a peculiarly Scottish staple: haggis.[3] Here, as elsewhere in Burns's poetry, food encodes a specific regional identity, indicating that the geography of dietary difference in eighteenth-century literature could work to differentiate between consumers *within* Britain, as well as to demarcate those from without.

Certainly, food provides an important fulcrum for eighteenth-century debates about Anglo-Scottish difference. Poets such as Burns and his compatriot Robert Fergusson (whose works inspired Burns) feared that increased commerce with England, signified by Scotland's rising importation of luxurious 'eistacks' [dainties] (Fergusson 1956b, l. 73), would result in the post-Union Scots identity 'being consumed' by a homogenizing cosmopolitanism, as Carol McGuirk suggests (2003, 140). A range of hostile English satires similarly employed images of food to express their opposition to cultural syncretism. The notoriously 'Scottophobic' Charles Churchill's satirical poem *The Prophecy of Famine*, for instance, depicts Scotland as a barren land, whose starving inhabitants, locust-like, threaten England's plenitude: the personification of Famine tells the poem's Scottish protagonists, Jockey and Sawney: 'For our advantage shall their [England's] harvests grow / And *Scotsmen* reap what they disdain'd to sow' (1763, 23). References to Scots' supposed predilection for offal-based dishes were also used in English print culture to emphasize Caledonian otherness. *Humphry Clinker*'s Jery is physically sickened by the prospect of haggis and regards sheep's heads as being as alien to English consumers as cannibalism: they 'put me in mind of the history of Congo, in which I had read of negros' heads sold publickly in the markets', he writes during a stay in Edinburgh (Smollett 1984, 222).

Rather than playing down such outlandish associations, Burns's panegyric to the haggis consistently and exuberantly amplifies them, comically representing the consumption of this dish as a kind of anthropophagy. Personified as the 'Great Chieftain o' the Puddin-race' (l. 2), the haggis is accorded human features such as an 'honest, sonsie [cheerful] face' (l. 1) and 'hurdies [buttocks] like a distant hill' (l. 8), while its sheep's stomach casing is compared to perspiring skin – 'thro' your pores the dews distil / Like amber bead' (ll. 11–12) – and its offal-and-oatmeal contents to 'gushing entrails bright' (l. 15).[4] As Robert Crawford suggests, 'there is in Burns's [poem] a sense that the bill of fare may appear joyfully outrageous, but this is relished as part of its appeal' (1997, 7). While working to scandalize the polite reader, the visceral imagery in 'To a Haggis' also serves a patriotic function, evoking Scotland's proud heritage of martial prowess. Whereas the effete (and implicitly Anglicized) consumer of refined delicacies is figured as wholly 'unfit' (l. 36) to take to the 'bluidy . . . field' (l. 35), the haggis-fed Rustic, used to battling for his fair share of the food, is a ferocious warrior, who draws strength from his hearty diet:

> But mark the Rustic, *haggis-fed*,
> The trembling earth resounds his tread,
> Clap in his walie nieve a blade,   [firm fist]
> He'll make it whissle;
> An' legs, an' arms, an' heads will sned   [cut off]
> Like taps o' thrissle.   [tops of thistle]
>   *(ll. 37–42)*

This comic-defiant stanza, with its combative vernacular diction, could be interpreted as a kind of imaginary compensation for what Alan Bold calls Scotland's 'massive spiritual hangover' following the failed Jacobite rising of 1745–1746 (1982, 219). Alternatively, it might be read, in light of the British army's active recruitment of Scottish soldiers post-Culloden, as a tacit reminder that the comfortable existence enjoyed by the nation's 'feckless' (l. 32) consumers of luxuries depends upon battle-hardy, Scots-born troops, fortified by a diet of traditional Scottish fare.[5]

A similar, though more obviously archaic, appeal to martial glory is made via food in Fergusson's 'The Farmer's Ingle'. After describing a humble rural supper, the poem's speaker breaks off to declare that 'On sicken [such] food has mony a doughty [many a mighty] deed / By Caledonia's ancestors been done' (1956a, ll. 37–38), including the repulsion of Danish and Roman invaders. This evocation of 'antient days' (l. 42) implies that an enduring bond connects the 'gudeman' (l. 14) who currently works the land to his resilient precursors, who were sustained by identical fare, conjuring an impression of continuity and stability that serves to mitigate contemporary anxieties about the social and agricultural changes then sweeping through Scotland.[6] The food that fuels the farmer's labours in Fergusson's poem is not the iconic haggis, but a meal of steaming-hot '*kail*' [cabbage broth] (l. 25) and 'butter'd *bannocks*' [traditional Scottish flatbreads] (l. 23). These plain and lowly comestibles may seem, at first, to present less of an affront to the 'gentler gabs' (l. 28) addressed in the poem than Burns's anthropomorphized offering; significantly, though, both dishes could be made with oatmeal or barley, polemicizing ingredients in eighteenth-century Britain that are frequently used by Fergusson and Burns to challenge Anglocentric authority and celebrate autochthonous Scottish culture. Whereas wheat was the staple grain in the south of Britain in the eighteenth century, the north was governed by what Nigel Leask terms a 'meal and barley nexus' (2010, 126). Perhaps unsurprisingly, this culinary-geographic distinction came to be loaded with ideological meaning, as shown by Samuel Johnson's notorious dictionary definition of oats: 'a grain, which in England is generally given to horses, but in Scotland supports the people' (1785, n.p.). Burns and Fergusson's strategic approbation of meal-and-barley-based foods represents a subtle but deliberate rebuttal to such dietary stereotyping, challenging the notion that Scottish fare was coarse, tasteless and dehumanizing.

Fergusson's endorsement of native nutriment becomes more pugnacious in his lively address 'To the Principal and Professors of the University of St Andrews', where he openly invites Johnson to eat his words regarding Scotian food. The poem is an indignant response to the news that, during their famous tour of Scotland, Johnson and his travelling companion James Boswell were treated to a lavish dinner at St Andrews. It begins by criticizing the University Regents for serving their guests fashionable (and costly) foreign delicacies rather than authentic Scots cuisine, before imagining a replacement menu of 'gudely hamel [home-bred] gear' (Fergusson 1956b, l. 34) with which to satisfy Johnson's 'mow' [mouth] (l. 42). This alternative bill of fare, comprising haggis, sheep's head and trotters, broth, white and black puddings and toasted farls, is not only 'distinctively Caledonian' but also audaciously rich in oats, as Crawford points out (1997, 7). For Rhona Brown, its signal purpose is to emphasize the abundance of 'Scotland's natural larder' (2012, 203); for Matthew Simpson, however, it is an intentionally 'punitive meal', in which the foods are 'not so much served to Johnson' as proactive in forcing themselves upon him (2003, 110), 'hirstl[ing]' [sliding] (l. 48) abrasively down his throat and causing him to 'skirl' [cry out] (l. 52) with thirst.[7] This alimentary culture clash is re-enacted with rhetorical gusto in lines such as 'What think ye neist, o' gude fat brose [broth] / To clag his ribs? a dainty dose!' (ll. 49–59), where Fergusson's rhyming macaronics gleefully juxtapose earthy Scottish dialect with Anglicized *politesse*. Obliged to dine on the kind of unpretentious food that is 'our cottar childer's boon' (l. 76), Johnson, the envoy of English values and learning, is here given a salutary lesson in Scottish taste and culture.

Where 'To the Principal' raucously and hyperbolically rams Scottish fare down the 'gabs', or mouths, of its genteel readers, Burns's 'The Cotter's Saturday Night' offers a version of culinary nationalism more palatable to the metropolitan middle classes. Written in contemplative Spenserian stanzas, it celebrates the modest supper that 'crowns' a hardworking cotter-family's 'simple board' (2001b, l. 91): 'the hale-some *Porritch*, chief o' SCOTIA'S food; / The soupe [milk] their *only Hawkie* [cow] does afford' (ll. 92–93), and, later, some 'weel-hain'd kebbuck [well-matured cheese]' (l. 96), brought out in honour of a visiting suitor. Like 'The Farmer's Ingle', 'The Cotter' applauds the frugal self-sufficiency of rural labourers; instead of focus-ing on issues of hunger, the poem identifies in the 'very spareness' of the meal 'a symbol of Scottish self-reliance', as McGuirk suggests (2003, 142). Yet, the poem's idealization of the peasantry's diet and insinuation that domestic contentment might compensate for material poverty also generate more conservative readings. Significantly, in his 1797 enquiry into *The State of the Poor*, social commentator Frederick Eden quotes line 92 of Burns's 'Cotter' in order to bolster his recom-mendation that England's labouring classes adopt a Scottish-style meal-and-barley diet, which is praised for its economy and nutritional value (1797, 497). The poem's suggestion that the '*Cottage* leaves the *Palace* far behind' (l. 168), meanwhile, seems to anticipate William Paley's disingenuous assertion in *Reasons for Contentment* (1793) that the lives of the industrious poor are more physically and spiritually nourishing than those of the indolent rich (1793, 8–9).

Despite these intersections with the politics of quietism (a politics that also structures Hannah More's didactic fictions, considered below), 'The Cotter' retains something of the spirit that more typically infuses Burns's and Fergusson's culinary verse. As John Barrell suggests, in the context of the harvest failures and food shortages of the late 1700s, even 'apparently conventional' pastoral poetry could seem 'to the literate poor . . . excitingly subversive', offering up the image of a recent past 'when nature gave everyone enough to eat' (1980, 87). In this light, the nostalgic sentimentalism of Burns's 'chearfu' Supper' (l. 100) takes on a more political flavour, for in the gap between his poem's idealized representation of late eighteenth-century agrarian life and the reality lies a critique of the prevailing ideology of 'improvement' and an affirmation of the labouring classes' right to proper sustenance.

Charlotte Smith, *Desmond* (1792); Hannah More, *The Way to Plenty* (1795) and *The Cottage Cook* (1797)

During the turbulent 1790s, the political meanings around food in literature took on a new potency and urgency. A rising population, falling wages and a costly and unpopular war with revolutionary France combined with bad weather and poor harvests to cause widespread scarcity in Britain, inflating the price of provisions and leading to protests and food riots in a number of towns and cities.[8] As various critics have noted, the dearth of food during this decade was supplemented by an abundance of printed matter on the subject, ranging from reactionary political pamphlets on managing the diet of the poor to radical tracts and handbills that threatened the ruling classes with the ultimatum 'bread or blood'. The female-authored fiction of the period considered here further contributed to the debates surrounding the twin demands for sustenance and rights, though with markedly different aims. While Charlotte Smith's epistolary novel *Desmond* shows a degree of sympathy for the idea that insurrection is a justifiable outcome of entrenched social and alimentary inequality, Hannah More's contributions to the Cheap Repository Tracts – a series of chapbooks and ballads published with the aim of supplying the 'inferior ranks' with 'wholesome' reading matter (More 1830, vii) – promote a more conservative politics, suggesting that poverty can be ameliorated by the adoption of domestic economy and dietary reform.

Set during the early years of the French Revolution (an event intimately linked to questions of consumption in the contemporary cultural imaginary)[9] and located alternately in England and France, *Desmond* challenges the dietary stereotypes cultivated in late eighteenth-century graphic satires, which frequently juxtaposed images of well-fed, contented British subjects with pictures of starving French citizens. This binocular visual strategy, evident in Thomas Rowlandson's *The Contrast* (1792), Isaac Cruikshank's ironically titled *French Happiness, English Misery* (1793) and James Gillray's equally ironic *French Liberty, British Slavery* (1792), typically associates rational British constitutionalism with prosperity and plenty, and fanatical French republicanism with famine and want. Smith's novel, however, questions such easy associations. To her liberal-minded hero Lionel Desmond's description of the running of a model French estate, in which the happy, well-nourished labourers 'possess something more than the mere necessaries of life' (2001, 115), Smith appends a lengthy footnote challenging readers to reconsider their complacent, chauvinistic assumptions:

> The English have a custom of arrogantly boasting of the fortunate situation of the common people of England. – But let those, who, with an opportunity of observation, have ever had an enquiring eye and a feeling heart on this subject, say whether this pride is well founded. At the present prices of the requisites of mere existence, a labourer, with a wife and four or five children, who has only his labour to depend upon, can taste nothing but bread, and not always a sufficiency of that. . . . Yet we are always affecting to talk of the misery and beggary of the French – And now impute that misery, though we well know it existed before, to the revolution; – To the very cause that will in a very few years remove it.
>
> *115*

Smith's insistence here that revolution is the understandable response (and potential remedy) to scarcity, rather than the cause, is reaffirmed later in the novel when its heroine, Geraldine Verney, avers that the food shortages experienced in Paris in 1789 (the stimulus for the *poissardes'* famous march on Versailles) were 'artificial', engineered 'by those, who not only had the power to monopolize for their own profit, but others, who had it in view to reduce the people by famine to obedience' (325–326). This attribution of hunger to political and economic rather than providential causes would have resonated strongly with radical assessments of the contemporaneous situation in Britain, where a breakdown in paternalist relations between the classes and a concomitant increase in sharp commercial practices such as jobbing and engrossing were frequently blamed for the high price of provisions.[10]

Smith, then, 'draws constant parallels' between the excesses and abuses of the French *ancien régime* and 'the current ruling classes in England' in order to highlight the social injustices underlying *domestic* deprivation, as Anne Mellor suggests (2000, 111). A major target is aristocratic extravagance: one of *Desmond*'s earliest alimentary incidents involves Lord Newminster, a decadent young nobleman, indulging his dog with chocolate, bread and butter intended for the breakfast table, while telling the animal: 'I would rather all the old women in the country should fast for a month, than thou shouldest not have thy belly-full' (69).[11] The troubling corollary to Newminster's warped dietary priorities becomes apparent a few pages later when Desmond encounters a starving woman with two sick children in tow, begging for money on the streets. The novel's deliberate collocation of thoughtless dissipation and essential need demonstrates Penny Bradshaw's point that, 'in *Desmond*, we are never allowed to forget the interdependence of absence and excess' (2004, 67). As in the medieval and early modern critiques of hunger discussed in Chapters 1 and 2, the gluttonous and wasteful habits of the rich are directly implicated in the hunger of the poor.

This theme is further developed in *Desmond* in relation to the unscrupulous epicure Sir Robert Stamford, whose political guile has enabled his rapid rise from country attorney to baronet. In a storyline reminiscent of the Baynard subplot in *Humphry Clinker*, Stamford 'sacrifice[s]' the once-scenic grounds of his Linwell estate 'to the luxuries of the table', cutting down the 'beautiful little wood' where Desmond and Geraldine first met to make way for 'an immense range of forcing and succession houses, where not only pines are produced, but where different buildings, and different degrees of heat, are adapted to the ripening cherries in March, and peaches in April, with almost every other fruit out of its natural course' (194). The corruption of nature that Desmond's correspondent Erasmus Bethel identifies in these un-seasonably cultivated fruits is also discernible, in political form, at Stamford's magnificent dinner parties, which function as a kind of gastronomic bribery; we are told that it is by 'the luxury of his table' that Stamford 'strengthens his interest' with those in positions of power and influence (121). Desmond's disgusted response to what Diana Bowstead calls Stamford's 'grotesque notion of husbandry' indicates that the ethical and economic implications of luxurious consumption cannot be disaggregated (1986, 244); in a provocative reworking of Edmund Burke's infamous reference to a 'swinish multitude' (1790, 117), Desmond suggests that Stamford's 'swinish excess' is enjoyed 'at the expence' of ordinary people, 'hundreds of whom might be fed by the superfluities of his luxurious table' (202).

It is not only the profligacy of the ruling classes that is critiqued in *Desmond*, however. As Antje Blank and Janet Todd note, Smith is equally censorious of 'avaricious, middle-class *nouveaux riches* for their espousal of a capitalist culture rooted in economic inequality' (2001, 25). One representative of this class is Mr Sidebottom, a corpulent former tavern-keeper who has 'retired upon a fortune', and whom Desmond overhears disquisiting on current affairs in a library in Dover (81).

Sidebottom's discourse reveals him to be obsessed with matters of consumption, both dietary and economic: his conversation covers, by turns, 'the price of soals and mackerel that morning at market' (79), an excoriation of French cuisine ('most of their provisions are nothing to be compared to ours' [79–80]) and an appreciation of 'the good things for the table' that are to be found in Kent, such as 'some delicate fat ducks and pigeons, of peculiar size and flavour' he has sourced from a nearby farm (82). Tellingly, his fierce antipathy towards the French Republic stems in part from a conviction that the new regime will mismanage the nation's gastronomic resources: he bewails the fact that the country's plentiful game and vineyards will fall into the hands of 'taylors and tinkers and frisseurs', and advocates invasion in order to 'give [the French] a little taste of the liberty of us Englishmen' (80). The reference to liberty here is rendered ironic by Sidebottom's support for the game laws, oppressive legislation that restricted the right to pursue and kill game to the socially privileged.[12] His evident lack of concern for dietary inequality is again signalled when he dismisses the heart-rending appeals of a destitute Frenchwoman on the grounds that the 'the small money he [has] about him' will be required in his 'tour after good dishes' (83). His affronted claim that the woman is attempting 'to take the bread out of the mouth of our own people' (82) overlooks the fact that his own fortune is derived from the parasitic exploitation of overseas labour. While discussing a turtle dinner he has in prospect, Sidebottom discloses that he owns a 'West-Indian farm; a little patch of property . . . in Jamaica', from which he has transported both the turtle he plans to eat and a 'negro fellow' to serve as his cook (81). This incidental reference to slavery forms part of what Bradshaw calls Smith's 'radical reappropriation' of late eighteenth-century food imagery (2004, 68). In an ironic rejoinder to the hyperbolic alimentary metaphors deployed by conservative commentators such as Burke, who famously associated French revolutionaries with 'cannibal appetites' (1790, 211), Smith here suggests that it is in fact 'bloated' colonial capitalists, such as the slave-holder Sidebottom, who metaphorically grow fat off their fellow beings (79).

If, in *Desmond*, the 'consumer-orientated' middle classes are as guilty of immoral consumption as their aristocratic counterparts, as Bradshaw suggests (2004, 69), then in Hannah More's didactic fictions the middle classes are, by contrast, valued for their philanthropy and economizing zeal. Part of the counter-revolutionary discourse of the 1790s, More's Cheap Repository Tracts not only challenge the political message contained in texts such as Smith's but also engage directly with topical events such as the food scarcity of 1795–1796, when successive cold winters depleted the wheat harvest, causing the price of bread to rise sharply from 7 ½ *d.* to 12 ½ *d.* per quartern loaf. More's writings tend to preach passivity and forbearance in relation to this subsistence crisis. Her famous anti-Jacobin ballad *The Riot*, for instance, places faith in the workings of Providence and the benevolent paternalism of 'Gentlefolks' rather than popular protest: 'What a whimsey to think we shall mend our spare diet / By breeding disturbance, by murder and riot!' (More 1795a). More also implies that the effects of scarcity can be countered by a simple policy of dietary retrenchment and effective household organization. As Samantha Webb notes, the Cheap Repository 'presents the scarcity as something manageable, reconstituting it from actual event with national and political implications into pure discourse, something . . . that needs no activity beyond what any competent housewife can accomplish' (2006, 430). Indeed, drawing on the kinds of ideologies of self-sufficiency and self-help seen earlier in *Humphry Clinker*, More repeatedly suggests that practical advice on domestic and dietary reform is more useful to the poor than pecuniary charity, and encourages her readers to 'find out ways of doing much good with little money; or even without any money at all' (1797, 3).

Two of More's exemplary middle-class activists are Mrs Jones from *The Cottage Cook* and Mrs White from *The Way to Plenty*, both of whom set about improving the morals and culinary habits of their respective communities, under the guidance of local clergymen. The so-called 'luxurious' appetites of the labouring classes provide an immediate target for their reforming energies. At a parish meeting in *The Way to Plenty*, Dr Shepherd informs his impoverished congregation that their 'present hardships' are 'owing to BAD MANAGEMENT' (1795c, 24), before calling on Mrs White to supply the assembled housewives with recipes for 'nice, cheap dishes' that will wean them from their taste for expensive commodities such as shop-bought white bread (25). Similarly, in *The Cottage Cook*, Mrs Jones (who, we are told in an interesting intertextual reference, has read *The Way to Plenty*) urges the poor women of her village 'to bake large brown loaves at home instead of buying small white ones at the shop' (1797, 9) and to follow one local paragon, Patty Smart, in renouncing expensive products such as tea, butter, sugar and gin. Another key economizing strategy promoted in the tracts is substitution. In a 1795 handbill, the President of the Board of Agriculture recommended that British people should eat mixed loaves (in which wheat flour was combined with other, cheaper grains or potatoes) and increase their consumption of vegetables, meat and fish in order to mitigate the effects of the reduced wheat harvest (Board 1795, 579–580). While such advice was lampooned in a number of graphic satires (among them James Gillray's *The British Butcher* [1795], which portrays Prime Minister William Pitt telling a ragged John Bull that if he cannot afford a 12 *d.* quartern loaf, he should replace it with a crown's worth of meat), it appears to have been adopted enthusiastically by certain members of the gentry, keen to provide a good example to the lower classes.[13] Indeed, dietary substitution is invested with spiritual authority in More's tracts; echoing the association of brown bread with Christian humility found in *Piers Plowman* (Chapter 1), Dr Shepherd reminds his parishioners that 'our blessed Saviour ate barley bread' (1795c, 23–24).

As well as endorsing the use of coarse brown or mixed bread, *The Way to Plenty* and *The Cottage Cook* supply readers with recipes for dishes featuring alternative forms of carbohydrate such as potatoes and rice. The former are frequently recommended to bulk out soups and stews, while the latter, combined with a quart of milk, some allspice and brown sugar, 'will make a dainty and cheap dish', according to Mrs White (1795c, 27). This validation of frugal consumption aligns More's heroines with the ideological position of eighteenth-century agricultural reformers such as Arthur Young, who praised the cost-effectiveness of rice, together with its 'wholesome and nourishing' qualities (1795, 578), and Frederick Eden, who described the potato as a 'valuable root' owing to its easy cultivation, abundance and ability to 'nourish men completely' for little outlay (1797, 505, 503). This enthusiasm for economical alternatives to traditional foodstuffs was not universal, however. In *The Poor Man's Friend*, Alexander Dalrymple observed that even 'the poorest industrious Englishman thinks he has a *right* to eat *good wheaten Bread*' (1795, 4), while in a footnote to his *Essay on Population* Thomas Malthus suggested that, though potatoes represented 'a most valuable subsidiary' in times of crisis, he 'should be very sorry ever to see them the principal dependence of our labourers' (1803, 579). If (as the present volume argues) foods are habitually imbued with symbolic meaning, then in the late eighteenth- and early nineteenth-century imagination bread and potatoes were vested with particular ideological significance. As Catherine Gallagher and Stephen Greenblatt note, whereas wheaten bread was associated with a 'satisfyingly social and symbolic cycle of planting, germination, sprouting, growing, ripening, harvesting, thrashing, milling, mixing, kneading and baking', the potato represented 'mere subsistence, unorganized into a reciprocal economy of rights and duties, expectations and negotiations' (2000, 114, 126).[14] Given this ideologically freighted discourse, it is perhaps unsurprising to find that a range of eighteenth- and early nineteenth-century commentators characterized potatoes as debased and degrading fare; for the political writer William Cobbett, for instance, it was 'an undeniable fact that, in the proportion that this root is in use, as a substitute for bread, the people are wretched' (1926, 69).

In order to counter such ideological objections to cheap dietary substitutes, More's fictions participate in their cultural rehabilitation, demonstrating that they can be rendered palatable to *all* classes, including members of the gentry. During a visit to Mrs Jones's cookery class in *The Cottage Cook*, the local squire remarks that 'your pot really smells as savoury as if Sir John's French Cook had filled it' (1797, 13) and, after being furnished with a bowl of aromatic soup, goes on to solicit the recipe so that he can pass it to his cook at home. Correspondingly, in *The Way to Plenty*, Mrs White's economical cookery is validated by Dr Shepherd, who comments that 'you really get me an appetite, Mrs White, by your dainty receipts . . . I am resolved to have this dish at my own table' (1795c, 29). In presenting such middle-class testimonials to the merits of inexpensive cuisine, 'More capitalizes on the notion that the poor will naturally imitate their "betters"', as Webb points out (2006, 430). Ironically, then, her fictions depend, at times, on the very social mimicry that is deplored when it involves the lower-class emulation of 'luxurious' tastes. The extent of More's culinary egalitarianism is fairly limited, however. The Cheap Repository elsewhere reinstates the idea of proper dietary stratification when both Mrs Jones and Dr Shepherd instruct the better-off members of their communities to buy only the best cuts of meat from the butcher, so that the cheaper cuts (which the rich use merely to enrich their stocks and gravies) can be purchased by the poor.

The reforming, yet politically reactionary, agenda inherent in this directive, and in More's didactic culinary literature more generally, has, over recent years, generated a mixed critical response. While Sandra Sherman describes *The Cottage Cook* as 'an insidious little tract' that 'devalues paternalist obligations toward the poor, legitimating dietary alternatives that accommodate – rather than resist – the high price of grain' (2001, 50, 47), other scholars have identified a more subversive potential within More's work. Webb, for instance, detects 'traces of critique in More's representation of scarcity measures', noting that some of her fictions depict 'poverty that is too intractable even for retrenchment' (2006, 430, 431). An example of this can be found in the second part of *The Shepherd of Salisbury Plain*, in which we are presented with an impoverished agrarian family 'devoutly begg[ing] the blessing of heaven' for the 'dish of potatoes' and 'piece of coarse loaf' before them (1795b, 5). The obvious inadequacy of this meal renders its description as 'homely fare' bleakly ironic (5); patently, the kind of domestic economy that More sponsors elsewhere cannot improve this family's lot. Indeed, they are lifted from dire poverty only when, at the end of the tract, the Shepherd is offered the role of parish clerk following the textually fortuitous death of the previous incumbent. As Anne Stott notes, the tearful gratitude with which the Shepherd and his family greet this news calls into question their previous professions of contentment and poses a number of questions for the reader: does the story ultimately 'preach submission or aspiration'? Are the poor 'meant to be content or to hope for the arrival of a *deus ex machina*' (2003, 181)? If, as Stott concludes, the contradictions in this tale complicate its final moral message, the tract is nevertheless unambiguous in demonstrating that 'the agricultural wage of a shilling a day was insufficient to support a family, however pious, prudent, and enterprising' (2003, 185).

As well as drawing attention to the failure of economizing measures to alleviate the effects of scarcity, More further challenges conservative orthodoxy by presenting the poor as discriminating consumers with their own gastronomic tastes. This is significant for, according to Sherman, in the bulk of eighteenth-century dietary reform literature, the labouring classes are abstracted and homogenized as 'machines that eat' and, consequently, denied individual appetites and preferences (2001, 10). More, by contrast, claimed that she was 'resolved, in trying to *reform* the poor, to *please* them too, a point which I think we do not sufficiently attend to. We are very apt to forget they have the same tastes, appetites, and feelings with ourselves' (qtd. in Chatterton 1861, 275–276). Although this belief in labouring-class discernment is sometimes obfuscated by the authoritarian didacticism of the Cheap Repository, it does come across in More's insistence that the poor should have access to flavoursome, meat-based dishes. It is striking that, unlike the bland meal-and-vegetable soups favoured in many dietary reform tracts, the recipes incorporated into *The Way to Plenty* and *The Cottage Cook* invariably include meat among their ingredients. Implicitly challenging the doctrine that, in times of scarcity, the lowest orders of society could (and should) subsist on potatoes, More repeatedly sanctions strategies by which the poor can retain animal protein in their diets, noting that 'it is a great mistake . . . to think a bit of meat so ruinous' to a household's budget that it must be relinquished entirely (1795c, 25). In this way, her social mission comes into some kind of proximity with the democratizing vision of Smith's *Desmond*, for, although More does not enlist the same language of dietary and political rights as her literary counterpart, she does explicitly and persistently counter the dehumanizing ideology that, when it comes to food, '*any thing is good enough for the poor*' (1797, 14).

Mary Birkett, *A Poem on the African Slave Trade* (1792)

The politicized rhetoric surrounding food in the 1790s did not only involve domestic produce, such as bread and potatoes; questions regarding the rights, responsibilities and ethics of consumption also coalesced around a popular colonial import: sugar. Once considered an exotic luxury and used predominantly by the rich as a medicine or spice (see Chapter 3), sugar, by the late eighteenth century, had been 'transformed into a proletarian necessity', as Sidney Mintz suggests (1986, 180). Its extensification was linked to the 'tea complex' that 'gradually came to characterize British society top to bottom'; sugar was not only used as a sweetener within tea itself, but also formed 'a fundamental ingredient' of the foods that typically accompanied the beverage (Mintz 1986, 121). Yet, despite its increasingly widespread use amongst the labouring classes (a habit criticized as economically improvident and morally deleterious by Hannah More and others), sugar 'still retained something of its former status as a luxury item', as Deirdre Coleman points out, owing to its tropical origins and perceived nutritional superfluity (1994, 344); for Samuel Taylor Coleridge, for instance, sugar represented an *imaginary* want rather than an essential bodily need (1970, 132). In addition to its luxuriousness, sugar was endowed with what Keith Sandiford calls superordinate values of 'purity and perfection' (2000, 23). For the anonymous author of a 1752 essay, sugar was superlatively 'wholesome and innocent', the natural substance with the 'greatest resemblance' to breast-milk, for which it could happily deputize (Anon. 1752, 4, 6). According to Benjamin Moseley, an eighteenth-century doctor, meanwhile, sugar was infused with quasi-magical 'restorative power', frequently providing a cure for apparently intractable diseases (1799, 142).

Contra such positive associations, sugar also stood as the primary emblem of plantation slavery (a connection noted in the discussion of *Robinson Crusoe* in Chapter 3), and as such became a focus for eighteenth-century abolitionists. Following the defeat of William Wilberforce's 1791 parliamentary bill to end the slave trade, activists turned to consumer politics to advance their cause, advocating abstention from West Indian sugar until such time as plantation owners desisted from the use of enslaved labour. One of the supporters of this campaign was Mary Birkett, a young Quaker woman from Dublin, who in 1792 published *A Poem on the African Slave Trade* to encourage the renunciation of slave-produced sugar. The poem is addressed specifically to members of the author's 'own sex' for, notably, women were constructed as the main consumers of sugar in eighteenth-century society. Exploiting this connection, Birkett accentuates the potential power wielded by female consumers:

> Say not that small's the sphere in which we move,
> And our attempts would vain and fruitless prove;
> Not so – we hold *a most important share*,
> In all the evils – all the wrongs they [slaves] bear,
> And tho' their woes *entire* we can't remove,
> We may th' *increasing* mis'ries which they prove,
> Push far away the plant for which they die,
> And in this one small thing our taste deny.
>
> *(1792, ll. 295–302)*

The reference here to women's 'share' in the enterprise of slavery, via their taste for sweetened produce, is significant, for it fuses the language of moral responsibility with that of commercial interest, indicating that female consumers have an economic as well as an ethical stake in the slave trade. This dual signification is also present in line 270 ('And in our brethren's sufferings hold no share') and highlights one of the complexities that characterized the abstention campaign. If, on the one hand, the boycotting of sugar represented a 'form of resistance to mercantilism', as Charlotte Sussman suggests (2000, 39), then, on the other, it was a strategy fully implicated in and dependent on the dynamics of eighteenth-century consumerism. As Timothy Morton notes, 'the choice *not* to consume was in itself a self-reflexive way of defining oneself as a consumer' (2004, 3). By denying their taste for 'one small thing' – sugar – women could simultaneously adopt a critical moral stance on colonial capitalism and participate actively within the commercial sphere, exerting their influence as discerning economic agents.

While advancing this political viewpoint, Birkett, in common with other female abolitionist writers, is careful to modulate her language, voicing her critique through what Claire Midgley calls 'the acceptably "feminine" means of poetic sentiment' (1992, 34). In a clear appeal to the cult of female sensibility, Birkett aims to foster a sympathetic identification between her poem's addressees and its protagonist, an unnamed African male, whose pre-slavery existence is rendered in familiar, homely terms: a devoted 'father, husband, brother, son [and] friend' (l. 110), he takes on a nurturing, semi-maternal role within his household, not only hunting but also preparing his family's food with 'ceaseless love and anxious care' (l. 103). The domestic felicity evoked in this romanticized vignette inevitably heightens the 'agony of grief' that accompanies the African's later kidnap by slave-traders (l. 121). More obliquely, his simple, organic mode of consumption invites comparisons with sophisticated European luxury, in which consumers are typically alienated from producers; as Birkett reminds her readers, it is the abstract, depersonalized entity 'Commerce' (rather than individuated labourers) that 'to you . . . its choice stores [does] impart' (l. 309).

As well as idealizing the dietary relations of pre-industrial societies, *A Poem* seeks to make visible the obfuscated chains linking African slaves to Western consumers. The former are the 'sad vassals of our lux'ry' (l. 168), Birkett suggests, and the sugar they cultivate the material symbol of their physical suffering and occluded labour, although this connection is rarely recognized among the cultured environs of the eighteenth-century tea-table:

> How little think the giddy and the gay
> While sipping o'er the sweets of charming tea,
> How oft with grief they pierce the manly breast,
> How oft their lux'ry robs the wretch of rest,
> And that to gain the plant we idly waste
> Th' *extreme of human mis'ry* they must taste!
> *(ll. 21–26)*

The antithetical language deployed in this stanza emphasizes the contrasting fates of leisured, middle-class tea-sippers and wretched, overtasked slaves, who drink not from porcelain dishes of sweetened tea, but rather from the metaphorical 'cup of mis'ry' (l. 4). Further disparity emerges between the unremitting distress alluded to in the anaphoric refrain 'how oft' and the consumer indifference suggested in the phrase 'how little think', implying that 'the giddy and the gay' *should* reflect more frequently than they do on the 'grief' and 'mis'ry' subsumed within their saccharine beverages.

The notion that the tea-table might be contaminated by the taint of human suffering is crystallized in a later stanza, in which the speaker insists that women have the power to mitigate the anguish of slaves,

> If we the produce of their toils refuse,
> If we no more the blood-stain'd lux'ry choose;
> If from our lips we push the plant away
> For which the liberties of thousands pay.
> *(ll. 263–266)*

The lurid reference to 'blood-stain'd lux'ry' here marks an interesting shift in rhetorical direction: Birkett's poem moves away from the language of sentimental identification to a lexis of aversion, insinuating that British consumers metaphorically cannibalize West-Indian slaves every time they ingest sugared produce. This '"blood sugar" topos', as Morton (1998, 87) labels it, is a common feature of abolitionist writing, appearing perhaps most famously in William Fox's polemical *Address to the People of Great Britain*, in which the author posits that 'so necessarily connected are our consumption of the commodity, and the misery resulting from it, that in every pound of sugar used, (the produce of slaves imported from Africa) we may be considered as consuming two ounces of human flesh' (1791, 4). It also appears in Coleridge's 1796 essay on the slave trade, which berates the false sensibility of fine ladies who sip 'a beverage sweetened with human blood, even while . . . weeping over the refined sorrows of Werter' (1970, 139), and in Robert Southey's 1797 sonnets on the slave trade, which echo Coleridge in their contempt for those 'who at [their] ease / Sip the blood-sweeten'd beverage!' (2004, ll. 9–10).

The continual redeployment of the blood-sugar trope during the 1790s is testament to its emotional and psychological power; however, as a number of critics have noted, its effects can also be highly ambiguous. The reference to flagellated slaves' 'reeking backs' (l. 191) in Birkett's poem, for instance, implies that the presence of blood in West Indian sugar may not be merely metaphorical. A correspondingly queasy logic pervades other abolitionist writings: Timothy Touchstone's *Tea and Sugar* (1792) stresses that, during their labours, 'the plunder'd . . . / Are made to sweat, nay bleed through every pore' (2010, 2.5–6), while, in a perverse horticultural image, the speaker of William Cowper's 'The Negro's Complaint' (1789) suggests that the sweat and tears of enslaved plantation workers 'dress the soil' in which the sugar cane grows (1967, l. 20). More dramatically, James Gillray's print *Barbarities in the West Indies* (1791) depicts a white slave-holder immersing a black slave in a vat of boiling sugar juice, in a horrific visualization of the blood-sugar topos that the cartoon's legend assures us is based on true events. The blurring of the figurative and the literal in these examples is designed to intensify the reader/spectator's repugnance towards slave-produced sugar; however, as Sussman observes, the 'supererogatory negative affect' generated by such representations could also 'work against the explicit political intention' of the abolitionists (2000, 15), relegating the porous, contaminating body of the slave to abjection in order to maintain the physical and psychical purity of the white consuming subject.

The disgust-inducing rhetoric of the blood-sugar topos thus exposes the limits of the political identification between slave and consumer, demonstrating Coleman's point that the 'recuperative features of abolitionism always coexist with a panicky and contradictory need to preserve essential boundaries and distinctions' (1994, 359). These limits become further apparent in Birkett's *Poem* when the speaker sets out her preferred model for post-slavery relations between Britain and Africa. Trade between the two should not cease, she suggests; in fact, Britain should look to cultivate Africa's 'fertile land' (l. 237) and 'plant . . . colonies' there (l. 245), taking advantage of the continent's 'rich plain[s]', which are so naturally fruitful they 'scarce [need] the ploughman's toil' (l. 240). Positioning this scheme as an ethical alternative to the 'rav'nous' slave trade (l. 37), Birkett apparently fails to notice that it leaves the exploitative power relations underpinning eighteenth-century slavery unchanged; within her fantasy vision, it remains the role of the fecund periphery to nourish and sustain the colonial centre. The unacknowledged perpetuation of anthropophagic metaphorics here calls into question the distaste for colonial enterprise expressed elsewhere in the poem. Though Birkett undoubtedly seeks to renovate imperial producer–consumer relations through her sponsorship of abstention, her work by no means dislodges British subjects from their position at the top of the symbolic food chain.

Jane Austen, *Sense and Sensibility* (1811), *Mansfield Park* (1814) and *Emma* (1816)

As Maggie Lane suggests, although the domestic plots of Jane Austen's novels 'inevitably [cohere] around the give and take of meals', references to food itself tend to be 'rationed' in her corpus, limited 'to a few particulars which are made to do a great deal of work' (1995, xi). When, for instance, in *Northanger Abbey* (1818) General Tilney tells Catherine Morland that his pinery yielded one hundred fruits in the last year, his ostensibly casual reference to plentiful hot-house produce (considered an exotic luxury in Georgian society) communicates his obsession with wealth, status and social display (Austen 2003, 130). By contrast, the 'beautiful pyramids of grapes, nectarines, and peaches' served at Pemberley in *Pride and Prejudice* (1813) are described as the 'finest fruits *in season*' (Austen 1972, 287, my emphasis); although these, too, signify wealth, the reference to seasonality here implies that Mr Darcy's estate is managed in sympathetic concert with the organic rhythms of nature. The symbolic nuances of food are also evident in *Mansfield Park*: Sir Thomas Bertram's declaration that he 'would rather have nothing but tea' (the 'blood-stained' beverage decried by eighteenth-century abolitionists) on his return from his West-Indian sugar plantations cements his status as a colonial capitalist (1996, 151). In *Emma*, meanwhile, clergyman Mr Elton's preoccupation with his own bodily nourishment – on a visit to the home of some impoverished parishioners he provides a lengthy account of the various dishes he has previously consumed at a friend's party (1966, 113) – signals his deficiencies as a spiritual instructor to the people of Highbury.[15] The structure and timings of meals are similarly freighted with meaning in Austen's works. In *Pride and Prejudice*, Mrs Bennet reveals she will 'take care to have two full courses' at the ostensibly informal 'family dinner' to which she has invited Mr Bingley, signalling her eagerness to impress her affluent guest (1972, 161). In the aborted early novel *The Watsons* (1804–1805), meanwhile, embarrassment ensues when Tom Musgrave and his friend Lord Osborne call on the Watson family at 'five minutes before three', just as they are about to have their dinner (Austen 2003, 276). The Watsons' 'early hours' indicate their provincialism and relatively low social status (278); Tom, by contrast, dines at the fashionably late hour of eight (285).

As well as revealing such minutiae of Regency domestic life, Austen's works are highly attuned to the broader cultural meanings surrounding food – and, particularly, food refusal – in early nineteenth-century culture. Her novels contain a number of disorderly eaters whose self-destructive patterns of consumption are shown to be symptomatic of a wider social malaise. Women, in particular, are revealed to be vulnerable to injurious eating habits. The characters of Marianne Dashwood in *Sense and Sensibility*, Fanny Price in *Mansfield Park* and Jane Fairfax in *Emma* each restrict their intake of food in self-abnegating gestures that are linked directly to the possession of a heightened sensibility. The ideological conflation of limited appetite and female delicacy was commonplace in late eighteenth- and early nineteenth-century literature and culture, as Mary Wollstonecraft indicates in her derogation of 'weak' women of fashion who consider a 'puny appetite the height of all human perfection' and proof of an 'exquisite sensibility' (1994, 111). In her Juvenilia, Austen exhibits an equally cynical view, mocking the sentimental novel's privileging of exalted etherealism over the 'mean and indelicate employment of Eating and Drinking' (1993, 82). Her satirical treatment of abstemiousness continues in *Sense and Sensibility*, where the narrator knowingly observes of Marianne's 'unwilling[ness] to take any nourishment', following Willoughby's abrupt departure for London, 'her sensibility was potent enough!' (1995, 83). Abandoned by the lover to whom she has openly committed herself (without the security of a formal engagement), Marianne sustains herself on emotion alone, a damaging behaviour that only intensifies her suffering, while distressing her mother and sisters. Tellingly, the exclamatory status of the usually equable narrator's interjection here encourages us to interpret Marianne's self-denial as excessive and self-indulgent. As the novel progresses, however, and Marianne's health declines – after Willoughby snubs her in London, 'she neither ate, nor attempted to eat any thing' (172), and she eventually succumbs to an unnamed but life-endangering illness that her friends attribute to 'the many weeks of previous indisposition which [her] disappointment had brought on' (293) – Austen invites us to undertake a more nuanced reading, which challenges the cultural expectations surrounding female sensibility. As Claudia Johnson shrewdly notes, *Sense and Sensibility* questions how the ideals of romantic love promoted in sentimental fiction can ever '[serve] women if the same charms of sensibility that render them alluring . . . also induce febrile morbidity' (1988, 67). While ridiculing the excessive nature of Marianne's passions, on the one hand, Austen also indicts, on the other, a cultural ideology that invests so extensively in notions of female delicacy that it actually elicits acts of quasi-anorexic 'self-destruction' (1995, 322).

Like Marianne, the sensitive Jane Fairfax is shown to reject her bodily appetites following romantic disappointment. When she first appears in *Emma*, Jane is described as occupying 'a most becoming medium, between fat and thin' (1966, 180). Her body soon begins to waste, however, as, compromised by a secret engagement to Frank Churchill and tormented by his public flirtation with Emma, she is 'reduced to refusing food simultaneously to reassert control of herself and signal her trauma', as Sarah Moss suggests (2003, 203). Unlike the ascetic Shakespearean heroines discussed in Chapter 2, who use food refusal as an overt form of protest, Jane does not explicitly comment on her alimentary self-denial. Instead, her physical decline is recorded in scrupulous detail by her well-meaning but loquacious aunt, Miss Bates, for the general consumption of Highbury society: an initial report outlining 'exactly how little bread and butter [Jane] ate for breakfast, and how small a slice of mutton for dinner' (182) is superseded by the announcement that 'she really eats nothing – makes such a shocking breakfast, you would be quite frightened if you saw it' (244). After Jane breaks off her clandestine engagement, we are further informed that every item of food her family and neighbours try to tempt her with is 'distasteful' to her (382), and even Mr Perry, the local apothecary, confirms that her 'appetite [is] quite gone' (381). Though romantic reconciliation eventually removes Jane from any danger of self-starvation, it is telling that, just as Marianne's friends and family were quick to assume that in keeping with fictional convention she would die from her decline (Mrs Jennings, for instance, prematurely grieves Marianne's 'rapid decay [and] early death' [1995, 292]), Jane's fate is assumed to be that of a typical sentimental heroine. In her representation of female food refusal, then, Austen both demonstrates and critiques the powerful cultural hold of romantic ideas regarding alimentary self-denial and 'proper' femininity, condemning a literary ideology that seemingly compels women to be ill.

In the case of Fanny Price in *Mansfield Park*, delicacy of appetite pre-dates romantic upset. From her very arrival at Mansfield as a child, Fanny is associated with the rejection of foods, managing only 'two mouthfuls' of the placatory 'gooseberry tart' offered to her as a salve to homesickness (1996, 13). According to Michael Parrish Lee, the young Fanny transcends the culinary field: her tastes are aesthetic rather than gustatory, with 'books, letters, and experience' supplying metaphorical 'food' for her fancy (2012, 382). Later, when the disreputable Mr Crawford discloses his romantic interest in her, her negative emotions are, unsurprisingly, sublimated into food refusal: 'her comfort in that day's dinner was quite destroyed; she could hardly eat any thing' (251). Interestingly, though, it is Fanny's enforced return to her parent's lower-class home in Portsmouth that represents the greatest trial to her finely tuned sensibilities. She is disgusted by the lack of cleanliness she finds there: 'the tea-board never thoroughly cleaned, the cups and saucers wiped in streaks, the milk a mixture of motes floating in thin blue, and the bread and butter growing every minute more greasy' (363). Indeed, 'so little equal' is Fanny to the unsavoury cookery produced in her family home, she is put 'in the most promising way of being starved', very often 'defer[ring] her heartiest meal, till she could send her brothers in the evening for biscuits and buns' (342). Whether this refined taste for dainty baked goods is acquired – the result of 'being nursed up' (342) in the sophisticated milieu of Mansfield – or the manifestation of 'natural delicacy' (337) remains a matter of ambiguity in the text. As Lane suggests, the novel adopts an uncertain stance on the issue, vacillating between 'a reading which posits an effete nobility and gentry invigorated and reinvented by the values and attitudes of the class below' and one in which 'a Cinderella figure ascends to the position from which she has been wrongfully excluded, and the old order goes on as before' (1995, 89).

Yet, if *Mansfield Park* is evasive regarding the class implications of Fanny's ascetic sensibility, it is unequivocal in its condemnation of Dr Grant's voracity. One in a long line of gluttonous literary clergymen (see, for instance, the religious figures described in *Piers Plowman* and *The Canterbury Tales* in Chapter 1 and *Joseph Andrews* in Chapter 3), Dr Grant is described as being 'very fond of eating': he 'would have a good dinner every day, and Mrs Grant instead of contriving to gratify him at little expense, gave her cook as high wages as they did at Mansfield Park' (27). This suggestion of un-Christian extravagance is compounded by Mary Crawford's denouncement of the Doctor as 'an indolent selfish Bon vivant, who must have his palate consulted in every thing' and who refuses to 'stir a finger for the convenience of any one' (93). Not only does Dr Grant's fetishistic relationship to food render him personally obnoxious – he blames his wife for their cook's blunders, argues with Mrs Norris about the provenance of an apricot tree, and at one point drives the Crawfords from the Parsonage with his grumblings about a green goose – it also makes him unproductive, in every sense of the word. It is hinted that his professional indolence is matched by sexual impotence for, although his wife is 'about fifteen years his junior', he has 'no children' (22), implying that physical appetite has supplanted sexual desire – an insinuation reinforced by Tom Bertram's sly observation: 'a desperate dull life [Mrs Grant's] must be with the doctor' (100). The correlation between lavish consumption and social and economic inutility was well-recognized in the Georgian period; according to the political economist Nathaniel Forster, 'luxury' not only dampened 'the spirit of industry', but also had the 'pernicious and fatal' effect of being 'an enemy to population' (1767, 44). Childless and idle, Dr Grant becomes socially useful only in death. When he fulfils Tom's description of him as an 'apoplectic sort of fellow' (22) by expiring after consuming 'three great institutionary dinners in one week' (387), his demise has the fortuitous effect of freeing up the Mansfield living for Edmund Bertram, Fanny's husband. This event occurs just after the couple have 'been married long enough to begin to want an increase of income', we are told, in a strong hint of actual or impending pregnancy (390). The novel ends, then, not only with the punishment of excess, but also with the intimation that Fanny's own once-unproductive appetite has given way to socially beneficial fruitfulness.

Like Dr Grant, *Emma*'s Mr Woodhouse is a disorderly male eater whose habits are suggestive of an emasculated sexuality. Whereas the Doctor is a glutton, however, Mr Woodhouse's fastidious tastes are more reminiscent of the constrained appetites of Austen's female consumers. He screens his daily fare with hypochondriacal obsessiveness, rejecting anything that might prove remotely harmful to his health and expressing a preference, above all, for 'a small basin of thin gruel' (1966, 55) – a bland, semi-liquid food, redolent of pap, that the celebrated cookery-writer Maria Rundell lists under 'Cookery for the Sick' in her *New System of Domestic Cookery* (1808, 286). For Gwen Hyman, Mr Woodhouse's food also bears similarities to the diet 'prescribed to women to suppress the signs and urges of the body'; however, she argues, we should not assume from this that Mr Woodhouse is simply 'a mass of stereotypical feminine traits, a cross-dresser who replaces the skirt with the invalid's rug' (2009, 20). Crucially, Mr Woodhouse's valetudinarian regimen works to augment his cultural authority, rather than to indicate his powerlessness. As the narrator of *Emma* notes, 'what was unwholesome to him, he regarded as unfit for any body' (49–50), and this culinary zealotry invariably affects the eating behaviours of those Highbury residents whose social position is lower than his own. Time and again, Mr Woodhouse imposes his idiosyncratic tastes on his friends and neighbours: he tries 'earnestly' to 'dissuade them' from eating the Westons' wedding cake (50), advises against the consumption of custard at a Hartfield evening party (55), and disappoints his friend Mrs Bates by sending back 'a delicate fricassee of sweetbread and some asparagus' (a favourite dish of hers) because the asparagus is deemed to be 'not . . . quite boiled enough' (326). His alimentary foibles also compromise his patriarchal obligations: when a pig is killed at Hartfield, he prevaricates over sending a loin to the dependent Bateses, for he cannot 'be sure of their making it into steaks, nicely fried, as [his] are fried . . . and not roast it, for no stomach can bear roast pork' (185–186). His dereliction of duty is offset in the text by Emma's hospitable attentions (she makes 'all the amends in her power . . . for whatever unwilling self-denial' her father imposes on their guests [223]) and Mr Knightley's generosity (in contrast with Mr Woodhouse's reticence regarding the gift of pork, Knightley willingly bestows his personal supply of apples on Jane Fairfax and the Bateses after hearing how much Jane enjoys them [246]).[16]

Yet, while endorsing such gestures of munificence, Austen's novels also hint at the more problematic aspects of paternalist benevolence: namely, the unequal power relations it upholds and the obligations it places on recipients. This burden is made explicit by Marianne in *Sense and Sensibility*, who represents the hospitality of the sociable Sir John Middleton as suffocatingly excessive: 'The rent of this cottage is said to be low; but we have it on very hard terms, if we are to dine at [Barton] park whenever any one is staying . . . with them' (1995, 106). In *Emma*, meanwhile, 'an ostensibly pastoral economy of food gifts is revealed to us as a mystification of the realities of class and money underlying it', as Lisa Hopkins suggests (1998, 67). Mr Knightley's liberality with the produce from his estate visibly reaffirms his status and authority as local squire, while culinary donations similarly consolidate Emma's position at the top of Highbury's social hierarchy, marking her out as established gentry in a world where social mobility threatens to blur traditional class boundaries. Unlike the *arriviste* Mrs Elton, who is more concerned with the quality of the rout-cakes and the lack of ice at Highbury card parties than with the welfare of the poor (291), Emma is aware of her responsibilities to those less fortunate than herself, dutifully undertaking charitable visits to local cottagers and inviting the child of one 'poor sick family' (108) to fetch a pitcher of restorative broth from the kitchens at Hartfield. Her benevolence in this instance is not entirely disinterested, however. After loftily declaring that the sight of poverty 'do[es] one good' and congratulating herself on her 'compassion' and 'exertion' for the underprivileged (111), Emma's attention is quickly diverted by the rather less worthy activity of matchmaking, indicating that her public-spiritedness stems less from instinctive altruism than from a superficial sense of social obligation. What is more, though Austen here ironizes her heroine's lack of self-awareness in comic fashion, any textual recognition that 'to find a destitute family on the doorstep of a large and beautiful house overflowing with good food suggests a greater social ill than can be remedied with a pitcher of broth' is 'conspicuously missing', as Moss notes (2003, 197). It seems that although the metaphorical hungers of those middle-class women disempowered by patriarchal ideology are amply represented in Austen's novels, the material hunger of the lower classes – and, perhaps more importantly, its causes – are much less visible, occluded by hospitable and ostensibly unstinting flows of food.

Percy Bysshe Shelley, *Queen Mab; A Philosophical Poem with Notes* and *A Vindication of Natural Diet* (1813); Mary Shelley, *Frankenstein, or the Modern Prometheus* (1818)

The revolutionary fervour that inflected writings on food in the 1790s re-emerged forcefully in the 1810s, a decade similarly troubled by war, scarcity and hunger. During this period, Romantic writers such as Percy Shelley deployed representations of consumption not only to convey the current, degraded state of humankind but also to imagine its future perfectibility. In *Queen Mab* (a visionary poem deemed so controversial by its author that it was initially distributed only privately to a select circle of fellow progressives) the Fairy Queen of the title transports the Soul of the sleeping Ianthe to her ethereal palace, where she conjures images of the past, present and future. In a suggestive allusion to Regency dissipation, the vision of the present centres on a king who is 'a slave / Even to the basest appetites' (2002b, 3.32–33) and whose regal gluttony inures him to the hungry cries of his people:

> that man
> Heeds not the shriek of penury; he smiles
> At the deep curses which the destitute
> Mutter in secret, and a sullen joy
> Pervades his bloodless heart when thousands groan
> But for those morsels which his wantonness
> Wastes in unjoyous revelry.
>
> *(3.33–39)*

The reference to 'unjoyous revelry' here recalls James Gillray's famous 1792 caricature *A Voluptuary under the Horrors of Digestion*, which depicts a grossly bloated George, Prince of Wales (later Prince Regent and George IV), impassively picking at his teeth with a fork, while surrounded by the debris of gluttonous carousal. Shelley's oxymoronic phrase further indicates that his imaginary king is an 'unnatural being', whose alimentary instincts have been utterly corrupted by luxury and surfeit (3.103). Rather than being motivated by a healthy, spontaneous hunger, *Queen Mab*'s jaded monarch 'drags / His palled unwilling appetite' (3.45–46) to each 'meal / Of silence, grandeur, and excess' (3.44–45), apparently anaesthetized to the wholesome sensory pleasure that would arise from more temperate gustatory experience.

Shelley explicitly links such regal luxury with political tyranny. Turning his attention to the social relations that exist within the court, he uses transecting metaphors of industry and feeding to demonstrate the pervasive inequality of the king's debauched regime:

> Those gilded flies
> That, basking in the sunshine of a court,

Fatten on its corruption! – what are they?
– The drones of the community; they feed
On the mechanic's labour: the starved hind
For them compels the stubborn glebe to yield
Its unshared harvests; and yon squalid form,
Leaner than fleshless misery, that wastes
A sunless life in the unwholesome mine,
Drags out in labour a protracted death,
To glut their grandeur.

(3.106–116)

The competing lexica of plenitude and deprivation here highlight the entrenched injustices of monarchical reign: there is evidently sufficient food available
within the kingdom, but it is not distributed equally. Shelley adapts the popular
eighteenth-century comparison of the aristocracy to drones and the masses
to worker bees to imply that relations between the ruling and lower classes
are inherently parasitic. The courtiers' figurative and literal fattening is implied
to be inversely correlated to the attenuation of workers' bodies, whose 'wasting'
(both physical and temporal) is underscored by the double syntax at the end of
line 113.

While deploring the current state of things, *Queen Mab* does not despair for the
future of civilization. In Canto 8, Mab presents Ianthe's spirit with what Alan
Bewell calls a 'biosocial utopia' (1999, 211) and Timothy Morton an 'ecotopian
vision' (2006, 58): the prospect of an abundant, bountiful future in which humanity
and Nature exist in harmonious synchronicity, and relations between producers,
eaters and eaten are radically redefined. In a potent image of maternal nourishment,
designed to counter Malthusian claims that 'at nature's mighty feast there is no
vacant cover' for members of a surplus population (Malthus 1803, 531), Mab
describes the 'fertile bosom of the earth' giving 'suck / To myriads, who still grow
beneath her care' (8.109–110). This populous future world exists conveniently in a
state of constant fruition, alternating between the 'virgin bloom' of spring and
autumnal fecundity (8.122): 'fruits are ever ripe, flowers ever fair, / And autumn
proudly bears her matron grace, / Kindling a flush on the fair cheek of spring'
(8.119–121). As part of this global eco-transformation, even the previously inhos-
pitable frozen wastes at the poles, 'where matter dared not vegetate or live' (8.61),
are 'unloosed' into productivity (8.63), while the 'deserts of immeasurable sand'
(8.70) at the equator 'Now teem with countless rills and shady woods, / Corn-fields
and pastures and white cottages' (8.75–76). As Bewell wryly notes, the evocation
of 'corn-fields, pastures, and white cottages' here 'shows how difficult it is, even
for the most radical of English anti-imperial poets, to avoid using English landscapes
as the measure of utopia' (1999, 219). Yet, if the domestic countryside provides a
seemingly conservative topographic model for effective agronomics in *Queen Mab*,
the poem's reconfiguration of human–animal alimentary relationships reveals a
more revolutionary turn.

Crucially, in Shelley's utopian vision, all sentient beings live together in universal vegetarian concord, in a paradisiacal environment which closely resembles the prelapsarian Eden described by Milton in Book 4 of *Paradise Lost* (see Chapter 3). Shelley imagines that

> The lion now forgets to thirst for blood:
> There might you see him sporting in the sun
> Beside the dreadless kid; his claws are sheathed,
> His teeth are harmless, custom's force has made
> His nature as the nature of a lamb.
> *(8.124–128)*

Moreover, that previously predatory figure, 'man', no longer 'slays the lamb that looks him in the face',

> And horribly devours his mangled flesh,
> Which still avenging nature's broken law,
> Kindled all putrid humours in his frame,
> All evil passions, and all vain belief,
> Hatred, despair, and loathing in his mind,
> The germs of misery, death, disease, and crime.
> *(8.212–218)*

These passages bring into play a complex series of meanings around eating, nature and culture, in which vegetarianism is figured as both a means to rise above 'carnal animality, and a way of returning to nature' (Morton 2006, 59). In the first quotation, the lion's apparently instinctual 'thirst for blood' has been civilized, his ferocious 'nature' refined into one of lamb-like docility. Yet the notion of cultivation implicit in the reference to 'custom's force' is countered by the language of forgetting in line 124, which implies that the lion's taste for blood was itself a learnt behaviour. In this light, the lion's present vegetarianism is figured not in terms of evolutionary progression, but rather as the *restoration* of a previous natural state.

A parallel logic marks humans' relationship to meat-eating, which is similarly characterized as a corruption or perversion of nature's originary laws, as well as the root of all society's subsequent ills. The point is elaborated in an extensive footnote to *Queen Mab*, subsequently published as a separate essay, *A Vindication of Natural Diet* (1813), in which Shelley deploys a series of discourses – moral, medical, ana-tomical, economic – in justification of vegetarianism.[17] Following the arguments set out by his friend John Frank Newton in *The Return to Nature* (1811), Shelley also cites biblical and mythological sources to support his claim that 'at some distant period man forsook the path of nature, and sacrificed the purity and happiness of his being to unnatural appetites' (1884, 9). The shift to carnism provides the key to all Fall narratives, Shelley suggests: 'the allegory of Adam and Eve eating of the tree of evil . . . admits of no other explanation, than the disease and crime that have flowed from unnatural [i.e. animal-based] diet', while Prometheus's theft of fire from the gods in Greek mythology (the catalyst for the loss of the Golden Age) is similarly attributed to the inauguration of meat-eating, cookery being necessary to render dead flesh physically and psychologically palatable by disguising its sanguinity and 'screening' out 'the horrors of the shambles' (1884, 9, 10–11).

Interestingly, as Carol J. Adams notes, it is from the shambles or slaughterhouse that Mary Shelley's 'Modern Prometheus', Victor Frankenstein, retrieves many of the materials required to form his Creature, 'a Being who, like the animals eaten for meat, finds itself excluded from the moral circle of humanity' (2010, 158). Forced to fend for himself in the forests around Ingolstadt following Frankenstein's abandonment of him, the Creature intuitively adopts a vegetarian diet – 'I ate some berries which I found hanging on the trees, or lying on the ground. I slaked my thirst at the brook' (Shelley 1980, 103) – validating Percy Shelley's point that 'unsophisticated instinct is invariably unerring' in determining 'what aliment is natural or otherwise' (1884, 15). Although the Creature does, on one occasion, taste meat in the form of roasted offal (the discarded meal of some itinerant beggars) and declares it to be 'savoury', he swiftly reverts to his usual foraged regimen of 'berries', 'nuts and roots', an ascetic diet that the text typically associates with an ethical worldview (105). After requesting that Frankenstein manufacture him a mate, with whom he could live in Romantic isolation in the 'vast wilds of South America', the Creature affirms:

> My food is not that of man; I do not destroy the lamb and the kid to glut my appetite; acorns and berries afford me sufficient nourishment. My companion will be of the same nature as myself, and will be content with the same fare . . . the sun will shine on us as on man, and will ripen our food.
>
> *146*

In terms strikingly similar to those used by Percy Shelley in Canto 8 of *Queen Mab*, the Creature here imagines the foundation of an Edenic community, in which beneficent nature provides a constant sufficiency and all life-forms co-exist in humane fellowship. The idyllic, co-operative form of existence envisioned here appears to contrast sharply with the more imperialist mode of settlement represented in *Robinson Crusoe*, where, as Chapter 3 notes, meat-eating is aligned with colonial exploitation and violent domination. *Frankenstein*'s investment in the Romantic association of vegetarianism and peaceability is somewhat compromised, however, by the Creature's earlier threats to 'glut the maw of death, until it be satiated with the blood of [Frankenstein's] remaining friends', should Frankenstein not accede to his wishes (99). The manifestation of savage violence in Mary Shelley's text certainly undermines radical vegetarian Joseph Ritson's claims, in his *Essay on Abstinence from Animal Food, As a Moral Duty*, that it is carnivorousness that 'disposes man to cruel and ferocious actions', 'while the frugivorous live together in constant peace and harmony' (1802, 86, 88).

Nevertheless, the notion that abstention from animal food could 'reverse malignancy throughout the world' by 're-establishing natural health and freeing humanity from the cause of disease, violence and crime' remains a focal point of Romantic writing, as Tristram Stuart points out (2008, 383–384). According to Percy Shelley's meliorist vision in *A Vindication*, the nationwide adoption of a natural diet would inevitably result in social reform, with the 'excessive complication' of existing relations between the classes being 'so far simplified, that every individual might feel and understand why he loved his country, and took a personal interest in its welfare' (1884, 21). What this inclusive, socially levelling rhetoric leaves unsaid, of course, is that the possibility of *choosing* to renounce meat (an expensive commodity in Regency Britain) was restricted to a privileged elite, for whom vegetarianism functioned as 'a *habitus*, a socially distinctive way of living' (Morton 1994, 158). It is no accident that Percy Shelley describes his vegetable diet as 'a system of perfect *epicurism*', a term freighted with notions of connoisseurship (1884, 24, my emphasis). Far from simplifying class relations in the way that *A Vindication* proposes, vegetarian texts such as George Nicholson's *On Food* (1803) and Martha Brotherton's *A New System of Vegetable Cookery* (1821), which present middle-class readers with recipes for the kinds of poverty-foods included in Hannah More's Cheap Repository Tracts, endorse 'a complex or sophisticated use of simple food', elevating a vegetable diet 'into an ideologically-coded form of self-presentation', as Morton suggests (1994, 18, 17). Thus, much like the anti-saccharites of the 1790s, with whom they were often ideologically aligned, Romantic vegetarians can be seen to adopt a reflexive consumer stance in relation to diet through their deployment of an aversive rhetoric that works as much to signal their social as their ethical position.

George Gordon, Lord Byron, *The Corsair* (1814) and *Don Juan* (1819–1824)

The self-conscious association of ascetic lifestyle with Romantic identity is nowhere more apparent than in Byron's poetry. As Tom Mole notes, 'cultivated slenderness' became 'central to [Byron's] self-presentation' (2006, 26) as, at various points during his adult life, the poet dieted obsessively to achieve the lean body-image demanded by Romantic celebrity culture. It was during one of these periods of severely restricted eating that Byron composed his bestselling narrative poem *The Corsair*, in which the recognizably Byronic pirate chief Conrad is distinguished from other men by his frugal vegetarianism:

> Earth's coarsest bread, the garden's homeliest roots,
> And scarce the summer luxury of fruits,
> His short repast in humbleness supply
> With all a hermit's board would scarce deny.
> *(1981, 1.71–74)*

Conrad's limited diet is complemented by his strict teetotalism. Whereas the members of his pirate crew 'carouse' (1.48) during their time ashore, 'Ne'er for his lip the purpling cup they fill, / That goblet passes him untasted still' (1.67–68). This exacting somatic self-discipline is presented as a crucial component of the innate nobility deemed integral to Byronic heroism. Conrad's wife, Medora, admiringly observes that 'what others deem a penance is thy choice' (1.432), while the poem's speaker equates Conrad's alimentary rigour with intellectual vitality, perceiving that 'his mind seems nourished by that abstinence' (1.76).

Ironically, though, Conrad's singularizing capacity for self-denial almost proves his undoing. Alerted to an incipient raid by the Turkish pacha, Seyd, Conrad decides to launch a pre-emptive attack and infiltrates his enemy's halls disguised as a Dervise. Here, he finds Seyd hubristically hosting a luxurious 'feast for promised triumph yet to come' (2.4). When invited to partake of the 'sumptuous fare' on offer, Conrad cannot hide his disgust, shunning the banquet 'as if some poison mingled there', to the surprise of his host (2.113–114). It is only by his quick thinking that Conrad is able to deflect suspicion; he attributes his aversion to religious piety, explaining that 'my stern vow and order's law oppose / To break or mingle bread with friends or foes' (2.125–126). Such putative observance contrasts strongly with Seyd's own disregard for Islamic law regarding intoxicants; whereas the principled Conrad is 'more than Moslem when the cup appears' (1.430), the hedonistic Seyd reputedly 'dare[s] to quaff' 'forbidden draughts' (2.32). As Mole suggests, through these orientalist portraits of heroism and villainy, Byron associates abstention from food and drink with 'charisma, self-sufficiency and mastery' and excessive consumption with 'luxury, self-indulgence and callousness' (2006, 32).

This representational paradigm continues in Byron's unfinished mock-heroic epic *Don Juan*. Notably, the poem's witty and irreverent speaker appears to share his creator's ascetic tastes, professing a Diogenic preference for 'simple olives' and 'bread' (1986, 15.577, 581) over *haute cuisine*, and promising readers that, in the course of his narration, he 'will not dwell upon ragoûts or roasts' (13.789). In fact, despite this alleged lack of interest in culinary concerns, *Don Juan* abounds with references to food and feasting, in which, as usual, simple tastes and self-control are validated, and gluttony and lavishness reviled. Yet Peter Graham suggests the work also acknowledges – indeed, has some sympathy for – the idea that the 'lower, more visceral claims' of the body 'coexist with and often supersede' moral and aesthetic imperatives (1992, 115). The stomach's controlling influence over elevated human emotion is made particularly clear in Canto 2 of the poem, where, aboard the ship the *Trinidada*, Juan's declarations of devotion for his absent love Julia are bathetically interrupted by bouts of sea-sickness; as the speaker wickedly observes, 'No doubt [Juan] would have been much more pathetic, / But the sea acted as a strong emetic' (2.167–168).

The case for the primacy of the body is made even more vehemently a few stanzas later when the *Trinidada* is shipwrecked. Instead of 'hoarding' their provisions, the survivors fall upon the remaining victuals 'ravenously' (2.544, 543), with the result that, a few days later, they are driven 'wild' by 'hunger's rage' (2.558). In desperation, they kill and eat first Juan's pet spaniel and then his tutor, Pedrillo, who draws the short straw in the shipmates' lottery 'for flesh and blood' (2.583). A number of critics have suggested that the comic-horrific description of the Catholic

Pedrillo's exsanguination and devourment can be read as a critique of the cannibalistic tendencies of the Eucharist and its doctrine of transubstantiation (see Graham 1992, 116; Kolb 1995, 105).[18] *Don Juan*'s anthropophagic episode could also, however, be interpreted in relation to the ideology of Romantic vegetarianism. For the radical writer Joseph Ritson, cannibalism was the natural corollary to meat-eating, a link he substantiated by reference to 'the deliberate coolness with which seamen, when their ordinary provisions are exhausted, sit down to devour such of their comrades as chance or contriveance [*sic*] renders the victim of the moment' (1802, 125).[19] Although Byron's forthright declaration that 'man is a carnivorous production' (2.529) would seem to militate against a Ritsonian reading by naturalizing human carnism, careful analysis of the stanza in which this line appears reveals that its initial 'apparently assured statement' is subsequently 'whittled away by qualification and temporizing', as Christine Kenyon Jones suggests:

> In the second line ['And must have meals, at least one meal a day'] the expected 'meat' is replaced twice with the weaker 'meals.' In the fourth line we are told that humans 'must have prey,' but the sanguinary connotations of 'prey,' again a substitute for 'meat,' warn us that this is not a straightforward statement of fact, but a particular representation of humanity, which is not the way it 'must' be at all.
>
> *1998, 53–54*

Thus, while appearing to essentialize humans as carnivores, Byron's 'tongue-in-cheek claim' actually 'denaturalizes carnivorousness by turning man into a "carnivorous *production*"' – a creature of custom rather than of nature – as Denise Gigante observes (2005, 125–126).

Significantly, the sailors who indulge in the cannibalization of Pedrillo's body subsequently suffer 'madly, / For having used their appetites so sadly' (2.639–640); crazed with thirst (a state that Percy Shelley associates with fall from originary vegetarianism [1884, 11]), they take to drinking sea-water and as a result '[die] despairing' (2.632). By contrast, Juan abstains from feasting on his former tutor, sustaining himself instead by 'chewing a piece of bamboo, and some lead' (2.654). As in *The Corsair*, asceticism is here associated with heroism. Juan's exemplary appetitive self-discipline sets him apart from his fellow shipwreck survivors: although 'three or four / Who were not quite so fond of animal food' initially refuse the taboo meal (2.617–618), eventually all except Juan make 'a little supper' of Pedrillo (2.652). When the 'faint, emaciated' Juan eventually reaches the shore of a Cycladian island, his previous self-restraint is immediately rewarded (2.841), for, unlike that other famous literary shipwreck survivor, Robinson Crusoe (Chapter 3), Byron's hero has no need to source his own food. Discovered by the beautiful Haidée and her maid Zoe, he is supplied with a hearty, natural breakfast of 'eggs, fruit, coffee, bread, fish, [and] honey' (2.1159), as well as 'a most superior mess of broth' (2.981) – 'a thing which poesy but seldom mentions', the speaker reminds us in a dry interjection (2.982).

Once again, then, in this part of the poem, Byron deflates the exalted language of love through references to food and feeding, satirically suggesting that affection is fortified by, and perhaps even dependent on, physical sustenance. In a humorous stanza, reminiscent of Fielding's bathetic commentary on the relationship between food and passion in *Tom Jones* (Chapter 3), the speaker declares that 'While Venus fills the heart', 'Ceres presents a plate of vermicelli, – / For love must be sustain'd like flesh and blood' (2.1353, 1355–1356). Problematically though, while nourished by Haidée's love and Zoe's cookery, Juan slips from disciplined consumption into easeful indulgence. As Kolb notes, he 'ignores the paradisiacal connotations' of the meal initially presented to him 'and longs instead for a beefsteak' (1995, 106), a foodstuff associated more with the sexual virility of Fielding's Tom Jones than the stoical self-discipline of Byron's Conrad. Further, when Haidée's father, Lambro, returns from his travels as a slave-trader, he finds his daughter and her lover sat before a lavish, exotic banquet of 'about a hundred dishes':

> Lamb and pistachio nuts – in short, all meats,
> And saffron soups, and sweetbreads; and the fishes
> Were of the finest that e'er flounced in nets,
> Drest to a Sybarite's most pamper'd wishes;
> The beverage was various sherbets
> Of raisin, orange, and pomegranate juice,
> Squeezed through the rind, which makes it best for use.
> *(3.489–496)*

As Jones points out, 'even before it is interrupted by the avenging Lambro, we know that Haidée's and Juan's idyll is doomed because the ostentation and orientalization of the food betokens decadence and loss of purposefulness' (1998, 45). Indeed, Timothy Morton notes, the very language in this part of *Don Juan* has become luxuriant and excessive: 'the writing gluts the eye and ear as much as its content' (2000, 21). This voluptuous linguistic turn contrasts sharply with the semiotics of natural consumption in evidence at the earlier meal on the beach and signals that Juan's relationship to food has fundamentally changed. His heroic status is threatened by the effeminizing opulence of Haidée's sybaritic feast; as Morton puts it, 'arabesqued pleasure' here 'becomes its own warning' (2000, 21).

The corrupting potential of feasting is again signalled in Canto 15, where the speaker spends no less than thirteen stanzas describing an elaborate banquet, hosted by Lord and Lady Amundeville, at which Juan is a guest. Here, however, Byron's satire is less concerned with the damaging effects of Eastern luxury on heroic masculinity than with the debased tastes of the English aristocracy. Among the numerous dishes that furnish the table at Norman Abbey,

> There was a goodly 'soupe à la *bonne femme*,'
> Though God knows whence it came from; there was too
> A turbot for relief of those who cram,

> Relieved with dindon a la Périgueux;
> There also was – the sinner that I am!
> How shall I get this gourmand stanza through? –
> Soupe à la Beauveau, whose relief was Dory,
> Relieved itself by pork, for greater glory.
>
> *(15.497–504)*

A litany of further lavish dishes – 'fowls à la Condé' (15.513), 'glazed Westphalian ham' (15.517), 'young Partridge fillets, deck'd with truffles' (15.528) – is supplied in subsequent stanzas. Indeed, such is the excessive character of the meal, adapted from a series of menus in celebrity-chef Louis Eustache Ude's *The French Cook* (1813),[20] that the speaker struggles to catalogue the various dishes on offer, as indicated by his comic-plaintive 'How shall I get this gourmand stanza through?' in line 502. His later use of apophasis – 'Alas! I must leave undescribed the gibier, / The salami, the consommé, the purée' (15.561–562) – similarly gestures towards the bewildering profusion of consumables on display. Ironically though, given the copious amounts of food available, the assembled company appears to have little interest in eating. Byron makes clear that the younger guests, in particular, are more concerned with romantic intrigue and flirtatious socializing than with gourmandizing. Plainly, the food at the Amundeville banquet does not function straightforwardly as bodily sustenance; rather than working to relieve essential physical hunger, it has been transposed, through its very oversufficiency, into a signifier of superfluous luxury.

Byron shows himself to be only too aware of the historical and political implications of luxurious consumption in *Don Juan*. His references to the celebrated epicures Apicius (15.518) and Lucullus (15.527) invite readers to draw connections between the notorious decadence of Rome (habitually blamed for the decline of its empire) and the gluttonous dissipation of contemporary high society.[21] However, whereas the poet allows the epicures of antiquity, whose 'names lend lustre' (15.536) to modern culinary culture, a certain nobility, the modern Amundeville banquet is lampooned for its 'sham greatness', as Carol Shiner Wilson suggests (1991, 43). Tellingly, the feast is reminiscent of the kinds of sumptuous and costly entertainments hosted by the Prince of Wales, whose famously prodigious appetite Byron attacks in a caustic aside on the state of the nation. Evoking the food scarcity that afflicted Ireland in 1822, the poet juxtaposes the hunger of the people with royal satiety, observing that 'Gaunt Famine never shall approach the throne – / Though Ireland starve, great George weighs twenty stone' (8.1007–1008).

In light of this politicized commentary, which accentuates the disjunction between necessitous and conspicuous consumption, the speaker's later mock-heroic efforts to enumerate the myriad dishes at the Amundeville feast can be read as part of a sustained social critique of the dietary extravagances and vitiated tastes of the English aristocracy. The 'tumult of fish, flesh, and fowl' that crowds the table at Norman Abbey signals a perversion of the natural limits of need (15.585). As the ascetic speaker muses,

Who would suppose, from Adam's simple ration,
That cookery could have call'd forth such resources,
As form a science and a nomenclature
From out the commonest demands of nature?

(15.549–552)

Luxurious dining is characterized here, as in so much Romantic literature, as a *sophistication*: a distortion or corruption of the simple 'demands of nature'. Notably, we are told that the foodstuffs at the banquet have been refined out of all recognition from their original state: 'all in masquerade' (15.586), they contain 'more mystery' than 'witches, b——ches, or physicians brew' (15.494, 496). This culinary artistry is symbolic of the cultural pretensions of Regency society – pretensions that Byron is evidently keen to deflate. Playing with the differing French and English interpretations of '*goût*' (meaning taste/discernment) and 'gout' (an inflammatory disease traditionally associated with gluttony), he wittily implies that while the Norman Abbey diners believe the food before them has been 'refine[d] / From nature' in service of the former (15.569–570), '*after*, there are sometimes certain signs / Which prove plain English truer of the two' (15.573–574).

Yet, for all its condemnation of decadent dining, *Don Juan* appears consistently to revel in the description of eatables, repeatedly inviting readers to 'enjoy the aural and visual pleasures' of lists of food, as Jane Stabler suggests (2004, 156). From the outrageous description of the sailors' anthropophagic meal to the intoxicating plenty of Haidée's feast and the culinary profusion of the Amundeville banquet, Byron's evocations of food are (like one of the many dishes at Norman Abbey) 'drest / Superbly, and [contain] a world of zest' (15.591–592). The sense of relish implicit in this phrase – and in so many of the culinary images in *Don Juan* – indicates that a subtle shift in poetic perspective has occurred from the sober asceticism of *The Corsair*. Though, in his later work, Byron continues to associate male heroism with dietary discipline, he also acknowledges the vitalizing power of food, together with the interdependence of bodily appetite and elevated spirit, comically conceding that in literature, as in life, 'much depends on dinner' (13.792).

John Keats, *Endymion* (1818), *The Fall of Hyperion* (written c. 1819–1821), *The Eve of St Agnes* and 'La Belle Dame sans Merci' (1820)

In an 1819 letter to Charles Wentworth Dilke, John Keats suddenly breaks off from discussing pecuniary matters to remark:

> this moment I was writing with one hand, and with the other holding to my Mouth a Nectarine. Good god how fine. It went down soft pulpy, slushy, oozy; all its delicious embonpoint melted down my throat like a large beatified Strawberry.

Keats 2002, 356

Whereas much eighteenth- and early nineteenth-century literature sought to distinguish 'natural' from 'luxurious' foods – and to police the value-laden boundary between the two – Keats here renders natural produce luxurious, aestheticizing the sensory experience of consumption. His discourse is inspired by the etymological rapport between taste and touch; he carefully delineates the texture of the fruit as well as the tactile sensation of deglutition. His organizing simile ('like a large beatified Strawberry'), meanwhile, has a curiously circular quality to it: the experience of eating fruit is compared to the experience of eating fruit, referring back on itself in a reflexive gesture that works to intensify the impression of pure alimentary pleasure.

The synaesthetic enjoyment evoked in this anecdote represents in miniature one of the signature aspects of Keats's work. As Denise Gigante notes, 'references to gustatory taste inform not only [Keats's] poetry but also much of his poetic theory . . . His "poetical character" is defined by its ability to "taste" and "relish" the world it perceives' (2005, 139–140). In particular, Keats uses food and drink as a sensory supplement to amatory or erotic experience in his verse. In stanza 30 of *The Eve of St Agnes*, for instance, sexual consummation is famously delayed by the arrangement of a 'sumptuous' feast (1988d, l. 273). After watching his would-be lover Madeline fall into 'an azure-lidded sleep' (l. 262), Porphyro begins to remove from the closet where he has been hiding

> a heap
> Of candied apple, quince, and plum, and gourd,
> With jellies soother than the creamy curd,
> And lucent syrups, tinct with cinnamon;
> Manna and dates, in argosy transferred
> From Fez; and spicèd dainties, every one,
> From silken Samarkland to cedared Lebanon.
>
> *(ll. 264–270)*

Simple, organic produce is self-consciously transposed (or sophisticated) here into the register of exotic luxury by what Timothy Morton calls Keats's 'poetics of spice' (2000, 223). Like Haidée and Juan's banquet in *Don Juan*, Porphyro's feast is a fantasy of oriental excess, its profusion underscored by Keats's polysyndetic sentence structure ('and plum, and gourd . . . and lucent syrups . . . and dates . . . and spicèd dainties'). It is also, like Keats's description of eating a nectarine, deliberately reflexive: Morton notes that the 'phrase "tinct with cinnamon" could be paraphrased as "spiced with spice"' (2000, 31), a rhetorical doubling that heightens the perception of sensory overload within the stanza.

The luxuriousness of Porphyro's feast is further underscored by its fundamental inutility; as a range of critics have pointed out, Porphyro and Madeline never actually consume the copious delicacies on display. Despite the 'heap' of alimentary signifiers loaded into the verse, then, stanza 30 is less about direct gustatory experience than about the pleasures of the literary imagination. As Marjorie Levinson argues, 'by the magnificent onomatopoeia of lines 264–270 – a virtuoso display of alliteration and assonance – Keats effectively designates the *word* the object of consumption' (1988, 123). The oral sensations created by Keats's rich language both evoke and displace the gustative act: Betsy Tontiplaphol refers to 'the molasses-like sonority' of the phrase 'lucent syrups' (2011, 62), while Laura Betz highlights the accumulation of 'mouth-filling' plosives ('apple', 'plum') and 'oozing' sibilants ('soother', 'syrups') in the festal scene (2008, 310). Language elicits its own oral pleasures here: though Levinson speculates that we might sicken if actually obliged to ingest Keats's cloyingly saccharine banquet, she maintains that we can nevertheless 'enjoy reading [it], for what we consume is the concrete sensuous particularity of the words' (1988, 121).

A similar kind of aesthetic enjoyment is offered in *Endymion*, where we (and the poem's eponymous shepherd) are invited to 'feast on' the luxurious natural spread prepared by Venus for her slumbering lover, Adonis (1998c, 2.454). A cupid sets out the Elysian menu:

> here is cream,
> Deepening to richness from a snowy gleam;
> Sweeter than that nurse Amalthea skimmed
> For the boy Jupiter: and here, undimmed
> By any touch, a bunch of blooming plums
> Ready to melt between an infant's gums:
> And here is manna picked from Syrian trees,
> In starlight, by the three Hesperides.
> *(2.446–453)*

Brimming with quasi-maternal forms of nourishment in anticipation of Adonis's reawakening/rebirth, this paradisiacal repast offers temporary hope and refreshment to Endymion as he continues his quest for the moon-goddess, Cynthia. In other poems from Keats's corpus, however, the fetishization of ethereal foods results in distaste rather than healthy repletion. In 'La Belle Dame sans Merci', for instance, a natural diet comprising 'roots of relish sweet, / And honey wild, and manna-dew' apparently fails to satisfy the ailing knight-at-arms who is in thrall to the beautiful woman of the title (1988b, ll. 25–26). Despite the poem being set 'in the same luscious, overripe world' as Keats's odes, the knight exists in a nauseated condition, Gigante suggests, because he can no longer appreciate 'the beauty surrounding him' or 'relish the world as the true "poetical character" should' (2005, 143, 146). His dangerously palled appetite is reflected back to him in the guise of the 'death-pale' kings, princes and warriors who haunt his dreams (l. 38), 'their starved lips' 'gap[ing] wide' with 'horrid warning' of his fate (ll. 41–42).

Appetitive aversion materializes again in *The Fall of Hyperion*, although initially the poem seems to promise an encounter with the same kind of delectable picnic-feast found in Adonis's bower in *Endymion* – or, indeed, the bounteous natural meal that Eve prepares for Raphael in Book 5 of *Paradise Lost* (see Chapter 3), a text to which Keats's poem is thematically and stylistically indebted.[22] In the first canto, the visionary poetic persona is transported to a lush and verdant landscape, framed by 'plantain, and spice-blossoms' (1988e, 1.21). From this initial, exoticized vista, Keats's verse pans round cinematographically to an arbour wreathed in vines and 'a mound / Of moss', on which is spread what looks like an Edenic 'feast of summer fruits' (1.28–29). On closer inspection, however, the expected banquet turns out to be the

> refuse of a meal
> By angel tasted, or our Mother Eve;
> For empty shells were scattered on the grass,
> And grape-stalks but half bare, and remnants more.
> *(1.30–33)*

As Gigante suggests, the detritus of this post-lapsarian meal would seem to augur 'nausea far more than delight' (2004, 186). Nevertheless, the poet-speaker seems fascinated by the 'sweet-smelling' cornucopian leftovers (1.34), which are more plentiful 'than the fabled horn / Thrice emptied could pour forth at banqueting' (1.35–36). Suddenly experiencing an 'appetite / More yearning than on earth I ever felt' (1.38–39), the speaker gluts himself with Eve-like abandon and, soon after, slakes his thirst with similar gusto from a 'cool vessel of transparent juice' (1.42). Indulgence in this ambrosial liquid does not result in unambiguous pleasure, however; rather, as in the poem's Miltonic antecedent, gluttonous ingestion precipitates an unsettling loss of control. The speaker is intoxicated by the 'domineering potion' (1.54) and, though he struggles hard against its effects, he is eventually 'rapt . . . away' by its heady force (1.51).

Further queasy images of consumption ensue as the poet's 'cloudy swoon' (1.55) gives way to mythological visions of the fallen Golden Age. The defeated Titan Saturn complains (in an ironic reversal of his fabled ingestion of his children) that he and his siblings 'are swallowed up / And buried from all godlike exercise' following the Olympians' triumph (1.412–413). Meanwhile, in his sun palace, Saturn's brother Hyperion is troubled by unpalatable effusions from the mortal world:

> when he would taste the wreaths
> Of incense breathed aloft from sacred hills,
> Instead of sweets, his ample palate takes
> Savour of poisonous brass and metals sick.
> *(2.30–33)*

If Keats's verse here conflates the related senses of taste and smell, it does not repeat the pleasurable synaesthesia of *The Eve of St Agnes* or the poet's joyful epistolary reflections on eating a nectarine. What Hyperion experiences is the metallic tang of disgust, a sickening sensory image that Gigante relates to Keats's own consumption of mercury for medical purposes, and to the wracking digestive complaints from which he suffered during the advanced stages of tuberculosis (2004, 186–187; 2005,

151–152). Although perhaps best known for his evocations of 'mellow fruitfulness' (1988a, l. 1) and sensual gratification, Keats, in the alimentary references that suffuse his poetry, thus articulates the full range of gustatory experience, from transcendental tasting to nauseated satiety, while blurring the fragile boundaries that separate 'natural' from luxurious consumption.

Keats's sensorily rich representations of food and eating may seem less overtly political than those of some of his Romantic contemporaries, such as Shelley and Byron; however, as this chapter has shown, the very act of writing about dietary matters (including alimentary pleasure) in the period 1750 to 1830 was politically charged. In the second half of the eighteenth century, food in literature was pivotal to the expression of anxieties about the growth of consumerism, providing a material focus for the ideological debates that raged regarding the social, moral and economic effects of luxurious consumption, on the one hand, and domestic retrenchment, on the other. Food was also, as we have seen, central to competing articulations of regional and national identity; to explorations of gendered power relations; to the revolutionary politics of the 1790s and 1810s, when scarcity precipitated calls for a radical reorganization of the social hierarchy; and to the ethical campaigns of the anti-saccharites and vegetarians, who embraced their roles as autonomous consumers in their efforts to restructure colonial and human–animal relations. The precise political associations of food examined here inevitably come to shift and change in the literature of the later nineteenth century, explored in the next chapter; nevertheless, the contentiously labelled 'consumer revolution' of the eighteenth century lays much of the groundwork for the representations of food-as-commodity found in Victorian culture, as well as for the concerns about appetitive desire and alimentary rights that would proliferate in the writings of the period.

Notes

1 For further discussion of turtle in eighteenth-century literature, see the section on *Robinson Crusoe* in Chapter 3.
2 In his *Essay on Modern Luxury*, Samuel Fawconer makes a similar complaint: 'Our luxury might be less unpardonable, if the only good effects of it were suffered to circulate among ourselves. But the materials of our splendour and profusion are, for the most part, exotic: nothing, that is the produce of our own climate, is barely supportable. . . . What a strange infatuation! that we should be at so great pains and expence to feed our natural rivals in trade, and sworn enemies to the welfare of our country!' (1765, 40–41).
3 Joy Fraser suggests that it is 'highly unlikely' that haggis actually originated in Scotland, noting that similar dishes exist around the world (2003, 2). Nevertheless, by the eighteenth century haggis had come to signify 'Scottishness' in the British literary imagination.
4 These cannibalistic connotations continue in an earlier version of the poem's final stanza, recorded in *The Canongate Burns*: 'Ye Pow'rs wha gie us a' that's gude / Still bless auld Caledonia's brood, / Wi' great John Barleycorn's heart's bluid / In stoups or luggies' (Burns 2001a, 214).
5 Linda Colley suggests that, following the final failure of the Jacobite rising, the British army began to recruit men 'on a massive scale' from Scotland; she quotes Lord Barrington, the Secretary of War, telling Parliament in 1751: 'I am for having always in our army as many Scottish soldiers as possible . . . because they are generally more hardy [than those of any other country we can recruit from]' (2009, 104, 121).

6   Nigel Leask suggests that at the time Fergusson's poem was written the traditional figure of the 'gudeman' was 'beginning to metamorphose into the capitalist farmer' (2010, 217).

7   Interestingly, Fergusson's mock-vengeful desire to acculturate Johnson's taste finds its mirror in James Boswell's attempts to 'Scottify' his friend's palate, as recorded in his *Journal of a Tour to the Hebrides* (1786): 'I bought some *speldings*, fish (generally whitings) salted and dried in a particular manner, being dipped in the sea and dried in the sun, and eaten by the Scots by way of a relish. [Johnson] had never seen them, though they are sold in London. I insisted on *scottifying* his palate; but he was very reluctant. With difficulty I prevailed with him to let a bit of one of them lie in his mouth. He did not like it' (Johnson and Boswell 1984, 185). The incident is also illustrated in a Thomas Rowlandson print, *Scottifying the Palate at Leith* (1786), which depicts a gleeful Boswell force-feeding speldings to a resistant Johnson, much to the amusement of a group of Scottish fishwives in the background.

8   See Bohstedt (2010) and Wells (1988).

9   As Antje Blank and Janet Todd note, the history of the Revolution 'seethes with rumours of "famine plots", conspiracies instigated by the nobility and the royal family to starve the people into political submission' (Smith 2001, 438n24). It was the shortage of bread in Paris in autumn 1879 that triggered the *poissardes*' march on Versailles.

10   John Bohstedt points out that 'suspicions of middlemen and market manipulations' during periods of hunger have a long history, 'going back to Anglo-Saxon times, at least' (2010, 65). Notably, a number of the medieval writings discussed in Chapter 1 feature corrupt practices around food; millers, in particular, are associated with dishonesty in *The Canterbury Tales*.

11   The trope of the pampered pet is common in late eighteenth- and early nineteenth-century radical writing. In Percy Shelley's *The Mask of Anarchy*, for instance, 'Hope' tells the people that it is slavery 'to hunger for such diet / As the rich man in his riot / Casts to the fat dogs that lie / Surfeiting beneath his eye' (2002a, ll. 172–175). See also note 12 below.

12   In her *Vindication of the Rights of Men*, Mary Wollstonecraft complains that 'the game laws are almost as oppressive to the peasantry as press-warrants to the mechanic . . . How many families have been plunged, in the *sporting* countries, into misery and vice for some paltry transgression of these coercive laws, by the natural consequence of that anger which a man feels when he sees the reward of his industry laid waste by unfeeling luxury? – when his children's bread is given to dogs!' (1994, 16).

13   In his diary entry for 20 April 1796, for instance, the country parson and *bon-vivant* James Woodforde records attending a dinner party where, though meat was abundant, there was 'no kind of Pastrey, no Wheat Flour made use of . . . and the Bread all brown Wheat-Meal with one part in four of Barley Flour' (1999, 345).

14   Nick Groom makes a similar point about the contrasting symbolic meanings of potatoes and wheat: 'Potatoes were of the earth and water, subterranean and covert, massy, rhizomic: examples of vegetal otherness . . . Wheat had a completely different symbolic vocabulary: it was golden, swayed in the air, and ripened in the sun; it was the Biblical staple enshrined in the Lord's Prayer, a prayer enacted at a domestic level every day in the miraculous, metamorphic, living process of breadmaking' (2004, 28).

15   Mr Elton's interest in food situates him as one in a long line of religious literary figures who prioritize their own appetites over their responsibilities towards their parishioners: see, for instance, the figure of Sloth in *Piers Plowman* (Chapter 1), the corrupt friars and summoners described in *The Canterbury Tales* (Chapter 1) and Mr Barnabas in *Joseph Andrews* (Chapter 3), as well as Dr Grant in Austen's own *Mansfield Park*.

16   Jane Austen's letters reveal the importance of the food-gift economy in the early nineteenth century. See, for instance, her 1808 letter to her sister Cassandra, telling her that the family has received '4 brace of Birds lately, in equal Lots from Shalden & Neatham' (2011, 145), and her 1816 letter to her niece Anna Lefroy, thanking her for the gift of a turkey (2011, 228).

17 Although the term 'vegetarian' was not coined until the 1840s (Shelley's contemporaries used terms such as 'Pythagorean' or 'Brahmin'), the practice of abstaining from meat for religious, ethical or health reasons has a long history in European culture. See Stuart (2008).

18 Representations of the Eucharist as cannibalistic are commonly found in anglophone literary history: see, for instance, the sections on Spenser's *Fairie Queene* in Chapter 2; Milton's *Paradise Lost* in Chapter 3; and Joyce's *Ulysses* in Chapter 6.

19 According to some critics, a link between carnism and cannibalism can also be identified in *Robinson Crusoe*, where instances of meat-eating are loaded with overtones of savagery (see Chapter 3).

20 See, in particular, Ude's dinners for 'Twelve or Fourteen Persons' and 'Sixteen or Twenty Persons' (1822, xi–xiii).

21 The Roman epicure Apicius is also a reference point for Ben Jonson's social satire in *The Alchemist* (see Chapter 2).

22 For further analysis of the relationship between the meals in *The Fall of Hyperion* and *Paradise Lost*, see Gigante (2005).

References

Adams, Carol J. 2010. *The Sexual Politics of Meat: A Feminist-Vegetarian Critical Theory*. New York and London. Continuum.

Anon. 1752. *An Essay on Sugar, Proving it the Most Pleasant, Salubrious, and Useful Vegetable to Mankind; especially as Refin'd and Brought to its Present Perfection in England*. London. E. Comyns.

——. 1757. *The Tryal of the Lady Allurea Luxury, Before the Lord Chief-Justice Upright, on an Information for a Conspiracy*. London. F. and J. Noble.

——. 1758. *An Essay on Monopolies, or Reflections upon the Frauds and Abuses Practised by Wholesale Dealers in Corn and Flour*. London. R. and J. Dodsley.

——. 1777. *An Essay on Tea, Sugar, White Bread and Butter, Country Alehouses, Strong Beer and Geneva, and Other Modern Luxuries*. Salisbury. J. Hodson.

Austen, Jane. 1966. *Emma*. Ed. Ronald Blythe. London. Penguin.

——. 1972. *Pride and Prejudice*. Ed. Tony Tanner. London. Penguin.

——. 1993. *Catharine and Other Writings*. Eds. Margaret Anne Doody and Douglas Murray. Oxford. Oxford University Press.

——. 1995. *Sense and Sensibility*. Ed. Ros Ballaster. London. Penguin.

——. 1996. *Mansfield Park*. Ed. Kathryn Sutherland. London. Penguin.

——. 2003. *Northanger Abbey, Lady Susan, The Watsons and Sanditon*. Eds. James Kinsley and John Davie. Oxford. Oxford University Press.

——. 2011. *Jane Austen's Letters*. 4th edn. Ed. Deirdre Le Faye. Oxford. Oxford University Press.

Barrell, John. 1980. *The Dark Side of the Landscape: The Rural Poor in English Painting 1730–1840*. Cambridge. Cambridge University Press.

Berry, Christopher J. 1994. *The Idea of Luxury: A Conceptual and Historical Investigation*. Cambridge. Cambridge University Press.

Betz, Laura Wells. 2008. 'Keats and the Charm of Words: Making Sense of *The Eve of St Agnes*'. *Studies in Romanticism* 47.3. 299–319.

Bewell, Alan. 1999. *Romanticism and Colonial Disease*. Baltimore, MD, and London. Johns Hopkins University Press.

Birkett, Mary. 1792. *A Poem on the African Slave Trade. Addressed to Her Own Sex*. Part 1. 2nd edn. Dublin. J. Jones.

Blank, Antje and Janet Todd, eds. 2001. Introduction to *Desmond*. By Charlotte Smith. Peterborough, ON. Broadview. 7–33.

Board of Agriculture. 1795. 'On the Present Scarcity of Provisions'. *Annals of Agriculture and Other Useful Arts*. Vol. 24. Ed. Arthur Young. Bury St Edmunds. J. Rackham. 579–581.

Bohstedt, John. 2010. *The Politics of Provisions: Food Riots, Moral Economy, and Market Transition in England, c. 1550–1850*. Farnham and Burlington. Ashgate.

Bold, Alan. 1982. 'Robert Burns: Superscot'. *The Art of Robert Burns*. Eds. R. D. S. Jack and Andrew Noble. London and Totowa, NJ. Vision and Barnes & Noble. 215–238.

Bowstead, Diana. 1986. 'Charlotte Smith's *Desmond*: The Epistolary Novel as Ideological Argument'. *Fetter'd or Free? British Women Novelists, 1670–1815*. Eds. Mary Anne Schofield and Cecilia Macheski. Athens. Ohio University Press. 237–263.

Bradshaw, Penny. 2004. 'The Politics of the Platter: Charlotte Smith and the "Science of Eating"'. *Cultures of Taste/Theories of Appetite: Eating Romanticism*. Ed. Timothy Morton. Basingstoke. Palgrave Macmillan. 59–76.

Brotherton, Martha. 1821. *A New System of Vegetable Cookery; with an Introduction Recommending Abstinence from Animal Foods and Intoxicating Liquors, by a Member of the Society of Bible Christians*. 2nd edn. Salford. The Academy Press.

Brown, Rhona. 2012. *Robert Fergusson and the Scottish Periodical Press*. Farnham. Ashgate.

Burke, Edmund. 1790. *Reflections on the Revolution in France, and on the Proceedings in Certain Societies in London Relative to That Event*. London. J. Dodsley.

Burns, Robert. 2001a. 'Address to a Haggis'. *The Canongate Burns*. Vol 1. Eds. Andrew Noble and Patrick Scott Hogg. Edinburgh. Canongate. 212–214.

——. 2001b. 'The Cotter's Saturday Night'. *The Canongate Burns*. Vol 1. Eds. Andrew Noble and Patrick Scott Hogg. Edinburgh. Canongate. 87–92.

Byron, George Gordon, Lord. 1981. *The Corsair. Lord Bryon: The Complete Poetical Works*. Vol. 3. Ed. Jerome J. McGann. Oxford. Clarendon Press. 148–214.

——. 1986. *Don Juan. Lord Byron: The Complete Poetical Works*. Vol. 5. Ed. Jerome J. McGann. Oxford. Clarendon Press. 1–661.

Chatterton, Lady Georgiana. 1861. *Memorials, Personal and Historical of Admiral Lord Gambier, G.C.B.* Vol. 1. London. Hurst and Blackett.

Churchill, Charles. 1763. *The Prophecy of Famine: A Scots Pastoral*. 2nd edn. London. G. Kearsly.

Cobbett, William. 1926. *Cottage Economy*. London. Peter Davies.

Coleman, Deirdre. 1994. 'Conspicuous Consumption: White Abolitionism and English Women's Protest Writing in the 1790s'. *ELH* 61.2. 341–362.

Coleridge, Samuel Taylor. 1970. *The Watchman*. Ed. Lewis Patton. *The Collected Works of Samuel Taylor Coleridge*. Bollingen Series 75. London and Princeton, NJ. Routledge & Kegan Paul and Princeton University Press.

Colley, Linda. 2009. *Britons: Forging the Nation 1707–1837*. New Haven, CT, and London. Yale University Press.

Cowper, William. 1967. 'The Negro's Complaint'. *Cowper: The Poetical Works*. 4th edn. Ed. H. S. Milford. London. Oxford University Press. 371–372.

Crawford, Robert. 1997. 'Robert Fergusson's Robert Burns'. *Robert Burns and Cultural Authority*. Ed. Robert Crawford. Edinburgh. Edinburgh University Press. 1–22.

Cruikshank, Isaac. 1793. *French Happiness, English Misery*. Cartoon. London. British Museum. BM sat. 8288.

Dalrymple, Alexander. 1795. *The Poor Man's Friend*. London. P. Elmsly.

Eden, Frederick. 1797. *The State of the Poor: or, An History of the Labouring Classes in England, from the Conquest to the Present Period*. Vol. 1. London. B. and J. White.

Fawconer, Samuel. 1765. *An Essay on Modern Luxury: or, an Attempt to Delineate its Nature, Causes, and Effects*. London. James Fletcher and J. Robson.

Fergusson, Robert. 1956a. 'The Farmer's Ingle'. *The Poems of Robert Fergusson*. Vol. 2. Ed. Matthew P. McDiarmid. Edinburgh and London. William Blackwood & Sons. 136–140.

——. 1956b. 'To the Principal and Professors of the University of St Andrews, on Their Superb Treat to Dr Samuel Johnson'. *The Poems of Robert Fergusson*. Vol. 2. Ed. Matthew P. McDiarmid. Edinburgh and London. William Blackwood & Sons. 182–185.

Forster, Nathaniel. 1767. *An Enquiry into the Causes of the Present High Price of Provisions.* London. J. Fletcher & Co.

Fox, William. 1791. *An Address to the People of Great Britain, on the Utility of Refraining from the Use of West India Sugar and Rum.* 5th edn. London. M. Gurney.

Fraser, Joy. 2003. '"Gie her a Haggis!": Haggis as Food, Legend and Popular Culture'. *Contemporary Legend.* n.s. 6. 1–43.

Gallagher, Catherine and Stephen Greenblatt. 2000. *Practicing New Historicism.* Chicago, IL, and London. University of Chicago Press.

Gigante, Denise. 2004. 'The Endgame of Taste: Keats, Sartre, Beckett'. *Cultures of Taste/ Theories of Appetite: Eating Romanticism.* Ed. Timothy Morton. Basingstoke. Palgrave Macmillan. 183–201.

——. 2005. *Taste: A Literary History.* New Haven, CT. Yale University Press.

Gillray, James. 1791. *Barbarities in the West Indies.* Cartoon. London. National Portrait Gallery. NPG D12417.

——. 1792. *French Liberty, British Slavery.* Cartoon. London. British Museum. BM sat. 8145.

——. 1792. *A Voluptuary under the Horrors of Digestion.* Cartoon. London. National Portrait Gallery. NPG D33359.

——. 1795. *The British Butcher, Supplying John Bull with a Substitute for Bread.* Cartoon. London. British Museum. BM sat. 8665.

Graham, Peter W. 1992. 'The Order and Disorder of Eating in Byron's *Don Juan*'. *Disorderly Eaters: Texts in Self-Empowerment.* Eds. Lilian R. Furst and Peter W. Graham. University Park. Pennsylvania State University Press. 113–123.

Groom, Nick. 2004. 'William Henry Ireland: From Forgery to Fish 'N' Chips'. *Cultures of Taste/Theories of Appetite: Eating Romanticism.* Ed. Timothy Morton. Basingstoke. Palgrave Macmillan. 21–40.

Guest, Harriet. 2000. *Small Change: Women, Learning, Patriotism, 1750–1810.* Chicago, IL, and London. University of Chicago Press.

Hanway, Jonas. 2010. 'Essay on Tea'. *Tea and the Tea-Table in Eighteenth-Century England, Vol. 3: Tea, Commerce and the East India Company.* Ed. Matthew Mauger. London. Pickering & Chatto. 63–107.

Hopkins, Lisa. 1998. 'Food and Growth in *Emma*'. *Women's Writing* 5.1. 61–70.

Hume, David. 1752. *Political Discourses.* Edinburgh. A. Kincaid and A. Donaldson.

Hyman, Gwen. 2009. *Making a Man: Gentlemanly Appetites in the Nineteenth-Century British Novel.* Athens. Ohio University Press.

Jacobsen, Susan L. 1996. '"The Tinsel of the Times": Smollett's Argument against Conspicuous Consumption in *Humphry Clinker*'. *Eighteenth-Century Fiction* 9.1. 71–88.

Johnson, Claudia L. 1988. *Jane Austen: Women, Politics and the Novel.* Chicago, IL, and London. University of Chicago Press.

Johnson, Samuel. 1785. *A Dictionary of the English Language.* 6th edn. London. William Strahan.

Johnson, Samuel and James Boswell. 1984. *A Journey to the Western Isles of Scotland and The Journal of a Tour to the Hebrides.* Ed. Peter Levi. London. Penguin.

Jones, Christine Kenyon. 1998. '"Man Is a Carnivorous Production": Byron and the Anthropology of Food'. *Prism(s): Essays in Romanticism* 6.1. 41–58.

Keats, John. 1988a. 'To Autumn'. *The Complete Poems.* 3rd edn. Ed. John Barnard. London. Penguin. 434–435.

——. 1988b. 'La Belle Dame sans Merci'. *The Complete Poems.* 3rd edn. Ed. John Barnard. London. Penguin. 334–336.

——. 1988c. *Endymion. The Complete Poems.* 3rd edn. Ed. John Barnard. London. Penguin. 106–216.

——. 1988d. *The Eve of St Agnes. The Complete Poems.* 3rd edn. Ed. John Barnard. London. Penguin. 312–324.

——. 1988e. *The Fall of Hyperion. The Complete Poems.* 3rd edn. Ed. John Barnard. London. Penguin. 435–449.

——. 2002. *Selected Letters of John Keats.* Ed. Grant F. Scott. Cambridge, MA, and London. Harvard University Press.

Kolb, Jocelyne. 1995. *The Ambiguity of Taste: Freedom and Food in European Romanticism.* Ann Arbor. University of Michigan Press.

Kowaleski-Wallace, Elizabeth. 1997. *Consuming Subjects: Women, Shopping, and Business in the Eighteenth Century.* New York. Columbia University Press.

Lane, Maggie. 1995. *Jane Austen and Food.* London. Hambledon Press.

Leask, Nigel. 2010. *Robert Burns and Pastoral: Poetry and Improvement in Late Eighteenth-Century Scotland.* Oxford: Oxford University Press.

Lee, Michael Parrish. 2012. 'The Nothing in the Novel: Jane Austen and the Food Plot'. *Novel: A Forum on Fiction* 45.3. 368–388.

Lehmann, Gilly. 2003. *The British Housewife: Cookery Books, Cooking and Society in Eighteenth-Century Britain.* Totnes. Prospect.

Levinson, Marjorie. 1988. *Keats's Life of Allegory: The Origins of a Style.* Oxford. Basil Blackwell.

McGuirk, Carol. 2003. 'The "Rhyming Trade": Fergusson, Burns, and the Marketplace'. *'Heaven-Taught Fergusson': Robert Burns's Favourite Scottish Poet.* Ed. Robert Crawford. East Linton. Tuckwell. 135–159.

McKendrick, Neil, John Brewer and J. H. Plumb. 1983. *The Birth of a Consumer Society: The Commercialization of Eighteenth-Century England.* London. Hutchinson.

McKeon, Michael. 2003. 'Aestheticising the Critique of Luxury: Smollett's *Humphry Clinker*'. *Luxury in the Eighteenth Century: Debates, Desires and Delectable Goods.* Eds. Maxine Berg and Elizabeth Eger. Basingstoke. Palgrave Macmillan. 57–67.

Malthus, Thomas. 1803. *An Essay on the Principle of Population.* 2nd edn. London. J. Johnson.

Mauger, Matthew. 2010. 'Jonas Hanway, "Essay on Tea"'. *Tea and the Tea-Table in Eighteenth-Century England, Vol. 3: Tea, Commerce and the East India Company.* Ed. Matthew Mauger. London. Pickering & Chatto. 58–61.

Mellor, Anne K. 2000. *Mothers of the Nation: Women's Political Writing in England, 1780–1830.* Bloomington and Indianapolis. Indiana University Press.

Midgley, Claire. 1992. *Women against Slavery: The British Campaigns, 1780–1870.* London and New York. Routledge.

Mintz, Sidney. 1986. *Sweetness and Power: The Place of Sugar in Modern History.* Harmondsworth. Penguin.

Mole, Tom. 2006. '"Nourished by That Abstinence": Consumption and Control in *The Corsair*'. *Romanticism* 12.1. 26–34.

More, Hannah. 1795a. *The Riot; or, Half a Loaf Is Better Than No Bread.* London and Bath. J. Marshall and S. Hazard.

——. 1795b. *The Shepherd of Salisbury Plain.* Part 2. London and Bath. J. Marshall and S. Hazard.

——. 1795c. *The Way to Plenty; or, the Second Part of Tom White.* London and Bath. J. Marshall and S. Hazard.

——. 1797. *The Cottage Cook; or, Mrs Jones's Cheap Dishes: Shewing the Way to Do Much Good with Little Money.* London. J. Evans and Co.

——. 1830. Advertisement for the Cheap Repository Tracts. *The Works of Hannah More.* Vol. 3. London. T. Cadell. vii–viii.

Morton, Timothy. 1994. *Shelley and the Revolution in Taste: The Body and the Natural World.* Cambridge. Cambridge University Press.

——. 1998. 'Blood Sugar'. *Romanticism and Colonialism: Writing and Empire, 1780–1830.* Eds. Tim Fulford and Peter J. Kitson. Cambridge. Cambridge University Press. 87–106.

——. 2000. *The Poetics of Spice: Romantic Consumerism and the Exotic.* Cambridge. Cambridge University Press.

——. 2004. 'Consumption as Performance: The Emergence of the Consumer in the Romantic Period'. *Cultures of Taste / Theories of Appetite: Eating Romanticism.* Ed. Timothy Morton. Basingstoke. Palgrave Macmillan. 1–17.

——. 2006. 'Joseph Ritson, Percy Shelley and the Making of Romantic Vegetarianism'. *Romanticism* 12.1. 52–61.

Moseley, Benjamin. 1799. *A Treatise on Sugar.* London. G. G. and J. Robinson.

Moss, Sarah. 2003. 'Fetching Broth from Hartfield: Sustaining the Body Politic in Jane Austen's *Emma'*. *Eating Culture: The Poetics and Politics of Food.* Eds. Tobias Döring, Markus Heide and Susanne Mühleisen. Heidelberg. Universitätsverlag Winter. 195–206.

——. 2009. *Spilling the Beans: Eating, Cooking, Reading and Writing in British Women's Fiction, 1770–1830.* Manchester. Manchester University Press.

Newton, John Frank. 1811. *The Return to Nature, or, A Defence of the Vegetable Regimen.* London. T. Cadell and W. Davies.

Nicholson, George, ed. 1803. *On Food.* Poughnill. G. Nicholson.

Paley, William. 1793. *Reasons for Contentment; Addressed to the Labouring Part of the British Public.* London. R. Faulder.

Peckham, Ann. 1771. *The Complete English Cook; or, Prudent Housewife.* 2nd edn. Leeds. J. Ogle.

Porter, Roy. 1993. 'Consumption: Disease of the Consumer Society?' *Consumption and the World of Goods.* Eds. John Brewer and Roy Porter. London and New York. Routledge. 58–81.

Ritson, Joseph. 1802. *An Essay on Abstinence from Animal Food, As a Moral Duty.* London. Richard Phillips.

Rowlandson, Thomas. 1786. *Scottifying the Palate at Leith.* Cartoon. London and Edinburgh. Royal Collection Trust. RCIN 810208.

——. 1792. *The Contrast.* Cartoon. London. British Museum. BM sat. 8149.

Rundell, Maria. 1808. *A New System of Domestic Cookery; Formed upon Principles of Economy and Adapted to the Use of Private Families.* London. John Murray.

Sandiford, Keith A. 2000. *The Cultural Politics of Sugar: Caribbean Slavery and Narratives of Colonialism.* Cambridge. Cambridge University Press.

Shelley, Mary. 1980. *Frankenstein, or the Modern Prometheus.* Ed. M. K. Joseph. Oxford. Oxford University Press.

Shelley, Percy Bysshe. 1884. *A Vindication of Natural Diet.* London. F. Pitman.

——. 2002a. *The Mask of Anarchy. Shelley's Poetry and Prose.* 2nd edn. Eds. Donald H. Reiman and Neil Fraistat. New York and London. W. W. Norton & Company. 316–326.

——. 2002b. *Queen Mab. Shelley's Poetry and Prose.* 2nd edn. Eds. Donald H. Reiman and Neil Fraistat. New York and London. W. W. Norton & Company. 16–71.

Sherman, Sandra. 2001. *Imagining Poverty: Quantification and the Decline of Paternalism.* Columbus. Ohio State University Press.

Simpson, Matthew. 2003. '"Hame Content": Globalization and a Scottish Poet of the Eighteenth Century'. *Eighteenth-Century Life* 27.1. 107–129.

Smith, Charlotte. 2001. *Desmond*. Eds. Antje Blank and Janet Todd. Peterborough, ON. Broadview.

Smith, Nicholas D. 2004. "'The Muses *O'lio*": Satire, Food, and Tobias Smollett's *The Expedition of Humphry Clinker*'. *Eighteenth-Century Fiction* 16.3. 403–418.

Smollett, Tobias. 1984. *The Expedition of Humphry Clinker*. Ed. Lewis M. Knapp. Oxford. Oxford University Press.

Southey, Robert. 2004. 'Oh he is worn with toil! the big drops run'. *Robert Southey: Poetical Works 1793–1810*. Vol 5. Ed. Lynda Pratt. London. Pickering and Chatto. 51–52.

Stabler, Jane. 2004. 'Byron's World of Zest'. *Cultures of Taste/Theories of Appetite: Eating Romanticism*. Ed. Timothy Morton. Basingstoke. Palgrave Macmillan. 141–160.

Stott, Anne. 2003. *Hannah More: The First Victorian*. Oxford. Oxford University Press.

Stuart, Tristram. 2008. *The Bloodless Revolution: A Cultural History of Vegetarianism from 1600 to Modern Times*. New York and London. W. W. Norton & Company.

Sussman, Charlotte. 1994. 'Lismahago's Captivity: Transculturation in *Humphry Clinker*'. *ELH* 61.3. 597–618.

——. 2000. *Consuming Anxieties: Consumer Protest, Gender and British Slavery, 1713–1833*. Stanford, CA. Stanford University Press.

Tontiplaphol, Betsy Winakur. 2011. *Poetics of Luxury in the Nineteenth Century: Keats, Tennyson, and Hopkins*. Burlington, VT. Ashgate.

Touchstone, Timothy. 2010. *Tea and Sugar, or the Nabob and the Creole; A Poem, in Two Cantos. Tea and the Tea-Table in Eighteenth-Century England, Vol. 1: Literary Representations of Tea and the Tea-Table*. Ed. Markman Ellis. London: Pickering & Chatto. 197–204.

Ude, Louis Eustache. 1822. *The French Cook*. 7th edn. London. John Ebers.

Webb, Samantha. 2006. 'One Man's Trash Is Another Man's Dinner: Food and the Poetics of Scarcity in the Cheap Repository Tracts'. *European Romantic Review* 17.4. 419–436.

Wells, Roger. 1988. *Wretched Faces: Famine in Wartime England, 1793–1801*. Gloucester. Alan Sutton.

Wilson, Carol Shiner. 1991. 'Stuffing the Verdant Goose: Culinary Esthetics in *Don Juan*'. *Mosaic: A Journal for the Interdisciplinary Study of Literature* 24.3/4. 33–52.

Wollstonecraft, Mary. 1994. *A Vindication of the Rights of Men; A Vindication of the Rights of Woman; An Historical and Moral View of the French Revolution*. Ed. Janet Todd. Oxford. Oxford University Press.

Woodforde, James. 1999. *The Diary of a Country Parson 1758–1802*. Ed. John Beresford. Norwich. Canterbury Press.

Young, Arthur. 1795. 'Substitutes for Wheat Flour'. *Annals of Agriculture and Other Useful Arts*. Vol. 24. Ed. Arthur Young. Bury St Edmunds. J. Rackham. 576–578.

5

'COME BUY, COME BUY . . . I HAVE NO COPPER IN MY PURSE'

Hunger, indulgence, desire and adulteration (1830–1898)

Charlotte Boyce

Following the so-called 'consumer revolution' of the eighteenth century (discussed in the previous chapter), the inhabitants of nineteenth-century Britain had access to a greater range of foodstuffs than ever before. Trans-global trading networks combined with technological advances in food production and preservation to provide Victorian consumers with such far-flung produce as bananas and pineapples from the West Indies, corned beef from Uruguay and frozen lamb from New Zealand.[1] Yet, as the literature of the period makes clear, access to the basic staples of sustenance, as well as to these transoceanic imports, was unequally distributed amongst the population. In his 1844 essay on *National Distress*, Samuel Laing pointed to one of the fundamental contradictions structuring Victorian society: that 'amidst the intoxication of wealth and progress', 'destitution . . . preys, like a consuming ulcer, in the heart of our large cities and densely-peopled manufacturing districts' (1844, 8). Of course, the bodily hunger of the lower classes had long been a matter of literary concern, influencing texts as diverse as *Piers Plowman* (Chapter 1), *The Faerie Queene* (Chapter 2), Swift's 'Modest Proposal' (Chapter 3) and More's Cheap Repository Tracts (Chapter 4). Following on from these examples, in Victorian literature issues of access and entitlement to food shape some of the most iconic moments in Dickensian fiction, in particular: the eponymous Oliver Twist's petition for 'more' gruel while incarcerated in the workhouse, Ebenezer Scrooge's haunting encounter with the ghostly figures of 'Ignorance' and 'Want' in *A Christmas Carol*, and Abel Magwitch's menacing demand for victuals in *Great Expectations* all highlight hunger's status as an entrenched social problem, underwriting the representations of sumptuous feasting located elsewhere in Dickens's novels.

While physical famishment remained a pressing cultural concern for much of the nineteenth century, it was not the only type of want to preoccupy Victorian writers. During the period, a number of female authors sought also to highlight the less tangible forms of hunger that afflicted the nation's middle-class women. Drawing a direct – and contentious – comparison between corporeal and mental deprivation, Florence Nightingale provocatively argued:

> If we have no food for the body, how we do cry out, how all the world hears of it, how all the newspapers talk of it, with a paragraph headed in great capital letters, DEATH FROM STARVATION! But suppose one were to put a paragraph in the 'Times', *Death of Thought from Starvation*, or *Death of Moral Activity from Starvation*, how people would stare, how they would laugh and wonder! One would think we had no heads nor hearts, by the total indifference of the public towards them. Our bodies are the only things of any consequence.
>
> *1993, 220*

The novels of Anne, Charlotte and Emily Brontë, and later in the century Sarah Grand, share Nightingale's concern with the intellectual and emotional malnourishment of Victorian women, while also demonstrating the problems inherent in resisting the stereotypical version of nineteenth-century femininity, the self-denying but continually nurturing 'angel in the house'. Aware that their 'bodies are the only things of any consequence' in patriarchal culture, heroines such as *Wuthering Heights*'s Catherine Earnshaw, *Shirley*'s Caroline Helstone and *The Beth Book*'s Beth Caldwell Maclure undertake a complex range of food-refusing behaviours that, like those depicted in Jane Austen's fiction (see Chapter 4), represent simultaneously a form of protest *against* and conformity *to* the gender roles prescribed for them.

'Hunger' also emerges in Victorian writing in the form of consumer desire. As the newly industrialized labouring classes became increasingly dislocated from agricultural food sources, they were obliged 'for the first time to purchase their food rather than produce it' (Houston 1994, 8) – to become consumers, in other words – and a burgeoning marketplace arose to meet their alimentary needs. Within this commercial arena, food underwent a metaphorical transformation, morphing from object of basic sustenance into fetishized agent of desire. Notably, many of the marketplace wares imagined by Dickens, Christina Rossetti and George Eliot, in *A Christmas Carol*, 'Goblin Market' and 'Brother Jacob' respectively, resemble the commodities critiqued by Karl Marx in *Capital* and exercise a seductive hold over shoppers. In keeping with long-standing fears regarding the dangers of female appetite (articulated most famously in Milton's *Paradise Lost* [Chapter 3]), women were deemed particularly susceptible to the de-moralizing pleasures of purchase and consumption in Victorian culture. However, consumer desire also generated more general, non-gendered anxieties about national morality, as the demand for visually appealing comestibles resulted in the widespread practice of commercial frauds such as food adulteration, another recurring theme in this study and the cause of a major mid-nineteenth-century public-health scandal.

The polite, middle-class home was supposed to provide a stable safe-haven from the vicissitudes and iniquities of the marketplace; however, as the texts considered in this chapter repeatedly reveal, the ideological segregation of the commercial and private spheres was, in fact, untenable. The bourgeois dining-room could engender displays of appetite the equal of those stimulated by grocers' shop windows, undermining assumptions about the civilizing effects of domesticity. *Vanity Fair*'s Jos Sedley (one in a long line of literary gluttons considered in this book) is metaphorically animalized by his gustatory overindulgence, while, in Lewis Carroll's *Alice* books, the tea-table and dinner-table elicit acts of disorderly, and sometimes savage, ingestion rather than genteel consumption. In fact, a disturbing trace of predatory violence runs through many of the meals considered in this chapter, lending new meaning to Mrs Beeton's declaration in her famous *Book of Household Management* (1861) that 'man . . . is a dining animal' (2000, 363). As we shall see, hunger, in its various Victorian literary incarnations, has the capacity to destabilize prevailing ideological assumptions, bringing to light a voracity that belies nineteenth-century narratives of civility and social and moral advancement.

Charles Dickens, various works

In common with the canonical works of William Shakespeare, the writings of Charles Dickens are famously crammed with representations of food and eating; indeed, Margaret Lane calculates that *The Pickwick Papers* alone contains thirty-five breakfasts, thirty-two dinners, ten luncheons, ten teas and eight suppers, as well as numerous allusions to drink (1970, 166). In light of this prodigiousness, the following section mirrors the critical approach adopted in relation to Shakespeare's drama in Chapter 2; rather than concentrating exclusively on just a couple of examples from Dickens's substantial oeuvre, this section provides an overview of the food-based themes that emerge across his novels, with particular focus on the leitmotifs of feasting, hunger, female culinary labour, alimentary violence and consumer desire.

Within Dickens's extensive corpus of gastronomic references, depictions of festive plenty enjoy particular cultural prominence. One of his earliest newspaper sketches celebrates the 'good humour and hospitality' of a family Christmas dinner, where the communal glee that greets the arrival of 'a gigantic pudding, with a sprig of holly in the top', is matched by the applause that attends 'the astonishing feat of pouring lighted brandy into mince-pies' ('Tibbs' 1835, 1). Equally convivial are the Christmas Eve revelries at Dingley Dell in *The Pickwick Papers* (1836–1837), where the Pickwickians join the Wardles for 'a substantial supper, and a mighty bowl of wassail . . . in which the hot apples were hissing and bubbling with a rich look, and a jolly sound, that were perfectly irresistible' (2003, 378). The synaesthetic pleasures conjured here contribute to the scene's cosy ambience and comforting sense of nostalgia, an impression enhanced by the inclusive, commensal character of the festivities. As Mr Wardle explains, participation in the yuletide celebrations at Dingley Dell is not restricted by social class; rather, in an echo of the open hospitality represented in Arthurian literature (Chapter 1), it is customary for 'every body [to sit] down with us on Christmas eve . . . servants and all' (378).

Commensality is similarly important to festal merriment in *A Christmas Carol* (1843), where the sharing of food strengthens bonds of kinship and seems, superficially, to compensate for material deprivation. At the Cratchits' Christmas dinner, the family's apostrophizing of the fare – 'Oh, a wonderful pudding!' (2006, 51) – and joyous participation in rituals of domestic intimacy, such as roasting chestnuts and drinking toasts, work to assuage repeated narratorial hints at straitened circumstances: we are told that a goose is as rare as a 'black swan' in the Cratchit household (50); that the present meal is 'eked out by apple-sauce and mashed potatoes' (51); and, in a telling use of apophasis, that 'nobody said or thought it was at all a small pudding for a large family' (51). Jolly communal consumption also marks Ebenezer Scrooge's reintegration into the social and familial spheres at the end of *A Christmas Carol*. As Tara Moore suggests, Scrooge's conversion from misanthropic miser to benevolent patriarch is predicated on 'his relinquishment of the incorrect Christmas food, such as his pre-visitation gruel, for the proper food markers of a Christmas Englishness' (2008, 498): the prize turkey he purchases for the Cratchits, the bountiful dinner he shares with his nephew's family, and the bowl of smoking bishop (a kind of mulled wine) he consumes with Bob Cratchit on Boxing Day. Yet, these images of festal abundance, paternalistically dispensed, fail to eliminate entirely the spectre of want that haunts the text both figuratively and literally ('Want' is one of the 'ragged' phantoms to emerge from the cloak of the Ghost of Christmas Present in Stave Three [61]). If, on the one hand, Scrooge's charitable provision of the Cratchits' Christmas dinner challenges *laissez-faire* economics by attesting to 'the right of the poor to eat', as Sally Ledger suggests (2007, 122), then, on the other, his 'benign, seasonally redistributive capitalism' has only peripheral effects, as Andrew Smith points out, leaving untouched 'the central mechanisms of economic power' that give rise to social deprivation (2010, 35). The lingering prospect of hunger thus undercuts the Bacchanalian plenty that is popularly considered the keynote of a Dickensian Christmas.

The positive connotations of yuletide feasting in Dickens's works are further destabilized by the repeated incursion of images of violence into the festal scene. The description of Mrs Cratchit preparing to 'plunge' her carving-knife into the breast of the Christmas goose, which subsequently 'issue[s] forth' a 'gush of stuffing' (2006, 51), has a disconcertingly visceral quality, recalling Robert Burns's haggis with its 'gushing entrails bright' (see Chapter 4). Elsewhere, the Christmas-morning breakfast enjoyed by the medical students Bob Sawyer and Benjamin Allen in *The Pickwick Papers* is peppered with incongruous references to dismemberment:

> 'Nothing like dissecting, to give one an appetite,' said Mr Bob Sawyer, looking round the table.
> Mr Pickwick slightly shuddered.
> 'By the bye, Bob,' said Mr Allen, 'have you finished that leg yet?'
> 'Nearly,' replied Sawyer, helping himself to half a fowl as he spoke. 'It's a very muscular one for a child's.'
> *2003, 392–393*

As Gail Turley Houston notes, this 'conflation of alimentation and dissection magnifies the work of eating as cannibalism', an insinuation that recurs throughout Dickens's work, resurfacing most prominently in *Great Expectations* (1860–1861), where 'tales of the eating or dissection of children act as appetizers for the adults' during the Christmas celebrations at Gargery's forge (1994, 18, 164). Over the course of the pickled pork dinner prepared by Mrs Joe, Uncle Pumblechook catalogues what would have been the young hero Pip's fate, had he been born a pig:

> You would have been disposed of for so many shillings according to the market price of the article, and Dunstable the butcher would have come up to you as you lay in your straw, and he would have whipped you under his left arm, and with his right he would have tucked up his frock to get a penknife from out of his waistcoat-pocket, and he would have shed your blood and had your life.
>
> *Dickens 1994, 27*

The discursive fusion of boy/swine and eater/eatable here mirrors the earlier moment when the escaped convict Magwitch configures Pip as food and threatens to devour the boy's 'fat cheeks' and 'heart and liver', should he fail to do his bidding (4, 5). Punctuated by such unsettling references to butchery and instances of aggressive orality, Christmastide in *Great Expectations* is figured not in nostalgic terms of alimentary harmony, but rather as a 'festal travesty', as Sarah Gilead points out (1988, 236).

Miss Havisham's abandoned wedding breakfast in the ironically named 'Satis House' represents another failed feast in *Great Expectations*. The decomposing, arachnid-infested bride-cake at its centre is symbolically aligned with Miss Havisham's own decaying body; she tells Pip, 'it and I have worn away together. The mice have gnawed at it, and sharper teeth than teeth of mice have gnawed at me' (87). The figurative reference to 'sharper teeth' here indicates that, for all Dickens's fascination with culinary violence and the horrors of cannibalism (a fascination he shares with a number of the writers considered in this volume, including Defoe, Swift and Conrad), it is the predatory character of the Victorian social and economic system, rather than the prospect of literal devourment, that poses the greatest threat to the self in his fiction.[2] Miss Havisham is revealed to have been the casualty of the mercenary schemes and social ambitions of her half-brother and her former lover; consumed by the desire for revenge, she subsequently gluts herself on bitterness throughout her spinsterhood, while refusing to take material food or drink in public. At the other end of the social spectrum, Magwitch's 'ravenous' (327), semi-canine mode of consumption, which Pip attributes to innate criminality – 'in all his ways of . . . eating and drinking . . . there was Prisoner, Felon, Bondsman, plain as plain could be' (334) – is shown to originate rather in the desperate hunger that arises from entrenched poverty. As Magwitch himself notes, the phrenologists who 'measured [his] head' for evidence of a criminal disposition would have done better to have 'measured [his] stomach' (342), for it was the desire for basic sustenance – for 'eat and drink' (344) – that originally propelled him along his morally aberrant course.

The qualified sympathy that readers are encouraged to feel towards Magwitch here indicates a cultural shift in attitudes towards the hungry. Whereas in the medieval and early modern texts discussed in Chapters 1 and 2 hunger was seen as an inevitable, and perhaps necessary, part of the human condition – one that 'taught the lazy and indigent the moral discipline of labor' (Vernon 2007, 2) – in Dickens's works hunger is reconfigured as a *social* problem and the hungry as figures of humanitarian concern.[3] This compassionate response to hunger, which highlights physical suffering in order to engender readerly sympathy, emerges perhaps most famously in *Oliver Twist* (1837–1839), where parish-boy Oliver's famous demand for 'more' food is prefigured by 'the tortures of slow starvation' in the workhouse (1985, 56). Driven 'voracious and wild with hunger' by their meagre regimen, Oliver and his companions employ themselves 'in sucking their fingers most assiduously, with the view of catching up any stray splashes of gruel that might have been cast theron' (56), their autophagic actions anticipating the findings of social commentator John Lhotsky's 1844 enquiry into cases of starvation, which stated that the hungry often '[dilacerate] the arms and other parts of their body with their teeth, for the sake of satisfying, in some degree, the cravings of a ravenous, and as it were, beastly appetite' (1844, 3). The boys' autophagy quickly gives way to the possibility of anthropophagy, as one of their number, who was 'tall for his age' and unused to privation, 'hinted darkly . . . that unless he had another basin of gruel *per diem*, he was afraid he might some night happen to eat the boy who slept next to him' (56). His outlandish threats are designed to testify to the brutality inculcated by Victorian political economy, the ideology that underpinned the poor-relief system and operated according to the 'all-consuming force of self-interest' (Ledger 2007, 98). Schooled in this doctrine since birth, Oliver naturally assumes, when presented with additional rations prior to being apprenticed, that the workhouse board are 'fatten[ing] him up' for consumption (63). His instincts are not far off the mark, for, as Ledger suggests, almost all of the individuals and institutions that feed Oliver during the course of the novel do so with a view to feeding *off* him: they invest in his appetite 'with an eye to the kind of return they might get' (2007, 97). Chief amongst these calculated provisioners are Fagin and his gang of thieves, who use food to lure Oliver into their criminal world. On the road to London the Artful Dodger treats Oliver to 'a long and hearty meal' of beer, bread and ham (101), while, on arrival in the capital, the demonized Jew Fagin furnishes his new recruit with a (presumably non-kosher) supper of sausages, in a twisted parody of nourishing maternal care (105).

That Oliver is better nourished by his felonious friends than he is by the Parish is a crucial tenet of Dickens's social critique; denied a proper quotient of food in the workhouse, in the thieves' kitchen Oliver is allowed to '[eat] his share' (106). Indeed, the sharing of food forms an important part of the criminals' code. When Bill Sikes is taken ill following the bungled Chertsey burglary, Fagin, the Artful Dodger and Charley Bates (in perverted imitation of middle-class philanthropic

visiting) bring him a food-parcel, the contents of which are itemized with gusto by
Charley:

> Sitch a rabbit pie, Bill . . . sitch delicate creeturs, with sitch tender limbs, Bill,
> that the wery bones melt in your mouth, and there's no occasion to pick 'em;
> half a pound of seven and sixpenny green, so precious strong that if you mix
> it with biling water, it'll go nigh to blow the lid of the tea-pot off; a pound
> and a-half of moist sugar that the niggers didn't work at all at, afore they got
> it up to sitch a pitch of goodness, – oh no! Two half-quartern brans; pound
> of best fresh; piece of double Glo'ster; and, to wind up all, some of the richest
> sort you ever lushed!
>
> *(347–349)*

Unlike the unsolicited spiritual sustenance that the self-righteous do-gooder Mrs
Pardiggle mechanically distributes to the impoverished brick-makers in *Bleak House*
(1852–1853), Fagin's material gift of food is most welcome and helps to soothe Bill's
cantankerous temper. Yet, as Simon Edwards notes, the positive commensality of the
thieves' meal is supplemented by a typically Dickensian 'vein of violence and cruelty':
'the promise of immediate and complete gratification from the "very bones" of the
anthropoid rabbits complements and contrasts with the slave labor that produces
the sugar' (1990, 62). The text's passing allusion to slavery also introduces questions
around culinary origins and access; we might assume that, unlike the plantation slaves
who work to produce food that they don't consume, the thieves here consume food
for which they have not worked. Interestingly, though, Fagin repositions his gang as
useful participants in the Victorian economy when he insists that they have 'spent all
[their] money' (347) on the contents of Bill's food-parcel (just as, in an earlier chapter,
the Artful Dodger *buys* rather than steals a meal for Oliver). In the voracious world
of *Oliver Twist* it seems that 'even ill-gotten gains from criminal activity are somehow
retrievable to the extent that they can be reinvested into a consumption economy',
as Ledger astutely notes (2007, 97).

While deploring the dietary injustices inherent in Victorian consumer society,
where moral worth is no guarantee of alimentary fulfilment, Dickens's fiction also
betrays a fascination with food *qua* commodity in capitalist culture. In the semi-
autobiographical *David Copperfield* (1849–1850), the eponymous young hero is
enthralled by the confected offerings of the local pastry-cook's and pudding-shop
and, when his juvenile finances have run out, sates himself visually on the produce
of a venison-shop in Fleet Street and the exotic pineapples on display in Covent
Garden (1997, 156). Elsewhere, the narrator of *A Christmas Carol* slips into raptures
over the abundant edibles displayed in grocers' windows on Christmas Eve,
rhapsodizing about the 'pot-bellied baskets of chestnuts . . . tumbling out into the
street in their apoplectic opulence'; the 'pears and apples, clustered high in blooming
pyramids'; the 'bunches of grapes' dangling from 'conspicuous hooks, that people's
mouths might water gratis as they passed'; and the 'Norfolk Biffins . . . urgently
entreating and beseeching to be carried home in paper bags and eaten after dinner'
(2006, 46). The commercial context here transforms the goods described from

simple items of sustenance into commodities, self-advertising articles of desire whose visual arrangement coerces consumers into misrecognizing them as objects of exigent need.[4] However, the longing elicited by Dickens's delectable cornucopia also has the potential to segue into nausea. Along with the 'raisins . . . so plentiful and rare', 'almonds so extremely white' and 'sticks of cinnamon so long and straight' listed by the *Carol*'s narrator are 'candied fruits so caked and spotted with molten sugar as to make the coldest lookers-on feel faint and subsequently bilious' (47). The queasiness evoked here is ostensibly the result of optical and imaginatory surfeit, but Dickens also hints at the possibility that the grocers' exceptional comestibles (*so* plentiful, *so* rare) may in fact be too good to be true. Although, as the earlier chapters in this book show, the problem of food adulteration had existed for centuries, the industrialized, capitalistic society of the mid-nineteenth century 'created unprecedented prospects' for the perpetration of large-scale marketplace deceptions, as Rebecca Stern suggests (2003, 483). Following an investigation taken in conjunction with the medical journal *The Lancet*, Victorian chemist Arthur Hill Hassall proved that adulterants 'possessing highly deleterious and even in some cases poisonous properties' were frequently added to foodstuffs for aesthetic effect, with confectionery, of the kind depicted in *A Christmas Carol*, a particular target for fraudsters (1855, iii). Indeed, Dickens's weekly magazine *Household Words* warned in an article entitled 'Death in the Sugar Plum' that, although 'captivating to the eye' and 'tempting to the taste', sugary sweetmeats such as the *Carol*'s candied fruits could in fact represent 'rank poison', a 'deadly evil' responsible for the deaths of 'hundreds per annum' ([Wills] 1851, 426).

Within Dickens's works, the cherished middle-class domestic space offers a putative safe-haven from such unsavoury commercial perils. Chris Vanden Bossche observes that the 'idyllic portrayal of the home' in Dickensian fiction 'implies the concept of unalienated labor', unsullied by market economics (1986, 103). Inevitably, this household labour is gendered as feminine. As Houston notes, in Dickens's novels 'the mythic figure of the self-denying, always nourishing, seemingly never hungry, domestic female' is deployed 'to counter the debilitating effects on men of industrialization and the voracious nature of the marketplace' (1994, 155). The exemplary character of Ruth Pinch in *Martin Chuzzlewit* (1843–1844), for instance, glories in the 'elevated responsibilities' of keeping house for her brother Tom (a journeyman architect) and takes particular pleasure in making dishes to gratify his palate (1984, 513). Her culinary efforts are, in turn, a source of delight to the narrator, who records in fetishistic detail the exertions that go into the construction of a beef-steak pudding:

> It was a perfect treat . . . to see her with her brows knit, and her rosy lips pursed up, kneading away at the crust, rolling it out, cutting it up into strips, lining the basin with it, shaving it off fine round the rim; chopping up the steak into small pieces, raining down pepper and salt upon them, packing them into the basin, [and] pouring in cold water for gravy.

517

The concatenation of active participles here blazons the narrator's cathexic investment in female culinary labour. Revealingly, Ruth's baking skills are ultimately rewarded with a happy marriage to John Westlock, who joins with Tom in declaring her cookery an 'unalloyed' success (527). Her gastronomic competence is also the subject of intertextual endorsement: notably, among the recipes in Eliza Acton's *Modern Cookery in All Its Branches* is one for 'Ruth Pinch's Beef-Steak Pudding' (1845, 369), an allusion that implicitly positions Ruth as the consummate model of domestic competence for Acton's middle-class female readers.

The notion that home-cooking, of the kind practised by Ruth, might secure domestic happiness underpins many nineteenth-century recipe books, including *What Shall We Have for Dinner?* (1852) by Dickens's wife Catherine, published under the alias 'Lady Maria Clutterbuck'. In an introduction commonly attributed to Charles himself (see Rossi-Wilcox 2005, 81–82), 'Lady Maria' proudly recalls that her attentions to the requirements of her late husband's appetite brought her 'many hours of connubial happiness' and 'the possession of his esteem until the last', though she is aware that 'others are not so happy in their domestic relations':

> their daily life is embittered by the consciousness that a delicacy forgotten or misapplied; a surplusage of cold mutton or a redundancy of chops; are gradually making the Club more attractive than the Home, and rendering 'business in the city' of more frequent occurrence than it used to be.
>
> *'Clutterbuck' 2005, 23–24*

Implicit in this observation is the understanding that the housewife's role is to fortify the domestic space against the external world of commerce and industry by supplying her husband with delicious home-cooked dinners.[5] This ideology also permeates Dickens's fiction, enjoying particular traction not only in *Martin Chuzzlewit*, as we have seen, but also in *David Copperfield* and *Our Mutual Friend*, where two decorative but domestically ineffectual young heroines – Dora Spenlow and Bella Wilfer – attempt to fashion themselves into capable wives by consulting cookery books, with varying degrees of success.

In *David Copperfield*, Dora fails to engage properly with the instruction contained in the cookery book purchased for her by David, her fiancé, instead allowing her dog Jip to use the tome as a play-thing. Her lack of domestic knowledge means that, following the couple's marriage, she is incapable of protecting their home from the invasion of marketplace frauds: she is sold lobsters that are 'full of water' (1997, 623) and joints of mutton that are 'deformed' (625), and is serially overcharged for every-day items such as butter and pepper (624). She and David are also plagued by various culinary disasters: joints of meat that never 'hit any medium between redness and cinders' (624), oysters that cannot be opened (626), and condiments that bear the footprints of the irrepressible Jip, who is permitted to 'walk about the table-cloth during dinner' (625). As Houston notes, Dora's 'inability to emotionally' – or, we might add, materially – 'nourish' David 'effectually ends her life' (1994, 115). Her 'want of system and management' (673) is incompatible with the maturation and growth required by the *Bildungsroman* genre and she is therefore killed off, enabling David to marry the angelic Agnes Wickfield, who from the first has been idealized as a perfect 'little housekeeper' (217).

Like Dora, Bella in *Our Mutual Friend* (1864–1865) is at first figured as an ornamental, rather than a practical, woman; tellingly, her only culinary efforts prior to her marriage result in her parents being served raw fowls for their anniversary dinner (1971, 514).[6] She also, like Dora, initially finds the didactic guidance in her cookery book – *The Complete British Family Housewife* – as perplexing as if it had been written in a foreign tongue. Unlike Dora, however, Bella perseveres with her task of self-improvement, overcoming her feelings of exasperation with the *Housewife*'s impenetrable culinary instructions and eventually cultivating 'a perfect genius for home' (748). Her gastronomic endeavours (like those of Ruth Pinch) are recompensed by the love of an affectionate husband, John, who, we are told, deems her 'a most precious and sweet commodity' (750). Yet, while intimating John's uxorious regard, this metaphoric attestation to the value of Bella's newly developed domestic skills also problematically undermines Dickens's vaunted sacralization of the home. The adjective 'sweet' aligns Bella with the food she produces, rendering her passively consumable, a move that has troubling implications in light of Houston's argument that, at the end of the novel, Bella simply disappears from the narrative, as though cannibalistically assimilated into her husband's person (1994, 181). The designation 'commodity', meanwhile, admits marketplace economics into the couple's supposedly insulated domestic idyll, demonstrating Vanden Bossche's point that beneath the textual 'opposition of home and commercial world lies their basic identity' (1986, 102–103). Just as images of hunger and violence invariably haunt representations of commensal feasting in Dickens's work, it seems that the spiritually nourishing depictions of blissful domestic economy that interleave his fiction are habitually shadowed by the consumer culture that is purportedly their repudiated 'other'.

William Makepeace Thackeray, *Vanity Fair* (1847–1848)

As Thackeray acknowledges in the preface to *Vanity Fair*, 'there is a great quantity of eating and drinking' to be found in the bustling Regency world of his novel (1968, 33). One of the most capacious feeders within its pageant of consumption is Jos Sedley, the wealthy Nabob and aspiring dandy, who is variously described as a 'stout, puffy man' (55), 'a *bon-vivant*' (59) and a 'fat *gourmand*' (93). In common with earlier literary gluttons, such as Falstaff and Lazarello (see Chapter 2), Jos is motivated primarily by the satisfaction of his immense appetite. On a visit to Vauxhall Pleasure Gardens, he is so preoccupied with '[making] the salad', 'uncork[ing] the Champagne', 'carv[ing] the chicken' and eating and drinking 'the greater part of the refreshments' on offer (including an entire bowl of rack punch) that he neglects to make his planned proposal of marriage to Becky Sharp, the novel's ambitious anti-heroine (92). Later on, while stationed in Brussels on the eve of the Battle of Waterloo, Jos shows more concern for his appetite than for the historic events unfolding before him. As the narrator wryly observes, 'the dinner-hour' was an event 'of daily importance to Mr Joseph': 'Warriors may fight and perish, but he must dine' (368).

Whereas the medieval and early modern texts explored in Chapters 1 and 2 of this study tend to focus primarily on the sinful connotations of gluttony, *Vanity Fair*'s interest in overeating is more medically and aesthetically oriented. Jos's compulsive habit of 'gobbling' (a word used frequently to describe his voracious mode of consumption) has damaging implications for both his body-image and his digestive health. The narrator explains that 'his bulk caused Joseph much anxious thought and alarm', and 'now and then he would make a desperate attempt to get rid of his superabundant fat'; however, 'his indolence and love of good living speedily got the better of these endeavours at reform', and so he soon 'found himself again at his three meals a day' (59). Jos's intermittent attempts at dieting indicate a consciousness of the increasingly negative valence surrounding corpulence in the nineteenth century. As Joyce Huff observes, 'body fat was interpreted as the residue of aberrant acts of consumption' and thus 'served to stigmatize a body if it appeared in places or amounts considered anomalous' (2001, 51, 50). In a study published two years after *Vanity Fair*, Dr Thomas Chambers characterized fatness as a 'disease in the human subject' (1850, 39), while in his 1863 *Letter on Corpulence* Victorian dieter William Banting demonized obesity as a 'parasite' and noted that 'any one so afflicted' was liable to be 'often subject to public remark' (1864, 22, 13). Certainly, Jos's weight serves to demarcate him visibly from the norm, transforming him into a spectacle of unbridled appetite. At Vauxhall the crowd gives an ironic 'cheer for the fat gentleman' (90) as he emerges majestically from his carriage, while, following his virtuoso feats of ingestion at supper, one wag compares him to Daniel Lambert, the legendary 'fat man' who exhibited his fifty-stone frame in early nineteenth-century London and whose name became a byword for corpulence in Victorian literature (93).[7]

If Jos's uninhibited consumption results in the 'grotesque distortion' of his exterior form, as Christoph Lindner suggests (2002, 576), then it also adversely affects his inner bodily workings. He claims to suffer from a persistent liver complaint (presumably some form of steatosis, the result of gluttony), for which he regularly takes blue pills (mercury-based purgatives). Pathologizing his overindulgence by this means, Jos participates in the nineteenth century's anxious fascination with the process of digestion – a fascination that manifests itself in the reams of articles and pamphlets on gastro-enteric complaints and advertisements for peptic powders, laxatives and cathartics found in Victorian print culture. An 1845 article on 'Dyspepsia' in *Chambers's Edinburgh Journal* suggested that the vagaries of the stomach exercised an 'immense influence' over Victorian Britain (Anon. 1845, 11), while the satirical tract *Memoirs of a Stomach* (a kind of comic descendant of the early modern dietaries discussed in Chapter 2) attributed 'the larger portion of the ills' of nineteenth-century life to 'errors in diet' ([Whiting] 1853, 126). Narrated by a disgruntled stomach, the text records the various abuses to which the human gut is typically exposed: repeated bouts of overindulgence, followed by doses of physic which prove 'worse than useless' (46). According to the stomach, 'all I required was light diet' (47); unfortunately, though, its master presumes that 'the penalty of taking medicine' absolves him from 'the necessity of a strict regimen', with the result that the stomach grows 'rather worse than better' (49–50). A similarly disingenuous dietary policy is followed by Thackeray's Jos. The narrator sarcastically notes that, 'being an invalid', Jos 'contented himself with a bottle of claret besides his Madeira at dinner', as well as 'a couple of plates full of strawberries and cream, and twenty-four little rout cakes' (62) – a saccharine and saturate-rich collation more likely to exacerbate than ameliorate his digestive maladies.

Despite Jos's much-touted pretensions to refinement and claims of delicate health, he in many respects resembles that stout, hale and hearty emblem of Britishness, John Bull. On a number of occasions, Jos is associated with Bull-esque beef-eating: in Belgium, he fantasizes about 'good streaky beef, really mingled with fat and lean', for which, he contends, there is 'no country like England' (327), and, after docking at Southampton later in the novel, he is invigorated by the sight of 'a magnificent round of beef' at the Royal George Hotel (670). The security of Jos's Englishness is endangered, however, by his immoderate appetites, which tacitly align him with the native population he has lived amongst in India, a land that was presumed by Victorian imperialist ideology to welcome 'unchecked desires' (Cozzi 2010, 112). As Parama Roy suggests, colonized peoples 'were irreducibly somaticized' by Western discourse, 'incarnated in bodies whose appetites, expressions, and comings and goings' were assumed to require rigorous fashioning by their European rulers (2010, 7). Isabella Beeton's famous *Book of Household Management* (1861), for instance, sets out the differences between 'eating' and 'dining' in conspicuously racialized terms, positing that 'some races of men do not dine any more than the tiger or the vulture' (2000, 363). 'Dining' is deemed to be the exclusive 'privilege of civilization'; implicitly, only the inhabitants of Western cultures possess 'the will and the skill to reduce to order . . . the more material conditions of human existence', such as eating and drinking (Beeton 2000, 363). Jos's corpulence (visual signifier of *his* inability to reduce appetite to order) thus serves to orientalize him in Thackeray's novel, destabilizing and rendering ambiguous his English national identity.

Anxieties regarding transculturation are amplified in *Vanity Fair* by Jos's much-emphasized taste for Indian cuisine. On returning to England from Bengal, Jos brings with him 'chests of mangoes, chutney, and currie-powders' (685), as well as a 'native' servant, Loll Jewab, whose task it is to teach his European counterpart the 'art of preparing curries, pilaus, and pipes' (688). This importation of Indian culinary culture demonstrates Nupur Chaudhuri's point that the effects of nineteenth-century imperialism were both 'centripetal' and 'centrifugal' (1992, 231). Like many East India Company employees in the early nineteenth century, Jos has fully assimilated the tastes and traditions of India into his own diet. On his return to England, he admits to having developed a preference for the goats' milk customarily used by Bengalis in place of cream (62), talks of 'tiffin' instead of lunch (75) and, with the air of a connoisseur, assesses the authenticity of his mother's attempts at curry ('perhaps there was *not* enough citron juice in it – no, there was *not*' [64]). As Helen Pike Bauer suggests, 'by appropriating indigenous food' in this way,

'Anglo-Indians could assert their power' over the colonial sphere; however, in doing so, they also risked 'being consumed by the culture they had come to rule' (2007, 104), a danger that assumed greater significance following the events of the contentiously titled 'Indian Mutiny' of 1857. After this point, Anglo-Indians tended to adopt a stricter policy of dietary ethnocentrism, eschewing 'tactile, oral, and olfactory contact' with Indian produce and endeavouring instead to 'procure and serve European foodstuffs' wherever possible (Roy 2010, 60).[8] *Vanity Fair* to some extent anticipates this ontological and epistemological shift, articulating concerns regarding colonial incorporation and intimating the potentially transformative effects of foreign food on the British self. In a series of zoomorphic references, the curry-loving Jos is insistently conflated with an animal connoting Indian-ness: the elephant.[9] In the build-up to the Battle of Waterloo, Jos's brother-in-law, George, quips that, 'as there is one well-known regiment of the army which travels with a goat heading the column', so 'his regiment marched with an elephant' (326). A portrait of Jos hunting tigers on elephant-back, bought by Becky for a knock-down price at the Sedleys' house-sale, works similarly to 'associat[e] the lumbering beast with its loafing human burden', as Lindner suggests (2002, 576). Indeed, so insistent is this cross-species identification that, when the narrator later refers to 'Becky [taking] down her elephant', it is unclear whether the designation refers to the animal or the rider in the picture (787). According to *Vanity Fair*'s alimentary logic, it seems that ingesting the food of the Other, or 'going native', has the potential to compromise not only one's national but also one's *human* identity (a concern that earlier emerged in Swift's *Gulliver's Travels* in Chapter 3).

If colonial proximity necessitated a strategy of culinary segregation, then, Uma Narayan suggests, for many Victorians the domestic space offered a comparatively safe environment in which to sample Indian fare, for at 'home' the British did not have to work so assiduously 'at distinguishing themselves from their colonial subjects' (1997, 166). In *Vanity Fair*, however, the ingestion of Indian cuisine has debilitating somatic consequences, regardless of location. While staying with the Sedleys in London, Becky (as part of her plan to snare Jos) expresses an interest in trying some of the curry that Mrs Sedley has prepared for her son:

> Rebecca had never tasted the dish before.
> 'Do you find it as good as everything else from India?' said Mr Sedley.
> 'Oh, excellent!' said Rebecca, who was suffering tortures with the cayenne pepper.
> 'Try a chili with it, Miss Sharp,' said Joseph, really interested.
> 'A chili,' said Rebecca, gasping. 'O yes!' She thought a chili was something cool, as its name imported, and was served with some. 'How fresh and green they look!' she said, and put one into her mouth. It was hotter than the curry; flesh and blood could bear it no longer. She laid down her fork. 'Water, for Heaven's sake, water!' she cried.

61

Unable to digest the exotic food of the empire in its unadulterated form, Becky quickly attempts to reconstitute her oriental culinary experience in more familiar – and palatable – narrative terms, noting good-humouredly, 'I ought to have remembered the pepper which the Princess of Persia puts in the cream-tarts in the *Arabian Nights*' (61). Nevertheless, the idea that Indian cuisine has incapacitating effects on the fragile British constitution remains strong in Thackeray's novel: mirroring Becky's unfortunate encounter with the chilli, Jos's nephew Georgy later 'half-kill[s] himself' with eating 'preserves and pickles' sent by Major Dobbin from Madras, because 'they were so hot' (464).

Although Becky is unable to assimilate wholly the food of the Other, she does eventually succeed in (metaphorically) devouring Jos, who makes her the beneficiary of a hefty life-insurance policy shortly before his highly suspicious death. From the very beginnings of the novel, Jos's father has predicted his son 'is destined to be a prey to woman' (67); however, as Susan Zlotnick suggests, 'Sedley's parental anxieties' (which centre on the prospect of Jos being 'reeled in' by a 'black daughter-in-law') prove, in the event, to be 'inappropriately focused' (2003, 77). Jos is ensnared and consumed not by an Indian woman, as Mr Sedley fears, but by the predacious Becky, whom the narrator compares to the mythological man-eaters the sirens: 'fiendish marine cannibals, revelling and feasting on their wretched pickled victims' (738). Reversing the cannibalism trope that was so often used to provide narrative justification for British imperialism, Thackeray thus closes his novel with the suggestion that the real threats to English masculinity and national security reside not in India but at home, in the guise of the voraciously acquisitive and socially ambitious female consumer, epitomized by Becky Sharp.

Anne Brontë, *The Tenant of Wildfell Hall* (1848); Charlotte Brontë, *Jane Eyre* (1847) and *Shirley* (1849); Emily Brontë, *Wuthering Heights* (1847)

Written during the decade that would come to be known as the 'hungry forties', the novels of Anne, Charlotte and Emily Brontë are, perhaps unsurprisingly, brimming with references to famishment, both literal and metaphorical. This thematic preoccupation was noted by some of their earliest readers: Matthew Arnold suggested that Charlotte Brontë's mind contained 'nothing but hunger, rebellion and rage' (1974, 201), while, in a review of *Jane Eyre*, Elizabeth Rigby contested that the attitudes evident in the novel were comparable with those that had 'fostered Chartism' (1974, 110), a movement keenly associated with 'knife-and-fork' questions in the early Victorian consciousness.[10] As avid consumers of contemporary newspapers and periodicals, the Brontës can hardly have been unaware of the political urgency of hunger in the 1840s; publications to which they had regular access, such as the *Leeds Intelligencer*, *Leeds Mercury* and *John Bull*, frequently carried stories about the deprivation that prevailed in Britain's northern manufacturing towns. Nor can the sisters have been ignorant of the harrowing reports of famine in Ireland (birthplace of their father, Patrick) that supplemented media accounts of domestic distress following the failure of the potato crop in 1845. Yet, unlike their contemporary Elizabeth Gaskell, whose *Mary Barton* (1848) is set amongst starving Manchester mill-workers, the Brontës rarely evoke the hungers of the English working classes or Irish Famine victims in direct form. Instead, their fiction tends to deal with the matter of Victorian hunger obliquely, displacing it temporally (each of the novels considered here is set in the late eighteenth or early nineteenth century) and refocalizing it, often through the disordered eating practices of middle- and upper-class men and women.

Charlotte Brontë's *Shirley*, for instance, relocates the political protests of the 1840s to the Luddite disturbances of the 1810s, but largely obscures the starving proletarian body. As Terry Eagleton observes, the unemployed mill-workers whose agitations ostensibly underpin the action of the novel are 'distinguished primarily by [their] absence' (1975, 47). Their sufferings are typically expressed in depersonalized terms: the narrator refers abstractedly to 'the famished and furious mass of the Operative Class' (Brontë 1981, 344), whose destiny it is to '[eat] the bread, and [drink] the waters of affliction' (31). The only representative of this class to be properly individuated is William Farren, whose personal experience of hunger is nevertheless subsumed into the language of collectivity and universal human rights when he tells the mill-owner Robert Moore:

> we're ill off, – varry ill off: wer families is poor and pined. . . . What is to be done? Mun we say, wisht! and lig us down and dee? Nay; I've no grand words at my tongue's end, Mr Moore, but I feel that it wad be a low principle for a reasonable man to starve to death like a dumb cratur'.
>
> *137*

The balanced rhetorical structure and concerted appeal to reason in this speech work to distance and deflect the visceral experience of starvation and, in the absence of more radical vocalizations of working-class hunger, it is left to the children of *Shirley* to articulate the raw immediacy of alimentary need. When Farren returns home to 'such dinner as [his wife] had to give him' – 'porridge, and too little of that' – his children, Oliver Twist-like, affectingly ask for more, having finished off their meagre portions (138–139). Their plaintive demand (which draws silent tears from their father) mirrors the earlier textual moment when six-year-old Abraham Gale 'lifted up his voice and wept sore' for his share of a spice-cake that has been wholly devoured by his mother's locust-like lodger, Mr Donne, and his friends (9). Paralleling the deprivation of the unemployed mill-hands, Abraham's experience of dispossession neatly demonstrates that physical hunger in *Shirley* typically has less to do with food scarcity than with issues of access and entitlement.

Children again function as substitutes for the hungering working classes in *Wuthering Heights* and *Jane Eyre*, where localized patterns of dietary inequity deputize for the wider alimentary injustices of the 'hungry forties'. In *Wuthering Heights,* the young Heathcliff is repeatedly excluded from scenes of consumption owing to his foundling status and 'gipsy' appearance (Brontë 2003, 50). Debarred from the genteel interior of Thrushcross Grange, he can only watch through a window as his playmate and foster-sister Catherine is presented with a tumbler of negus and a plateful of cakes by the refined Linton family; as he bitterly recognizes, 'she was a young lady and they made a distinction between her treatment and mine' (51). He is further expelled from the commensal board at the Heights when the Lintons come to visit; his hostile foster-brother Hindley directs that he be sent 'into the garret till dinner is over', for 'he'll be cramming his fingers in the tarts, and stealing the fruit, if left alone with them a minute' (59). In *Jane Eyre*, the ten-year-old orphan Jane is similarly 'excluded' from festivities such as the Reed family's Christmas at Gateshead (Brontë 1996b, 36).[11] While she hungers, her 'stout' cousin John Reed 'gorge[s] himself habitually at table' and questions, in Malthusian style, her right to any kind of sustenance: 'you are a dependent, mamma says; you have no money; your father left you none; you ought to beg, and not to live here with gentleman's children like us, and eat the same meals we do' (16, 17). As Linda Schlossberg points out, by means of this reference to Jane as a childhood parasite, whose 'redundant' but 'growing body threatens to take resources away from other hungry mouths', Brontë's novel dramatizes the anxieties regarding population and food supply that shaped much political policy towards the lower classes in the 1840s (2001, 497).

In their angry responses to deprivation, Jane and Heathcliff further align themselves with the Victorian proletariat, who were often stereotyped in popular discourse in terms of animal hunger and rage. After rebelling against her Aunt Reed's uncaring treatment, Jane admits, 'something of vengeance I had tasted for the first time; as aromatic wine it seemed, on swallowing, warm and racy' (47). The young Heathcliff is similarly sustained by thoughts and acts of vengeance: he retaliates against Edgar Linton's snobbery by hurling 'a tureen of hot apple-sauce' at his face (2003, 59) and fantasizes about painting the front of the Heights with his oppressor Hindley's blood (49). His violent inclinations only intensify as he matures; at one point, he states that he would have 'torn [Edgar's] heart out, and drank [*sic*] his blood', had it not been for Catherine's regard (148), while on another occasion, we are told, his 'mouth watered to tear [Hindley] with his teeth' (181). As Matthew Beaumont notes, these anthropophagic tendencies have symbolic resonances, placing Heathcliff on a metaphoric continuum with the English working classes, who were often 'abominated in terms of the image of the cannibal in mid-Victorian Britain' (2004, 150).[12]

Heathcliff's vengeful appetites also affiliate him with the Irish, who had been popularly associated with starvation-cannibalism since the sixteenth century (see the section on Spenser in Chapter 2) and were frequently stereotyped in English print culture as savages with 'a spirit of revenge, not to be satiated except by blood' (qtd. in Michie 1992, 131). For Eagleton, indeed, 'Heathcliff is a fragment of the Famine' (1995, 11): a ferocious, primitive force, who both devours and is himself devoured by his monomaniacal desire for retribution. Certainly, during the period of (involuntary or deliberate) aphagia that portends his death, Heathcliff comes to resemble the skeletal Famine victims described in the British press.[13] His housekeeper Nelly compares him to 'a person starving with hunger' (333), registering his 'bloodless hue' and 'shivering' frame (328), 'ghastly paleness' (329) and 'hollow' cheeks (333). These kinds of gothicized tropes also emerge in *Jane Eyre* following Jane's flight from Thornfield. Having discovered the pining heroine on their doorstep, the Rivers family observe how 'very thin, and how very bloodless' she is, before labelling her 'a mere spectre!' (1996b, 377). The privations that Jane undergoes at Lowood School are similarly coded in terms of Irish hunger. The 'nauseous mess' of 'burnt porridge' that the ravenous girl receives for her first breakfast is, tellingly, compared to 'rotten potatoes', a meal that Jane suggests would sicken 'famine itself' (56). Such references to potatoes and hunger are by no means accidental, Schlossberg suggests; rather, they serve subtly to connect 'the suffering of England's so-called charity children and the condition of the rural Irish', gesturing towards the existence of 'a crisis of "nurturance" on a national scale' (2001, 490).[14]

Yet Charlotte Brontë's work also indicates the limits to Victorian sympathy for the starving. Despite the periods of hunger experienced by Jane Eyre at Gateshead, Lowood and following her departure from Thornfield (when desperation reduces her to eating discarded pig-swill [369]), Jane conspicuously fails to identify with the impoverished labouring classes whose sufferings mirror her own. Her childhood conviction that she 'should not like to belong to poor people', whom she associates with 'ragged clothes, scanty food' and 'rude manners' (32), persists into adulthood; while teaching peasant children at Morton, she expresses 'disgust' at the 'coarseness' of the poverty around her (402). In *Shirley*, too, the eponymous heroine's sympathy for the hungry is carefully qualified. Although Shirley disdains the 'vain philosophy' underpinning the ruling classes' attitude to the poor – 'for those who are not hungry, it is easy to palaver about the degradation of charity' (267) – her benevolence is motivated, in essence, by a reactionary fear of working-class unrest, for, as William Farren notes, 'starving folk cannot be satisfied or settled folk' (325). Should her tranquilizing measures fail, the heiress declares, her pity would evaporate and she would mutate from munificent nurturer to man-eater: 'if . . . my property is attacked, I shall defend it like a tigress' (267). The bounds to Shirley's empathy for the poor are further signified by her wasteful domestic management – at a meeting with her cook, she fails to 'retrench' even 'a single pound of butter' from her household expenditure (265) – and her provision of an incongruously 'recherché supper' for the community leaders who meet at her home to discuss relief for the hungry (273). Her delight at having gratified the palates of these guests with 'choice wines' and 'scientific dishes' (275) sits uncomfortably alongside the previously disclosed information that 'there are some families almost starving to death in Briarfield' (266).

The tempered sympathy for working-class malnourishment in the Brontës' fiction is countered by an acute textual awareness of the figurative forms of starvation endured by Victorian middle-class women (an awareness that earlier emerged in Jane Austen's novels in Chapter 4). Constrained by the cultural roles scripted for them and divested of emotional and/or intellectual sustenance, female characters such as *Shirley*'s Caroline Helstone and *Wuthering Heights*'s Catherine Earnshaw 'internalize' their privation 'as self-starvation', transforming metaphorical famishment into material hunger (Lashgari 1992, 141). Caroline's diminished appetites (like those of the anorectics diagnosed by physician Charles Lasègue in the 1870s) stem initially from romantic disappointment.[15] Her adored cousin Robert Moore cynically rescinds his affections for her during a period of economic crisis at his mill and instead courts her financially independent friend, Shirley. Bound by the conventions of Victorian propriety, Caroline cannot verbalize her subsequent distress, as the narrator makes clear in a sadistic image of ingestion:

> You expected bread, and you have got a stone; break your teeth on it, and don't shriek because the nerves are martyrized: do not doubt that your mental stomach – if you have such a thing – is strong as an ostrich's – the stone will digest.
>
> *105*

Heartache is again conceptualized in alimentary terms when Caroline is figured as 'a bystander at the banquet' (252); 'having no pleasant food to nourish [her mind] – no manna of hope', she must subsist instead 'on the meagre diet of wishes' (350). Her 'famished heart' (252) is soon reduplicated in her attenuated frame: her once 'girlish, light, and pliant' (75) figure begins to fall away (176, rpt. 253); her 'bloom . . . vanish[es]' and her 'flesh waste[s]' (189), as she 'eat[s] nothing' (242). Caroline's food-refusing behaviour only intensifies after she overhears her cousins speculating about Robert's relationship to Shirley; during the aetiologically ambiguous illness that follows, 'palatable food was as ashes and sawdust to her' (421) and she maintains that she 'cannot eat' (423).

It is not simply romantic disappointment that motivates Caroline's seemingly masochistic abjuration of food, however. Brontë makes clear that her heroine is also starved of purpose in a world that directs her to 'stick to' domestic pursuits such as needlework and 'pie-crust-making' (98). Longing for some occupation, Caroline extemporizes, in an extended interior monologue, on the current 'stagnant state of things' – a state that inexorably causes women to 'decline in health' (391). Her 'rejection of what her society has defined as nourishing' leads Sandra Gilbert and Susan Gubar to argue, in their classic account, that her self-starvation should be interpreted as a form of 'hunger strike', 'a kind of protest' against a dysfunctional social order (1979, 391). For Anna Krugovoy Silver, however, casting Caroline's anorexia 'as conscious rebellion exaggerates her subversiveness by conflating disease with social protest'; crucially, Silver notes, 'Caroline does not *set out* to starve herself in order to make a political point' (2002, 90, 91). The problem of how to read representations of female food refusal extends across the literary history considered in this volume: religious fasts, of the type undertaken by medieval women such as Margery Kempe (Chapter 1), are clearly motivated primarily by Christian piety, yet for some critics they can also be understood in terms of a more secular desire to take control of the body. More recently, scholars have debated whether it is legitimate to interpret Marian MacAlpin's food refusal in *The Edible Woman* as a form of anorexia (see Chapter 6). Critical disparity likewise emerges in analyses of Catherine Earnshaw's brief but intense bout of food refusal in *Wuthering Heights*. In Chapter 12 of the novel, Catherine shuts herself in her room and 'fast[s] pertinaciously' for three days (120) in order to punish her husband for demanding that she give up her friendship with Heathcliff, in an act that has generated conflicting readings. Whereas Susan Rubinow Gorsky claims (following Gilbert and Gubar) that this self-starvation 'resonates with metaphors of anorexia' – 'when [Catherine] cannot "stomach" her life or "swallow" the demands a relationship entails, her stomach rebels and she stops swallowing food as well' (1999, 180) – Dennis Bloomfield suggests that there is 'no medical support' for such a reading (2011, 295), and Beth Torgerson argues that Catherine's three-day abstention is 'hardly time enough to develop into the chronic life-threatening disease we know as "anorexia"' (2005, 156n1).

Although the precise nature of, and nomenclature for, Caroline and Catherine's food refusal may be critically contested, some kind of consensus coalesces around the idea that the culture in which the Brontës were writing idealized proto-anorexic behaviours such as female abstemiousness and self-denial. This insidious 'anorexic logic', to use Silver's term (2002, 3), is energetically excoriated by Rose Markham in Anne Brontë's *The Tenant of Wildfell Hall*. On being instructed by her mother (a model of self-sacrificing femininity, whose main pleasure is to cater to the appetites of others) to make some fresh tea for her brother Gilbert, who has returned home late, Rose rails against the gendered codes of consumption at work in the Markham household:

> Well! – if it had been *me* now, I should have had no tea at all . . . It's always so – if there's anything particularly nice at table, Mamma winks and nods at me, to abstain from it, and if I don't attend to that, she whispers, 'Don't eat so much of that, Rose, Gilbert will like it for his supper' – *I'm* nothing at all . . . In the kitchen [it's] – 'Make that pie a large one, Rose, I dare say the boys'll be hungry; – and don't put so much pepper in, they'll not like it I'm sure' – or, 'Rose, don't put so many spices in the pudding, Gilbert likes it plain' . . . If I say, 'Well Mamma, *I* don't', I'm told I ought not to think of myself – 'You know Rose, in all household matters, we have only two things to consider, first, what's proper to be done, and secondly, what's most agreeable to the gentlemen of the house – anything will do for the ladies'.
>
> *Brontë 1996a, 57*

As Rose's diatribe reveals, self-renunciation is sanctioned and normalized amongst the Victorian middle classes as integral to the performance of 'proper' femininity, while appetitive indulgence and the exercise of individual taste are culturally enshrined as male rights.

The damaging consequences of this gendered dietary logic are elucidated not only in the Brontës' representation of food-refusing women, such as Caroline Helstone and Catherine Earnshaw, but also in their representation of disorderly male consumers. In Anne Brontë's *Tenant*, in particular, masculine alimentary excess is figured as both individually and socially damaging. Arthur Huntingdon, the leisured gentleman whose physical and moral decline dominates the narrative, is an epicure who dedicates his existence to the selfish gratification of his appetites. His 'predilection for the pleasures of the table' (265) is accompanied by a debilitating intemperance; his wife, Helen, records that alcohol has become 'something more to him than an accessory to social enjoyment' (260), gradually 'degenerat[ing] his once noble constitution, and vitiat[ing] the whole system of his organization' (432). As with the alcoholic Hindley Earnshaw in *Wuthering Heights*, who drinks himself to death, Huntingdon's dependence eventually proves fatal; after falling from his horse, he sustains injuries that would 'have been but trifling to a man of temperate habits' (423–424), but which are lethally inflamed by his continued 'infatuation' with 'stimulating drink' (440). Unable to follow Helen's advice to fortify himself against temptation, Huntingdon functions in Brontë's novel as a re-gendered Eve: a case study in the perils of insatiable appetite.

Huntingdon's alcoholism forms part of a wider culture of masculine excess in *Tenant*; his coarse and brutal behaviour while inebriated is replicated by that of his debauched circle of friends. By focusing on the sottish habits of the gentry in this way, Brontë's novel enlarges the scope of contemporary debates on the 'drink question', as Torgerson notes (2005, 20), demonstrating that the problem of intoxication was not restricted to the labouring classes whose 'tyrannical drinking usages' were the main targets of early Victorian temperance literature (Anon. 1848, 11). Indeed, it is Huntingdon's gentlemanly status that enables his immoderate alcohol consumption: Helen frets, 'I wish he had something to do, some useful trade, or profession, or employment – anything to occupy his head or his hands for a few hours a day, and give him something besides his own pleasure to think about' (225). The prevailing gender values of his society militate against such sublimation, however. Immersed in a culture that validates the capacious ingestion of alcohol as a positive attribute of manliness, Huntingdon has little incentive to abstain from excessive drinking. Notably, when his friend Lord Lowborough becomes a teetotaller, he is roundly derided for his sobriety, which is seen as incompatible with a proper, manly spirit. Similarly, when Helen reveals that she has done all she can to make her son Arthur detest 'the very sight of wine', Mrs Markham warns that she will render him 'the veriest milksop that ever was sopped' (31) – 'a mere Miss Nancy' (33) – explicitly linking abstention with effeminization.

Helen's controversial determination to prevent Arthur from becoming a 'little toper' (370) stems from her fears regarding his father's contaminating influence and her concomitant lack of faith in masculine alimentary self-restraint ('for . . . five hundred men that have yielded to temptation, show me one that has had virtue to resist' [31–32]). Her defensive stratagems, which include adulterating little Arthur's wine with tartar-emetic – an ironic dramatization of *The Moral Reformer*'s warning that 'the connection of *poison* with intoxication is *direct*' (Anon. 1833, 324) – eventually succeed in giving the boy 'an absolute disgust for all intoxicating liquors' (369). Nevertheless, Brontë's novel implies that the corrupting culture of masculine excess is too socially pervasive to be entirely contained by a maternal cordon. Ominously, many of the injurious alimentary behaviours exhibited by Huntingdon are also enacted by his ostensible foil, *Tenant*'s narrator-hero Gilbert Markham. Both men expect women to cater to their culinary needs: pampered as a child by an indulgent mother, Huntingdon presumes that his wife will perform a similarly facilitative role during his adult years, while Gilbert's culinary preferences take priority in the Markham household, as noted earlier. What is more, Helen's fear that Huntingdon might ultimately 'give himself up to luxury' and 'plunge into the grossest excesses' (284) is echoed in Gilbert's acknowledgement that *he* 'might sink into the grossest condition of self-indulgence' from the 'mere habit of being constantly cared for' and 'having all [his] wants anticipated or immediately supplied' by his doting mother (57–58).

Both Huntingdon and Gilbert are also complicit with what Maggie Berg calls *Tenant*'s 'carno-phallogocentric order' (2010, 21), whereby the privileging of male appetite is accompanied by violent patterns of consumption. Huntingdon, for instance, is figured as predatory via his much-emphasized taste for blood sports. Unlike the hunts represented in Arthurian literature (see Chapter 1), those in *Tenant* are not associated with noble character. Rather, as Gwen Hyman points out, they are configured as exercises in masculine excess: 'nothing more than a mock pursuit of sustenance, a meticulously staged enactment of the stereotypical role of brutal provider . . . played out on estates carefully stocked with the requisite victims' (2009, 67). Portentously, it is during the game season that Huntingdon undertakes his pursuit of Helen: when he walks across the lawn to meet her 'all splattered and splashed' with the blood of his quarry (161), and later airily promises to 'murder' her uncle's 'birds by wholesale' (185), the clear implication is that she will become his next item of prey. Gilbert, too, is fond of hunting (he first perceives Helen while out with his dog and gun) and, like Huntingdon, is complicit in her metaphorical consumption. We are told that he 'devoured' (397) the contents of her private journal, a quasi-cannibalistic action that is reduplicated and literalized in the physical organization of *Tenant*; here, Helen's logistically and hermeneutically central first-person account is suggestively swallowed up by Gilbert's framing narratives.

Significantly, such male alimentary aggression is a common feature of Brontë-authored fictions. While the women in these texts starve or, like Helen, are left to subsist on 'bitter fruits' (399), their male counterparts frequently exhibit 'wolfish' (2003, 103, 138) or 'canine' (1981, 63) appetites; notably, even the 'milk-blooded' Edgar Linton is at one point compared to a cat with a 'half eaten' bird (2003, 115, 73). According to the Brontës, then, the corollary to the pervasive 'anorexic logic' that governs Victorian culture is the widespread corruption and brutalization of male appetites. The cultural script of male dietary indulgence and female self-denial that is learned and internalized by the characters of *Jane Eyre*, *Wuthering Heights*, *The Tenant of Wildfell Hall* and *Shirley* is shown to damage *both* genders, highlighting the moral and structural dysfunctionality of a society that permits some to glut themselves while others (literally or figuratively) starve.

Christina Rossetti, 'Goblin Market' (1862)

Grounded in the familiar literary topos of 'passionate yearning' for 'fruit forbidden' (Rossetti 2008, ll. 266, 479), 'Goblin Market' has often been read as an allegory of the Fall, in which Laura (one of the poem's two sister-protagonists) serves as the typological descendant of Genesis's hungry Eve. Tempted by the preternaturally luscious fruits hawked by an itinerant troop of goblin men, 'Curious Laura' (l. 69) disregards the counsel of her own 'cautioning lips' (l. 38) – 'We must not look at goblin men, / We must not buy their fruits' (ll. 42–43) – and purchases the salesmen's produce with a lock of golden hair. Her punishment for capitulating to physical craving is the 'exceeding pain' of 'baulked desire' (ll. 271, 267); unable to see the goblins or hear their 'customary cry' (l. 231) after gorging herself on their wares, Laura slips into a life-threatening decline and is saved only by the altruistic actions of her more circumspect sister Lizzie, who procures a 'fiery antidote' (l. 559) from the mysterious traders while resisting their sinister attempts to make her eat their merchandise.

Within this poetic 'paradigm of temptation' (Hill 2005, 458), Laura clearly exhibits the self-indulgence that Christina Rossetti associates with Eve in her devotional commentary *The Face of the Deep*. The description of Laura's zealous ingestion of the goblin fruit – 'she sucked and sucked and sucked the more' (l. 134) – resonates intertextually with Eve's unrestrained gorging in Milton's *Paradise Lost* (see Chapter 3), while the punitive longing Laura experiences after tasting the goblin fruit – 'she dreamed of melons, as a traveller sees / False waves in desert drouth / . . . And burns the thirstier in the sandful breeze' (ll. 289–292) – similarly invites comparison with what Rossetti calls the 'sentence' of unsatisfied desire imposed upon her biblical antecedent (1893, 312).[16] Lizzie, by contrast, embodies the 'self-oblation' and 'submission' that Rossetti identifies in the Virgin Mary (1893, 310). Fearful that her sister seems to be 'knocking at Death's door' (l. 321), Lizzie seeks out the goblin men and offers them a silver penny for a take-away portion of their fruits, politely but firmly declining their invitations to sit down and eat with them. Even when the frustrated vendors turn violently against her, 'squeez[ing] their fruits / Against her mouth' (ll. 406–407) and 'pinch[ing] her black as ink' (l. 427), she remains resolute, enduring their assault in the hope that her juice-stained body will provide proxy nourishment for her ailing sister.

Returning home, Lizzie invites Laura to

> Come and kiss me.
> Never mind my bruises,
> Hug me, kiss me, suck my juices
> Squeezed from goblin fruit for you,
> Goblin pulp and goblin dew.
> Eat me, drink me, love me;
> Laura, make much of me.
>
> *(ll. 466–472)*

Laura obeys, 'kiss[ing] and kiss[ing]' Lizzie 'with a hungry mouth' (l. 492), before experiencing what Mary Wilson Carpenter describes as 'a masochistic orgy' (1991, 429). 'Writhing as one possessed' (l. 496), Laura 'gorge[s] on bitterness without a name' (l. 510), before falling into a death-like swoon from which she eventually awakes, restored. The twinning of 'erotic desire and spiritual satisfaction' in this extraordinarily sensually charged passage is of a piece with the 'evocative and eroticized descriptions of the union between God and humans' that Marylu Hill locates in the Tractarian writings that influenced Rossetti's religious faith (2005, 455, 467). Sanctifying the corporeal, Lizzie offers her body to Laura as a regenerative, sacramental meal, her self-sacrifice apparently transforming the once-toxic juices of the goblin fruits into a Eucharistic source of revitalization and renewal. Eating thus both endangers and redeems Laura in the poem, signalling that 'consumption and the desire to consume are not *in themselves* sinful' in 'Goblin Market', as Anna Krugovoy Silver points out (2002, 149). What matters more, for Rossetti, is the mode or manner of consumption: whereas non-spiritual self-indulgence is shown to corrupt, 'Eucharistic ecstasy heals' (Silver 2002, 151).

While inviting such religiously inflected readings on the one hand, 'Goblin Market' also licenses more secular interpretations on the other. During the past twenty years, a wealth of criticism has sought to 'put the *market* back in "Goblin Market"' (Tucker 2003, 117), identifying in its narrative of buying and selling 'salient critical commentary about the deceptions and seductions of the capitalist marketplace' (Stern 2003, 477). Significantly, the poem suggests that, prior to their dealings with the goblins, Laura and Lizzie have occupied a self-sufficient pastoral idyll (similar to that conjured by Matthew Bramble in *Humphry Clinker* in Chapter 4), their lives apparently removed from commercial concerns:

> Neat like bees, as sweet and busy,
> Laura rose with Lizzie:
> Fetched in honey, milked the cows,
> Aired and set to rights the house,
> Kneaded cakes of whitest wheat,
> Cakes for dainty mouths to eat,
> Next churned butter, whipped up cream,
> Fed their poultry, sat and sewed.
> *(ll. 201–208)*

The sisters are portrayed here living autonomously off the land, producing 'with their own labor the food that sustains them', as Terrence Holt suggests, and 'enacting on an economic level the hermeticism of their domestic scene' (1990, 53). The poem's tentative segregation of home and marketplace cannot hold, however. After 'sweet-tooth Laura' (l. 115) succumbs to the goblins' 'sugar-baited' sales-pitch (l. 234), the sisters' self-reliant domesticity breaks down; instead of baking cakes and fetching honey (a natural product, which contrasts with the refined saccharinity of the goblins' words), Laura idles listlessly around the house and refuses to eat, substituting morbid dreams of commodified produce for healthy, solid nutriment.[17]

The market's insidious infiltration of the domestic sphere is further signalled by Laura's shifting discourse. When she arrives home after tasting the goblin fruits, she begins conspicuously to mimic the sales-patter of their vendors. Her promise to bring Lizzie 'plums to-morrow / Fresh on their mother twigs' (ll. 170–171) repeats and reinforces the emphasis on naturalness and organicity in the goblins' promotional spiel, in which references to 'fresh', 'wild' and 'free-born' fruits are prominent (ll. 20, 11). Likewise, Laura's deployment of a lexis of exceptionality – 'You cannot think what figs / My teeth have met in' (ll. 173–174) – echoes the goblins' verbal assurances of rarity and uniqueness. Her fetishization of visual appearances, evident in the evocation of 'pellucid grapes' (l. 179), further indicates that she has bought into the goblins' sophisticated marketing hype: translucency is speciously conflated here with trustworthiness, as that which is 'sound to eye' (l. 30) is fallaciously assumed to be wholesome to the self. However, Rossetti's verse furnishes us with a number of hints that the goblin fruit is not to be taken at face value. As Mary Arseneau points out, there is 'something inherently unnatural, illusory, and deceptive about the fruit and the satisfaction it offers' (1993, 86). Like the commodities described by Karl Marx in *Capital* (1867), the goblins' wares are constructed as 'strange thing[s], abounding in metaphysical subtleties' (1976, 163). 'Bloom-down-cheeked peaches' (l. 9) and 'swart-headed mulberries' (l. 10) – reminiscent of the animated commercial foodstuffs described by Dickens in *A Christmas Carol* – exhibit the anthropomorphism that Marx associates with commodified consumer objects.[18] What is more, the goblins' edible goods seem strangely abstracted from natural cycles of production: comprising both native and foreign fruits, summer and autumnal produce, their harvest is inexplicably 'All ripe together' (l. 15). Just as the marketplace commodity mystifies and obfuscates its origins as a product of labour according to Marxist philosophy, so the goblins' 'fantasy cornucopia' is 'unseasonably deracinated', as Herbert Tucker notes (2003, 122), stripped of its social, historical and geographical context.

The question of where the goblins' uncanny market produce comes from haunts Rossetti's poem. The verse is loaded with enigmatic references to 'unknown orchard[s]' (l. 135) and mysterious 'bowers / Where summer ripens at all hours' (ll. 151–152), and it is twice parenthetically noted of the fruits that 'Men sell not such in any town' (ll. 101, 556). Even suggestible Laura initially betrays some scepticism about the fruits' derivation: 'Who knows upon what soil they fed / Their hungry thirsty roots?' (ll. 44–45). Her suspicion quickly transmutes into fascination, however, as she succumbs to the goblins' marketing tactics, which purposely deploy mystification to stimulate desire. Not long after anxiously questioning the terroir that has yielded such omniperfect, hyperreal produce, Laura begins to speculate about its origins in a more positive manner: 'How fair the vine must grow / Whose grapes are so luscious; / How warm the wind must blow / Through those fruit bushes' (ll. 60–63). Consumption of the goblins' fantasmatic offerings only strengthens her imaginative convictions: 'Odorous indeed must be the mead / Whereon they grow, and pure the wave they drink' (ll. 180–181). As Richard Menke suggests, 'the epistemological aporia between the product and the knowledge of its production' serves here not as threat but as a spur to longing (1999, 117). Seduced by the goblins' advertising strategy, Laura romanticizes the origins of their wares, reconstituting her consumer desires as 'truth'.

Given the uncertain provenance and health-destroying properties of the goblin fruit, some critics have suggested that 'Goblin Market' can be read not only as an indictment of nineteenth-century consumer capitalism, but also as a specific commentary on the food-adulteration scandals that dogged mid-Victorian culture. Rebecca Stern notes that during the period in which the poem was composed and published 'the number of people who ate ostensibly nutritious food, only to wither and die in consequence, provoked both governmental and popular alarm'; thus, she suggests, the 'problem of food adulteration provides [an] apt framework for [Rossetti's] tale of a young woman sickened by the food she consumes' (2003, 482). Certainly, the poem is alive to the dangers of false-seeming (a recurrent motif in the literature considered in this study), closing with the warning that that which tastes 'like honey to the throat' can nevertheless be 'poison in the blood' (ll. 554–555). Although fresh produce of the kind hawked by the goblins represented less of a concern to mid-Victorian food reformers than potted or preserved fruits (which were often contaminated with toxins such as copper), an 1856 article in the *Scottish Review* noted that the adulteration of fertilizers and manures in British agriculture was 'extensive and systematic' (Anon. 1856, 149), lending credence to Laura's anxious concerns regarding the 'soil' that 'fed' the goblins' orchard crops. Victorian newspapers and magazines also warned consumers about the aesthetic and economic frauds practised on them by fruiterers and costermongers. An article in *Chambers's Edinburgh Journal* alerted readers to the problem of traders who 'purchase for a trifle damaged raisins and currants' and then 'have them well sodden in treacle and water' to give the appearance of 'new fruit' (Anon. 1849, 297). A later report in the *Pall Mall Gazette* exposed the trickery of fruit-sellers who inserted new crowns of leaves into the tops of imported pineapples to create the semblance of fresh, hothouse produce. 'If fruit and flowers once take to artificial methods of enhancing their attractions, all confidence in the garden will be destroyed', the newspaper thundered, adding that 'the plan of concocting fictitious fruit is injurious to commercial morality, whose standard requires raising rather than lowering' (Anon. 1873, 5).

Whereas Laura is dangerously susceptible to the kind of marketplace deceptions uncovered in the Victorian press, Lizzie is portrayed as an altogether more savvy shopper. From the outset, she recognizes that the goblins' seductive 'offers should not charm us' (l. 65), and when she finally enters the marketplace, she is determined not 'to pay too dear' a price for her purchases (l. 311). Whereas Laura's dealings with the goblins are ruled by her appetitive cravings, Lizzie comes 'not to consume but to transact', as Tucker points out (2003, 126). When the goblins refuse to trade with her on her terms, she continues to abjure desire, eventually escaping not only with her silver penny but also with a free sample of fruit juice, 'the symbolic representation of the power she has wrenched from the goblins' (Campbell 1990, 408). In this way, Lizzie succeeds in subverting Victorian market values: 'without becoming either the subject or the object of exchange, [she] transforms pure exchange-value (the commodity of goblin fruit) into pure use-value (the "fiery antidote" that saves Laura)', as Menke suggests (1999, 128). Her act of economic defiance has the additional effect of opening Laura's eyes to the manipulations of the marketplace. Tellingly, when the goblin fruits are given to Laura in love rather than vended in commercial exchange, and stripped of their aggrandizing promotional hype, they are no longer misrecognized by her as 'succous pasture' (l. 258); rather, their 'juice was wormwood to her tongue' and 'she loathed the feast' (ll. 494–495).

Laura's epiphany is accompanied by a subtle textual return to representations of organic harvest and unalienated rural labour: on the morning that Laura wakes from her illness 'as from a dream' (l. 537), Rossetti notes that 'early reapers plodded to the place / Of golden sheaves' to resume their gleaning of corn (ll. 531–532). The poem's retreat from the commercial sphere continues in its closing coda, which imagines the sisters, now 'wives / With children of their own' (ll. 544–545), safely ensconced in the kind of hermetic domestic idyll they occupied before Laura's 'fall'. Perhaps inevitably, though, the spectre of mercantilism continues to haunt this fairy-tale ending. The fact that Laura feels the need to gather the children round her and retell them cautionary tales of 'wicked, quaint fruit-merchant men' (l. 553) – to school them, in other words, in the doctrine of *caveat emptor* – attests to the enduring power of the marketplace and its attendant gustatory temptations. Just as commercial concerns habitually invade the security of the domestic space in the Dickensian fiction considered earlier in this chapter, so, within the moral economy of 'Goblin Market', the home is never entirely invulnerable to the corrupting forces of consumer desire.

George Eliot, 'Brother Jacob' (1864)

Like 'Goblin Market', George Eliot's satirical short story 'Brother Jacob' foregrounds the moral and social dangers of alimentary desire. The fable's protagonist is David Faux, an 'exceptional . . . confectioner' (Eliot 1999, 67) whose patronymic is indicative of not only the artifice associated with his trade but also the deceitful complexion of his character. After absconding from home with his mother's life-savings, David travels to the West Indies, where he imagines he shall make his fortune and enjoy 'a life of Sultanic self-indulgence' (68). In reality, though, he can find employment only as a lowly Kingstown cook and so, after a six-year absence, he returns to his native land, concocts a new identity for himself and opens a pastry-cook's shop in the provincial town of Grimworth. Here, under the alias of 'Edward Freely', he disrupts the dynamics of the previously self-contained local economy and warps the community's time-honoured domestic values, enticing its men and womenfolk to abandon their traditional home-cooked dishes in favour of his own commercialized wares. The 'gradual corruption of Grimworth manners from their primitive simplicity' is ultimately checked, however, by a 'fine peripateia [*sic*]' (64). David's brother Jacob, an 'idiot' (52) with a fetish for saccharine produce, discovers the whereabouts of the shop and, in the course of devouring its contents, publicly exposes David's true identity.

Food and alimentary pleasure are consistently figured in 'Brother Jacob' as low bodily concerns, suggestive of animal instinct and intellectual immaturity. During his consumptional rampage around David's shop, Jacob is tellingly likened to 'a heavy animal stamping about and making angry noises' (80), while, elsewhere in the story, his fascination with food is twice compared to the wasp's inexorable attraction to the 'sugar-basin' (59) or 'honey-pot' (86). Jacob's obsessive taste for sweet things can be traced to the box of yellow lozenges he is given by David as a culinary bribe early in the text (the gift is designed to distract him from David's theft of their mother's savings). Sucking on these 'propitiatory delicacies', Jacob abandons himself to the 'unprecedented pleasure' of palatal sensation, while 'making inarticulate sounds of gustative content' (54), his 'erotogenic, gurgling satisfaction' sexualizing his orality in an 'infantile way', as Susan de Sola Rodstein points out (1991, 308). The narratorial comparison of Jacob's alimentary 'ecstasy' to that of 'Caliban at the taste of Trinculo's wine' (53) works further to animalize and sexualize his consumption, for the 'drunken monster' of *The Tempest* (discussed in Chapter 2) is notably associated with both ingestive and carnal appetites (Shakespeare 1999, 2.2.175).[19] Although Jacob, in contradistinction to Caliban, is repeatedly configured by those around him as an 'innicent' (60, rpt. 84), his insatiable hunger for food nevertheless threatens to slip over into the cannibalism with which Shakespeare's savage is metathetically associated.[20] Linking David 'with the flavour of yellow lozenges' in his 'rudimentary mind' (56), Jacob comes to perceive his brother as a 'sort of sweet-tasted fetish' (55), eroding the distinction between the wily confectioner and his edible produce in what Carl Plasa terms 'a frequent metonymic slide' (2005, 297).

Importantly, though, Jacob is not the only character in Eliot's tale to be influenced by visceral culinary cravings; as Karen Mann suggests, in 'Brother Jacob' the whole of 'humanity is conceived of as a species of animal ruled by its stomach' (1981, 198). When, for instance, David is obliged by his father to decide on a future trade, he does so 'with a rashness inspired by a sweet tooth', having long subscribed to 'the pleasing illusion that a confectioner must be at once the happiest and the foremost of men, since the things he made were not only the most beautiful to behold, but the very best eating' (49). His juvenile passion for saccharinity finds its mirror in the society of Grimworth, where the townspeople's taste for sweet things overwhelms their initial reservations about purchasing commercialized confectioneries. In a further affirmation of the animal power of appetite, David reproduces the cannibalistic tendencies associated with his voracious brother: just as Jacob views David as a 'sweet-flavoured' (58) source of nourishment, David – 'a fastidious connoisseur of the fair sex' (68) – repeatedly conceives of women as food for his delectation.[21] Notably, one of his sweethearts, Sarah, is familiarly known as 'Sally' Lunn, which is also the name of a kind of tea-cake. A later romantic target, Penny Palfrey (the daughter of the leading family in Grimworth), is similarly figured in comestible terms: David thinks 'her prettiness comparable to the loveliest things in confectionery' (71), and, in a subsequent and rather more unsettling metaphor of devourment, Penny is described as 'a fresh white-heart cherry going to be bitten off the stem' (79) following her engagement to Freely.

Of course, Penny's name is also indicative of money, signalling the conceptual overlap between alimentary and pecuniary desire in 'Brother Jacob'. As a number of critics have suggested, food and money are consistently linked in Eliot's text. Helen Small points out that '[Jacob] exactly replicates David's ravenous greed' but, having 'no concept whatsoever of the value of enterprise, profit, or property', his voracity is 'distorted into the cruder form of an insatiable appetite for food' (1999, xxxiii). In a further instance of fraternal doubling, David's belief that food can be converted into money via his culinary skill finds its inverted image in Jacob's mis-guided conviction that money can be transformed into food. When the bag of guineas that David has stolen fatefully 'vomit[s] forth' its misappropriated contents in Jacob's presence (53), David convinces his credulous sibling that the coins are a kind of seed from which the yellow lozenges he fetishizes can be grown: 'Look, Jacob! . . . Put guineas in the hole – they'll come out like this!' (55). As Peter Allan Dale observes, this 'miracle of transubstantiation' (1985, 21) takes place, ironically, on a Sunday, when the rest of the family is at church, for, with typical cunning, David has decided that the Sabbath presents 'so singularly favourable an opportunity for sons who [want] to appropriate their mothers' guineas, that . . . it must have been kindly intended by Providence for such purposes' (Eliot 1999, 52).

The perverted religiosity inherent in this egocentric assumption presages the moral corruption that David's self-serving entrepreneurship will wreak on Grimworth society. Beginning with Mrs Steene, the vet's wife (who, unhappy with the quality of her own mince-pies, sends out just '*this once*' for a dish from the new pastry-cook's [65]), the women of the town gradually forsake 'the shops where their fathers and mothers had bought before them' (61) and abandon the exercise of their own culinary skill in favour of 'buying at Freely's' (65). At stake in the text's disapprobation of this social change is an ideological investment in the morality of domestic labour: as we saw earlier in Hannah More's Cheap Repository Tracts (Chapter 4), the purchase of ready-made baked goods signifies very differently from the purchase of raw ingredients, to be transformed by female industry into wholesome family meals. The Grimworthians' shift in consumer practice – satirically characterized by the narrator as an 'infection' (65) – is further associated with connubial dishonesty, as the townswomen take to comforting themselves with sophistic arguments – 'You paid a little more for [ready-made mince-pies], but there was no risk of waste' – while garbling their household accounts to hide their increased expenditure from their husbands (65). As the narrator drily notes, the Grimworthians' newfound taste for shop-bought produce may have enhanced the palatablity of their meals, but it does nothing to improve the moral probity of their domestic relations: 'many husbands, kept for some time in the dark . . . innocently swallowed at two mouthfuls a tart on which they were paying a profit of a hundred per cent, and as innocently encouraged a fatal disingenuousness in the partners of their bosoms by praising the pastry' (65).

The petty frauds and domestic deceptions encouraged by David's commodities are matched by the air of false-seeming that envelops both the confectioner and his wares. If the surname 'Faux' ironically provides a true estimation of David's character, the soubriquet 'Freely' that 'shone in gilt letters' over the entrance to his new shop (63) gives a sham impression of generosity; unlike the liberal Miss Matty in Elizabeth Gaskell's *Cranford* (1853), who cheerfully depletes her profits by making gifts of almond-comfits to her young customers 'by way of make-weight' (1998, 148), Eliot's impostor holds 'that the desire for sweets and pastry must only be satisfied in a direct ratio with the power of paying for them' (63).[22] Questions of veracity and authenticity also cleave to Freely's stock of goods: the narrator wryly observes that 'the sweet-tasted swans and other ingenious white shapes crunched by the small teeth of [Grimworth's] rising generation' have an oddly 'calcareous' quality to them, coupled with a strangely 'inorganic flavour' of 'tobacco-pipes' (66), in a strong hint that Freely's sugar-work is adulterated with chalk or clay.[23]

The merchandise displayed in David's shop window is similarly shadowed by the sense of being too good to be true:

> On one side, there were the variegated tints of collared and marbled meats, set off by bright green leaves, the pale brown of glazed pies, the rich tones of sauces and bottled fruits enclosed in their veil of glass – altogether a sight to bring tears into the eyes of a Dutch painter; and on the other, there was a predominance of the more delicate hues of pink, and white, and yellow, and buff, in the abundant lozenges, candies, sweet biscuits and icings, which to the eyes of a bilious person might easily have been blended into a faëry landscape in Turner's latest style.
>
> *62–63*

Although this visual cornucopia appears superficially desirable, Eliot's account is littered with clues that potential buyers of David's produce should beware. For instance, the narrative insistence on the painterly attributes of the window display lends its consumables a fantastical, unreal quality, while its spectacular 'blaze of light and colour' (62) gestures towards artificial means of chromatic enhancement. Significantly, during his investigations into food adulteration in the 1850s, the chemist Arthur Hill Hassall found that 'articles of sugared confectionery' like David's lozenges and candies were frequently 'subject to gross and injurious adulteration' (1857, 484), with poisonous contaminants such as vermilion and chromate of lead often deployed to achieve the kind of pretty hues of pink and yellow described by Eliot. Readerly suspicions regarding the possibility of culinary trickery here may be further fuelled by the narrator's reference to consumer biliousness, and by the subtle figuration of the glass receptacles encasing David's preserves in terms of obscurement rather than transparency. The reference to fruits enclosed in a 'veil of glass' is suggestive of masking or concealment, rather than the limpidity we might more usually associate with glassware; in this light, it is notable that bottled fruits, like sweets, were common articles of adulteration in the nineteenth century.[24]

Given the co-existent optical attractions and epistemological uncertainties of Freely's commercialized provisions, it is little wonder that shop windows such as those evoked in 'Brother Jacob' functioned simultaneously as sources of fascination and anxiety in mid-Victorian culture. Whereas one contributor to Dickens's family magazine *All the Year Round* celebrated the 'perpetual and . . . inexhaustible feast' (Anon. 1869, 37) afforded by retailers' window displays, another writer for the *Leisure Hour* was less sanguine in his assessment, arguing that, owing to 'the covetousness of greedy and dishonest traders', 'the influence of shop-windows is not everywhere and always to the advantage of mankind' (Anon. 1855, 669). For Eliot, it seems, David's 'rainbow' (62) display of eatables is symptomatic not only of commercial avarice, but also of an alienating modernity. As Andrew Miller suggests, while 'distancing consumers from the goods they desire[d]' and 'simultaneously heightening that desire', the shop window's 'invisible wall of solid crystal was also seen to encourage an increasing distance between people' (1995, 5). Notably, in another of Eliot's fictional towns – the nostalgically conceived St Ogg's in *The Mill on the Floss* (1860) – the shop windows are 'small', 'unpretending' and absent of 'plate-glass' (1979, 125), because consumers and traders know and trust one another, negating the need for promotional ostentation: 'the farmers' wives and daughters who came to do their shopping on market days were not to be withdrawn from their regular, well-known shops; and the tradesmen had no wares intended for customers who would go on their way and be seen no more' (1979, 125–126). In 'Brother Jacob', by contrast, David's depersonalized 'commercial organ' (66) disrupts Grimworth's finely tuned social order by introducing a promiscuous or 'vagrant spirit in shopping' (62). Prior to its arrival, we are told, the various classes and religious affiliations each had their own grocer, to whom they extended loyal patronage (61); this non-competitive retail system is deranged, however, by Freely's sudden appearance on the high street.

   The alienating effects of free-market capitalism are further felt within the domestic dwellings of Grimworth's private families. As the narrator notes, in a sceptical rebuttal of Smithian economics:

> I am not ignorant that this sort of thing is called the inevitable course of civilization, division of labour, and so forth, and that the maids and matrons may be said to have had their hands set free from cookery to add to the wealth of society in some other way. Only it happened at Grimworth . . . that the maids and matrons could do nothing with their hands at all better than cooking; not even those who had always made heavy cakes and leathery pastry. And so it came to pass, that the progress of civilization at Grimworth was not otherwise apparent than in the impoverishment of men, the gossiping idleness of women, and the heightening prosperity of Mr Edward Freely.

66

Eliot's sardonic refusal here to grant Grimworth's women any useful function outside of culinary activity contrasts sharply with the position adopted in the Brontëan fiction discussed earlier, where domestic labour is generally linked with female disempowerment. Certainly, Eliot appears to deny the women of Grimworth the same kind of intellectual hunger she grants to other of her heroines, such as *Middlemarch*'s Dorothea Brooke and *The Mill on the Floss*'s Maggie Tulliver. Given the relentlessly satirical tone of 'Brother Jacob', however, we might question how seriously we are to take the narrator's pronouncements here; as Small points out, 'comedy, especially in the satiric mode, is always its own get-out clause' (1999, xxxiv).

The inexorable social and moral decline that Eliot's narrator identifies in Grimworth society is eventually halted by 'Edward Freely's' unmasking as David Faux at the end of the text. Following his subsequent flit, 'the demoralization of Grimworth women was checked' and the 'secrets' of traditional home-cookery 'revived in [their] breasts' (87) – a restoration that is superficially endorsed in the narrative, as noted above. The means by which this reversal is achieved differ dramatically, though, from the 'ethics of renunciation' favoured in texts such as 'Goblin Market' (Menke 1999, 128). As Rodstein notes, '"Brother Jacob" presents a curious instance of desire itself providing the familiar, moralizing, Eliotic correction of desiring characters' (1991, 303–304), for it is Jacob's insatiable craving for sweetness that ultimately proves to be David's nemesis. Drawn to the 'paradise [of] his brother's shop' (85), where seemingly endless supplies of yellow lozenges and Bath buns await, Jacob innocently debunks the false history that David has confected for himself and brings about, as a result, the latter's exile from polite society. Thus, in a complex and ironic pattern of narrative reduplication, the libidinal desire for saccharine produce is implicated in both the demoralization *and* remoralization of Grimworth's populace, as well as in the making and unmaking of the duplicitous David Faux.

Lewis Carroll, *Alice's Adventures in Wonderland* (1865) and *Through the Looking-Glass, and What Alice Found There* (1871)

According to Lewis Carroll's nephew and biographer Stuart Dodgson Collingwood, the hearty appetites of little girls were a source of great alarm to the abstemious author: 'when he took a certain one of them out with him to a friend's house to dinner, he used to give the host or hostess a gentle warning, . . . "Please be careful, because she eats a good deal too much"' (1899, 390). Similar anxieties regarding the propensities of girlish appetite emerge repeatedly in Carroll's famous *Alice* books, the child-heroine of which 'always took a great interest in questions of eating and drinking' (1998, 65). At the Mad Hatter's tea-party, Alice impulsively interrupts the Dormouse's story of the three sisters who lived at the bottom of a well in order to enquire, 'what did they live on?' (65), while, in *Through the Looking-Glass*, she repeatedly asks the same question of the Gnat as it introduces her to a variety of fantastical insects: a 'rocking-horse-fly' that eats 'sap and sawdust' (149); a 'snap-dragon-fly' that consumes 'frumenty and mince-pie' (150); and a 'bread-and-butter-fly' that subsists on 'weak tea with cream' (151). For inquisitive Alice, it seems that diet is an important classificatory tool: like the writers of the early modern dietaries explored in Chapter 2, she subscribes to the philosophy that 'you are what you eat'. Indeed, at one point she suggests that regimen has a determining effect on character, speculating that it is 'pepper that makes people hot-tempered . . . vinegar that makes them sour – and camomile that makes them bitter' (78). However, if eating habits represent a (parodic) way of knowing and systematizing life-forms in Carroll's nonsense stories, they also work to undermine notions of stable and coherent identity. Alice's unthinking ingestion of items of food and drink invariably precipitates radical forms of bodily transformation, causing her to ponder periodically, 'who in the world am I?' (17–18). Although she eventually gains some measure of bodily control by regulating her consumption, the continual slippage in the *Alice* books between eaters and eaten, and predators and prey, works insistently to trouble alimentary ontologies.

It seems fitting that Alice's otherworldly adventures begin with a symbolically freighted 'fall', for, as Nina Auerbach observes, like 'Milton's Eve, the ever-ravenous Alice is a creature of curiosity and appetite' (1982, 49). While associating her with the fallen heroine of *Paradise Lost* (Chapter 3), Alice's hunger also aligns her with what Rémy Saisselin calls the 'modern Eve' (1984, 39): the figure of the nineteenth-century 'female consumer . . . lured by the dazzling commodities exhibited in shop windows' (Talairach-Vielmas 2007, 49). Notably, during her protracted fall down the rabbit-hole, Alice finds herself in a shelf-lined space which seems to stimulate unconscious desire:

> She took down a jar from one of the shelves as she passed: it was labelled 'ORANGE MARMALADE', but to her great disappointment it was empty: she did not like to drop the jar, for fear of killing somebody underneath, so managed to put it into one of the cupboards as she fell past it.
>
> *10*

Like the tempting sauces and bottled fruits displayed in Freely's shop window in 'Brother Jacob', the marmalade jar functions here as an orectic agent, to which Alice – juvenile avatar of the Victorian female shopper – finds herself impulsively drawn. However, the jar turns out to be but an 'empty sign of gratification', incapable of satisfying longing, as Nancy Armstrong points out, and this discovery quickly 'reverses the trajectory of [Alice's] desire' (1990, 15). In a striking demonstration of the auto-functioning of disciplinary power, Alice suddenly grows anxious about the consequences of her actions and places the emblematic commodity in a cupboard as she falls past it, self-mastery overcoming instinctual desire. Significantly, this appetitive struggle provides the template for subsequent alimentary encounters in Wonderland; as Armstrong argues, during the course of Alice's adventures it becomes clear that '*all possibility for pleasure splits off from appetite and attaches itself to self-control*' (1990, 20, emphasis in original).

Initially, however, alimentary desire consistently overpowers self-restraint as Alice devours the consumables she chances upon with relish, much like her literary predecessor Laura in 'Goblin Market'. Despite having been schooled in the cautionary values of didactic Victorian children's literature – 'she had never forgotten that, if you drink much from a bottle marked "poison", it is almost certain to disagree with you, sooner or later' (13) – Alice greedily finishes off the multi-savoury contents of the mysterious bottle labelled 'DRINK ME', before scoffing down the cake marked 'EAT ME' in similarly cavalier fashion (14). By the time she enters the White Rabbit's house, Alice is so in thrall to the demands of appetite that textual invitations to consume are no longer required: 'when her eye fell upon a little bottle that stood near the looking-glass', she immediately 'uncorked it and put it to her lips' even though 'there was no label this time with the words "DRINK ME"' to incite her actions (32). Her indiscriminate ingestion invariably leads to a disquieting loss of physical control; Alice's body either 'shut[s] up like a telescope' (14) following her consumption, or surges upwards in a dizzying parody of the corporeal transformations that await the prepubescent girl. Interestingly, the prospect of maturation is later rejected by Alice; while crammed into the White Rabbit's house following one of her growth spurts, she muses that 'there's no room to grow up any more *here* . . . That'll be a comfort, one way – never to be an old woman' (33). Symbolically associated with female sexuality and a concomitant loss of childhood innocence, appetite becomes a denigrated sign in the *Alice* books, one that Alice gradually learns to abjure. Instead of compulsively eating or imbibing the various items that offer themselves to her, Alice starts to consider how her body and its desires are 'to be managed' (38). After discovering that the right-hand side of the Caterpillar's mushroom causes her to contract when consumed, while the left side causes her to shoot upwards, Alice embarks on a programme of orderly shrinking and growing, 'nibbling' carefully at each side of the fungus until she reaches her desired height (49). As Armstrong notes, 'this behavior stabilizes the body that appetite has disfigured' (1990, 18) and aligns Alice with the dietetic abstemiousness demanded of Victorian bourgeois femininity. Tellingly, by the penultimate chapter of *Alice's Adventures*, Alice's consuming desires appear to be almost entirely under her control; although she gazes hungrily at a large dish of tarts during the Knave of Hearts' trial and fleetingly wishes that the courtiers would hurry up and 'hand round the refreshments', she quickly recognizes the futility of her longing ('there seemed to be no chance of this') and instead passes the time by 'looking at everything about her' (95).

Alice's new-found appetitive docility continues in *Through the Looking-Glass*, where, as Carol Mavor observes, the withholding of food and drink 'keeps desire in check' (2008, 96). When Alice tells the Red Queen she is thirsty, she is offered only a '*very* dry' biscuit in return (143), and when she announces that she doesn't 'care for jam', the White Queen responds that she 'couldn't have it if [she] *did* want it', the rule in this topsy-turvy world being 'jam to-morrow and jam yesterday – but never jam *to-day*' (171). In a further act of gustatory deprivation, Alice is instructed to hand round the cake at the battle of the Lion and the Unicorn, and then to 'cut it afterwards' – a nonsensical directive that leaves her holding an 'empty dish', having 'kept none for herself' (203). Her dispossession here links her with the self-denying women earlier found in the fiction of Dickens and the Brontës, who are typically expected to cater to the appetites of others while disregarding or renouncing their own bodily needs. Indeed, in a telling manifestation of the disciplinary logic governing Victorian female appetite, Alice is even left hungry at the feast intended to mark her own coronation; informed on arrival that she has missed the soup and fish courses, she is subsequently forbidden to serve up the leg of mutton set before her because, according to the Red Queen, 'it isn't etiquette to cut any one you've been introduced to' (229–230).

As this latter comment indicates, the *Alice* books are preoccupied not only with questions of female appetite but also with polite dining behaviour. In particular, the issue pervades both the closing banquet in *Through the Looking-Glass* and its narrative double, the Mad Hatter's tea-party in *Alice's Adventures*. As an ambassador of middle-class values, Alice expects both meals to be conducted in line with the norms and mores outlined in Victorian etiquette guides such as *The Habits of Good Society* (1859), which emphasizes the importance of good table manners and cautions readers that 'however agreeable a man may be in society, if he offends or disgusts by his table traits, he will soon be scouted from it, and justly so' (Anon. 1859, 257). In Carroll's nonsense works, by contrast, meals are invariably marked by discourteousness and disorderly comportment. The coronation banquet is troubled by 'a mutiny of food and dinnerware', as Anna Krugovoy Silver points out (2002, 78), while, at the Mad Hatter's party, Alice is rebuffed ('No room!'), contradicted ('You mean you ca'n't take *less* . . . than nothing') and repeatedly denied nourishment (60, 65). Having initially been offered only non-existent wine, she is afterwards obliged to forgo even the tea and bread-and-butter to which she has helped herself when the Hatter announces 'I want a clean cup . . . let's all move one place on' (66). This anarchic disregard for the rules of dining disorientates Carroll's heroine, troubling her culturally acquired sense of propriety. As Julie Fromer notes, although Alice presumes that she 'knows what to expect and how to act' at the tea-table, events such as the Hatter's party frustrate her suppositions by 'violat[ing] the boundaries of time' and subverting 'expectations of hospitality and civility' (2008, 170–171, 172). They also underline the absurdity always-already inherent in socially sanctioned protocols about eating, a notion that Carroll earlier addresses in a comic squib entitled 'Hints for Etiquette: or, Dining Out Made Easy' (1855). Here, the celebrated nonsense-writer offers up such parodic counsel as 'to use a fork with your soup . . . is a practice wholly exploded' (1899, 33). The *Alice* books extend this Carrollian critique, satirically deflating complacent assumptions about the politeness of Victorian society; as the March Hare firmly reminds Alice, by sitting down without first being invited, she is as guilty of breaking the rules of dinner-time decorum as the Wonderland creatures whom she continually reprimands.

While exposing the arbitrariness of dining conventions, the disorderly meals in *Alice's Adventures* and *Through the Looking-Glass* also reveal the savagery that underpins consumption by introducing 'a catastrophic series of substitutions and reversals' between eater and eaten (Guyer 2004, 161). As Michael Parrish Lee suggests, 'Carroll gives us a world in which . . . everything and everyone is potentially on the menu' (2014, 490). The Hatter's tea-party concludes with the disturbing image of the Dormouse being forcibly inserted into a teapot, while, at Alice's coronation feast, an animated plum-pudding demands to know of Carroll's knife-wielding heroine 'how you'd like it, if I were to cut a slice out of *you*[?]' (230). If, as Margaret Visser suggests, 'it is one of the chief roles of etiquette to keep the lid on the violence which the meal being eaten presupposes' (1991, 4), then Carroll's nonsense unmasks that alimentary aggression, undermining Victorian culture's easy conflation of 'dining' with 'civilization' (see, for instance, Beeton 2000, 363). Like her colonizing eighteenth-century predecessor Robinson Crusoe (Chapter 3), Alice represents a threat to the native creatures whose territory she invades. Although, like Crusoe, she tends complacently to associate ingestive violence with the animalized Other, supposing that it is *she* who is most at risk of being consumed – she fears, for instance, that an 'enormous puppy' is 'very likely to eat her up' (37) and is wary of the Cheshire Cat's 'great many teeth' (56) – her encounters with the inhabitants of Wonderland force her repeatedly to confront her own status as predator. She talks insensitively of having sampled various creatures, such as lobster and whiting, to whom she is introduced and is accused by a nesting pigeon of being a 'serpent' with a voracious taste for eggs (48) – a charge that 'harks back to the first destruction of life by eating in the Garden of Eden', according to Helena Michie (1987, 28).

Oral aggression also marks the songs that Alice misremembers during her travels. The didactic children's poem 'Against Idleness and Mischief' is transformed in her recital from a celebration of organic food production, in which a 'little busy Bee' gathers 'Honey all the Day' (Watts 1857, 28), into a tale of predation in which a crocodile 'cheerfully' 'welcomes little fishes' into his 'gently smiling jaws' (19). The second stanza of Isaac Watts's moralistic 'The Sluggard' is similarly renovated by Alice as a fable of carnivorous consumption:

> I passed by his garden, and marked, with one eye,
> How the Owl and the Panther were sharing a pie:
> The Panther took pie-crust, and gravy, and meat,
> While the Owl had the dish as its share of the treat.
> When the pie was all finished, the Owl, as a boon,
> Was kindly permitted to pocket the spoon:
> While the Panther received knife and fork with a growl,
> And concluded the banquet by ——.
>
> *(93)*

The closing ellipsis here invites readers to supply the rhymically consistent ending: the panther concludes the banquet by eating the owl. The poem's amalgamation of superficial politeness with culinary violence matches Alice's own 'courteously menacing relationship' to the animals of Wonderland; as Auerbach notes, Carroll's heroine is 'almost always threatening' to the creatures she meets, eyeing them with 'a strange hunger' reminiscent of that displayed by the Walrus in *Through the Looking-Glass*, who weeps for the oysters he has lured from the sea while greedily devouring them (1973, 37, 35). Thus, although Alice, on the one hand, appears to conform to normative Victorian values in her relationship to food, internalizing the ideological insistence on female alimentary self-discipline, and enforcing dietary etiquette wherever she goes, on the other, she subverts such cultural expectations, revealing the voracious hunger that potentially lingers behind the supposed innocence of juvenile femininity.

Sarah Grand, *The Beth Book, Being a Study of the Life of Elizabeth Caldwell Maclure, a Woman of Genius* (1897)

When Mina Harker, the capable heroine of Bram Stoker's *Dracula* (1897), records in her diary that she and her friend Lucy 'should have shocked the "New Woman" with [their] appetites' at tea (2003, 99), she draws on a pervasive cultural association of progressive femininity with gluttonous appetency. Within the *fin-de-siècle* periodical press, in particular, the politically enlightened 'New Woman' was cast as an insatiable Sybarite, whose alimentary avidity was mirrored by her rapacious sexuality. In Sarah Grand's New Woman *Künstlerroman The Beth Book*, however, feminine consumption is treated rather more ambiguously than in Victorian popular stereotype. Although, as Ann Heilmann points out, Grand made efforts to reclaim 'the pleasures of the body for feminist purposes' in her writing, she also 'stressed that the New Woman's impulse was not for self-indulgence' (2004, 35, 34). Rather, in the guise of Elizabeth Caldwell Maclure – *The Beth Book*'s titular 'woman of genius' – the New Woman displays an instinct for dietary renunciation that leads Abigail Dennis to draw parallels between this 'supposedly radical' figure and the self-abnegating heroines 'of earlier, iconic Victorian female starvation narratives' (2007, 19), such as those previously discussed in the sections on Dickens and the Brontës.

The motif of immolation finds early articulation in *The Beth Book*. Whilst heavily pregnant with Beth, Mrs Caldwell watches 'with interest' (Grand 2013, 32) as a butcher slaughters a lamb outside his shop in an image that 'foreshadows [her] later sacrificial attitude towards her daughter', as Heilmann notes (2004, 85). During her youth, Beth is obliged repeatedly to forgo both the intellectual nourishment of an education and the physical nourishment required to satisfy her growing body so that the little money her family possesses can be spent on her brothers' schooling; the narrator explains that Mrs Caldwell 'starved herself and her daughters in mind and body to scrape together the wherewithal to send her sons out into the world' (300). Ironically, though, 'all her privation' is undertaken in 'vain', for, like the men represented in Anne Brontë's *Tenant of Wildfell Hall*, her boys simply drift 'along the commonest course of self-seeking and self-indulgence' (300). In particular, Beth's older brother Jim fritters away the small inheritance Beth received from her Great-Aunt Victoria on drink and high living in his efforts to 'keep up with the best of his bar-loafing acquaintances' (247). Meanwhile, Beth bravely attempts to 'do without enough, to make it as if there were one mouth less to feed', and becomes 'torpid from excessive self-denial' as a result (236). Significantly, her stoical abstemiousness is neither acknowledged nor appreciated by her immediate family; instead, in a revealing authorization of male excess, Beth is told by her mother 'to leave the table' and 'have nothing but bread and water for the rest of the day' (178) on the one occasion that she obliquely challenges Jim's dissipated habits.

Like the Brontëan fiction discussed earlier, then, *The Beth Book* is governed by an 'anorexic logic' and, by this means, tenders a damning indictment of the gendered division of resources within the nineteenth-century family unit. In particular, it demonstrates the ways in which dietary inequalities become entrenched and naturalized through a process of inter-generational internalization. Born into a matrilineage of abjuration, Beth is indoctrinated in the self-denying behaviours of 'old-world women' (300) via her mother's 'long' marital 'sacrifice of herself' (299), while Jim's imbibitional and sexual intemperance is implicitly learned from his father. This inveterate cycle of female abstinence and male immoderation continues during Beth's own unhappy marriage to the egocentric and adulterous Dr Dan Maclure. Beth quickly discovers that

> what [Dan] had to eat was a matter of great importance to him. He fairly gloated over things he liked, and in order to indulge him, and keep the bills down besides, she went without herself; and he never noticed her self-denial.
>
> *359*

Perhaps more disconcertingly, gendered patterns of consumption and food refusal also structure Beth's romantic relationship with the putative hero of the novel, Arthur Brock, whom Beth nurses through a period of illness to the detriment of her own bodily health. Wracked with hunger-pangs, Beth spends the last of her meagre funds on 'a dainty little feast' for the 'thriving convalescent' (523), telling herself (in a disturbing proof of the power of social conditioning) that she would 'die of hunger rather than spend two precious shillings on herself while there was that poor boy at home, suffering in silence, gratefully content with the poorest fare she brought him' (522). Worryingly, Beth's allusion to death by famishment almost becomes reality when she collapses from hunger following her unremitting exertions on the oblivious Arthur's behalf; whereas he regains strength from her altruistic ministrations, she becomes 'a study in starvation' as a result of her self-denial (528).

If Arthur ('that poor boy') is implicitly infantilized by his nutritional dependence on Beth, then she, conversely, derives an intangible moral authority from her quasi-maternal domestic role. Taking issue with her culture's 'prejudice against domestic duties', Grand argues in her journalism that 'there can be no higher calling' than housekeeping, 'none . . . nobler or more ennobling' (2000, 123–124). Her assertion chimes with her contemporary Elizabeth Robins Pennell's defence of female cookery in her collected food-writing:

> why should not the woman of genius spend [her life] in designing exquisite dinners, inventing original breakfasts, and be respected for the nobility of her self-appointed task? For in the planning of the perfect meal there is art; and, after all, is not art the one real, the one important thing in life?
>
> *1900, 12*[25]

The coalition of cookery and creativity posited here also emerges in *The Beth Book*, which links 'storytelling and cooking from the start', as Beth Sutton-Ramspeck points out (2004, 167). Beth first learns to cook from Harriet, a servant with a 'brilliant imagination', who regales her with a never-ending 'stream of narrative' during her kitchen apprenticeship (146). In similar fashion, the adolescent Beth goes on to nourish *her* friends with stories and poems, while also feeding their bodies. When serving Sammy Lee a mouth-watering dish of 'whiting on toast, all hot and brown' (199), Beth recites him a fragment of verse of her own composition and, later, a ballad of Beth's invention runs through the head of Charlotte Hardy as she consumes the picnic of Melton Mowbray pie, sausage-roll, sponge-cake, lemon cheesecake and brandy snaps that her friend has collated for her (287).

As these examples of food provision indicate, the generous redistribution of alimentary resources is central to Beth's notion of domestic economy. Whereas her wealthy but parsimonious Uncle James – 'a great stout man' (113), similar to *The Magic Toyshop's* tyrannical Uncle Philip (Chapter 6) – obsessively monitors his cook's use of storeroom ingredients and seeks to limit his household's consumption, hypocritically declaring that 'people are much healthier and happier when they do not eat too much' (120), Beth's instinct is always to nourish those around her. This urge to be 'an agent for good by allocating resources in . . . just ways' prompts her to subvert both patriarchal and capitalist systems, as Melissa Purdue points out (2013, para. 8). Adopting the masculine persona of 'Loyal Heart the Trapper', Beth takes to poaching on Uncle James's Fairholm estate whenever her family's larder is empty, relieving the ever-present threat of hunger through her illicit activities. As well as providing much-needed sustenance, the rabbits and birds she snares function tacitly as a non-monetary form of restitution for social injustice; convinced that her Uncle has cheated her mother of her rightful inheritance, Beth 'does not scruple to poach' on his grounds (180), seizing his game in reparation for his moral debt. Certainly, her 'primitive' form of hunting and fishing (197), born out of 'dire poverty' (180) and restricted to what her family actually needs, is presented as more morally justifiable than her Uncle's voracious 'sport' (121), which has more in common with the brutal carno-phallogocentrism earlier identified in *The Tenant of Wildfell Hall*. In one salutary scene, which serves as an indictment of masculine violence and excess, Beth watches as Uncle James casually selects a guinea-fowl, a drake and a turkey from his poultry yard to be 'executed' for his dinner-table, before turning his gun on three sedentary pigeons for the purposes of an additional 'pigeon-pie' (120).

As Dennis notes, Beth's necessitous poaching forms part of a wider 'feminine conspiracy of food appropriation' in Grand's novel (2007, 22). When the young Beth is punished for her outspokenness by being deprived of pudding, Uncle James's cook later compensates her with 'a big cheesecake from a secret store' (122); in return, Beth turns a blind eye to Cook's secret requisition of 'tea, sugar, raisins, currants, and other groceries from Uncle James's carefully guarded treasure', with which to feed her family (131). Beth's bond with Harriet, the maid, is similarly cemented through food; the two frequently become 'so hungry over the recipes for good dishes' in Harriet's copy of the *Family Herald* that they fry up some 'eggs and potatoes, or a slice stolen from the joint roasting at the fire', and feast together in secret communion (151). The positive effects of sharing food have, of course, been noted elsewhere in this study, but in *The Beth Book* it is striking that commensal behaviours are specifically gendered.

Whereas male relationships to food in Grand's novel are invariably acquisitive, their female equivalents tend to be co-active and replenishing. Indeed, the only characters to repay Beth's culinary selflessness in the text are girls and women. Whereas Arthur Brock is 'too self-satisfied' to suspect that Beth might be 'starving herself that [he] might have all [he] required' (529), Charlotte Hardy supplies her 'famished' friend with meals of chicken, ham, cold apple-tart and cream (288), and fried ham, boiled eggs and hot buttered rolls (290), in return for the picnic of 'good things to eat' (287) that Beth has thoughtfully prepared for her.

A further example of mutual female nourishment occurs when the adult Beth is living alone in her rented London garret-room. Here she is frequently joined for tea by her landlady's daughter, Ethel Maud Mary, who 'never came empty-handed' (507). Their shared meals take the form of a spiritually enriching ritual:

> 'Miss Maclure, may I come in?' [Ethel Maud Mary] would say, after knocking.
>
> And Beth would answer, rising from her work with a smile of welcome, 'Yes, by all means. I'm delighted to see you. You take the big chair and I'll make the tea. I'm dying for a cup.'
>
> Then Ethel Maud Mary would uncover something she held in her hand, which would prove to be cakes, or hot buttered toast and watercresses, or a bag of shrimps and some thin bread and butter; and Beth, sparkling at the kindness, would exclaim, 'I never was so spoilt in my life!' to which Ethel Maud Mary would rejoin, 'There'll not be much to boast about between two of us.'
>
> *507*

Such scenes of frugal, but homely, shared consumption act as a narrative counterpoint to the more masochistic paradigms of female food refusal in Grand's fiction that have long frustrated her feminist readers. If asceticism is vested with moral value in *The Beth Book*, signalling the New Woman's ennobling 'self-possession' (522) and providing a necessary contrast to the Old Man's self-indulgence, female commensality represents a less exalted but more soul-nourishing alternative, furnishing women with the physical and emotional sustenance required to challenge patriarchy and renovate the social order.

In its presentation of different types of hunger, from the literal to the metaphorical, *The Beth Book* consolidates the various manifestations of that theme to have emerged in this chapter: corporeal famishment; ascetic self-denial; intellectual, emotional and spiritual longing; and ravenous desire. Like so much of the literature considered here, Grand's novel takes a particular interest in female relationships to food; yet, in common with the Brontëan fiction examined earlier, it does not seek to isolate feminine alimentary experience, instead demonstrating how the gendered ideologies of consumption ingrained in Victorian culture work to damage the social fabric more generally, affecting both women *and* men. In its attitude to cookery, by contrast, *The Beth Book* appears closer to the works of Dickens, Eliot and Rossetti, where female food preparation is validated as socially and morally beneficial. The complex and contested picture that emerges in relation to women and food in nineteenth-century literature continues into the writing of the twentieth and twenty-first centuries, explored in the next chapter, where consumption is endowed with the symbolic power to affirm shared humanity and recondition social relationships, but also to fragment individual subjectivities and wider ontological categories, amplifying the interrogation of culinary identities initiated in Victorian literature and culture.

Notes

1 For more on the history of Victorian food importation from the colonies and beyond, see Burnett (1989, 115–119).
2 Dickens's fascination with cannibalism is discussed at length in Marlow (1983) and Stone (1994).
3 For more on changing attitudes to hunger in the nineteenth century, see Boyce (2012).
4 The advertisement of foods is also seen in earlier descriptions of the marketplace (see, for instance, *Piers Plowman* in Chapter 1). However, it is Dickens's representation of shop produce as quasi-*autonomous* – the goods on display appear to speak directly to consumers – that enables the comparison with Marx's idea of the commodity in capitalist society (see note 18 below).
5 A similar point is made by Mrs Beeton in the preface to *Beeton's Book of Household Management*:

> I have always thought that there is no more fruitful source of family discontent than a housewife's badly-cooked dinners and untidy ways. Men are now so well served out of doors, – at their clubs, well-ordered taverns, and dining-houses, that in order to compete with the attractions of these places, a mistress must be thoroughly acquainted with the theory and practice of cookery.
>
> (2000, 3)

6 Notably, the serving of underdone meat is one of Dickens's most frequently deployed signs of female domestic incompetence: in *David Copperfield*, Dora serves Traddles a 'plateful of raw meat' at her and David's first dinner-party (1997, 626), while in *Bleak House* Mrs Jellyby's domestic deficiencies are signalled by the fact that the dinner of cod-fish, roast beef, cutlets and pudding she provides for her family and guests has had hardly 'any cooking to speak of', being 'almost raw' (1996, 50).
7 For instance, Joe, the 'fat boy' in *The Pickwick Papers*, is referred to as 'the infant Lambert' (2003, 95), while in Thackeray's novel *Barry Lyndon* (1844) Tim the valet grows so 'enormously fat' he 'would have fitted almost into Daniel Lambert's coat' (1984, 197).
8 The effects of this alimentary culture change can be identified in Flora Annie Steel and Grace Gardiner's *The Complete Indian Housekeeper and Cook* (1888), which segregates its eight recipes for 'Native Dishes' into a separate chapter. The chapter's dismissive prefatory comment – 'It may be mentioned incidentally that most native recipes are inordinately greasy and sweet, and that your native cooks invariably know how to make them fairly well' – further indicates the distaste for culinary integration amongst late-Victorian memsahibs (2010, 305).
9 Interestingly, the gluttonous figure of Lust in Book Four of Spenser's *Faerie Queene* (Chapter 2) is also figured as elephantine; however, Lust's physical appetites are presented as more brutal than Jos's, extending to rape and cannibalism.
10 At the great Chartist meeting on Kersal Moor in Lancashire, on 24 September 1838, Reverend Joseph Rayner Stephens declared that the Chartists' demand for universal

manhood suffrage was 'a knife-and-fork question; a bread-and-cheese question' (qtd. in Anon. 1838, 7).

11 Refusal to share an eating space also figures as a form of social exclusion/punishment in *The Book of Margery Kempe* (Chapter 1).

12 In a literal association of impoverishment and cannibalism, the Victorian social campaigner John Lhotsky suggested that 'starvation . . . encroaches upon the tenderest, upon the innermost feelings of human nature; and it is known, that when a mother has found herself in this state, she has even murdered her child, for the sake of banquetting [*sic*] upon the offspring of her own body' (1844, 3).

13 For more detailed analysis of the description of Famine victims in the British press, see Boyce (2012).

14 Susan Schorn identifies further allusions to the Famine in her essay 'Punish Her Body to Save Her Soul: Echoes of the Irish Famine in *Jane Eyre*' (1998), while, in *Charlotte Brontë: Critical Issues*, Carl Plasa explores the ways in which 'the Famine's unspoken presence is ventriloquised in *Shirley*' (2004, 102).

15 According to Lasègue, his typical anorectic patient was 'a young girl, between fifteen and twenty years of age', who 'suffers from some emotion which she avows or conceals. Generally it relates to some real or imaginary marriage project . . . or to some more or less conscient desire' (1873, 265).

16 For more detailed analysis of the intertextual parallels between 'Goblin Market' and *Paradise Lost*, see Gilbert and Gubar (1979) and Maxwell (1999).

17 Catherine Maxwell identifies here an intertextual relationship between 'Goblin Market' and Keats's 'La Belle Dame sans Merci' (discussed in Chapter 4); like Laura, the knight-at-arms of Keats's poem falls into a state of listlessness after being seduced by 'a bewitching song and enchanted foods' (1999, 82). Maxwell notes that 'luscious fruits' are also 'an aid to seduction' (1999, 82) in *The Eve of St Agnes* (also discussed in Chapter 4).

18 One of the central ironies governing nineteenth-century capitalism, according to Marx, is that while the producers of goods become objectified, the objects of their labour assume a semi-mystical autonomy. Once an 'ordinary' object, such as a wooden table, emerges into the marketplace as a commodity, Marx suggests, 'it changes into a thing which transcends sensuousness': 'it not only stands with its feet on the ground, but, in relation to all other commodities, it stands on its head, and evolves out of its wooden brain grotesque ideas' (1976, 163). Although Marx does not explicitly consider food as a commodity in *Capital*, figuring it rather as one of humanity's 'natural needs' (1976, 275), representations of marketplace foods in Victorian literature often resonate uncannily with his description of the animated commodity, as this chapter argues.

19 Shortly after his arrival on stage in *The Tempest*, Caliban declares: 'I must eat my dinner'; he then boasts that he would have 'peopled . . . / This isle with Calibans', had Prospero not prevented him from violating Miranda (Shakespeare 1999, 1.2.331, 351–352). The wine to which Eliot alludes is in fact given to Caliban by Stephano, not Trinculo.

20 Critics have long suggested that 'Caliban' can be read as a deliberate anagram of 'Can[n]ibal'. See Vaughan and Vaughan (1991, 26–32).

21 Representations of women as food recur throughout the literature considered in this volume, ranging from the literal (e.g. Lust's cannibalistic taste for female flesh in Spenser's *Faerie Queene* in Chapter 2) to the metaphorical (e.g. Marian's self-identification as food in *The Edible Woman* in Chapter 6).

22 It is only when Miss Matty is advised how 'unwholesome' almond-confits are for children that she curbs her generous practice (Gaskell 1998, 148).

23 According to the leading Victorian food reformer Arthur Hill Hassall, chalk, pipe-clay and plaster of Paris were common adulterants of sugar in the first half of the nineteenth century (1855, 600–601).

24 As a number of postcolonial analyses of 'Brother Jacob' have pointed out, David's shop window also undertakes another form of symbolic 'veiling', masking the slave-produced

origins of its sugared confectionery (see Rodstein [1991] and Plasa [2005]). For more on the relationship between sugar and slavery, see the sections on Birkett's *Poem on the African Slave Trade* (Chapter 4) and Levy's *Fruit of the Lemon* (Chapter 6).

25 The notion that there is 'art' in the preparation of the 'perfect meal' can also be identified in Woolf's *To the Lighthouse* (see Chapter 6).

References

Acton, Eliza. 1845. *Modern Cookery in All Its Branches: Reduced to a System of Easy Practice, for the Use of Private Families.* 2nd edn. London. Longman, Brown, Green and Longmans.

Anon. 1833. 'Intoxication'. *The Moral Reformer, and Protestor against the Vices, Abuses, and Corruptions of the Age* 3.10. 324.

——. 1838. 'West Riding Meeting'. *Northern Star.* 20 October. 6–7.

——. 1845. 'Dyspepsia'. *Chambers's Edinburgh Journal.* 5 July. 11–12.

——. 1848. *The Eleventh Annual Report (Being for the Year 1847) of the York Temperance Society.* York. John Coultas.

——. 1849. 'Further Progress of Adulteration'. *Chambers's Edinburgh Journal.* 12 May. 297–298.

——. 1855. 'Shop-Windows'. *The Leisure Hour* 199. 667–669.

——. 1856. 'Adulteration of Food, and Other Articles of Commerce'. *Scottish Review* 4.14. 145–154.

——. 1859. *The Habits of Good Society: A Handbook of Etiquette for Ladies and Gentlemen.* London. James Hogg & Sons.

——. 1869. 'Looking in at Shop Windows'. *All the Year Round.* n.s. 2.28. 37–43.

——. 1873. 'Occasional Notes'. *Pall Mall Gazette.* 30 July. 4–5.

Armstrong, Nancy. 1990. 'The Occidental Alice'. *Differences: A Journal of Feminist Cultural Studies* 2.2. 3–40.

Arnold, Matthew. 1974. Letter to Mrs Forster. *The Brontës: The Critical Heritage.* Ed. Miriam Allott. Abingdon and New York. Routledge. 201.

Arseneau, Mary. 1993. 'Incarnation and Interpretation: Christina Rossetti, the Oxford Movement and *Goblin Market*'. *Victorian Poetry* 31.1. 79–93.

Auerbach, Nina. 1973. 'Alice and Wonderland: A Curious Child'. *Victorian Studies* 17.1. 31–47.

——. 1982. 'Falling Alice, Fallen Women, and Victorian Dream Children'. *English Language Notes* 20.2. 46–64.

Banting, William. 1864. *Letter on Corpulence, Addressed to the Public.* 3rd edn. London. Harrison.

Bauer, Helen Pike. 2007. 'Eating in the Contact Zone: Food and Identity in Anglo-India'. *Consuming Culture in the Long Nineteenth Century: Narratives of Consumption, 1700–1900.* Eds. Tamara S. Wagner and Narin Hassan. Lanham, MD. Lexington Books. 95–106.

Beaumont, Matthew. 2004. 'Heathcliff's Great Hunger: The Cannibal Other in *Wuthering Heights*'. *Journal of Victorian Culture* 9.2. 137–163.

Beeton, Isabella. 2000. *Mrs Beeton's Book of Household Management.* Ed. Nicola Humble. Oxford. Oxford University Press.

Berg, Maggie. 2010. '"Let me Have its Bowels Then": Violence, Sacrificial Structure, and Anne Brontë's *The Tenant of Wildfell Hall*'. *LIT: Literature, Interpretation, Theory* 21.1. 20–40.

Bloomfield, Dennis. 2011. 'An Analysis of the Causes and Effects of Sickness and Death in *Wuthering Heights*'. *Brontë Studies* 36.3. 289–298.

Boyce, Charlotte. 2012. 'Representing the "Hungry Forties" in Image and Verse: The Politics of Hunger in Early-Victorian Illustrated Periodicals'. *Victorian Literature and Culture* 40.2. 421–449.

Brontë, Anne. 1996a. *The Tenant of Wildfell Hall*. Ed. Stevie Davies. London. Penguin.

Brontë, Charlotte. 1981. *Shirley*. Eds. Herbert Rosengarten and Margaret Smith. Oxford. Oxford University Press.

——. 1996b. *Jane Eyre*. Ed. Michael Mason. London. Penguin.

Brontë, Emily. 2003. *Wuthering Heights*. Ed. Pauline Nestor. London. Penguin.

Burnett, John. 1989. *Plenty and Want: A Social History of Food in England from 1815 to the Present Day*. 3rd edn. London. Routledge.

Campbell, Elizabeth. 1990. 'Of Mothers and Merchants: Female Economics in Christina Rossetti's "Goblin Market"'. *Victorian Studies* 33.3. 393–410.

Carpenter, Mary Wilson. 1991. '"Eat Me, Drink Me, Love Me": The Consumable Female Body in Christina Rossetti's *Goblin Market*'. *Victorian Poetry* 29.4. 415–434.

Carroll, Lewis. 1899. 'Hints for Etiquette: or, Dining Out Made Easy'. *The Lewis Carroll Picture Book: A Selection from the Unpublished Writings and Drawings of Lewis Carroll, Together with Reprints from Scarce and Unacknowledged Work*. Ed. Stuart Dodgson Collingwood. London. T. Fisher Unwin. 33–34.

——. 1998. *Alice's Adventures in Wonderland and Through the Looking-Glass and What Alice Found There*. Ed. Hugh Haughton. London. Penguin.

Chambers, Thomas King. 1850. *Corpulence; or, Excess of Fat in the Human Body*. London. Longman, Brown, Green and Longmans.

Chaudhuri, Nupur. 1992. 'Shawls, Jewelry, Curry, and Rice in Victorian Britain'. *Western Women and Imperialism: Complicity and Resistance*. Eds. Nupur Chaudhuri and Margaret Strobel. Bloomington and Indianapolis. Indiana University Press. 231–246.

'Clutterbuck, Lady Maria' [Catherine Dickens]. 2005. *What Shall We Have for Dinner? Satisfactorily Answered by Numerous Bills of Fare for From Two to Eighteen Persons*. Reprinted in Susan M. Rossi-Wilcox. *Dinner for Dickens: The Culinary History of Mrs Charles Dickens's Menu Books*. Totnes. Prospect Books. 21–74.

Collingwood, Stuart Dodgson. 1899. *The Life and Letters of Lewis Carroll*. London. T. Fisher Unwin.

Cozzi, Annette. 2010. *The Discourses of Food in Nineteenth-Century British Fiction*. New York. Palgrave Macmillan.

Dale, Peter Allan. 1985. 'George Eliot's "Brother Jacob": Fables and the Physiology of Common Life'. *Philological Quarterly* 64.1. 17–35.

Dennis, Abigail. 2007. '"A Study in Starvation": The New Girl and the Gendered Socialisation of Appetite in Sarah Grand's *The Beth Book*'. *Australasian Journal of Victorian Studies* 12.1. 19–34.

Dickens, Charles. 1971. *Our Mutual Friend*. Ed. Stephen Gill. Harmondsworth. Penguin.

——. 1984. *Martin Chuzzlewit*. Ed. Margaret Cardwell. Oxford. Oxford University Press.

——. 1985. *Oliver Twist*. Ed. Peter Fairclough. London. Penguin.

——. 1994. *Great Expectations*. Ed. Margaret Cardwell. Oxford. Oxford University Press.

——. 1996. *Bleak House*. Ed. Stephen Gill. Oxford. Oxford University Press.

——. 1997. *David Copperfield*. Ed. Nina Burgis. Oxford. Oxford University Press.

——. 2003. *The Pickwick Papers*. Ed. Mark Wormald. London. Penguin.

——. 2006. *A Christmas Carol and Other Christmas Books*. Ed. Robert Douglas-Fairhurst. Oxford. Oxford University Press.

Eagleton, Terry. 1975. *Myths of Power: A Marxist Study of the Brontës*. London and Basingstoke. Macmillan.

———. 1995. *Heathcliff and the Great Hunger: Studies in Irish Culture*. London. Verso.

Edwards, Simon. 1990. 'Anorexia Nervosa versus the Fleshpots of London: Rose and Nancy in *Oliver Twist*'. *Dickens Studies Annual* 19. 49–64.

Eliot, George. 1979. *The Mill on the Floss*. Ed. A. S. Byatt. London. Penguin.

———. 1999. 'Brother Jacob'. *The Lifted Veil and Brother Jacob*. Ed. Helen Small. Oxford. Oxford University Press. 45–87.

Fromer, Julie E. 2008. *A Necessary Luxury: Tea in Victorian England*. Athens. Ohio University Press.

Gaskell, Elizabeth. 1996. *Mary Barton*. Ed. Macdonald Daly. London. Penguin.

———. 1998. *Cranford*. Ed. Elizabeth Porges Watson. Oxford. Oxford University Press.

Gilbert, Sandra M. and Susan Gubar. 1979. *The Madwoman in the Attic: The Woman Writer and the Nineteenth-Century Literary Imagination*. New Haven, CT, and London. Yale University Press.

Gilead, Sarah. 1988. 'Barmecide Feasts: Ritual, Narrative, and the Victorian Novel'. *Dickens Studies Annual* 17. 225–247.

Gorsky, Susan Rubinow. 1999. '"I'll Cry Myself Sick": Illness in *Wuthering Heights*'. *Literature and Medicine* 18.2. 173–191.

Grand, Sarah. 2000. 'Should Married Women Follow Professions?' *Sex, Social Purity and Sarah Grand*. Vol. 1. Eds. Ann Heilmann and Stephanie Forward. London and New York. Routledge. 121–125.

———. 2013. *The Beth Book*. Ed. Jenny Bourne Taylor. Brighton. Victorian Secrets.

Guyer, Sara. 2004. 'The Girl with the Open Mouth: Through the Looking Glass'. *Angelaki* 9.1. 159–163.

Hassall, Arthur Hill. 1855. *Food and Its Adulterations; Comprising the Reports of the Analytical Sanitary Commission of 'The Lancet' for the Years 1851 to 1854 Inclusive*. London. Longman, Brown, Green and Longmans.

———. 1857. *Adulterations Detected; Or, Plain Instructions for the Discovery of Frauds in Food and Medicine*. London. Longman, Brown, Green, Longmans and Roberts.

Heilmann, Ann. 2004. *New Woman Strategies: Sarah Grand, Olive Schreiner, Mona Caird*. Manchester. Manchester University Press.

Hill, Marylu. 2005. '"Eat Me, Drink Me, Love Me": Eucharist and the Erotic Body in Christina Rossetti's *Goblin Market*'. *Victorian Poetry* 43.4. 455–472.

Holt, Terrence. 1990. '"Men Sell Not Such in Any Town": Exchange in *Goblin Market*'. *Victorian Poetry* 28.1. 51–67.

Houston, Gail Turley. 1994. *Consuming Fictions: Gender, Class, and Hunger in Dickens's Novels*. Carbondale and Edwardsville. Southern Illinois University Press.

Huff, Joyce L. 2001. 'A "Horror of Corpulence": Interrogating Bantingism and Mid-Nineteenth-Century Fat-Phobia'. *Bodies out of Bounds: Fatness and Transgression*. Eds. Jana Evans Braziel and Kathleen LeBesco. Berkeley and London. University of California Press. 39–59.

Hyman, Gwen. 2009. *Making a Man: Gentlemanly Appetites in the Nineteenth-Century British Novel*. Athens. Ohio University Press.

Laing, Samuel. 1844. *National Distress; Its Causes and Remedies*. London. Longman, Brown, Green and Longmans.

Lane, Margaret. 1970. 'Dickens on the Hearth'. *Dickens 1970*. Ed. Michael Slater. London. Chapman and Hall.

Lasègue, Charles. 1873. 'On Hysterical Anorexia'. *Medical Times and Gazette*. 6 September. 265–266.

Lashgari, Deirdre. 1992. 'What Some Women Can't Swallow: Hunger as Protest in Charlotte Brontë's *Shirley*'. *Disorderly Eaters: Texts in Self-Empowerment*. Eds. Lilian R.

Furst and Peter W. Graham. University Park. Pennsylvania State University Press. 141–152.

Ledger, Sally. 2007. *Dickens and the Popular Radical Imagination*. Cambridge. Cambridge University Press.

Lee, Michael Parrish. 2014. 'Eating Things: Food, Animals, and Other Life Forms in Lewis Carroll's *Alice* Books'. *Nineteenth-Century Literature* 68.4. 484–512.

Lhotsky, John. 1844. *On Cases of Death by Starvation, and Extreme Distress among the Humbler Classes, Considered as One of the Main Symptoms of the Present Disorganization of Society*. London. John Ollivier.

Lindner, Christoph. 2002. 'Thackeray's Gourmand: Carnivals of Consumption in *Vanity Fair*'. *Modern Philology* 99.4. 564–581.

Mann, Karen B. 1981. 'George Eliot's Language of Nature: Production and Consumption'. *ELH* 48.1. 190–216.

Marlow, James E. 1983. 'English Cannibalism: Dickens after 1859'. *Studies in English Literature, 1500–1900* 23.4. 647–666.

Marx, Karl. 1976. *Capital: Volume One*. Trans. Ben Fowkes. London. Penguin.

Mavor, Carol. 2008. 'For-getting to Eat: Alice's Mouthing Metonymy'. *The Nineteenth-Century Child and Consumer Culture*. Ed. Dennis Denisoff. Aldershot. Ashgate. 95–118.

Maxwell, Catherine. 1999. 'Tasting the "Fruit Forbidden": Gender, Intertextuality and Christina Rossetti's *Goblin Market*'. *The Culture of Christina Rossetti: Female Poetics and Victorian Contexts*. Eds. Mary Arseneau, Antony H. Harrison and Lorraine Janzen Kooistra. Athens. Ohio University Press. 75–102.

Menke, Richard. 1999. 'The Political Economy of Fruit'. *The Culture of Christina Rossetti: Female Poetics and Victorian Contexts*. Eds. Mary Arseneau, Antony H. Harrison and Lorraine Janzen Kooistra. Athens. Ohio University Press. 105–136.

Michie, Elsie. 1992. 'From Simianized Irish to Oriental Despots: Heathcliff, Rochester and Racial Difference'. *Novel: A Forum on Fiction* 25.2. 125–140.

Michie, Helena. 1987. *The Flesh Made Word: Female Figures and Women's Bodies*. New York and Oxford. Oxford University Press.

Miller, Andrew H. 1995. *Novels behind Glass: Commodity Culture and Victorian Narrative*. Cambridge. Cambridge University Press.

Moore, Tara. 2008. 'Starvation in Victorian Christmas Fiction'. *Victorian Literature and Culture* 36.2. 489–505.

Narayan, Uma. 1997. *Dislocating Cultures: Identities, Traditions, and Third-World Feminism*. New York and London. Routledge.

Nightingale, Florence. 1993. *Cassandra and Other Selections from Suggestions for Thought*. Ed. Mary Poovey. New York. New York University Press.

Pennell, Elizabeth Robins. 1900. *The Feasts of Autolycus: The Diary of a Greedy Woman*. Chicago, IL, and New York. The Saalfield Publishing Company.

Plasa, Carl. 2004. *Charlotte Brontë: Critical Issues*. Basingstoke. Palgrave Macmillan.

——. 2005. 'George Eliot's "Confectionery Business": Sugar and Slavery in "Brother Jacob"'. *LIT: Literature Interpretation Theory* 16.3. 285–309.

Purdue, Melissa. 2013. '"She had Suffered so Many Humiliations for Want of Money": The Quest for Financial Independence in Sarah Grand's *The Beth Book*'. *The Latchkey: Journal of New Woman Studies* 5. www.oscholars.com/Latchkey/Latchkey5/essay/Purdue.htm

Rigby, Elizabeth. 1974. Unsigned review from *Quarterly Review*. *The Brontës: The Critical Heritage*. Ed. Miriam Allott. Abingdon and New York. Routledge. 105–112.

Rodstein, Susan de Sola. 1991. 'Sweetness and Dark: George Eliot's "Brother Jacob"'. *Modern Language Quarterly* 52.3. 295–317.

Rossetti, Christina. 1893. *The Face of the Deep: A Devotional Commentary on the Apocalypse.* 2nd edn. London. Society for Promoting Christian Knowledge.

——. 2008. 'Goblin Market'. *Poems and Prose.* Ed. Simon Humphries. Oxford. Oxford University Press. 105–119.

Rossi-Wilcox, Susan M. 2005. *Dinner for Dickens: The Culinary History of Mrs Charles Dickens's Menu Books.* Totnes. Prospect Books.

Roy, Parama. 2010. *Alimentary Tracts: Appetites, Aversions, and the Postcolonial.* Durham, NC, and London. Duke University Press.

Saisselin, Rémy G. 1984. *The Bourgeois and the Bibelot.* New Brunswick, NJ. Rutgers University Press.

Schlossberg, Linda. 2001. '"The Low, Vague Hum of Numbers": The Malthusian Economies of *Jane Eyre*'. *Victorian Literature and Culture* 29.2. 489–506.

Schorn, Susan. 1998. 'Punish Her Body to Save Her Soul: Echoes of the Irish Famine in *Jane Eyre*'. *Journal of Narrative Technique* 28.3. 350–365.

Shakespeare, William. 1999. *The Tempest.* Eds. Virginia Mason Vaughan and Alden T. Vaughan. London. Arden Shakespeare.

Silver, Anna Krugovoy. 2002. *Victorian Literature and the Anorexic Body.* Cambridge. Cambridge University Press.

Small, Helen. 1999. Introduction. *The Lifted Veil and Brother Jacob.* By George Eliot. Oxford. Oxford University Press. ix–xxxviii.

Smith, Andrew. 2010. *The Ghost Story, 1840–1920: A Cultural History.* Manchester. Manchester University Press.

Steel, Flora Annie and Grace Gardiner. 2010. *The Complete Indian Housekeeper and Cook.* Eds. Ralph Crane and Anna Johnston. Oxford. Oxford University Press.

Stern, Rebecca. 2003. '"Adulterations Detected": Food and Fraud in Christina Rossetti's "Goblin Market"'. *Nineteenth-Century Literature* 57.4. 477–511.

Stoker, Bram. 2003. *Dracula.* Ed. Maurice Hindle. London. Penguin.

Stone, Harry. 1994. *The Night Side of Dickens: Cannibalism, Passion, Necessity.* Columbus. Ohio State University Press.

Sutton-Ramspeck, Beth. 2004. *Raising the Dust: The Literary Housekeeping of Mary Ward, Sarah Grand, and Charlotte Perkins Gilman.* Athens. Ohio University Press.

Talairach-Vielmas, Laurence. 2007. *Moulding the Female Body in Victorian Fairy Tales and Sensation Novels.* Aldershot. Ashgate.

Thackeray, William Makepeace. 1968. *Vanity Fair.* Ed. J. I. M. Stewart. London. Penguin.

——. 1984. *The Memoirs of Barry Lyndon, Esq.* Ed. Andrew Sanders. Oxford. Oxford University Press.

'Tibbs' [Charles Dickens]. 1835. 'Scenes and Characters – No. X: Christmas Festivities'. *Bell's Life in London, and Sporting Chronicle.* 27 December. 1.

Torgerson, Beth. 2005. *Reading the Brontë Body: Disease, Desire and the Constraints of Culture.* New York and Basingstoke. Palgrave Macmillan.

Tucker, Herbert F. 2003. 'Rossetti's Goblin Marketing: Sweet to Tongue and Sound to Eye'. *Representations* 82.1. 117–133.

Vanden Bossche, Chris R. 1986. 'Cookery, Not Rookery: Family and Class in *David Copperfield*'. *Dickens Studies Annual* 15. 87–109.

Vaughan, Alden T. and Virginia Mason Vaughan. 1991. *Shakespeare's Caliban: A Cultural History.* Cambridge. Cambridge University Press.

Vernon, James. 2007. *Hunger: A Modern History.* Cambridge, MA, and London. Harvard University Press.

Visser, Margaret. 1991. *The Rituals of Dinner: The Origins, Evolution, Eccentricities, and Meaning of Table Manners*. New York and London. Penguin.

Watts, Isaac. 1857. *Divine and Moral Songs for Children*. London. T. Nelson and Sons.

[Whiting, Sydney]. 1853. *Memoirs of a Stomach*. 2nd edn. London. W. E. Painter.

[Wills, William Henry]. 1851. 'Chips: Death in the Sugar Plum'. *Household Words* 2.44. 426–427.

Zlotnick, Susan. 2003. 'Domesticating Imperialism: Curry and Cookbooks in Victorian England'. *The Recipe Reader: Narratives – Contexts – Traditions*. Eds. Janet Floyd and Laurel Forster. Aldershot. Ashgate. 72–87.

6

YOU ARE WHAT YOU EAT?

Food and the politics of identity (1899–2003)

Charlotte Boyce

Throughout literary history, food has been intrinsic to articulations of identity. As this study has shown, the semiotics of consumption – what, how and where characters eat – reveal much about individual subjectivities and collective identities. Perhaps unsurprisingly, then, the notion that 'you are what you eat' remains potent within the literature of the twentieth and twenty-first centuries; however, the straightforward association of consumption with selfhood is also challenged and subverted by the fictions analyzed in this chapter, which tend to emphasize the contingency of conventional categories of being and the permeability of culturally constructed binaries. For instance, postcolonial writers such as Salman Rushdie, Andrea Levy, Zadie Smith and Monica Ali destabilize the idea that diet functions as a reliable marker of race, nation or ethnicity, pointing instead to the ways in which apparently naturalized cuisines have been imported, hybridized and absorbed by host cultures over time. In doing so, their novels validate David Bell and Gill Valentine's contention that 'the nation's diet is a feast of *imagined* commensality' – one that is underpinned by 'complex histories of trade links, cultural exchange, and especially colonialism' (1997, 169, my emphasis).

Traditional relationships between food and gender are, likewise, complicated or disrupted in the works of Virginia Woolf, Margaret Atwood and Angela Carter. Although the conventional role of female nourisher is typically linked to political and domestic disempowerment in these novelists' writings, existing on a continuum with the self-denying femininity located in the fiction of Jane Austen, Charles Dickens and Sarah Grand (see Chapters 4 and 5), cookery and consumption are additionally figured as sources of artistry, pleasure, erotic self-expression and author-ity in their works, thus enabling female characters to resist or undermine socially scripted norms. Proto-anorexic abstemiousness, of the kind seen earlier in Charlotte Brontë's *Shirley* and Emily Brontë's *Wuthering Heights* (Chapter 5), represents a further ambivalent strategy of cultural resistance in Woolf, Carter and Atwood's fiction; however, the use of food refusal as a conscious or unconscious form of protest is not specifically gendered in twentieth-century literature, as the diversely motivated fasting behaviours of Joyce's Stephen Dedalus, Carter's Finn Jowle and Rushdie's Aadam Aziz indicate.

As well as interrogating specific forms of identity, modern literature also calls into question the category of the 'human', with challenges to this privileged ontological order frequently clustering around representations of the cannibal (a recurrent figure in this study). Typically constructed as the guarantor of absolute difference between the 'civilized', 'human' self and the 'savage', 'non-human' Other, the cannibal in Joseph Conrad's fiction (as in Defoe's *Robinson Crusoe* in Chapter 3) subtly dissolves that distinction, highlighting instead the savagery that lurks within so-called civiliza-tion and the civility that co-exists with so-called savagery. Eating as cannibalism also emerges in James Joyce's *Ulysses*, where human bodies are persistently conflated with meat and acts of consumption are governed by an animalistic hunger, and in Woolf's *The Waves*, where Rhoda is afflicted by a recurrent dread of being devoured. These representations build on and intensify the deconstruction of the human/animal binary found in previously examined eighteenth-century novels, such as *Gulliver's Travels* (Chapter 3), and Victorian fictions, such as *Great Expectations*, *Vanity Fair* and *Alice's Adventures in Wonderland* (Chapter 5).

Despite its affiliations with violence and aggression, death and dissolution, food is also integral to positive literary representations of commensality in modern and postmodern writing. Indeed, the quest for communion through food is one that tacitly underpins much of the literature considered in this chapter. As in earlier chapters, however, the sense of belonging and shared humanity achieved through acts of consumption tends always to be precarious and provisional; grounded in shifting subjectivities and imaginary identifications, culinary community is at best a transient and ephemeral phenomenon in twentieth- and twenty-first-century fiction, as we shall see.

Joseph Conrad, *Heart of Darkness* (1899) and 'Falk: A Reminiscence' (1903)

In the preface to his wife Jessie's *Handbook of Cookery for a Small House* (1921), Joseph Conrad posits that national happiness is 'elaborated mainly in the kitchen', and contrasts the 'righteous art of cooking' practised in the homes of suburban Britons with the 'ill-cooked food' of the 'Noble Red Men' (Native Americans), whose 'indigestible feasts' supposedly function as 'a direct incentive to counsels of unrea-sonable violence' (2010, 113). Facetiously distinguishing 'good' from 'bad' cookery in such racio-nationalistic terms, Conrad appears here to endorse the prevailing culinary assumptions of the nineteenth century, discussed in Chapter 5, which opposed the polite act of 'dining' to animalistic 'eating' and deemed the former the privilege of an implicitly Eurocentric civilization. In Conrad's fiction, however, a more complex picture emerges: if his works appear at times to resurrect the racist dietary tropes of earlier imperialist narratives, they also trouble and subvert the binary alimentary logic that typically underpins colonial discourse. In particular, Conrad's representations of cannibalism – *sine qua non* of the ideological distinction between 'civilized' European self and 'savage' non-European Other – are marked by a profound ambivalence that unsettles cultural stereotypes and dissolves traditional categories of identity.

Conrad's early readers would have been culturally conditioned to associate cannibalism with the central-African setting of *Heart of Darkness*, his classic tale of colonial exploitation. Stories of primitive, anthropophagic tribes were familiar not only from the imperial-adventure narratives of writers such as H. Rider Haggard and R. M. Ballantyne, but also from non-fictional sources, such as the *Encyclopædia Britannica*, which casually alleged in a 1902 entry on Congo Free State that 'in many districts' of this Belgian-controlled enclave 'cannibalism is rife' (qtd. in Conrad 2006, 107). Recent scholarship has challenged such unsupported claims, arguing that the practice of cannibalism in Africa was neither so widespread, so uniform nor so straightforward as Victorian and Edwardian novelists and ethnographers assumed.[1] Nevertheless, the stereotype of the 'man-eating African' was fully ingrained in the European cultural imaginary at the beginning of the twentieth century, serving as a useful motif for the inscription and securance of ontological difference; as Anthony Fothergill points out, 'stock-in-trade' representations of the cannibal helped to define the limits of Western selfhood, working to categorize 'all that "we are not"' (1996, 107).

Initially, *Heart of Darkness* appears complicit with this racialized discourse of dietary difference. The tale's main narrator, Marlow, nonchalantly introduces the indigenous crew of the steamship he has been hired to navigate into the heart of a Congo-esque ivory-trading state as cannibalistic savages with sharp, filed teeth. Largely unindividuated, these 'grunting', atavistic figures are given a voice only to confirm their already-asserted anthropophagic tastes: the crew's head-man at one point demands that Marlow catch a group of hostile natives on the riverbank and 'give 'im to us', so that he and his companions can 'eat 'im!' (Conrad 2006, 40). Yet, despite this seemingly unambiguous statement of cannibalistic intent, the crew are never actually depicted eating human flesh. Marlow reports that they originally brought along a provision of hippo-meat for the journey and that, when that turned rotten and was thrown overboard by their nauseated European shipmates, they subsisted instead on 'a few lumps of some stuff like half-cooked dough' (41) – a substance David Gill identifies as '*kwanga*, a type of bread made from manioc', an edible root (1999, 8). Indeed, the appetites of the imputed cannibals are for the most part marked by a restraint that Marlow finds hard to comprehend: 'Why in the name of all the gnawing devils of hunger they didn't go for us – they were thirty to five – and have a good tuck-in for once amazes me now when I think of it' (41). In the absence of verified knowledge – Marlow doesn't think to *ask* the crew about their ascetic dispositions – their alimentary self-control is framed in terms of Marlow's own struggle against 'inexorable physical necessity' (41); describing 'lingering starvation' as a form of 'torment', he avers that 'it takes a man all his inborn strength to fight hunger properly' (42). This projection of heroic masculinity onto the native crew suggests a consciousness of shared humanity, or 'remote kinship' as Marlow puts it elsewhere (36), subtly eroding the grounds of difference between respectable self and repudiated Other. The process of metaphoric assimilation is further vivified in Marlow's syntactically faltering fantasy of being selected for ingestion by his companions: 'I own to you that just then I perceived – in a new light, as it were – how unwholesome the pilgrims [white shipmates] looked, and I hoped, yes I positively hoped, that my aspect was not so – what shall I say? – so – unappetising' (41). Imaginatively identifying himself with both appraising cannibal and potential victim, Marlow here unsettles the discrete boundaries of colonial identity, dissolving the supposedly fixed distinctions between contraposed subject positions; significantly, he has already admitted in an earlier part of the text that 'being hungry' makes him 'savage' (23). This process of psychological identification has interesting resonances with *Robinson Crusoe*, in which the protagonist at one point muses that the cannibals on whose island he finds himself shipwrecked would likely consider *him* in the same light as that in which *he* considers the animals he kills for food (see Chapter 3).

The barely suppressed anxiety that unrestrained appetites might lurk within the 'civilized' European self manifests itself most ominously in *Heart of Darkness* in relation to Kurtz, the peerless company agent who, the text implies, has succumbed to anthropophagic urges following his immersion in African culture. His mooted participation in taboo culinary acts is enveloped, however, in 'a complicated and evasive semiotics', as Allan Simmons points out; whereas the native steamship crew are categorized as cannibals despite their non-participation in any cannibalistic act, Kurtz, by contrast, 'may well have done the deed but can't be described as a cannibal' (2002, 96). Leaving the interdicted act unnamed, Marlow only refers obliquely to 'inconceivable ceremonies of some devilish initiation' (48), 'unspeakable rites' and mysterious sacral offerings (50). In a further obfuscatory move, Kurtz's carnal tastes are tacitly attributed to his own figurative devourment by the African jungle; we are told that the 'wilderness . . . had taken him, loved him, embraced him, got into his veins, [and] consumed his flesh' (48). Such rhetorical efforts to displace cannibalistic desire onto the colonized landscape fail to erase the overriding image of Kurtz's ravenous orality, however. In a much-analyzed passage, Marlow watches, captivated, as the corrupted agent 'open[s] his mouth wide' in a gesture that '[gives] him a weirdly voracious aspect as though he had wanted to swallow all the air, all the earth, all the men before him' (59).

Kurtz's insatiable omnivorousness here replicates what Alan Bewell has labelled the '*geophagy*' of Western imperialism, whereby 'the capacity to rule the world is signified by one's ability to consume it' (1999, 143). Like Jonathan Swift before him (see Chapter 3), Conrad deploys the motif of cannibalism to critique the inherent rapacity of colonial enterprise, its 'asymmetrical extraction and exploitation' of resources and peoples (Roy 2010, 13).[2] What is more, he indicates that the effects of such 'capitalist anthropophagy' (Phillips 1998, 188) extend far beyond the African jungle, infiltrating the supposedly refined habitations of polite Europeans. Notably, in the continental drawing-room of Kurtz's 'Intended', Marlow observes a stately grand piano (whose ivory keys tacitly evoke the brutal plunder of the Inner Station) and compares it to 'a sombre and polished sarcophagus' (73) – etymologically, a 'flesh-eater' – thus 'locating the savage within the civilized', as John Rickard suggests (2007, 56).

The submerged presence of 'the savage within the civilized' is further explored in Conrad's short story 'Falk', a tale of survival cannibalism in which the opening frame narration provides proleptic clues to the themes of hunger *in extremis* and culinary violence that will follow. An 'execrable' dinner of chops at 'a small river-hostelry' provokes the initial, unnamed narrator to muse upon

> the night of ages when the primeval man, evolving the first rudiments of cookery from his dim consciousness, scorched lumps of flesh at a fire of sticks in the company of other good fellows; then, gorged and happy, sat him back among the gnawed bones to tell his artless tales of experience – the tales of hunger and hunt.
>
> *2002, 77*

The primal appetite imagined here bursts its prehistoric bounds and erupts violently into the present when one of the frame-narrator's dining companions begins to relate *his* 'artless tale' of Falk, a Scandinavian tug-boat captain in an Eastern seaport, whose peculiar physical tics – he habitually 'draw[s] the palms of both his hands down his face, giving at the same time a slight, almost imperceptible, shudder' (90) – and unwavering repugnance for meat arouse the curiosity of his acquaintances. In particular, Falk's unusual gastronomy is scrutinized by Schomberg, the owner of a local hotel, who deems it both unnatural and unmanly. In an extended diatribe, he tells the narrator that Falk

> has got hold now of a Madras cook – a blamed fraud that I hunted out of my cookhouse with a rattan. He was not fit to cook for white men. No, not for the white men's dogs either; but, see, any damned native that can boil a pot of rice is good enough for Mr Falk. Rice and a little fish he buys for a few cents from the fishing-boats outside is what he lives on. You would hardly credit it – eh? A white man, too . . . A white man should eat like a white man, dash it all . . . Ought to eat meat, must eat meat.
>
> *97–98*

As well as abjuring the carnivorous diet that Schomberg sees as essential to white subjectivity, Falk fails to participate in the sociable dining practices typically associated with middle-class civility. Schomberg reveals that Falk's Madras cook takes whatever frugal dish he has prepared for his employer 'up to the wheelhouse . . . with a cover on it, and [Falk] shuts both the doors before he begins to eat' (98), misanthropically rejecting the company of his crew who are expected to 'feed all alone' in their cabins (99).[3]

Falk's 'peculiar domestic arrangements' (121) contrast sharply with the welcoming commensality practised on board the *Diana*, a German vessel belonging to the narrator's friend Hermann. Populated by Hermann's 'growing family' (79), the

Diana is repeatedly figured as a homely space, 'devoted to the support of domestic virtues' (122). The cabin in which the narrator regularly enjoys the family's hospitality is furnished 'more like a farm kitchen than a ship's cuddy', with the result that 'the sea and all nautical affairs [seem] very far removed' (83) from its 'arcadian felicity' (86). The bourgeois contentment of this happy, convivial space is shaken, however, when Falk (who wishes to marry Hermann's niece) reveals to Hermann and the narrator that he has previously 'eaten man' (129) while stranded on board a broken-down ship in the Antarctic. His admission forces his auditors to confront their complacent assumptions about human subjectivity, for, as Tony Tanner suggests, the act of cannibalism precipitates the breakdown of 'hitherto unquestioned taxonomies':

> If we may allow that 'man' and 'food' are two categories which are usually considered necessarily distinct, then cannibalism . . . becomes an example of the wrong things in the wrong categories, i.e. man shifts into the food category, where he shouldn't be, just as he ends up in another human stomach, again where he shouldn't be.
>
> *1976, 28*

Unable to cope with such paradigmatic collapse, Hermann attempts to uphold the conventional boundaries of identity by excluding Falk from the order of the human. Asserting that 'the duty of a human being [is] to starve' in extreme circumstances, Hermann denounces Falk as 'a beast, an animal' (132), using the German verb 'fressen' (131) to accentuate Falk's declension from the human (whereas 'essen' conveys the human act of eating, 'fressen' is typically deployed in relation to animals).[4] Ironically, these 'outraged denunciations of Falk', which deny his human status, 'fail to get to grips with what is distinctively horrific about cannibalism', as Paul Vlitos points out (2008, 438). It is precisely *because* Falk is human that his act appals; it is the mutual humanity of eater and eaten that arouses Hermann's visceral – and hypocritical – disgust (notably, the self-proclaimed moralist is happy to surrender his niece to Falk's voracious sexual hunger).

What perturbs the narrator most, by contrast, is the rift between Falk's reported experience and his own 'preconceived notions as to how a case of "cannibalism and suffering at sea" should be managed' (135). Perhaps conditioned by literary representations such as the sinking of the *Trinidada* in Byron's *Don Juan* (see Chapter 4), the narrator assumes that Falk and his fellow seamen were shipwrecked or marooned – 'I had . . . supposed they had been starving in boats or on a raft – or perhaps on a barren rock' (135) – and that the stoic survivors would have drawn lots to determine who should sacrifice themselves to be eaten. Falk's bald response to this suggestion – 'What lots? Do you think I would have allowed my life to go for the drawing of lots? . . . It was everybody for himself' (135) – explodes the sentimentality of such thinking. The romanticized idea of 'the last extremity of sailors, overtaking a small boat or a frail craft . . . because of the direct danger of the seas' might seem 'easier to bear' to the narrator, but, crucially, Falk's Darwinian struggle for survival takes place on board a modern steamship: 'safe, convenient, roomy: a ship with beds, bedding, knives, forks, comfortable cabins, glass and china, and a complete cook's galley' (139). It is the schismatic disjunction between these trappings of modernity and the primitive, cannibalistic hunger that lurks amongst them that represents, for the narrator, 'the grotesque horror of this sombre story' (139).

By dislocating anthropophagy from its conventional temporal and geographical anchors in this way, 'Falk' makes 'a rupture in the monolithic discourse on cannibalism', as Harry Sewlall points out (2006, 171). Rather than containing cannibalism within a 'savage' colonial landscape or a mythic, primeval past, 'Falk' explores its manifestation within the modern European self. Cannibals might be 'fine fellows . . . in their place', as *Heart of Darkness*'s Marlow suggests (2006, 34), but out of place they function as an affront to Western self-knowledge, as demonstrated by the hypocritical Hermann; tellingly, he condemns Falk as much for having *admitted* to the breaking of culinary taboo – for forcing him to confront the possibility of European cannibalism – as for having undertaken the act. While acknowledging and exploiting the horror of cannibalistic consumption, then, Conrad's fiction also critiques complacent bourgeois thinking. Exploring 'the fascination of the abomination' (2006, 6), his works test the limits of 'civilized' Western selfhood by subverting the oppositional logic on which constructions of the cannibal typically depend.

James Joyce, *Ulysses* (1922)

Thoughts of food and acts of consumption are central to the quotidian dynamics of James Joyce's modernist classic *Ulysses*. The novel is strikingly attentive to the routine bodily processes of ingestion, digestion and excretion, its alimentary fixation emerging at the level of form as well as content; as Lindsey Tucker points out, protagonist Leopold Bloom's ambulations around Dublin city centre were designed by Joyce to be discernibly 'peristaltic in movement' (1984, 62). Food and eating are also implicated in wider cycles of life and death in the novel. After attending Paddy Dignam's funeral in the chapter titled 'Hades', Bloom conceives of the earth as a remorseless devourer of bodies, fancying that the soil of the graveyard is 'quite fat with corpse manure, bones, flesh, nails' that turn 'a tallowy kind of a cheesy. Then begin to get black, treacle oozing out of them' (Joyce 1993, 104). The macabre nature of this image of decomposition, in which the human body is reconstituted as food – a 'regular square feed' for rats, maggots and flies (110)[5] – is mitigated by the concomitant textual acknowledgement that necrophagy leads to regeneration: as Bloom observes, 'It's the blood sinking in the earth gives new life' (104). A similarly productive cycle of organic renewal is imagined at the end of 'Calypso' when the defecating Bloom contemplates growing vegetables in a corner of his garden, fertilized by faeces: 'droppings are very good top dressing . . . Always have fresh greens then' (66). If food is repeatedly linked to waste, death and decay in *Ulysses*, it is also figured as vital and re-energizing, the essential stuff of 'warm fullblooded life' (110).

Bloom, certainly, is invigorated by his relationship to food. We are told at the beginning of 'Calypso' that

> Mr Leopold Bloom ate with relish the inner organs of beasts and fowls. He liked thick giblet soup, nutty gizzards, a stuffed roast heart, liver slices fried with crustcrumbs, fried hencod's roes. Most of all he liked grilled mutton kidneys which gave to his palate a fine tang of faintly scented urine.
>
> *53*

In keeping with this much-emphasized predilection for offal (it is attested to again in 'Sirens'), Bloom's first meal of the day on 16 June 1904 is a pork kidney, fried in butter. 'Done to a turn', this renal feast is a clear source of gustatory pleasure: Bloom 'chew[s] with discernment the toothsome pliant meat' and eagerly sops up its gravy with chunks of bread and butter (63). Notably, though, the language of culinary desire at this meal is tinged by an antithetical lexis of disgust. The sarcous, sanguinary quality of Bloom's preferred breakfast dish – the raw kidney is described as 'ooz[ing] bloodguts' (57), while in its cooked form it is characterized as 'burnt flesh' (63) – blurs the boundary between animal and human, demonstrating Gilles Deleuze's contention that 'meat is the common zone of man and the beast, the zone of their indiscernibility' (2005, 17). The bloody kidney also hints at the violence inherent in carnivorous consumption, a common theme within this study, and something that Bloom later acknowledges while walking down Duke Street. Musing on the pain experienced by butchered animals and envisioning the stomach-churning sights of the shambles – 'Pulp. Rawhead and bloody bones' – Bloom admits that there's 'a lot' to be said for vegetarianism (163), a diet he has previously dismissed as 'wind and watery' (158).[6] Yet, even the meat-free lunch that Bloom subsequently selects at Davy Byrne's pub – a gorgonzola sandwich – has the potential to engender disgust, recalling as it does his earlier observation that cheese is the 'corpse of milk' (110). As Sandra M. Gilbert concludes in her reading of Joyce's 1914 short story 'The Dead', the meal in modernist fiction simultaneously 'seeks to triumph over' and 'struggles to hold off' the looming prospect of death (2014, 107).[7]

Bloom's cosmopolitan tastes and orderly mode of consumption – at Davy Byrne's he carefully and precisely 'cut[s] his sandwich into slender strips' before eating it (164) – work to distinguish him from the animalistic eaters he observes in another Duke Street pub, the Burton. On entering this establishment,

> Stink gripped his trembling breath: pungent meatjuice, slop of greens. See the animals feed.
>
> Men, men, men.
>
> Perched on high stools by the bar, hats shoved back, at the tables calling for more bread no charge, swilling, wolfing gobfuls of sloppy food, their eyes bulging, wiping wetted moustaches. A pallid suetfaced young man polished his tumbler knife fork and spoon with his napkin. New set of microbes. A man with an infant's saucestained napkin tucked round him shovelled gurgling

soup down his gullet. A man spitting back on his plate: halfmasticated gristle: no teeth to chewchewchew it. Chump chop from the grill. Bolting to get it over.

161

Bloom's assertion that he 'couldn't eat a morsel here' (161) stems not only from his visceral revulsion towards the bestial diners' retrogressive eating habits and lack of dietary hygiene, but also from the sense of estrangement and unhomeliness generated by this public dining-space. As Lauren Rich notes, 'food fails as a basis for community at the Burton, at least in part, because the patrons appear to be in desperate competition for it' (2010, 87). Instead of fostering humane inter-social relations, the Burton's restaurant activates the kind of 'survival-of-the-fittest' mentality described in Conrad's 'Falk', or, as Bloom puts it, 'Every fellow for his own, tooth and nail. Gulp. Grub. Gulp. Gobstuff. . . . Eat or be eaten. Kill! Kill!' (162).

The philanthropic alternative to this 'all for number one' (162) alimentary ideology is provided in *Ulysses* by Bloom himself, who, as well as being one of the novel's most enthusiastic consumers, is also its primary nourisher (a role more usually associated with women in the literature considered in this volume). During the text's circadian course, Bloom prepares a breakfast of tea and bread and butter for his wife, Molly (about whose gustatory needs he is particularly solicitous); pours a saucerful of 'warmbubbled milk' (54) for their pet cat; feeds the gulls by the river Liffey with two Banbury cakes from a nearby street-stall; gives away the 'lukewarm pig's crubeen [foot]' and 'cold sheep's trotter' (413) he has purchased from Olhousen's butcher's to a hungry dog; and considerately furnishes Stephen Dedalus with some coffee and a roll at the cabman's shelter following the pair's drunken adventures in Nighttown. As this inventory of alimentary altruism shows, Bloom's actions work to counter his own pessimistic suggestion that life necessarily involves 'everybody eating everyone else' (118). A further example of his culinary hospitality can be found in the chapter 'Ithaca', in which he drinks a mug of Epps's cocoa with Stephen in the kitchen at Eccles Street. Commonly interpreted as a form of secular communion, this shared meal comes close to achieving the kind of genuine fellowship that Bloom feels is lacking from non-spiritual environments, such as the Burton, but also from the contemporary religious sphere. Tellingly, while observing a Catholic mass at All Hallows in 'Lotus Eaters', he dismisses the traditional ritual of the Eucharist as both narcotic ('stupefies them') and cannibalistic ('rum idea: eating bits of a corpse'), and he later configures the priesthood as parasitic ('no families themselves to feed. Living on the fat of the land'), affiliating them with the 'all for number one' philosophy he stands against (77, 145).[8]

Bloom's quasi-maternal interest in nourishing Stephen can be attributed to the latter's consistent alignment with symbolic and material hunger. As Tucker points out, 'aside from his three cups of tea and [his housemate] Mulligan's accusation, "You have eaten all we left, I suppose", we have no view of Stephen eating' in *Ulysses* (1984, 31). Indeed, in 'Eumaeus', Stephen suggests that he hasn't dined since 'the day before yesterday' (610), an admission that leads Bloom to ascribe his subsequent collapse during their walk home to 'gastric inanition' (620). Stephen's apparent rejection of 'solid food' – he tells Bloom that 'liquids I can eat' (590) – not only contrasts with Bloom's hearty ingestion, but also connects Stephen to the 'famished ghosts' (163) of Ireland's past; as Miriam O'Kane Mara suggests (and as the earlier sections on Spenser and Swift in this study show), 'starvation, both willing and unwilling, is a recurring theme in Irish history' (2009, 94).[9] If, for Stephen, 'history . . . is a nightmare from which I am trying to awake' (34), his seemingly compulsive abstemiousness can be read in the light of a traumatic response to the particular horrors of the Irish Famine (an event that haunts Joyce's novel in allusive form, as it did the Brontëan fiction discussed in Chapter 5).[10] Stephen's hungering also resonates with his more immediate personal history, foregrounding, in particular, his troubled relationship with his mother, who is likewise associated with the abjuration of food. At the fractious Christmas dinner in *A Portrait of the Artist as a Young Man* (1916), Mrs Dedalus eats but 'little' of the festive meal she has prepared (Joyce 1992, 31), at one point laying down her knife and fork in a gesture of protest that distinguishes her from the voracious men at the table. In *Ulysses*, meanwhile, the memories of her that beset Stephen's 'brooding brain' repeatedly correlate her with alimentary self-denial and physical attenuation: he remembers 'her glass of water from the kitchen tap when she had approached the sacrament' (i.e. she fasted before mass) and, in a dream, he perceives 'her wasted body within its loose graveclothes' looming over him (10). As Julieann Ulin suggests, Stephen appears to have 'ingested the cultural memory of the Famine', the tropes of which he then redeploys 'to illustrate his own personal demons' (2011, 33).

Individual and collective histories of hunger intersect once again in *Ulysses* when Mrs Dedalus's 'emaciated' ghost materializes in 'Circe' (539). Significantly, the 'green rill of bile' (540) that trickles from her mouth recalls not only the cancer that eventually devoured her from within, but also the green-mouthed Irish men and women of Famine iconography, who consumed grass in their desperate attempts to stave off the insistent pangs of hunger (see Ulin 2011, 40). Such 'intertextual and . . . intergastrical allusions' to starvation were vested with particular potency around the time of *Ulysses*' publication for, during this period, republican hunger-strikers such as Terence MacSwiney were consciously transforming their bodies into 'the "quotations" of their forebears and reinscrib[ing] the cause of Irish nationalism in the spectacle of starving flesh' (Ellmann 1993, 14). Like these real-life protesters, Joyce's Stephen Dedalus is mindful of – and resistant to – his colonized status as 'servant' of 'the imperial British state' (20); however, his food refusal does not represent a straightforward endorsement of nationalist politics. He is, for instance, markedly sceptical of the culinary values of the Irish Revival, which advocated a return to simple, wholesome foods and national self-sufficiency. Writing in the *Irish Homestead* in 1913, Revivalist George William Russell (A.E.) argued that

> There is no doubt that the vitality of Irish people has seriously diminished and that the change has come about with a change in the character of the food consumed. When people lived with porridge, brown bread and milk,

> as main ingredients in their diet, the vitality and energy of our people were
> noticeable, though they were much poorer than they are now.
>
> *1978, 375*

In language reminiscent of the luxury debates of the eighteenth century (see
Chapter 4), Revivalists criticized the modern taste for items such as tea and white
bread, promoting instead the health-giving properties of native agricultural produce.
Milk, in particular, was lauded as the 'best all round food anyone could take' (Russell
1978, 70). Wholesome and of rural origin, it was held to 'strengthen both body and
mind and thus . . . to counteract the supposed impurity of modern experience', as
Helen O'Connell suggests (2013, 132).[11] In *Ulysses*, this ideologically freighted
lactic rhetoric is aped by Stephen's friend Buck Mulligan, who tells the aged woman
delivering milk to Martello Tower, 'if we could only live on good food like that
. . . we wouldn't have the country full of rotten teeth and rotten guts' (14). For
Stephen, however, the milk-woman embodies only a warped version of 'Mother
Ireland': one that signifies dearth rather than nutritious plenitude. Watching her
'pour into the measure and thence into the jug rich white milk, not hers', he focuses
mentally on her 'old shrunken paps' – symbolic tokens of her inability to adequately
nourish the nation – and mockingly labels her 'silk of the kine', a traditional name
for Ireland meaning 'the most beautiful of cattle' (13–14).

Stephen's scornful puncturing of Revivalist milk-fetishism represents a critique of
the idea that dietary nationalism can eliminate the problem of contemporary hunger.
Indeed, *Ulysses* abounds with indications that, in the early twentieth century, Irish
famishment was by no means consigned to the past. Among the modern hungerers
who inhabit the text's pages are the men Bloom sees carrying Hely's advertising
boards through the streets, who 'just keep skin and bone together' on a diet of 'bread
and skilly [broth]' (147), and the 'barefoot arab' who stands over the grating of
Harrison's confectionery store, 'breathing in the fumes' of 'newbaked jampuffs
rolypoly' in order to 'deaden the gnaw of hunger' (150). Stephen's sisters, too, are
emblems of modern-day dietary deprivation. Spotting one of them loitering outside
Dillon's auction rooms, Bloom exclaims, 'Good Lord, that poor child's dress is in
flitters. Underfed she looks too. Potatoes and marge, marge and potatoes' (145). His
speculations about the Dedalus family's poverty-diet are well founded: in a later
domestic scene that knowingly evokes the charity-food of Famine-era Ireland,
Maggy Dedalus responds to her sister Boody's demand, 'Crickey, is there nothing
for us to eat?' by directing her to a kettle of thick 'peasoup' on the range, donated
by local nuns (217). The poverty of the Dedalus household is again intimated when
Stephen's 'mind's eye' engages itself 'in repicturing his family hearth the last time he
saw it, with his sister Dilly sitting by the ingle, her hair hanging down, waiting for
some weak Trinidad shell cocoa that was in the sootcoated kettle to be done so that
she and he could drink it with the oatmeal water for milk' (576). By attesting to the
perpetuation of Irish malnourishment in this way, *Ulysses* demystifies Revivalist
discourse, indicating that the problem of hunger cannot 'be eradicated by either a
diet of milk or a rhetoric of wholeness', as O'Connell suggests (2013, 144).

Yet, despite its gloomy assessment of modern dietary relations, Joyce's novel ends on a surprisingly optimistic alimentary note. Its final section, 'Penelope', comprises the interior monologue of Bloom's wife, Molly, and here, once again, food is represented as a source of pleasure and rejuvenation. Unlike the physical famishment described elsewhere in *Ulysses*, Molly's hunger – for food, love and sexual satisfaction – is figured as regenerative and life-affirming. Like the speakers of the Keatsian poetry considered earlier in Chapter 4, Molly revels in the sensory pleasure of ingestion, stating at one point, 'I wished I could have picked every morsel of that chicken out of my fingers it was so tasty and browned and as tender as anything' (701), and, later, 'Id love a big juicy pear now to melt in your mouth' (729). Even the affiliated processes of digestion and elimination are a source of joyful liberation to her ('wherever you be let your wind go free' [714]), and foods that have previously functioned in the text as *memento mori*, such as Plumtree's potted meat (a product Bloom repeatedly associates with Paddy Dignam's dead body), are now reconceptualized in terms of gratification and repletion; dwelling on her recent sexual liaison with Blazes Boylan, Molly remembers 'we took the port and potted meat [to bed] it had a fine salty taste yes' (693). With her twinned gustatory and carnal appetites, Molly is a great 'ingester/assimilator of life' – a 'personification of rites of *plerosis*', or fulfilment – as Tucker suggests (1984, 146, 152). She is also, like Bloom, a nourisher of others. Recollecting the period when she nursed her infant daughter, Molly says, 'I had a great breast of milk with Milly enough for two' (705), her plenitude contrasting with the sterility of the milk-woman in 'Telemachus'. A subsequent memory – of feeding a 'bit of seedcake' to Bloom from 'out of [her] mouth' during their lovemaking on Howth Hill (731) – recalls Freud's claim that sexual desire is rooted in the desire for nourishment and that sexual satisfaction is 'analogous to the sating of hunger' (1953, 149).[12] The potential for Molly and Bloom to recover some of this mutually remembered gastronomic intimacy is hinted at via Molly's apparent willingness to prepare breakfast in bed for her husband in the morning: 'Ill throw him up his eggs and tea . . . I suppose hed like my nice cream too' (729). Whether this conciliatory gift of food, with its additional promise of sex, will in fact materialize or help to reinvigorate the Blooms' marital relations is left unclear by Joyce; however, the novel's closing affirmation – 'Yes' (732) – gestures towards the exhilarating possibility of such alimentary communion.

Virginia Woolf, *To the Lighthouse* (1927) and *The Waves* (1931)

In the opening chapter of her feminist manifesto *A Room of One's Own* (1929), Virginia Woolf suggests that it is a 'curious fact' that novelists 'seldom spare a word for what was eaten' at a luncheon party: 'It is part of the novelist's convention not to mention soup and salmon and ducklings, as if soup and salmon and ducklings were of no importance whatsoever' (1993, 9). The aliment-rich works considered in this volume would seem to contradict this assertion, as indeed would Woolf's own writings, which insistently explore the gustatory, olfactory and aesthetic qualities of foods, as well as their wider symbolic meanings. As Allie Glenny points out, 'states of hunger, ingestion, and repletion were not to her ordinary, unremarked phenomena but significant events with ontological implications' (1999, xvi). Acts of consumption work to foster a sense of identity and belonging: in an interesting metaphor of nourishment, Woolf wrote of the 'succulence' of her social group, the Bloomsbury Circle (qtd. in Glenny 1999, 140), and, notably, many of the meals in her novels involve a search for pleasurable communion through food. However, eating in Woolf's works can also presage a dizzying sense of non-identity or dissolution, as well as a consciousness of the self's inevitable mortality; tellingly, the centripetal meals in both of the texts considered here – *To the Lighthouse* and *The Waves* – have been compared by critics to the Last Supper (see Handley 1994, 26; Utell 2008, 15). While serving, then, to quicken the senses and sustain life and friendship, the Woolfian feast (like its Joycean counterpart) is invariably haunted by intimations of ephemerality and death.

For Janine Utell, the commensal meal that forms the climactic centre of *To the Lighthouse* can be interpreted as a form of proleptic mourning for the deaths that will soon follow in the novel (2008, 5): of Prue Ramsay, during childbirth; of Andrew Ramsay, a solider of the Great War; and, most significantly, of Mrs Ramsay, the dinner's hostess, who implicitly sacrifices herself to her role as spousal and maternal nurturer ('giving, giving, giving, she had died' [Woolf 2006, 124]). Woolf's sister, Vanessa Bell, famously identified in the depiction of Mrs Ramsay the figure of their mother, Julia Stephen, 'raised from the dead' (Bell 1972, 128), but *To the Lighthouse*'s matriarch also represents a more general apparition of the Victorian 'Angel in the House', a woman who, according to Woolf, 'sacrificed herself daily', always deferring to the wishes of others so that if, for instance, 'there was chicken' for dinner, 'she [would take] the leg' (1942, 150). Mrs Ramsay clearly conforms to this model of self-abnegating femininity (several examples of which are considered in Chapter 5); we are told that she devotes herself to the charitable nurturance of the poor and to the sustenance of her large family with 'an instinct like the swallows for the south, the artichokes for the sun' (2006, 160). At dinner, she diligently addresses the alimentary needs of others, helping her guests to the most 'tender piece[s]' of meat (85) and assuring those assembled that 'there is plenty for everybody' (86). Her nourishing disposition is further implied via her fixation with milk, a substance redolent of maternal care: like the Irish Revivalists considered in the previous section, Mrs Ramsay is eloquent on the health benefits of 'real butter and clean milk' (84), and she directs Mildred, the cook, to 'keep a plate of milk soup' for Mrs McNab, the housekeeper, to restore her after she has carried a heavy basket to the Ramsay household from town (112).

Such culinary ministrations are evidently a source of pleasure to Mrs Ramsay, as they were to earlier Victorian heroines such as Dickens's Ruth Pinch and Grand's Beth Caldwell (Chapter 5); we are told that 'every nerve of [Mrs Ramsay's] body' fills with a pure sense of 'joy' as she watches her 'husband and children and friends' eating together (85). However, her interior monologue also suggests her frustration with the limitations imposed on her by her domestic role. As her guests take their seats at the dinner party she has organized, she suddenly questions what she has done with her life, concluding that her existence amounts to little more than 'an infinitely long table and plates and knives' (68). Her ambivalent attitude here to her social role connects her in particular to the character of Caroline Helstone in Charlotte Brontë's *Shirley* (Chapter 5), who longs for some practical vocation other than needlework and cookery, and is wearied by the hospitable duties expected of her as the local rector's niece. Like Caroline, Mrs Ramsay is conscious of the burdensome nature of her obligations as hostess; if her dinner party is to be a sociable, communalizing affair, she realizes, 'the whole of the effort of merging and flowing and creating rested on her . . . for if she did not do it nobody would do it' (69). This renewed perception of duty engenders a sudden shift in mood in the text. After 'giving herself the little shake that one gives a watch that has stopped', Mrs Ramsay's sense of purpose returns: 'the old familiar pulse began beating, as the watch begins ticking – one, two, three, one, two, three', and she reverts to superintending the 'business' of hospitality (69). However, a nebulous ambivalence towards female domestic responsibility remains. By figuring the role of exemplary hostess as mechanized performance in this way, Woolf denaturalizes the idea that nurturance is intuitive to women, recognizing it instead as part of a stifling, socially certified 'code of behaviour' (74).

It is perhaps owing to the artificiality of this code that Mrs Ramsay's initial attempts to foster unity among her dinner guests prove unsuccessful. The first course is marred by an underlying impression of disparateness: Charles Tansley wishes 'he could be alone in his room working' (71); William Bankes, who does 'not enjoy family life', would prefer to be 'dining alone' at home (73), 'where his man cooked vegetables properly' (61); and the ascetic Mr Ramsay, whose relationship to food is purely functional and who hates social dining, declines to make polite conversation with his guests and scowls angrily when Augustus Carmichael requests another bowl of soup ('he loathed people eating when he had finished' [78]). Both Lily Briscoe and Mrs Ramsay recognize that 'something [is] lacking' from the occasion (77); however, this sense of deficiency is eventually assuaged by the lighting of the candles on the table. The illumination they provide has a curious, coalescing effect on the previously isolated diners: 'some change at once went through them all . . . and they were all conscious of making a party together in a hollow, on an island . . . against the fluidity out there' (80). The candlelight also has the effect of aestheticizing the contents of the meal. The diners feast their eyes on a centrepiece of fruit arranged by Rose Ramsay, which, 'brought up suddenly into the light . . . seemed possessed of great size and depth', its undulating forms and palette of overlapping purples and yellows resembling 'some picture' (79). The group's collective appreciation of this fructiform work of art cements their newfound communality: despite their different points of view, 'looking together united them' (79).

The synaesthetic effect of the meal is magnified by the arrival of the main course: a 'huge brown pot' of Boeuf en Daube (81), which the cook has spent three days preparing.[13] Its 'confusion' of colours, textures and aromas – 'savoury brown and yellow meats' (82) mingled with 'olives' (81), 'bay leaves' and 'wine' (82) – further stimulates the diners' senses and engenders communal contentment, the triumphant *mélange* of ingredients replicating in miniature the unification of heterogeneous elements that has taken place around the table. As Carolyn Korsmeyer observes, the dish exercises 'as much social force' over the assembly as Mrs Ramsay does (1999, 215). The aesthetic and emotional satisfaction generated by the Boeuf en Daube is only temporary, however. Although Mrs Ramsay, while 'helping Mr Bankes to a specially tender piece' of beef, feels that the perfect rightness of things at that moment partakes 'of eternity', the illusion of permanence is soon shattered (85). To her distress, a hand reaches out to take a pear from Rose's centrepiece, resolving it back from numinous artwork into material foodstuff. Moreover, as she rises from the table, Mrs Ramsay is 'suddenly overwhelmed' by an 'intuition of mortality', as Sandra Gilbert suggests (2014, 108). She realizes that the scene she is about to leave is 'vanishing' before her very eyes: 'it changed, it shaped itself differently; it had become, she knew, giving one last look at it over her shoulder, already the past' (90).

The sense of loss that Mrs Ramsay perceives here resonates throughout the remainder of the text. Following her death, the Ramsay household lacks its 'emotional, structural, or domestic centre', as Diane McGee points out (2001, 145), and mealtimes become disjointed and peripatetic as a result. Notably, in the final part of the novel, Lily Briscoe eats breakfast 'alone', while the lunch that Mr Ramsay, Cam and James share on the way to the lighthouse is a hastily put-together snack, Nancy having 'forgotten to order the sandwiches' (121). The domestic fragmentation experienced by the Ramsays resembles that described by the food-writer Agnes Jekyll in the preface to her *Kitchen Essays* (1922):

> when homes dissolve and re-form, or the main prop of a household is withdrawn, it is often found that a good tradition or a valued formula, painstakingly acquired, has vanished beyond recovery, and that the pleasant things we enjoyed in youth . . . or the *spécialité* of some clever long-lost cook, have all been swept irrevocably down Time's rolling stream.
>
> *2002, vii–viii*

In *To the Lighthouse*, Mrs Ramsay fulfils the role of domestic 'prop' to which Jekyll here alludes, helping to preserve her family's culinary heritage (the recipe for the Boeuf en Daube is, significantly, a matrilineal legacy, passed down from Mrs Ramsay's grandmother). The creative gastronomy over which she presides also provides artistic stimulus for subsequent generations; although Lily, the modern woman, rejects Mrs Ramsay's traditional brand of femininity, deeming it 'dusty and out of date' (144), she nevertheless takes inspiration from the older woman's culinary success, seeking to replicate the same 'spirit of unity' (Knapp 1988, 35) in her painting that Mrs Ramsay achieved with the Boeuf en Daube (though we might note that it was the Ramsays' cook, rather than Mrs Ramsay, who undertook the actual *labour* of cooking that venerated dish).[14] If Woolf famously felt the need to 'kill' the 'Angel in the House' in her writing (1942, 151), owing to the latter's complicity with patriarchal norms, then in her nuanced representation of Mrs Ramsay she, like her New Woman predecessor Sarah Grand (Chapter 5), nevertheless acknowledges the positive force exerted by such nutrifying, self-denying women.

A further ambivalent portrayal of nurturing femininity emerges in Woolf's experimental novel *The Waves*, in which Susan, one of the text's six interconnected speakers, embodies the same nourishing instinct as Mrs Ramsay. Like Mrs Ramsay, Susan is recurrently associated with milk and dairy produce; as a child, she relishes the sensation of sinking her teeth into 'soft bread and butter' and of lapping 'sweet milk' (2015, 13), and, as a young woman, she fantasizes about 'suckling' her future children in the manner of the gipsy women she sees by the roadside (57). In a potent symbolic alignment of food and maternity, Susan's body's fruitfulness is articulated in terms of agricultural production – she compares herself to 'a field bearing crops in rotation' (77) – while her culinary activity is described in terms of fecundity; during its proving stage, the bread-dough over which she has laboured 'rises in a soft dome under the clean towel' like a pregnant belly (58). In a further doubling of food production and child-rearing, Susan expends the same fastidious care on her farm produce as she does on her children; her lovingly 'netted over strawberry beds and lettuce beds', and her pears and plums 'stitched . . . into white bags' to protect them from insects, resemble her sleeping sons and daughters 'netted over like fruit in their cots' (112–113).[15] 'Netting' here of course implies protection, but, as Glenny notes, it can also signify 'entrapment' and significantly, as Susan matures, she finds herself inextricably 'woven into her own mesh', 'fenced in' by her domestic role (1999, 171). 'Pad[ding] about the house all day long in apron and slippers', Susan becomes disconnected from the outside world, no longer appreciating the passing of the seasons (101). Finally, she admits, in a faltering repudiation of her role as maternal nurturer, 'I am sick of natural happiness, and fruit growing, and children' (113).

If cultivation, cooking and feeding work jointly to constrain Susan's identity, then food and eating induce an altogether more radical form of crisis in her friend Rhoda. As Vicki Tromanhauser points out, 'Rhoda's being disintegrates over the course of the novel's meals' (2014, 87) as she comes to identify more with the status of 'eaten' than with that of 'eater'. Walking down London's Oxford Street, Rhoda feels estranged from the crowds around her, which she perceives as 'faces and faces, served out like soup-plates by scullions' (93). The thought of queuing alongside them fills her with disgust: 'I should . . . smell sweat, and scent as horrible as sweat; and be hung with other people like a joint of meat among other joints of meat' (94). Rhoda's self-identification with meat here is suggestive, given her recurrent dread of being devoured; she anxiously imagines being 'pluck[ed] at' and '[torn] . . . to pieces' by her friends (133), and, according to Bernard, she 'grasps her fork' like a 'weapon' against them (77). Beset by fears of being consumed, Rhoda is also troubled by the act of ingestion. For Glenny, indeed, she exemplifies the anorectic's abhorrence of corpulence (1999, 158). At an afternoon concert, Rhoda watches the 'heavy bodies' around her, 'gorged' with 'beef and pudding' (94), with a kind of fascinated repulsion, indicative of abjection.[16] Whereas another of the novel's speakers, Neville, enjoys the sensation of 'becoming weighed down with food', deriving a sense of stability and control from 'delicious mouthfuls of roast duck, fitly piled with vegetables' (80), Rhoda abjures the carnality of consumption, preferring instead the vertiginous prospect of dissolution. Notably, at various points in the text, she invites the universe to 'consume' her (36, 96, 121) – in other words, to rid her of the burden of embodied subjectivity.

Like Rhoda, Louis is plagued by feelings of isolation and alterity (the son of an Australian banker, he is morbidly conscious of his social and cultural 'Otherness'). Unlike Rhoda, however, he craves assimilation and uses food to cultivate a sense of belonging. He frequently spends time in a down-market eating-house, believing that among its plates of 'ham sandwiches' and vapours of 'beef and mutton, sausages and mash' (53) he will experience – and integrate with – autochthonous English culture. Sitting with his book of poetry propped 'against a bottle of Worcester sauce', he '[tries] to look like the rest' (53), mimicking his co-diners' eating behaviours while repeating the mantra 'I am an average Englishman' (54). Despite his best imitative efforts, however, Louis is unable to 'pass' as authentic: he cannot 'order [his] beef, with conviction' (54), and when he later tries to assert his preference for everyday working-class food – 'my favourite dish is liver and bacon' – his claim is rendered unconvincing by the ambivalent prefatory remark, 'I think' (100). Irrevocably 'alien', he is unable to attune himself to the 'rhythm of the eating-house' (54), its unspoken norms and practices; whereas his waitress serves other customers their 'apricots and custard unhesitatingly, like a sister', she responds to his 'too large a tip' with scornful laughter (56), effectively marking him out as an interloper. Thus, like the restaurant at the Burton in Joyce's *Ulysses*, the eating-house in *The Waves* fails to foster human (or humane) communality; as Louis despondently recognizes, as he watches the whirl of activity around him, 'I am not included' (54).

The quasi-mythic sense of community for which Louis yearns does emerge – albeit tentatively – when the novel's six speakers gather at a restaurant to bid farewell to their friend Percival, who is leaving for India. As with the dinner party in *To the Lighthouse*, the event does not initially augur well: Neville finds 'the hostility, the indifference' of other diners 'oppressive' (69); Louis and Susan are plagued by feelings of self-consciousness and self-doubt; while Rhoda is 'without anchorage anywhere, unconsolidated' (71). Unanimity emerges, however, with the arrival of Percival and the food, joint catalysts for a new consciousness of coming together. The group's senses are collectively 'widened' and heightened by the meal (79); Neville's palate is invigorated by the 'evanescent' wine (81) and even Rhoda is enriched by the experience of shared consumption, perceiving 'bloom and ripeness . . . everywhere' (78). Inevitably, though, this state of food-bound communality is only transient. Bernard recognizes that 'too soon the moment of ravenous identity is over, and the appetite for happiness, and happiness, and still more happiness is glutted' (83). In common with the picnic-feast described in Keats's *The Fall of Hyperion* (Chapter 4), figures of vitality – of mellowing and 'swollen' fruit (82) – are quickly supplanted by images of detritus and decay – of 'mottled peelings of pears' (83) and a 'litter of breadcrumbs' (84) – thus prefiguring Percival's imminent death. For Utell, indeed, *The Waves'* central meal should be understood as a 'symbolic funeral' for the departing Percival (2008, 10). However, as Bernard suggests, the farewell dinner also represents a form of agape or celebration: 'We have proved, sitting eating, sitting talking, that we can add to the treasury of moments' (85). If food, via its relationship to atrophy and abjection, threatens both individual subjectivity and inter-subjective relations in Woolf's fiction, it also forms the basis for fleeting moments of pleasurable communion, the fragility of which only intensifies their salience.

Angela Carter, *The Magic Toyshop* (1967); Margaret Atwood, *The Edible Woman* (1969)

Following the privations of wartime and post-war rationing, the 1960s represented a period of relative gastronomic plenty in Britain and North America and, during this time, women were addressed explicitly as consumers within a wide range of visual and textual media. Magazine advertisements for a bewildering range of edible goods (often placed strategically alongside cookery features) encouraged women to expand their product consumption (see Ballaster *et al.* 1991, 116), while recipe books such as Poppy Cannon's *The Frozen-Foods Cookbook* (1964) promised to help busy housewives create quick and tasty meals using shop-bought convenience foods. The not-so-subtle subtext of these publications was that, culinarily speaking, women had never had it so good. Yet, despite enjoying indubitable material and nutritional advantages over their historical predecessors, the 'Happy Housewife Heroines' of mid-century marketing ideology were in fact often troubled – like their Victorian and modernist literary antecedents – by a latent 'hunger that food [could not] fill', as Betty Friedan noted in her pioneering 1963 work *The Feminine Mystique* (2010, 21, 15). This hunger for 'something more' than the culturally vaunted role of homemaker (Friedan 2010, 20), laid bare by second-wave feminists, belied the construction of women as active, autonomous consumers, indicating instead the ways in which they were disenfranchised by the economic and gendered power structures of the 1960s. The early fictions of both Angela Carter and Margaret Atwood repeatedly use food as a metaphor by which to explore this social and political inequality, exposing the often damaging relationships that exist between gender, consumption and power, as well as the disordered modes of eating to which this insidious nexus can give rise. Unlike Friedan, however, Carter and Atwood dispute the notion that culinary culture is incapable of engendering feminine fulfilment; while acknowledging that dietary ideology is often implicated in female oppression, *The Magic Toyshop* and *The Edible Woman* also recognize that food can provide women with a potent symbolic medium through which to resist culturally scripted norms.

At the beginning of *The Edible Woman*, Marian MacAlpin is tacitly aligned with the unfulfilled women described by Friedan, whose work Atwood had read around the time of the novel's composition. Degree-educated Marian is stuck in a job with limited prospects, designing questionnaires for a marketing company that pitches convenience foods such as canned rice pudding and instant tomato juice to Canadian housewives, but she has little appetite for the alternative, socially sanctioned roles available to her: those of wife and mother. Her comparison of her friend Clara's pregnant body to 'a boa-constrictor that has swallowed a watermelon' (Atwood 2009, 30) is indicative of a nascent matrophobia that gradually increases through the text, ending with Marian refusing to eat eggs – a foodstuff freighted with reproductive connotations, as Sarah Sceats points out (2000, 97). The prospect of wifehood is scarcely more appealing: Marian's relationship with the chauvinistic Peter, a trainee lawyer, is repeatedly figured in terms of what Atwood calls 'symbolic cannibalism' (ix). Although Peter typically casts women as 'predatory' sirens, whose instinct is to lure hapless male victims into marriage (74), it quickly becomes clear that it is *he* who dominates over Marian, 'monopoliz[ing]' her life (32). He habitually expects her to fulfil the traditional female role of spousal nurturer, petulantly demanding of her, when she presents him with a boil-in-the-bag meal of smoked meat and frozen peas, 'Why can't you ever *cook* anything?' (73). He also expects her to cater to his sexual appetites and, on one occasion, bites into her shoulder after intercourse, in a gesture heavy with cannibalistic connotations.

The Edible Woman also deploys tropes of hunting and predation to convey (and critique) the inequalities of modern gender relations. After Marian has spent the day conducting market research for Moose Beer – a product that aims to foster a 'mystical identity' between modern, urban males and the primitive figure of the woodsman (23) – she is obliged to listen dutifully as Peter regales her friends with gory reminiscences of eviscerating a rabbit: 'I whipped out my knife . . . and slit the belly and took her by the hind legs and gave her one hell of a crack, like a whip you see, and the next thing you know there was blood and guts all over the place' (80). As in Anne Brontë's *The Tenant of Wildfell Hall* (Chapter 5), hunting is here associated less with masculine nobility than with carno-phallogocentric aggression. Notably, whereas Peter is amused by the violence he describes, Marian intuitively projects herself into his brutal memory, mentally conjuring the rifle-toting Peter surrounded by trees 'splashed with blood' (80). Tellingly, though, she is unable to 'see the rabbit' (80), the quarry whose place she has unconsciously supplanted. This imaginative identification with prey precipitates an alarming loss of self-control; overcome by a sudden feeling of panic, Marian 'let[s] go of Peter's arm and [begins] to run' (83).

Trapped within a culture that pays lip service to ideas of 'freedom' while upholding unequal power relations, Marian internalizes social disorder as psychological disorder. Notably, her feelings of self-fragmentation only intensify following her engagement to Peter, an event that is marked by a textual shift from autodiegetic to heterodiegetic narration. Marian's loss of narrative voice is mirrored by a debilitating loss of autonomy. During an ostensibly 'romantic' meal for two in a restaurant, she relinquishes her choice of food to Peter: we are told, 'she had fallen into the habit in the last month or so of letting him choose for her. It got rid of the vacillation she had found herself displaying when confronted with a menu' (179–180). Peter's taste is for rare steak, a preference that is consistent with his self-construction as primal huntsman, as well as with the long-standing literary association of beef and masculine virility (articulated, for instance, in *Tom Jones* in Chapter 3). As Roland Barthes suggests, beefsteak is implicated in a peculiarly 'sanguine mythology':

> It is the heart of meat, it is meat in its pure state; and whoever partakes of it assimilates a bull-like strength. The prestige of steak evidently derives from its quasi-rawness. In it, blood is visible, natural, dense, at once compact and sectile. One can well imagine the ambrosia of the Ancients as this kind of heavy substance which dwindles under one's teeth in such a way as to make one keenly aware at the same time of its original strength and of its aptitude to flow into the very blood of man.
>
> *2000, 62*

Watching Peter slice his fillet – 'a violent action' (184) – Marian becomes suddenly aware of the semiotics of sanguinary assimilation to which Barthes refers:

> She looked down at her own half-eaten steak and suddenly saw it as a hunk of muscle. Blood red. Part of a real cow that once moved and ate and was killed . . . when you went into a butcher shop they wrapped it up so efficiently and quickly that it was made clean, official. But now it was suddenly there in front of her with no intervening paper, it was flesh and blood, rare, and she had been devouring it. Gorging herself on it.
>
> *185*

Despite trying to convince herself that meat is 'natural' and 'good for you' (185), Marian finds herself (like the Romantic vegetarians discussed in Chapter 4) sickened by the prospect of consuming another life-form and can eat no more. Her loss of appetite ironically gratifies Peter as it fits with his assumptions about feminine docility and makes him 'pleasantly conscious of his own superior capacity' for ingestion (186); unsurprisingly, he has no qualms about devouring the whole of his steak and appears oblivious to the wider symbolic implications of his carnivorous appetite.

Marian, by contrast, remains troubled by the inherent brutality of consumption – the 'fiendishness' undertaken 'in kitchens across the country, in the name of providing food!' (190) – and is reluctant to collude in what Angela Carter calls the 'primal condition' of 'eat or be eaten' (1979, 140). She consequently develops a problematic relationship to food that causes her to renounce 'anything that had once been, or . . . might still be living' (220), until, finally, she 'can't eat anything at all' (325). Her eating disorder is not explicitly taxonomized in the novel but, as a number of critics have pointed out, its psychopathology bears some resemblance to that of anorexia nervosa.[17] Like the anorectic women described by the feminist psychoanalyst Susie Orbach, Marian finds eating with others 'tortuous' and develops a range of strategies to deflect attention away from her limited ingestion, such as 'hid[ing] the food on her plate under the lettuce leaves' or furtively dropping it 'into a convenient handbag or receptacle of some kind' (Orbach 1993, 93). In a further example of anorectic behaviour, Marian takes 'perverse delight in watching other people eat', even as her own relationship to food becomes more and more ambiguous (190). Although she does not exhibit the '*relentless pursuit of excessive thinness*' that Hilde Bruch identifies as the 'outstanding feature' of anorexia (2001, xxi), Marian does seem to have an unconscious repugnance for body-fat. She comments disgustedly on Clara's 'swollen mass of flesh' (139) and, at the office Christmas party, examines her co-workers' forms in quasi-anthropological detail, noting their 'roll[s] of fat', 'ham-like bulge[s] of thigh' and 'jellied' jowls (205) with a kind of nauseated fascination, reminiscent of that exhibited by Woolf's Rhoda in *The Waves*.

Crucially, Marian also identifies with the '*basic delusion*' of not 'owning [one's] body' that Bruch sees as symptomatic of disorderly eating (1973, 50). Time and again, she refers to the 'refusal of her *mouth* to eat' (187) or to 'her *body's* decision to reject certain foods' (219, my emphases), demonstrating a disorientating sense of alienation from her physical self. Her friend Duncan interprets her apparently involuntary food refusal as a form of somatic protest, telling her that she is 'rebelling' against the social system via her 'digestive system' (236).[18] However, if this is the case, Marian fails to derive a straightforward sense of empowerment from her dietary mutiny. Rather (again, like Rhoda in *The Waves*), she is beset by fears of 'dissolving', of 'coming apart layer by layer' (274). This dread of 'not being able to contain herself' (274) manifests itself via an identification with foods such as jelly and ice-cream that signify 'vulnerability, physical instability and a liability to melt – characteristics that mirror [Marian's] self-image', as Tracy Brain suggests (1995, 302). Of course, these foods are also associated predominantly with children and thus serve tacitly to signal the way in which the culture of the mid-twentieth century works to infantilize women.

Notably, Marian only regains a sense of autonomy when, at the end of the novel, she seizes control by baking a sponge-cake version of herself and offering it to Peter with the words, 'You've been trying to assimilate me. But I've made you a substitute, something you'll like much better . . . I'll get you a fork' (344). Exchanging silent corporeal protest for verbal and culinary remonstration against the symbolic cannibalism to which she has been subjected, Marian experiences both a return of appetite and a return of selfhood: 'Suddenly she was hungry. Extremely hungry' (344). Devouring her edible surrogate, she reintegrates herself into the social order by appropriating the role of 'consumer', as Duncan recognizes (353). However, this reclamation of subjectivity (marked by her return to thinking of herself in the first person singular) is not without its problems. If consumption enables female empowerment in Atwood's novel, it is also portrayed 'as both an act of aggression and a participation in the *status quo*', as Sceats points out (2000, 99). Marian may have 'learned assertiveness, that sexual politics means "eat or be eaten"', but her transformation does not resolve 'the conundrum of how she can live without either being consumed or becoming a predator' (Sceats 2000, 99): how she can *subvert* rather than simply *invert* the conventional alimentary order, a problem that Atwood leaves unsettled at the end of the text.

Angela Carter's *The Magic Toyshop* offers a differently focused, but no less powerful, reading of and response to the predatory power relations implicit in mid-twentieth-century culture. The novel opens by announcing that Melanie, its fifteen-year-old heroine, has 'discovered that she [is] made of flesh and blood' (1981, 1), a psychosexual development that engenders in her a new-found awareness of bodily pleasure, but also signals the potential for her to be culturally constructed, like Atwood's Marian, as 'meat'. Indeed, on the cusp of womanhood, Melanie seems already to have internalized the gendered expectations of her society; keen to maximize her marriageability, she harbours anxieties about housekeeper Mrs Rundle's ubiquitous bread pudding, fearing that 'if she ate too much of it she would grow fat and nobody would ever love her and she would die virgin' (3). As a result of these apprehensions, Melanie adopts the kind of proto-anorectic tactics undertaken by Marian in *The Edible Woman*, pushing her food 'around her plate with her spoon' and 'slyly' reallocating 'most of her helping' to her younger brother, Jonathon, who eats like a 'blind force of nature' (4). Her nascent food aversion further intensifies following a nocturnal adventure in her parents' Edenic garden, during which she wears and subsequently tears her mother's wedding dress on the branches of an apple tree (a literary signifier that is always symbolically charged where acts of female rebellion are concerned). At breakfast the next morning, Melanie cannot 'eat for the weight of guilt and shame which seemed to have settled on her stomach' (23), causing her to abandon her portion of toast and bacon to her greedy siblings. Her consciousness of having sinned is exacerbated by the revelation that her parents were killed that night in an aeroplane accident, news which provokes an immediate enteric response: feeling her stomach contract, Melanie runs 'upstairs to the lavatory and vomit[s]' (24), convinced that their deaths are a form of karmic punishment for her night-time escapade.

The dramatic change in domestic circumstances wrought by Melanie's orphanhood brings about a concomitant shift in her relationship to food. Uprooted from her former privileged existence, where the family dinner-table 'steamed' with 'hearty stews and puddings running with golden syrup' (93–94), Melanie no longer demonstrates anorectic tendencies. Instead, obliged to live as a dependant in her tyrannical Uncle Philip's lower-class home, where food is regularly withheld from the inhabitants in the service of patriarchal authority, she comes to realize (like her literary precursor Beth Caldwell in Sarah Grand's *The Beth Book* [Chapter 5]) the importance of maintaining a well-fed, 'resilient' body (138). As Emma Parker notes, power in *The Magic Toyshop* 'is connoted by consumption' (2000, 144). Whereas Uncle Philip presides 'magisterially' over the dinner-table (71), commandeering the lion's share of any meal for himself, his mute wife, Aunt Margaret – whom Melanie characterizes as 'Our Lady of Famine' (113) – subsists on 'the tiniest . . . Baby Bear portion' of food (73), although she is required to undertake all of the cooking. Aunt Margaret's alimentary subjugation manifests itself most vividly on Sundays when she is obliged to wear a 'barbaric' silver choker that so restricts her ability to swallow 'all she could do was to sip painfully at a meagre cup of tea and toy with a few shoots of mustard and cress' (113). Her sadistic husband derives 'a certain pleasure from her discomfort' (113), finding that the sight of it improves his own appetite for food, as well, it is implied, as for other forms of sensory gratification; Melanie discovers that it is following this ritual deprivation of sustenance that Uncle Philip chooses to exercise his conjugal rights each week.

With his shark-like grin and oppressive presence, Uncle Philip very much resembles the figure of the cannibal described in Carter's *The Sadeian Woman*, who 'turn[s] the other directly into a comestible' and 'abuse[s], exploit[s] and meatif[ies] the weak' (1979, 140). In a number of telling allusions, Melanie compares her uncle to mythical exponents of masculine alimentary violence, such as Bluebeard, the wife-murderer who in some variants of the tale is also a cannibal, and Saturn, the Roman god who devoured his children in order to prevent them from rising against him. Yet, Philip is not the only character in *The Magic Toyshop* to be governed by an aggressive instinct for assimilation. Complicating the conventional gender politics of consumption, Carter suggests that Melanie's younger sister Victoria is equally as capable of omnivorous voracity as her monstrous uncle. Although Victoria has not yet developed Philip's cruel pleasure in denying others' appetites, she demonstrates the same selfish preoccupation with the immediate satisfaction of her own bodily hunger that he does. The day after her parents' death, unconcerned by Melanie's inability to eat, Victoria clamours with typically thoughtless egocentricity, 'I want my pudding NOW!' (27), and later, like Uncle Philip, she grows fat from Aunt Margaret's cookery while showing little gratitude for the culinary treats with which she is indulged. Indeed, when Melanie flouts Philip's embargo on Christmas present-giving in order to furnish her sister with a festive tin of sweets, the little girl accepts the gift 'incuriously' and simply sets out to 'eat them at once' (159). So compulsive is her ingestive instinct, she occasionally fails to distinguish between the edible and inedible, at one point tearing 'the fringes off the hassocks' in church in order to consume them (9). Elsewhere, her consumption of the decorative robin that adorns her aunt's chocolate yule log hints at a lurking predaciousness that once again connects her to her uncle's savage gluttony. As Andrea Adolph concludes, Victoria represents *The Magic Toyshop*'s 'consumer *par excellence*': she is 'all impulse, all id' (2009, 119).

If alimentary rapacity is not restricted to men in Carter's fiction, then neither is dietary disempowerment the exclusive preserve of women. Although Melanie initially categorizes Margaret's brother Finn as orally threatening, focusing obsessively on his teeth and identifying herself as his potential 'prey' (45), she later realizes that he (like her) occupies the role of passive consumable rather than active consumer in her uncle's household. Watching him curled up in bed 'like a whiting on a plate', she muses that 'he should have been garnished with sprigs of parsley and lemon butterflies' (182) in tacit recognition of his vulnerability to devourment. Finn's ensuing remark – that Uncle Philip wears his false teeth 'all the better to eat me with' (182) – indicates that he shares Melanie's view of his status as food. As well as being threatened with figurative cannibalization, Finn is also subjected to the same kind of culinary deprivation as his sister. Owing to Philip's relentless bullying, he hardly eats at mealtimes; even when the family sits down to a special dinner of roast goose, Philip serves him nothing but 'a mean portion of skin and bone', which Finn then pushes 'moodily around his plate with his fork, not eating' (160). Finn's status as hunger-striker here not only resonates with his Irish heritage, but also subverts the simplistic notion that men automatically occupy positions of alimentary power.[19] As Margaret Atwood notes, 'although society may slant things so that women appear to be better candidates for meathood than men and men better candidates for meat-eating, the nature of men is not fixed by Carter as inevitably predatory, with females as their "natural" prey' (1994, 121). In Carter's fiction, such cultural roles are fluid and interchanging rather than rigidly gendered.

The power dynamics vested in acts of consumption are therefore unstable in *The Magic Toyshop*, working to challenge as well as to reinforce the status quo. Although Uncle Philip's voracity signifies his domestic dominance, it also infantilizes him, for, as Parker points out, in Freudian terms he is 'stuck in the oral (cannibalistic) phase of libidinal development', confined to perpetual immaturity (2000, 150). Similarly, though Aunt Margaret's limited ingestion and servile role would seem to construct her as the passive victim of domestic oppression, they in fact veil a dissident orectic agency. As in Sarah Grand's *The Beth Book* (Chapter 5), the provision of food represents a subversive source of satisfaction in Carter's novel; Sceats notes that Aunt Margaret is a 'beneficent creator' (2000, 20) who derives immense pleasure from her nurturing role, which encompasses both 'love and defiance' (1997, 100). Although her husband's 'towering, blank-eyed presence at the head of the table' has the capacity to '[draw] the savour from the good food she cook[s]' (124), during his intermittent absences from home Margaret transforms mealtimes into festive commensal experiences. The cream tea that she prepares to welcome her nieces and nephew on their arrival represents 'a touching and whole-hearted welcome' (41), while, on another occasion, a home-cooked dinner of steak pudding is eaten with 'exceptional appetite' and a joyous 'feeling of holiday' (97). The gratification that Margaret derives from her role as nourisher thus subtly undermines her husband's authority, lending her an intermittent substantiality that enables her to live 'under the weight' of his rule (77).

Uncle Philip's sporadic absences from home further enable Aunt Margaret to satisfy her concealed, though passionate, sexual appetites. During the lavish, carnivalesque breakfast that closes the novel – at which Margaret, like the others, eats 'a great deal' (184) – it is revealed that she is involved in an incestuous relationship with her brother Francie. Although transgressive, their mutual devotion is not condemned in the text but rather configured as emotionally and spiritually nourishing, as is their non-sexual, but intimate, love for their brother Finn. Earlier in the text, Melanie has already recognized that the siblings' affection for one another is as 'strong and soothing as sweet tea' (43). Later, it is also portrayed as expansive and inclusive: through repeated acts of culinary kindness – the provision of a 'cream bun as a token of friendship' (43) or the preparation of a 'nice cup of tea' (120) – Margaret, Francie and Finn 'reach out from the charmed circle of themselves' to incorporate Melanie into their mutually nurturing group (123). It is perhaps in this textual focus on the comforting aspects of commensality (a theme that recurs throughout this study) that *The Magic Toyshop* differs most from *The Edible Woman*, for whereas Atwood's novel cannot seem to escape from the violent implications of consumption, even in its depiction of Marian's culinary liberation, Carter's text emphasizes the positive affinities between food, conviviality and love. Even so, its ending is no less ambivalent than *The Edible Woman*'s: having escaped from her uncle's suffocatingly patriarchal regime, Melanie faces an uncertain future. Will she go on to achieve a rich and fulfilling selfhood, or will she end up realizing her stultifying vision of marriage to Finn: 'babies crying and washing to be done and toast burning all the rest of her life' (177)? While acknowledging the emancipatory potential of eating and feeding, Carter, like Atwood, refuses her readers the consolation of a fairy-tale ending, recognizing that the realities of mid-century power relations would invalidate any such overly optimistic resolution.

Salman Rushdie, *Midnight's Children* (1981)

Given Salman Rushdie's acknowledgement that his purpose in writing *Midnight's Children* was 'somewhat Proustian' (1992, 23), it is perhaps unsurprising to find that the novel's sensorily gifted narrator-protagonist, Saleem Sinai, experiences an epiphanic moment of remembrance via food. Gradually disconnected from history following the successive traumas of the 1965 Indo-Pakistan War, the 1971 Bangladesh War of Independence and the 1975–1977 State of Emergency, Saleem is precipitously re-immersed into his past at the end of Rushdie's novel by an unexpected encounter with a taste from his childhood. In the back-room of a seedy Bombay club, he is presented with a bowl of his former ayah Mary Pereira's grasshopper-green chutney, the savour of which provides a spur to memory:

> it carried me back to a day when I emerged nine-fingered from a hospital and went into exile at the home of Hanif Aziz, and was given the best chutney in the world . . . the taste of the chutney was more than just an echo of that long-ago taste – it was the old taste itself, the very same, with the power of bringing back the past as if it had never been away.
>
> *2008, 637*

Like the famous tea-soaked madeleine of Proust's *Remembrance of Things Past* (1913), Mary's chutney is vested with anamnestic power, facilitating a recollection of and reconnection with lost time. It also becomes the stimulus for a more far-reaching form of remembrance than mere individual nostalgia. Inspired by Mary's evocative cookery, Saleem embarks on a project of culinary and narratorial preservation, incorporating his personal history (which coincides fantastically with that of post-independence India) into thirty special blends of pickle, each of which corresponds to – and takes on the flavour of – a chapter of his autobiography.

This 'chutnification of history' (642) represents a challenge to traditional forms of recording the past. Immortalizing his story in both words and pickles, Saleem moves beyond the rigid inscription of facts to encompass 'memories, dreams, [and] ideas' (643) within his textual-culinary productions. His chutnified reminiscences self-reflexively position history as a confection. It is the writer-chef – postmodern descendant of the author-innkeeper conjured in Henry Fielding's *Tom Jones* (Chapter 3) – who determines 'what-must-be-pickled' (643) from the available raw ingredients and who gives 'shape and form – that is to say, meaning' (644) to those ingredients by blending and combining them. This process of narrative-gastronomic selectivity inevitably raises the possibility that some less palatable items will be omitted from the mix; as Saleem acknowledges, history 'has its proper dietary laws. One is supposed to swallow and digest only the permitted parts of it, the halal portions of the past, drained of their redness, their blood' (74). Although he goes on to assert his willingness to 'become the first and only member of [his] family to flout the laws of halal', 'letting no blood escape from the body of the tale' (74), some aspects of his story nevertheless seem to resist full disclosure. The state-sanctioned tortures to which he was subjected during the time of India's Emergency, for instance, are not easily incorporated or digested; when he reaches this point in his account, Saleem writes: 'here I record a merciful blank in my memory . . . there is no chutney or pickle capable of unlocking the doors behind which I have locked those days!' (605).

Yet, despite such obfuscation, Saleem still worries that, when 'unleashed upon the amnesiac nation' (643) of India, his 'pickles of history' will prove 'too strong for some palates' (644); that is, too piquant for those keen to conserve a blander, more easily assimilable version of the past. Aware of his status as unreliable narrator (he repeatedly questions his interpretation and sequencing of events), he also frets about the presence of 'discordant note[s] in the orchestrated flavours' of his story, or the unintentional inclusion of an 'occasional speck of dirt' (644). If historical inaccuracy is here conceived of as culinary adulteration or impurity, the concomitant possibility of narrative embellishment is configured by Saleem in terms of (over-)seasoning. Drawing on the long-standing literary association of spice with ornamentation or supplementarity (see Morton 2000), Saleem suggests that the chutnifier of history must steer a careful path between the legitimate enhancement and wholesale altera-tion of narrative flavours, navigating 'the intricacies of turmeric and cumin, the subtlety of fenugreek, when to use large (and when small) cardamoms', as well as 'the myriad possible effects of garlic, garam masala, stick cinnamon, coriander, [and] ginger' (644). Complex combinations of spices have the potential to transform utterly the raw materials to which they are added, Saleem suggests, and although he assures readers that his condiments/chapters 'possess the authentic taste of truth', his defensive interrogative, 'a certain alteration, a slight intensification of taste, is a small matter, surely?' (644), indicates that, in places, his story may well have been enlivened with some extra savoury 'zing'.

While struggling to synthesize the competing demands of history and auto-biography, memory and truth, Saleem ultimately reconciles himself to the 'inevitable distortions of the pickling process' (644), signalling that the benefits of (imperfect) cultural preservation outweigh the problematics. Indeed, as Judith Plotz suggests, the promiscuous 'mish-mash of antithetical flavours' involved in chutnification would seem to offer a more useful way of thinking about the history of postcolonial India than alternative 'metaphors of political coherence' (1996, 28), such as the classic 'melting pot', which, in its evocation of smooth liquescence, fails to account for the multiple religious and cultural identities that co-exist, sometimes antagonistically, on the subcontinent. Importantly, chutnifcation encompasses at once the contradictory ideas of amalgamation and diversity: it 'suggests the difficult unification more or less harmoniously, more or less positively', of miscellaneous elements, while also 'resist[ing] bland assimilation' and 'retain[ing] powerfully astringent differences' (Plotz 1996, 29). The metaphor thus works to communicate Rushdie's understanding of India as fundamentally plural, hybrid, mixed: a nation based on 'a *mélange* of elements as disparate as ancient Mughal and contemporary Coca-Cola American' (1992, 67).

The heterogeneity of modern India is rendered particularly clearly in Rushdie's representation of the culinary culture of Bombay. A city of 'highly-spiced non-conformity' (2008, 428), Bombay is home not only to vendors of beachfront-grown coconuts and locally produced street-food – 'hot-channa-channa-hot, . . . kulfi and bhel-puri and chutter-mutter' (632) – but also to Europeanized establishments such as 'Bombelli's the Confectioners', with its offerings of 'Marquis cake' and 'One Yard of Chocolates' (124). During his childhood there, Saleem's intake of food is correspondingly eclectic: at home, he dines not only on dishes indicative of his family's Kashmiri heritage, but also on the chips commonly associated with Western diets, while at the local cinema he has the option to feast on Coca-Cola, potato chips and Kwality ice-cream, as well as Indian samosas (except during the month of Ramzàn, when he fasts). His adolescence in Pakistan similarly fuses the tastes of East and West: it is here that he consumes his aunt's traditional birianis but also purchases 'warm fresh loaves' (438) from a hatch in the wall of Santa Ignacia convent to satisfy his sister Jamila's hankering for Western-style leavened bread, a 'last relic' of her former 'flirtation' with Christianity (439).[20] It is also in Pakistan that Saleem perfects his ability to distinguish by smell alone 'the twelve different available brands of fizzy drink': Pakola, Hoffman's Mission, Citra Cola, Fanta, Canada Dry, 7-Up, Pepsi, Coke, Double Kola, Kola Kola, Perri Cola and Bubble Up (441). The inclusion of both Asian and North American brands in this list of products over which Saleem achieves olfactory mastery demonstrates the globalized character of consumables in the twentieth century, their entanglement in transnational capitalist networks. Food is positioned by Rushdie as an object of worldwide commercial exchange: while importing foreign produce on the one hand, the subcontinent reciprocally exports its native cuisines to an avid global customer-base on the other. As Mary Pereira proudly informs Saleem, 'even in England they eat' her Bombay-produced Braganza Pickles (640).

As well as highlighting the prevalence of international culinary interchange in the twentieth century, Rushdie's fiction testifies to the *historical* patterns of trade, migration, colonization and imperial rule that have left their gustatory mark on India. Moraes Zogoiby, narrator of *The Moor's Last Sigh* (1995), points out that it was the European taste for pepper that originally 'brought Vasco da Gama's tall ships across the ocean, from Lisbon's Tower of Belém to the Malabar Coast' (1996, 4), a development that left a perceptible Portuguese influence on Indian culture. In

Midnight's Children, meanwhile, both the frozen dessert kulfi, sold by the vendors at Chowpatty Beach, and the rose-infused drink falooda, advertised at the Pioneer Café in Bombay, bear witness to the extensive temporal and geographic reach of the flavours of the Mughal empire (see Achaya 1998, 132, 65). The culinary influence of the British is rather more comically captured in the 'half empty pots of Bovril' and cocktail-hour rituals that William Methwold bequeaths to the Indian inheritors of his Bombay estate when he departs in 1947 (130); as the Indian-born author William Makepeace Thackeray noted in his novel *Vanity Fair* (discussed in Chapter 5), 'those who know the English colonies abroad know that we carry with us our pride, pills, prejudices, Harvey-sauces, cayenne-peppers, and other Lares, making a little Britain wherever we settle down' (1968, 744). By repeatedly emphasizing the gastronomic pluralism of India in this way, Rushdie exposes as fantasy the idea of a homogeneous, cohesive nation, united by its gustatory preferences and practices of consumption. He also issues a challenge to the kind of naïve natio-culinary essentialism espoused by Ayooba Baloch, a member of Saleem's military unit, who reductively characterizes Indo-Pakistani conflict as a confrontation between 'vegetarians' (Hindus) and 'beefy types' (Muslims) (484).

It is not only religious or cultural difference that engenders dietary diversity in Rushdie's fiction, however. As *Midnight's Children* makes clear, in modern India there also remains a huge gulf in alimentary experience between rich and poor. Whereas Saleem's middle-class upbringing furnishes him with a varied and nourishing regimen, four hundred and twenty of his fellow 'midnight's children' – those Indians born during the first hour of independence, to whom he is telepathically connected – fail to survive to adulthood because of 'malnutrition' and 'disease' (271). The divide between plenty and want (a recurrent theme in this study) is emphasized further during Saleem's juvenile experiments with extrasensory 'mind-hopping' (240). 'At one time', he records,

> I was a landlord in Uttar Pradesh, my belly roiling over my pajama-cord as I ordered serfs to set my surplus grain on fire . . . at another moment I was starving to death in Orissa, where there was a food shortage as usual: I was two months old and my mother had run out of breast-milk.
>
> *240–241*

Saleem's consciousness of dietary inequality is stoked by Shiva, the boy who was born, like him, at the stroke of midnight on 15 August 1947, and with whom he was exchanged at birth. Whereas Saleem harbours idealistic ideas about the ameliorative social function of the midnight's children, Shiva (who, as a result of the baby-swap, has grown up in impoverishment in the Bombay slums) tells him bluntly that 'the world is no place for dreamers or their dreams . . . five hundred million stay hungry' (354). Later on in the novel, Saleem goes on to experience the realities of famishment for himself. In an ironic reversal of fortune, Shiva achieves success as a major in the Indian army, initiating him into the feasts and banquets of high society, while Saleem is left to struggle for survival in the magicians' ghetto in Delhi, where the occupants subsist on scanty meals 'composed of twenty-seven grains of rice apiece' (623).

As such repeated narrative references to hunger suggest, access to food functions as a measure of social and political authority in Rushdie's novel – and not only in national contexts. In the domestic sphere, too, food denial and hunger serve as indices of power and powerlessness, most notably in the 'war of starvation' (51) that breaks out between Saleem's grandmother, known as 'Reverend Mother', and his grandfather, Aadam Aziz. When Aadam ejects his children's religious instructor for teaching them 'to hate Hindus and Buddhists and Jains and Sikhs and who knows what other vegetarians' (50–51), his devout wife responds by swearing that 'no food will come from my kitchen to your lips! No, not one chapati, until you bring the maulvi sahib back' (51). Aadam protests, in turn, by refusing to feed himself and is at risk of attenuating completely until his eldest daughter, Alia, intercedes with an alimental olive branch: a bowl of chicken soup. While bringing an end to the immediate spousal conflict, this détente does not, however, effect a democratization of dietary relations; Reverend Mother quickly reassumes her domestic influence within the Aziz household, once more asserting her control over all matters culinary. As Saleem notes, she defends the pantry and kitchen – 'her inalienable territory' – with tigerish ferocity (48) and rules over the dinner-table 'imperiously', marshalling the placement of the curry and crockery, and prohibiting her husband and children from choosing their own food (49).

As in a number of the texts considered in this chapter, then, food provision in *Midnight's Children* offers women a way to bypass or appropriate patriarchal authority while outwardly conforming to sanctioned versions of femininity. Cookery in Rushdie's novel is linked to both the assertion of individual agency and the vectoring of others' thoughts, feelings and desires; significantly, a number of the women in the text have the magical ability to imbue their dishes with powerful, transferable emotions, indicative of the 'personality of [the] creator' (190). Reverend Mother doles out to her family 'the curries and meatballs of intransigence' and 'the fish salans of stubbornness' (190), foods which fill Saleem's mother, Amina, with the determination necessary to restore her family's temporarily embarrassed finances; the Catholic Mary Pereira stirs into her pickles 'the guilt of her heart . . . so that, good as they tasted, they had the power of making those who ate them subject to nameless uncertainties and dreams of accusing fingers' (190–191); Saleem's embittered spinster aunt, Alia, serves up 'the birianis of dissension and the nargisi koftas of discord', dishes that introduce a sour note into the Sinais' previously happy marriage (459); and Parvati-the-witch seduces Shiva with 'a dinner of biriani so exquisite' that he devotes 'his undivided attention to her for four whole months' (574).

The incredible affective power of female cookery is nevertheless surpassed, Saleem maintains, by his own culinary achievements as history's 'pickler-in-chief' (459). 'To understand just one life', he argues, 'you have to swallow the world' (145) – an omnivorous task that is made possible by the 'symbolic value of the pickling process: all the six hundred million eggs which gave birth to the population of India could fit inside a single, standard-sized pickle-jar' (642). As well as aiming to capture the multiple histories of post-independence India in this way, Saleem's chutneys look forward to the future; one jar on the shelf always remains empty, emblematizing 'what cannot be pickled, because it has not taken place' (645). *Midnight's Children* thus moves beyond the conventional solaces of nostalgia to embrace what Laurent Milesi calls 'a more political and historical "remembering forward" or "promnesia" that would help to forge [India's] "re-membrance of future things"' (2001, 202). Although the novel closes with Saleem's prophetic visions of death, it also signals that his wares, when released into mass production, will engender a new understanding of history in all who consume them: a collective reprocessing/digestion of the chutnified past that will form the tentative basis for a more appetizing future. As another Rushdian cook, Ezekiel, puts it in *The Moor's Last Sigh*, 'we will cook the past and present also, and from it tomorrow will come' (1996, 273).

Andrea Levy, *Fruit of the Lemon* (1999); Zadie Smith, *White Teeth* (2000); Monica Ali, *Brick Lane* (2003)

In a much-quoted 2001 speech on multiculturalism and national identity, then British Foreign Secretary Robin Cook asserted that the enduring curry-house favourite chicken tikka masala should be considered 'a true British national dish', not only because of its massive popularity among consumers, but also 'because it is a perfect illustration of the way Britain absorbs and adapts external influences' (2001, n.p.). Encapsulating the cultural diversity of twenty-first-century Britain in culinary terms, Cook here draws on the long-standing assumption that food practices function as definitive components and dependable indices of nation. However, while making recourse to the politically expedient idea of a common 'national dish', Cook's speech simultaneously undermines such notions of dietary essentialism; foregrounding the hybrid origins of chicken tikka masala, Cook suggests that the 'chicken tikka' part derives from an authentic Indian dish, while the 'masala' sauce with which it is combined represents an Anglo-influenced addition, developed 'to satisfy the desire of British people to have their meat served in gravy' (2001, n.p.).[21] Chicken tikka masala thus serves as a classic example of what Ian Cook and Philip Crang call the 'contemporary fabrication or simulation of . . . "ethnic" cuisines'; an invented culinary tradition, it demonstrates the pivotal role played by food in 'the discursive construction of . . . imaginative geographies' (2003, 114, 115).

By highlighting the compound character of chicken tikka masala in this way, Robin Cook's speech implicitly recognizes and celebrates the processes of gastronomic borrowing, admixture, innovation and naturalization that underlie so-called 'national' dishes. His concomitant evocation of a cohesive multicultural community, vitalized and enriched by migrant foodways, overlooks, however, the fragmentizing histories of colonialism, social and economic inequality, and troubled race relations that subtend ostensibly progressive narratives of cross-cultural culinary exchange. These occluded political contexts are given thorough and nuanced consideration, by contrast, in a number of the literary texts to have emerged in Britain around the turn of the millennium. The three examples selected for discussion here – Andrea Levy's *Fruit of the Lemon*, Zadie Smith's *White Teeth* and Monica Ali's *Brick Lane* – each use food to explore questions of diasporic identity, cultural assimilation and appropriation, and the commodification of (dietary) difference. Though located in the kind of ethnically diverse society conjured by Cook – each novel is set wholly or partly in late twentieth-century London and is peopled by a combination of first-generation immigrants and their British-born descendants – the texts refuse to ratify the naïve fantasy of what Smith calls 'Happy Multicultural Land' (2001, 465). Instead, through collective engagement with the complexities and contradictions of the food–nation nexus, they convey the difficulties and tensions – as well as the positive, creative possibilities – that arise when different cultures are brought into a state of cohabitation.

Like many of the second-generation characters portrayed in the novels considered here, *Fruit of the Lemon*'s Faith Jackson, the London-born daughter of Jamaican immigrants, identifies primarily as British, an affiliation that is tacitly corroborated by her dietary choices. With no 'oral tradition' linking her to her Caribbean heritage (Levy 2004, 4), Faith partakes of a regimen largely indistinguishable from that of her white peers, a correspondence that contributes to her brother Carl's accusations of racial self-loathing. In the house she shares with friends Marion, Mick and Simon, Faith consumes 'indigestible macaroni cheese' and 'egg and chips' (41); in the canteen at work, she eats 'pork chop with two veg' (68); and at her parents' home in Crouch End, she binges on the sugar-laden staples of British tea-time, Fondant Fancies (40), all seemingly unremarkable alimentary behaviours. However, embedded in this latter 'quotidian act of consumption' is a 'complex set of historical connections linking an imperial past . . . and a postcolonial present', as Jeannette Baxter points out; via her taste for Fondant Fancies, Faith participates in the consumption of a commodity – sugar – 'with a long and incredibly bitter-sweet history' (2014, 91). For the first part of the text, however, that history (laid bare in the anti-saccharite poetry examined in Chapter 4) goes unrecognized. When Faith thinks of Jamaica at all, it is as an alien place, visited periodically by family friends who bring back with them 'strange fruits' (45). Indeed, so imbricated is Faith in mainstream British culture, it shocks her to discover that her parents still think of Jamaica as 'home'. As far as she is concerned, the Jacksons are thoroughly assimilated citizens whose preference is for 'muffins', 'cups of tea' and holidays in Devon 'because they liked to eat scones with jam and clotted cream' (45, 46). They have never regaled their children with nostalgic 'tales of life in Jamaica – of palm trees and yams and playing by rivers' (4) – and Mildred, Faith's mum, is as likely to cook dinners of roast lamb with roast potatoes and mint sauce as the Jamaican dish of rice and peas – a pluralist culinary tendency that leads Carl's girlfriend Ruth to accuse her of being insufficiently proud of 'black food' (144).

Yet, despite the Jacksons' evident acculturation (signified, notably, through their tastes and eating practices), British society persists in classifying them as 'Other' owing to their Caribbean roots. Faith receives an early lesson in the limits of self-identification when schoolyard bullies taunt her with the words 'Faith is a darkie and her mum and dad came on a banana boat' (3), a gibe that 'exoticizes and marginalizes Faith as a migrant', as Weihsin Gui points out (2012, 86). In fact, the Jamaica Producers' boat on which her parents travelled emblematizes Anglo-Caribbean interconnectedness, highlighting both 'the foreign produce that has become an integral part of Britain's domestic consumption and the immigrant labor force that supports domestic economy' (Githire 2010, 867).[22] The children in the playground have no awareness of this socio-economic context, however, and as a result 'the banana boat is appropriated and resignifed as a derogatory insult', the 'racist logic' of which becomes 'ingrained in Faith's imaginary as well' (Sáez 2006, 2). Notably, before Mildred explains that 'it was a proper boat with cabins and everything', Faith assumes that her parents simply 'curled up on the floor of [the] ship' like slaves during the Middle Passage, 'trying to find a comfortable place amongst the spiky prongs of unripe bananas' (4).

During adulthood, Faith encounters further insidious indicators of non-belonging, which, though less crude than the affronts she received at school, are no less psychically damaging. When she visits Marion's white, working-class family, she is ostensibly treated as a guest, the recipient of Marion's mother's endless offers of hospitality. However, the family's casual use of racist language to describe other black people makes it clear that Faith can never truly be at home there. A weekend trip to Simon's parents' house in the 'quintessentially English' countryside proves similarly alienating (115). Labelled 'exotic' by Simon's mother (125), Faith later finds her ancestry held to account in the village pub; when she responds to the question 'And whereabouts are you from, Faith?' with the answer 'London', her inquisitor rejoinders, 'I meant more what country are you from?' (130). These accumulating reminders of alterity contribute to an incipient crisis of subjectivity that comes to a head when Faith witnesses a racist attack by National Front thugs. Taking to her bed, she decides that she '[doesn't] want to be black any more' (160), a repudiation of selfhood that her parents decide to remedy by sending her on a recuperative journey of self-discovery to Jamaica.

Once relocated to her Aunt Coral's Kingston home, Faith acquires a new sense of rootedness via the piecemeal ingestion of her family's oral history – a history that is intimately bound up with the cultivation, cookery and commoditization of foods. She discovers, for instance, that her maternal grandparents were resourceful entrepreneurs who planted a small plot of land with oranges, lemons, coconuts, bananas, yams and sweet potatoes, and sold the resulting produce in their shop, along with homemade chocolate and hand-roasted coffee beans. Their story of enterprising commercial spirit is inevitably shadowed, however, by the history of colonialism and slave-produced commodities that haunts the Caribbean. Faith's ancestry is revealed to include a Mr Livingstone, a white plantation owner, and his black slave Katherine; Benjamin Hilton, a mixed-race servant who was favoured by his Spanish employers because of his ability to 'cook *bacalao*', a dish of 'spiced sweet potatoes, peppers, eggs and black olives' (260–261); and James Campbell, a dispossessed Scottish tenant farmer who emigrated, Robinson Crusoe-like, to find work on a sugar-estate. Linked to both independent living and enforced labour, empowerment and exploitation, food in Faith's family history plays a role that is intrinsically bitter-sweet, a collocation that is metaphorized in Faith's first taste of the symbolically charged foodstuff sugar-cane:

> as I bit down onto it, the sticky glutinous sweetness trickled into my mouth and slid effortlessly down my throat. But then it became horrible. A bitter sponge of sharp fibres that coated my mouth in woodchip wallpaper and started to soak up my saliva.
>
> *220*

The transition from palatal pleasure to pain here mirrors Faith's experience of acquiring an 'oral tradition', signifying the mixed emotions to which postcolonial acts of historical restitution can give rise. It also recalls the ambivalence of the 'blood sugar' topos deployed in eighteenth-century abolitionist writings (see Chapter 4), in which images of sweetness co-exist with images of disgust.

The motif of bitter-sweetness further underpins the story of Faith's great-aunt Matilda, a 'pass-for-white' woman (307) who disowns her black racial heritage while fetishizing 'the ways of the English' (312). In order to inculcate what she assumes to be Anglicized manners in her daughter and nieces, Matilda obliges them to eat 'lemons with sugar and a tiny spoon', assuring them 'as they grimaced and sucked in their cheeks' that 'this is what the English do' (312–313). Aunt Coral's reflection on this curious practice – 'the thing bitter no matter how much sugar you put on it' (313) – can be interpreted simultaneously as a remembrance of the literal experience of eating sweetened lemons and a judgement on the folly of such flawed cultural mimicry.[23] Yet, if Matilda's misguided emulative practices expose her to ridicule, they also – as invented traditions – denaturalize the assumed link between consumption and nation. While acknowledging, through Faith's story, that culinary heritage can instil a sense of belonging and facilitate temporal and geographic (re)connections, *Fruit of the Lemon* refuses, in its representation of Matilda, to reify food as the locus of authentic national identity.

Like Levy's Faith, Smith's Irie Jones (the mixed-race daughter of a Jamaican mother and English father) finds that food serves as a conduit to her Caribbean ancestry in *White Teeth*. During a period of teenage identity crisis, Irie seeks refuge in the Lambeth flat of her patois-speaking grandmother Hortense, a place she associates with 'unusual' fare such as 'pickled fish head' and 'chilli dumplings' (Smith 2001, 381). Comforted on arrival by a mountainous breakfast of home-cooked Jamaican-style plantain, Irie goes on to take intellectual nourishment from Hortense's 'small and eclectic library' of books on colonial history, 'voraciously' devouring titles such as '*In Sugar Cane Land*' and '*Dominica: Hints and Notes to Intending Settlers*' (399, 400). 'Cocooned' within this virtual portal to her matrilineal heritage (399), Irie begins to mentally supplant the actual prospect from her window (an allotment of tomato-vines) with visions of 'sugar, sugar, sugar' (400). Furthermore, she fancies that the smell of plantain from Hortense's kitchen sends her 'back to somewhere' – a 'somewhere' that the narrator admits is 'quite fictional, for [Irie had] never been there' (400). Just as *Fruit of the Lemon*'s Matilda constructs a fantasy England from rituals involving lemons and sugar, in *White Teeth* Irie transports herself to an imaginary Jamaica via the aromas of her grandmother's cookery. Paradoxically, it is by laying claim to this fabricated motherland that Irie finally achieves a much-longed-for sense of belonging: 'so *this* was where she came from' (400).

The powerful allure of '*homeland*' – a 'magical fantasy' word (402) – bewitches not only Irie but also her father's Bangladeshi friend Samad Iqbal (who is constantly misidentified as 'Indian' in the text). A first-generation immigrant, Samad struggles to reconcile his Westernized lifestyle with his Muslim faith; he lusts after his sons' white, middle-class music-teacher and admits to eating bacon and drinking Guinness, *haram* practices which he blames on his 'corruption' by British culture (149). Plagued by a range of 'spiritual, physical, [and] sexual' hungers (141), and concerned by the acculturation of his children's generation, who 'eat all kinds of rubbish' (190), Samad begins to idealize his Bangladeshi homeland as a repository of 'tradition' and 'untainted principles' (193) – an essentialist vision that is challenged by his wife, Alsana, who calls attention to Bangladesh's own history of cultural intermixture and assimilation with the aid of the *Reader's Digest Encyclopedia*: 'you go back and back and back and it's still easier to find the correct Hoover bag than to find one pure person, one pure faith, on the globe' (236). Samad, however, cannot accede to the pluralistic mindset by which he is surrounded – a philosophy summarized in Abdul-Mickey's declaration that 'we're all English now, mate' (192) – and attempts instead to engineer an unalloyed identity for his twin sons by sending them 'home' to Bangladesh. In the event, he is only able to afford a single airfare, so Magid is sent abroad while Millat remains in London, a decision that rebounds on Samad's deterministic assumptions in unexpected ways. Millat grows up to become 'a fully paid-up green bow-tie wearing fundamentalist' (407), albeit one whose commitment to Islamic asceticism occasionally lapses where alcohol is concerned, and whose obsession with Mafia gangster-movies means he is better able to cook a 'seafood linguine' than a 'lamb curry' (446). Magid, meanwhile, returns from his Bangladeshi upbringing a 'pukka Englishman' (407) who horrifies his father by ordering a bacon sandwich from Abdul-Mickey's halal refectory, thereby transgressing its 'most hallowed, sacred rule': 'NO PORK' (450). As Ashley Dawson notes, 'the absolute separation between East and West that Samad dreams of is an illusion, and even after he separates them his sons are constantly constructing new identities based on composites of the interpenetrating cultures of East and West' (2007, 164).

As well as highlighting the indeterminacy of multicultural identity through food, Smith's novel attests to the ways in which cultural difference is decontextualized, commodified and consumed in modern Britain. At the Palace, the garish West-end restaurant where Samad works as a waiter, his young colleagues ('whose furthest expedition East was the one they made daily, back home to Whitechapel, Smithfield's, [or] the Isle of Dogs') happily fabricate narratives about the exotic history and geography of the dishes on the menu (203) – dishes that 'do not exist in India', as the narrator wryly notes (59). Meanwhile, their inebriated post-pub customers make demands to be served 'egg fried rice whether or not it is a Chinese dish' (206), casually conflating all non-British cuisines into a fuzzy mass of Otherness.

The commercialization of ethnic difference within the food industry thus generates only a shallow kind of pluralism, Smith implies, one that invites white Britons to 'eat the Other', to use bell hooks' well-known phrase (2015, 21), while leaving unquestioned what Anita Mannur calls 'the conditions of race and class' which make it necessary 'for South Asian immigrants to enter into the business of making Indianness palatable to Western tastes' (2010, 4). A similar point about the commodification of decontextualized difference is made by Monica Ali in *Brick Lane*. Noticing the trend for local curry-houses to display statues of Ganesh, Krishna and Kali in their windows, Nazneen assumes that a new, Hindu community must have moved into the predominantly Bengali-Muslim area until her husband informs her that the deities are deployed because white consumers like to see them 'for authenticity'; as he sagely points out, 'marketing' is the 'biggest god of all' (2003, 373).

The Palace's unthinking dietary adventurers are by no means the worst exponents of 'eating the Other' in *White Teeth*, however.[24] The white, liberal, middle-class Chalfens demonstrate a fetishistic attitude to racial difference that is implicitly cannibalistic, illustrating hooks' point that, in modern society, ethnicity functions as 'spice', a form of 'seasoning that can liven up the dull dish that is mainstream white culture' (2015, 21). Before they meet Irie and Millat as part of a school-sponsored mentoring scheme, Joyce and Marcus Chalfen are palpably 'bored' by the 'mirrored perfection' of their family life (314) and 'looking for something new to get their teeth into', as Peter Childs suggests (2012, 222). Irie and Millat – 'stimulating', 'brown strangers' (326) – provide the requisite raw material to satisfy their hunger. Although Joyce, in particular, is initially figured as an inveterate nurturer, who loves nourishing others and '*hated* it' when her children, 'pop-eyed addicts of breast milk, finally kicked the habit' (315), the novel provides strong hints that the Chalfens have a co-existent capacity for violent devourment. Marcus's declaration that 'all Chalfens are healthy eaters' (318) is affirmed by the depiction of the family at Sunday dinner, 'tearing apart a chicken until there was nothing left but a tattered ribcage' (314). Further evidence of their rapacity is provided by their association with 'Canines: the Ripping Teeth' (the title of the chapter in which they first appear) and by Alsana's characterization of them as 'birds with teeth' who are devouring her son's alterity (345). These accumulative references to voracious consumption signal that the Chalfens' well-intentioned cross-cultural interactions may have outcomes as damaging as the literal violence wreaked by 'young white men who are *angry*' about multicultural diversity (327). As hooks points out, when 'cultural, ethnic, and racial differences' are served up as tantalizing 'dishes to enhance the white palate', there is always a danger that 'the Other' will be metaphorically obliterated: 'eaten, consumed, and forgotten' (2015, 39).

Like Smith's *White Teeth*, Ali's *Brick Lane* inhabits a conspicuously multicultural London, in which shops sell 'fish and chips and samosas and pizzas and a little bit of everything from around the world' (2003, 81). As a post-9/11 fiction, however, *Brick Lane* conveys a stronger sense of anxiety than its precursor that modern Britain's taste for 'ethnic' cuisines does not necessary translate into community cohesion and a tolerance for minorities. The racial tensions implicit in twenty-first-century society are highlighted via a series of right-wing pamphlets pushed through the letterbox of the Ahmed family's Tower-Hamlets flat, one of which warns of the enactment of 'multicultural murder' in British schools, intoning ominously that in domestic science lessons the nation's daughters are being taught 'how to make a kebab, or fry a bhaji' instead of learning how to cook so-called native dishes (207). The leaflet's hysterical culinary patriotism is rendered ironic by the thoroughly assimilated Ahmed girls' preference for 'baked beans' over 'dal' (147) and 'Birds Eye burgers' over 'fish head curry' (160) – Anglicized tastes that cause them to clash with their Bangladeshi-born father, Chanu, who occupies a conflicted position in relation to cultural integration. Theorizing the immigrant's situation as inherently tragic, Chanu explains:

> I'm talking about the clash between Western values and our own. I'm talking about the struggle to assimilate and the need to preserve one's identity and heritage. I'm talking about children who don't know what their identity is. I'm talking about the feelings of alienation engendered by a society where racism is prevalent.
>
> *92*

As Sara Upstone suggests, 'Chanu is a master of Fanonian contradictions' (2007, 337): an avid consumer of classic English literature, who drinks alcohol because 'it's part of the culture here' (90) and refuses to haggle while food-shopping on Brick Lane for fear of acting 'like a primitive' (73), he is also, like *White Teeth*'s Samad, afflicted by 'Going Home Syndrome' (24), a pining for Bangladesh that ultimately manifests itself as a physical hunger; yearning for the country of his birth, the previously portly Chanu gradually loses interest in food, his stomach eventually becoming 'flatter than a paratha' (401).

Chanu's intellectual agonizing over his diasporic identity is treated dismissively by Mrs Azad, who dresses in Westernized fashion, drinks beer and presents the Ahmeds with a meal of 'unidentified meat in tepid gravy with boiled potatoes' when they visit her home (89). Revelling in the code-switching enabled by her dual consciousness, Mrs Azad asks Chanu:

> Why do you make it so complicated? . . . Assimilation this, alienation that! . . . Listen, when I'm in Bangladesh I put on a sari and cover my head and all that. But here I go out to work. I work with white girls and I'm just one of them. If I want to come home and eat curry, that's my business.
>
> *93*

For Mrs Azad, living in Britain enables freedom and independence, and she contrasts her autonomous, hybrid existence with that of other immigrant women who 'spend ten, twenty years here' only to 'sit in the kitchen grinding spices all day' (93). This stereotypical picture of the female migrant experience seems initially to describe the life of Chanu's wife, Nazneen, who moves to Britain aged eighteen, an 'unspoilt girl' from a small Bangladeshi village (16). In the early chapters of *Brick Lane*, Nazneen's daily routine is ordered around food preparation; she makes breakfast for Chanu each morning, then busies herself with domestic chores before spending the afternoon cooking dinner. The monotony of her task is conveyed via a list-like succession of clauses: she 'washed the rice and set it to boil, searched through a cupful of lentils for tiny stones that could crack your teeth, put them in a pan with water but no salt and put the pan on the stove' (48). While outwardly conforming to the role of dutiful wife, however, Nazneen also engages in subversive behaviours that reveal what Angelia Poon calls 'the tactical nature of everyday practices' (2009, 429). When Chanu upsets her, Nazneen undertakes small acts of insurrection 'designed to destroy the state from within', such as secreting 'fiery red chillies', like hidden 'hand grenades', in his sandwiches (50). And although she refuses to eat in front of Chanu at mealtimes in order to 'make . . . visible' her wifely 'self-restraint' and 'self-denial', Nazneen takes solace in secret night-time feasts at the refrigerator, nourishing herself on foods that remind her of her mother and homeland (62).

If Nazneen's strategies of adaptation and survival indicate that she is more than just a stereotype, then Chanu, too, works to subvert readerly assumptions. Although he resembles, at times, a tragi-comic incarnation of the colonial mimic man, at others he is humanized as a tender and caring husband. When his baby son is hospitalized, Chanu brings feasts of perfectly cooked rice and 'velvety' dal from home for his anxiously watching wife, which she consumes 'like a zealot' (104). Later, when Nazneen succumbs to a nervous illness, Chanu, the 'excellent cook', lovingly prepares for her a succession of 'special dishes' in order to coax her back to health (269). Although Nazneen believes that it is her politically engaged lover Karim who sustains her most by 'feeding her slices of the world' (375), he is in fact a figure of 'false promise' (Poon 2009, 431) who reinstates patriarchal norms, expecting her to '[dance] attendance' on his casual demands for snacks and refreshments (248). It is Nazneen's relationship with Chanu, the narrative tacitly suggests, that is actually the more physically and emotionally nourishing. Despite this, the pair separate at the end of the text, Nazneen deciding that her future lies in England rather than in Bangladesh. The novel closes with an apparently positive message about female opportunity, multiculturalism and syncretic identity; on a day-trip to the local ice-rink, Nazneen and her daughters eat cream-cheese and mango pickle sandwiches (edible symbols of transcultural accommodation), while their friend Razia joyfully declares: 'This is England . . . You can do whatever you like' (413). Some critics have read this exuberant closing statement as overly optimistic in its assessment of modern British culture, but its potentially naïve faith in the idea of personal freedom is tempered by the knowledge that, in the first month of Nazneen's new life as a working single-mother, her family has had to subsist every day on 'rice and dal, rice and dal' because money is so limited (409). While celebrating Nazneen's successful negotiation of diasporic identity, *Brick Lane* is careful not to disregard the wider social and economic factors that shape migrant lives – and diets.

Fruit of the Lemon and *White Teeth* offer similarly nuanced denouements. At the end of Levy's novel, Faith's triumphant declaration that 'I am the bastard child of

Empire and I will have my day' (2004, 327) attests to her positive reclamation of her mixed cultural heritage. Importantly, though, this recuperation of the past does not take the form of deracinated nostalgia. As Elena Machado Sáez argues, Faith's 'acquisition of a historical context' – and concomitant sense of belonging – 'is invested or maintained by commodities' (2006, 1); her plan to take home to London authentic Blue-Mountain coffee beans and 'roast them as [her] grandfather used to do' (323), and to proudly re-tell the story of her parents' arrival in England on a banana boat, acknowledges that her family's story is inextricable from wider colonial histories of economic exploitation and international trade (histories that frame a number of the eighteenth- and nineteenth-century fictions considered in earlier chapters). *White Teeth*, too, suggests the importance of the past (including inherited foodways) to diasporic communities; however, its ambiguous ending implies that something will always resist or escape from attempts to forge pure or essentialized cultural identities. In the words of Irie, the roots of cross-cultural interaction run 'too damn deep' to be easily disentangled (Smith 2001, 527).

As the millennial fictions considered here show, representations of food provide writers with a means to explore the haphazard processes of intermixture and exchange, hybridity and fusion that make up modern culture, as well as the contingent identities that emerge from them. The foods we eat are deeply embedded in notions of subjectivity; yet they also expose the fictions and fabrications that underlie assertions of identity. If, as Roland Barthes contends, food is 'a system of communication' (2013, 24), then the meanings it produces are multiple and some-times contradictory. Indeed, in the literature analysed in this chapter, food both supports *and* challenges assumptions around gender, ethnicity and nation, both reinforces *and* subverts dichotomies between 'civilized' and 'uncivilized', and human and animal. This semantic border-crossing is perhaps unsurprising when we consider that food is, by its very nature, a substance involved in the transgression of boundaries: external matter, it becomes integral to the consuming subject via the bodily processes of ingestion, digestion and absorption. Although in twentieth- and twenty-first-century culture the idea that 'you are what you eat' has become something of an orthodoxy, appearing in the titles of multiple diet books, self-help manuals and television lifestyle programmes, in the fiction of the period the equation is repea-tedly reformulated as a question, as literary representations of food work to contest, as well as to construct, notions of identity and community.

Notes

1 According to Marianna Torgovnick, 'most scholars agree that cannibalism existed in parts of Africa, but spottily, with neighbouring groups often widely diverse in attitudes toward the practice' (1990, 258n47). Indeed, Dorothy Hammond and Alta Jablow suggest that 'writers were far more addicted to tales of cannibalism than the Africans ever were to cannibalism. Its prevalence was taken for granted, and no actual evidence was required to establish that a tribe was notoriously anthropophagous' (1977, 94). Where instances of cannibalism are known to have occurred, they tend to have been motivated by social and/ or religious function rather than gastronomic preference: Paul Armstrong notes that

'cannibals do not typically eat human flesh to appease hunger but for spiritual reasons as part of specific rituals' (1996, 30).

2 Notably, representations of colonialism as cannibalistic are found in a number of late nineteenth-century and early twentieth-century accounts, particularly those documenting Belgian atrocities in the Congo. One of the native witnesses quoted in Roger Casement's 'Congo Report' (1904) recalls being told by 'the white men' of King Leopold II's administration, 'you are only nyama (meat)' (qtd. in Conrad 2006, 139).

3 Solitary dining is similarly characterized as non-normative behaviour in earlier literatures, such as *The Book of Margery Kempe* (Chapter 1).

4 Cannibalism is frequently represented as animalistic in the works considered in this study: see, for instance, the representation of Lust in Spenser's *Faerie Queene* (Chapter 2) and Crusoe's comments about the brutality of cannibalism in *Robinson Crusoe* (Chapter 3).

5 Bloom's macabre imagery here seems indebted to Shakespeare's *Hamlet*: 'We fat all creatures else to fat us, and we fat ourselves for maggots' (2006, 4.3.21–22).

6 For more on attitudes to vegetarianism in *Ulysses*, see Freedman (2009) and Regan (2009).

7 Gilbert notes that underlying the plenitude at the feast in 'The Dead' is 'an extended military metaphor: the ham and beef are "rival ends"; the fruit stand is flanked by "sentries"; the other drinks are lined up in "squads" and known by "the colours of their uniforms"' (2014, 107). With its oblique references to death, the dinner reminds protagonist Gabriel Conroy that '"one by one", he, his aunts, and their other guests "[are] all becoming shades"' (108).

8 The idea of the Eucharist as cannibalistic has a long literary history; see, for instance, the sections on Spenser's *Faerie Queene* in Chapter 2; Milton's *Paradise Lost* in Chapter 3; and Byron's *Don Juan* in Chapter 4. Representations of the clergy as parasitic have a similarly extensive history; for early examples, see the sections on *Piers Plowman* and *The Canterbury Tales* in Chapter 1.

9 Drawing on Ellmann (1993), Mara highlights the practice of 'fasting to distrain' in medieval Ireland, 'whereby a creditor could fast against a debtor, or a victim of injustice could fast against the person who had injured him'. She notes that self-imposed starvation re-emerged in the early twentieth century as a form of nationalist protest against British rule in Ireland, and again in the hunger strikes of republican prisoners in Northern Ireland in the 1980s (2009, 94).

10 Julieann Ulin argues that 'eviction, exposure, poverty, the cessation of ritual burial, and the fear of dogs devouring bodies form an iconography of the Famine that is present throughout *Ulysses*' (2011, 24). For further analyses of Joyce's novel in terms of Famine memory, see Wurtz (2005), Roos (2006) and Mara (2009).

11 The construction of milk as a pure and wholesome substance extends back to the literature of the medieval period; see, for instance, the section on *The Canterbury Tales* in Chapter 1.

12 In 'Three Essays on Sexuality', Freud argues that sexual desire is connected to and emerges out of the infant's initial experiences of feeding:

> The satisfaction of the erotogenic zone is associated, in the first instance, with the satisfaction of the need for nourishment . . . No one who has seen a baby sinking back satiated from the breast and falling asleep with flushed cheeks and a blissful smile can escape the reflection that this picture persists as a prototype of the expression of sexual satisfaction in later life.
>
> (1953, 181–182)

13 In the holograph draft of *To the Lighthouse*, Woolf gives a partial recipe for Boeuf en Daube: 'you stand it in water for twenty four hours: you ~~add~~ stir continuously; you add a little bay leaf, & then a dash of sherry: the whole ~~being~~ never ~~been~~ being allowed, of course to come to the boil' (1982, 129).

14 The notion that there is artistry in the design and production of an exquisite meal is shared in the writings of late nineteenth-century feminists Sarah Grand and Elizabeth Robins Pennell (see Chapter 5).

15 Interestingly, Woolf deploys a comparable simile in *To the Lighthouse*: Mrs Ramsay describes her sleeping children as being 'netted in their cots like birds among cherries and raspberries' (2006, 50), suggesting again the existence of a continuum between Mrs Ramsay and Susan.

16 According to Julia Kristeva, the abject 'beseeches, worries', but also 'fascinates desire' (1982, 1). Significantly, this experience has strong links to consumption: Kristeva suggests that 'food loathing is perhaps the most elementary and most archaic form of abjection' (2). The abjection that Rhoda feels in response to corpulent human bodies and meat is replicated by Marian in Atwood's *The Edible Woman*, discussed later in this chapter.

17 See, for instance, Brain (1995), Sceats (2000) and Drautzburg and Halfmann (2010).

18 The extent to which female food refusal can be read as a form of (conscious or unconscious) social protest is a contentious critical issue in this study; see in particular the section on the Brontës' fiction in Chapter 5.

19 The historic link between Irish national identity, hunger and rebellion is discussed in more detail in the earlier section on *Ulysses* and in note 9 above.

20 Jamila's taste for the food of the Other mimics (but reverses the trajectory of) that found in Thackeray's *Vanity Fair* (Chapter 5), where Jos longs for authentic Indian curry during his sojourns in Britain.

21 For more on the (contested) origins of chicken tikka masala, see Collingham (2006, 3) and Mannur (2010, 3).

22 The interconnectedness of modern Anglo-Jamaican experience and colonial history is articulated powerfully in cultural theorist Stuart Hall's declaration that 'people like me who came to England in the 1950s have been there for centuries; symbolically, we have been there for centuries . . . I am the sugar at the bottom of the English cup of tea. I am the sweet tooth, the sugar plantations that rotted generations of English children's teeth' (1997, 48).

23 Eating behaviours offer postcolonial writers rich opportunities by which to explore the ambivalence of colonial mimicry, famously theorized by Homi Bhabha in *The Location of Culture* (2004, 121–131). Like Great-Aunt Matilda, Chanu in *Brick Lane* (discussed later in the section) can be interpreted as a colonial mimic.

24 Lisa Heldke discusses the modern phenomenon of 'food adventuring', as well as its relation to contemporary cultural and economic colonialism, in her autobiographically inflected study *Exotic Appetites* (2003).

References

Achaya, K. T. 1998. *A Historical Dictionary of Indian Food*. Oxford. Oxford University Press.

Adolph, Andrea. 2009. *Food and Femininity in Twentieth-Century British Women's Fiction*. Farnham. Ashgate.

Ali, Monica. 2003. *Brick Lane*. London. Doubleday.

Armstrong, Paul. 1996. '*Heart of Darkness* and the Epistemology of Cultural Differences'. *Under Postcolonial Eyes: Joseph Conrad after Empire*. Eds. Gail Fincham and Myrtle Hooper. Rondebosch. UCT Press. 21–41.

Atwood, Margaret. 1994. 'Running with the Tigers'. *Flesh and the Mirror: Essays on the Art of Angela Carter*. Ed. Lorna Sage. London. Virago. 117–135.

———. 2009. *The Edible Woman*. London. Virago.

Ballaster, Ros, Margaret Beetham, Elizabeth Frazer and Sandra Hebron. 1991. *Women's Worlds: Ideology, Femininity and the Woman's Magazine*. Basingstoke. Macmillan.

Barthes, Roland. 2000. *Mythologies*. Trans. Annette Lavers. London. Vintage.

———. 2013. 'Toward a Psychosociology of Contemporary Food Consumption'. *Food and Culture: A Reader*. 3rd edn. Eds. Carole Counihan and Penny Van Esterik. New York and London. Routledge. 23–30.

Baxter, Jeannette. 2014. 'Exquisite Corpse: Un/Dressing History in *Fruit of the Lemon/ The Long Song*'. *Andrea Levy: Contemporary Critical Perspectives*. Eds. Jeannette Baxter and David James. London. Bloomsbury. 79–94.

Bell, David and Gill Valentine. 1997. *Consuming Geographies: We Are Where We Eat*. London and New York. Routledge.

Bell, Quentin. 1972. *Virginia Woolf: A Biography*. Vol. 2. London. Hogarth Press.

Bewell, Alan. 1999. *Romanticism and Colonial Disease*. Baltimore, MD, and London. Johns Hopkins University Press.

Bhabha, Homi K. 2004. *The Location of Culture*. London and New York. Routledge.

Brain, Tracy. 1995. 'Figuring Anorexia: Margaret Atwood's *The Edible Woman*'. *LIT: Literature Interpretation Theory* 6.3/4. 299–311.

Bruch, Hilde. 1973. *Eating Disorders: Obesity, Anorexia Nervosa, and the Person Within*. New York. Basic Books.

——. 2001. *The Golden Cage: The Enigma of Anorexia Nervosa*. Cambridge, MA, and London. Harvard University Press.

Cannon, Poppy. 1964. *The Frozen-Foods Cookbook*. New York. Thomas Y. Crowell.

Carter, Angela. 1979. *The Sadeian Woman: An Exercise in Cultural History*. London. Virago.

——. 1981. *The Magic Toyshop*. London. Virago.

Childs, Peter. 2012. *Contemporary Novelists: British Fiction since 1970*. 2nd edn. Basingstoke. Palgrave Macmillan.

Collingham, Lizzie. 2006. *Curry: A Tale of Cooks and Conquerors*. London. Vintage.

Conrad, Joseph. 2002. 'Falk: A Reminiscence'. *Typhoon and Other Tales*. Ed. Cedric Watts. Oxford. Oxford University Press. 75–145.

——. 2006. *Heart of Darkness*. Ed. Paul B. Armstrong. New York and London. W. W. Norton & Company.

——. 2010. 'Cookery: Preface to Jessie Conrad's *A Handbook of Cookery for a Small House*'. *Last Essays*. Eds. Harold Ray Stevens and J. H. Stape. Cambridge. Cambridge University Press. 112–114.

Cook, Ian and Philip Crang. 2003. 'The World on a Plate: Culinary Culture, Displacement and Geographical Knowledges'. *The Consumption Reader*. Eds. David B. Clarke, Marcus A. Doel and Kate M. L. Housiaux. London and New York. Routledge. 113–116.

Cook, Robin. 2001. 'Robin Cook's Chicken Tikka Masala Speech: Extracts from a Speech to the Social Market Foundation in London'. *The Guardian*. 19 April. www.theguardian. com/world/2001/apr/19/race.britishidentity

Dawson, Ashley. 2007. *Mongrel Nation: Diasporic Culture and the Making of Postcolonial Britain*. Ann Arbor. University of Michigan Press.

Deleuze, Gilles. 2005. *Francis Bacon: The Logic of Sensation*. Trans. Daniel W. Smith. London and New York. Continuum.

Drautzburg, Anja and Miriam Halfmann. 2010. 'The Battle of the Bulge? Anorexia Nervosa in North American Fiction 1969–1981–2007'. *The Pleasures and Horrors of Eating: The Cultural History of Eating in Anglophone Literature*. Eds. Marion Gymnich and Norbert Lennartz. Goettingen. V&R Unipress/Bonn University Press. 429–445.

Ellmann, Maud. 1993. *The Hunger Artists: Starving, Writing and Imprisonment*. London. Virago.

Fothergill, Anthony. 1996. 'Cannibalising Traditions: Representation and Critique in *Heart of Darkness*'. *Under Postcolonial Eyes: Joseph Conrad after Empire*. Eds. Gail Fincham and Myrtle Hooper. Rondebosch. UCT Press. 93–108.

Freedman, Ariela. 2009. '"Don't eat a beefsteak": Joyce and the Pythagoreans'. *Texas Studies in Literature and Language* 51.4. 447–462.

Freud, Sigmund. 1953. 'Three Essays on Sexuality'. *The Standard Edition of the Complete Psychological Works of Sigmund Freud, Vol. VII*. Trans. and ed. James Strachey. London. Hogarth Press and the Institute of Psycho-Analysis. 123–245.

Friedan, Betty. 2010. *The Feminine Mystique*. London. Penguin.

Gilbert, Sandra M. 2014. *The Culinary Imagination: From Myth to Modernity*. New York and London. W. W. Norton & Company.

Gill, David. 1999. 'The Fascination of the Abomination: Conrad and Cannibalism'. *The Conradian* 24.2. 1–30.

Githire, Njeri. 2010. 'The Empire Bites Back: Food Politics and the Making of a Nation in Andrea Levy's Works'. *Callaloo* 33.3. 857–873.

Glenny, Allie. 1999. *Ravenous Identity: Eating and Eating Distress in the Life and Work of Virginia Woolf*. New York. St Martin's Press.

Gui, Weihsin. 2012. 'Post-heritage Narratives: Migrancy and Travelling Theory in V. S. Naipaul's *The Enigma of Arrival* and Andrea Levy's *Fruit of the Lemon*'. *Journal of Commonwealth Literature* 47.1. 73–89.

Hall, Stuart. 1997. 'Old and New Identities, Old and New Ethnicities'. *Culture, Globalization and the World-System: Contemporary Conditions for the Representation of Identity*. Ed. Anthony D. King. Minneapolis. University of Minnesota Press. 41–68.

Hammond, Dorothy and Alta Jablow. 1977. *The Myth of Africa*. New York. Library of Social Science.

Handley, William R. 1994. 'The Housemaid and the Kitchen Table: Incorporating the Frame in *To the Lighthouse*'. *Twentieth Century Literature* 40.1. 15–41.

Heldke, Lisa M. 2003. *Exotic Appetites: Ruminations of a Food Adventurer*. New York and London. Routledge.

hooks, bell. 2015. *Black Looks: Race and Representation*. New York and London. Routledge.

Jekyll, Agnes. 2002. *Kitchen Essays*. London. Persephone Books.

Joyce, James. 1956. 'The Dead'. *Dubliners*. London. Penguin. 199–256.

——. 1992. *A Portrait of the Artist as a Young Man*. Ed. Seamus Deane. London. Penguin.

——. 1993. *Ulysses* (1922 text). Ed. Jeri Johnson. Oxford. Oxford University Press.

Knapp, Bettina L. 1988. 'Virginia Woolf's "Boeuf en Daube"'. *Literary Gastronomy*. Ed. David Bevan. Amsterdam. Rodopi. 29–36.

Korsmeyer, Carolyn. 1999. *Making Sense of Taste: Food and Philosophy*. Ithaca, NY, and London. Cornell University Press.

Kristeva, Julia. 1982. *Powers of Horror: An Essay on Abjection*. Trans. Leon S. Roudiez. New York. Columbia University Press.

Levy, Andrea. 2004. *Fruit of the Lemon*. London. Review.

McGee, Diane. 2001. *Writing the Meal: Dinner in the Fiction of Early Twentieth-Century Women Writers*. Toronto, Buffalo and London. University of Toronto Press.

Mannur, Anita. 2010. *Culinary Fictions: Food in South Asian Diasporic Culture*. Philadelphia, PA. Temple University Press.

Mara, Miriam O'Kane. 2009. 'James Joyce and the Politics of Food'. *New Hibernia Review* 13.4. 94–110.

Milesi, Laurent. 2001. '"Promnesia" (Remembering Forward) in *Midnight's Children*; or Rushdie's Chutney versus Proust's *Madeleine*'. *Sensual Reading: New Approaches to Reading in Its Relation to the Senses*. Eds. Michael Syrotinski and Ian Maclachlan. Lewisburg, PA, and London. Bucknell University Press / Associated University Presses. 179–212.

Morton, Timothy. 2000. *The Poetics of Spice: Romantic Consumerism and the Exotic*. Cambridge. Cambridge University Press.

O'Connell, Helen. 2013. '"Food Values": Joyce and Dietary Revival'. *James Joyce in the Nineteenth Century*. Ed. John Nash. Cambridge. Cambridge University Press. 128–146.

Orbach, Susie. 1993. *Hunger Strike: The Anorectic's Struggle as a Metaphor for Our Age*. London. Penguin.

Parker, Emma. 2000. 'The Consumption of Angela Carter: Women, Food, and Power'. *ARIEL: A Review of International English Literature* 31.3. 141–169.

Phillips, Jerry. 1998. 'Cannibalism qua Cannibalism: The Metaphorics of Accumulation in Marx, Conrad, Shakespeare and Marlowe'. *Cannibalism and the Colonial World*. Eds. Francis Barker, Peter Hulme and Margaret Iverson. Cambridge. Cambridge University Press. 183–203.

Plotz, Judith. 1996. 'Rushdie's Pickle and the New Indian Historical Novel: Sealy, Singh, Tharoor, and National Metaphor'. *World Literature Written in English* 35.2. 28–48.

Poon, Angelia. 2009. 'To Know What's What: Forms of Migrant Knowing in Monica Ali's *Brick Lane*'. *Journal of Postcolonial Writing* 45.4. 426–437.

Proust, Marcel. 1981. *Remembrance of Things Past [À la Recherche du Temps Perdu]*. 3 vols. Trans. C. K. Scott-Moncrieff and Terence Kilmartin. London. Chatto & Windus.

Regan, Marguerite M. 2009. '"Weggebobbles and Fruit": Bloom's Vegetarian Impulses'. *Texas Studies in Literature and Language* 51.4. 463–475.

Rich, Lauren. 2010. 'A Table for One: Hunger and Unhomeliness in Joyce's Public Eateries'. *Joyce Studies Annual*. 71–98.

Rickard, John. 2007. 'Eating Like a White Man: Nibbling at the Edges of *Heart of Darkness*'. *L'Epoque Conradienne* 33. 49–57.

Roos, Bonnie. 2006. 'The Joyce of Eating: Feast, Famine and the Humble Potato in *Ulysses*'. *Hungry Words: Images of Famine in the Irish Canon*. Eds. George Cusack and Sarah Goss. Dublin and Portland, OR. Irish Academic Press. 159–196.

Roy, Parama. 2010. *Alimentary Tracts: Appetites, Aversions, and the Postcolonial*. Durham, NC, and London. Duke University Press.

Rushdie, Salman. 1992. *Imaginary Homelands: Essays and Criticism 1981–1991*. London. Granta Books/Penguin Books.

——. 1996. *The Moor's Last Sigh*. London. Vintage.

——. 2008. *Midnight's Children*. London. Vintage.

Russell, George William. 1978. *Selections from the Contributions to The Irish Homestead*. Vol. 1. Ed. Henry Summerfield. Gerrards Cross. Colin Smythe.

Sáez, Elena Machado. 2006. 'Bittersweet (Be)Longing: Filling the Void of History in Andrea Levy's *Fruit of the Lemon*'. *Anthurium: A Caribbean Studies Journal* 4.1. Article 5. 1–14. http://scholarlyrepository.miami.edu/anthurium/vol4/iss1/5/

Sceats, Sarah. 1997. 'The Infernal Appetites of Angela Carter'. *The Infernal Desires of Angela Carter: Fiction, Femininity, Feminism*. Eds. Joseph Bristow and Trev Lynn Broughton. London and New York. Longman. 100–115.

——. 2000. *Food, Consumption and the Body in Contemporary Women's Fiction*. Cambridge. Cambridge University Press.

Sewlall, Harry. 2006. 'Cannibalism in the Colonial Imaginary: A Reading of Joseph Conrad's "Falk"'. *Journal of Literary Studies* 22.1/2. 158–174.

Shakespeare, William. 2006. *Hamlet*. Eds. Ann Thompson and Neil Taylor. London. Arden Shakespeare.

Simmons, Allan. 2002. 'The Language of Atrocity: Representing the Congo of Conrad and Casement'. *Conrad in Africa: New Essays on 'Heart of Darkness'*. Eds. Attie de Lange and Gail Fincham with Wieslaw Krajka. New York. Columbia University Press. 85–106.

Smith, Zadie. 2001. *White Teeth*. London. Penguin.

Tanner, Tony. 1976. '"Gnawed Bones" and "Artless Tales" – Eating and Narrative in Conrad'. *Joseph Conrad: A Commemoration*. Ed. Norman Sherry. London and Basingstoke. Macmillan. 17–36.

Thackeray, William Makepeace. 1968. *Vanity Fair*. Ed. J. I. M. Stewart. London. Penguin.

Torgovnick, Marianna. 1990. *Gone Primitive: Savage Intellects, Modern Lives*. Chicago, IL, and London. University of Chicago Press.

Tromanhauser, Vicki. 2014. 'Eating Animals and Becoming Meat in Virginia Woolf's *The Waves*'. *Journal of Modern Literature* 38.1. 73–93.

Tucker, Lindsey. 1984. *Stephen and Bloom at Life's Feast: Alimentary Symbolism and the Creative Process in James Joyce's 'Ulysees'*. Columbus. Ohio State University Press.

Ulin, Julieann. 2011. '"Famished Ghosts": Famine Memory in James Joyce's *Ulysses*'. *Joyce Studies Annual*. 20–63.

Upstone, Sara. 2007. '"Same Old, Same Old": Zadie Smith's *White Teeth* and Monica Ali's *Brick Lane*'. *Journal of Postcolonial Writing* 43.3. 336–349.

Utell, Janine. 2008. 'Meals and Mourning in Woolf's *The Waves*'. *College Literature* 35.2. 1–19.

Vlitos, Paul. 2008. 'Conrad's Ideas of Gastronomy: Dining in "Falk"'. *Victorian Literature and Culture* 36.2. 433–449.

Woolf, Virginia. 1942. 'Professions for Women'. *The Death of the Moth and Other Essays*. London. Hogarth Press. 149–154.

——. 1982. *To the Lighthouse: The Original Holograph Draft*. Ed. Susan Dick. Toronto and Buffalo. University of Toronto Press.

——. 1993. *A Room of One's Own / Three Guineas*. Ed. Michèle Barrett. London. Penguin.

——. 2006. *To the Lighthouse*. Ed. David Bradshaw. Oxford. Oxford University Press.

——. 2015. *The Waves*. Ed. David Bradshaw. Oxford. Oxford University Press.

Wurtz, James F. 2005. 'Scarce More a Corpse: Famine Memory and Representations of the Gothic in *Ulysses*'. *Journal of Modern Literature* 29.1. 102–117.

CONCLUSION

Charlotte Boyce and Joan Fitzpatrick

One of the notable publishing trends of the past ten years has been the rise of the popular, hybridized genre, the 'literary cookbook': collections of recipes inspired by famous meals in literature. While some of these titles – *Cooking with Shakespeare* (2008), *Dinner with Mr Darcy* (2013) – focus on the culinary repertoires of individual authors, others, such as *Literary Feasts: Recipes from the Classics of Literature* (2005), *A Literary Feast: Recipes Inspired by Novels, Poems and Plays* (2015) and *Voracious: A Hungry Reader Cooks Her Way Through Great Books* (2015), reimagine dishes from an eclectic mix of canonical and non-canonical sources, many of which are also analyzed in the present volume. Collectively, literary cookbooks bear witness to the prevalence of food in literature, while extending to its logical conclusion the long-standing figurative association of cooking and story-telling, reading and eating – an association that has emerged repeatedly in this study, in texts such as *Sir Gawain and the Green Knight* and *The Canterbury Tales* (Chapter 1), *The History of Tom Jones* (Chapter 3) and *Midnight's Children* (Chapter 6). Literary cookbooks also share a sense that evocations of food in literature enrich the reading experience, providing a tangible link to the imaginary world of the text. In the preface to *Voracious: A Hungry Reader Cooks Her Way Through Great Books*, Cara Nicoletti confesses: 'I fell in love with cooking through reading . . . I connected deeply to the characters in my books, and cooking the foods that they were eating seemed to me a natural way to be closer to them' (2015, xi). This sentiment is echoed by Dinah Fried, creator of *Fictitious Dishes: An Album of Literature's Most Memorable Meals*: 'many of my most vivid memories from books are of the meals the characters eat. I read *Heidi* more than twenty years ago, but I can still taste the golden, cheesy toast that her grandfather serves her, and I can still feel the anticipation and comfort she experiences as she watches him prepare it over the open fire' (2014, 11).

Clearly, to a wide range of readers, representations of food in literature matter and, although the kinds of intensely personal responses outlined here may appear to be of limited critical value to literary scholars, such affective reactions to fictive meals intersect intriguingly with Pamela Gilbert's point that traditional metaphors of reading-as-ingestion position the text as a 'tangible substance' that enters, inhabits and influences the subject (1997, 84). What is more, by foregrounding the tastes, textures and aromas of fictional dishes, literary cookbooks and their generic variations draw attention to the inherent *materiality* of food in literature, issuing a tacit challenge to E. M. Forster's claim in *Aspects of the Novel* (1927) that 'food in fiction is mainly social', serving more to '[draw] characters together' in the interests of the plot than to excite their palates or nourish their bodies (1990, 61). Although the literary meal can, of course, function as narrative device, in the texts considered in this volume food has repeatedly manifested itself as reified object, the physical properties of which may be linked to bodily pleasure – one thinks of the 'seedcake warm and chewed' (Joyce 1993, 167) that Molly Bloom passes from her mouth to her husband's during their lovemaking in *Ulysses* (Chapter 6) – or corporeal pain, as Thackeray's Becky Sharp discovers to her cost when she samples a raw green chilli in *Vanity Fair* (Chapter 5). The literary representations of hunger examined here also testify, in inverted form, to food's materiality; little Oliver Twist's famous request for 'more' in Dickens's novel (Chapter 5) constitutes, in essence, a demand for solid matter with which to fill the hollow space of his stomach. Some critics have suggested that such references to food as concrete substance tend to be 'limited to the novel or to comedy, "low" genres that tolerate allusions to subjects excluded from tragedy or lyric and epic poetry' (Kolb 1995, 1). However, this study has shown that even such culturally vaunted forms as Shakespearean tragedy (Chapter 2) and Miltonian epic (Chapter 3) take a clear interest in the materiality of food: it is, for instance, the fleshy, human content of the pie served to Tamora in *Titus Andronicus* that cements the visceral horror of the play's final scene, while, in *Paradise Lost*, the description of Adam and Eve chewing on the 'savory pulp' of nectarines (Milton 1993, 4.335) affirms the palpability of Eden's garden produce, rendering paradise tantalizingly real.

The importance of food as material object is not limited to its ability to amplify the realism of the text, of course. As Matt Watson suggests, ultimately the 'materiality of food becomes the material of ourselves' (2013, 130); we are what we eat and, as a result of this corporal boundary crossing, food in literature is often implicated in a radical interrogation of subjectivity, working to call into question the physical and psychical integrity of the consuming self. For example, underpinning the sometimes comical references to (in)digestion, flatulence, vomit and excretion that interleave literary history, from Chaucer's *Canterbury Tales* (Chapter 1) and Jonson's *The Alchemist* (Chapter 2) to Byron's *Don Juan* (Chapter 4) and Atwood's *The Edible Woman* (Chapter 6), is an implicit understanding of food as foreign or extraneous matter, which, through the twin processes of ingestion and incorporation, destabilizes identity by problematizing the ostensibly clear-cut distinction between 'self' and 'Other'. Although eating is typically represented as an activity essential to the maintenance of the subject in the writings considered in this book, it can thus also engender feelings of queasiness or disgust: see, for instance, Gulliver's appalled response to Brobdingnagian breastfeeding in *Gulliver's Travels* (Chapter 3), or Rhoda's nauseated reaction to carnivorous consumption in *The Waves* (Chapter 6). Metaphysical concerns regarding the ingestion of food are particularly evident when the eater's mode of consumption is perceived as feral or animalistic, or when the personal hygiene of the cook or seller is less than assured; as we have seen, the disturbing corollary to the presence of human pus, skin, sweat or spittle in vended produce in *The Canterbury Tales* (Chapter 1), *Bartholomew Fair* (Chapter 2) and *The Expedition of Humphry Clinker* (Chapter 4) is the transformation of unwary consumers into accidental cannibals. Cultural anxieties regarding the ontological and epistemological implications of 'eating the Other', in literal or figurative form, also surface repeatedly in post-Reformation representations of the Eucharist and transubstantiation (see, for instance, the discussion of Milton in Chapter 3 and Joyce in Chapter 6) and in post/colonial literary contexts, as evidenced by the ambivalent attitudes towards assimilation and transculturation located in works by Defoe and Swift (Chapter 3), Birkett (Chapter 4) and Thackeray (Chapter 5), and Conrad and Smith (Chapter 6).

All this goes to show that the physicality of food in literature is not straightforwardly divisible from its role as mediator of intersubjective relations, nor from its function as repository of cultural or symbolic meaning. If literary food demands, on the one hand, to be understood *as* food – as authentic textual re-presentation of the material fare consumed by real people at various points throughout history – it also calls to be read as the 'embodiment of all kinds of social practices, including the formation of ideology', as Timothy Morton points out (2006, 1). The complex interplay between food's material and symbolic functions has come to light repeatedly in this study, but can be identified particularly clearly in the literary history of bread. As the foregoing chapters have illustrated, bread has long been constructed as 'the staff of life', an essential article of human subsistence. As a signifier, it often stands metonymically for 'ordinary food or victual' (*OED*), and it figures heavily in texts where hunger is a prevailing concern. A basic item of material nourishment, bread is also invariably loaded with social, political and historical meaning: in a variety of works, its physical composition signals not only the social station of the eater, but also his/her accordance with the hegemonic values constructed in the text. The modest bean-and-bran loaf provided by Piers Plowman in Chapter 1, for instance, connotes his lowly rank but also, importantly, his compliance with the principles of Christian humility; by contrast, the fine white bread that Chaucer's Prioress feeds to her dogs in the same chapter indicates her relative wealth, but also suggests a propensity towards extravagance incompatible with her religious vows of poverty. The ideologically freighted divide between white and brown bread continues into the literature of the eighteenth century; here, during a period of national subsistence crisis, food reformers such as Hannah More disdained expensive white loaves as unnecessary luxuries, while co-opting 'mixed' or barley breads as emblems of wholesome frugality (see Chapter 4). Diversely textured breads have also functioned across literary history as signifiers of national or cultural difference: in Chapter 4, we saw Robert Fergusson celebrate oatmeal-rich bannocks and farls as symbols of a distinctively Scottish identity, while, in *Midnight's Children* (Chapter 6), Rushdie's Jamila fetishizes leavened, white loaves as exotic, occidental alternatives to the flatbreads typically found in India and Pakistan. The intersection of bread's material and symbolic meanings emerges particularly powerfully in religious contexts; it is the Catholic belief in the literal transubstantiation of bread into the body of Christ that enables the figurative construction of the Eucharist as cannibalistic in a variety of writings, from Spenser's *Faerie Queene* (Chapter 2) to Joyce's *Ulysses* (Chapter 6).

The long-standing existence of motifs such as the cannibalistic Eucharist could be taken as an indication that certain textual staples, like bread, achieve a kind of trans-historical relevance in anglophone literature. However, as the preceding chapters of this book have demonstrated, food is a remarkably mobile signifier, capable of acquiring and transmitting a range of disparate and sometimes contradictory meanings over time. Beef is one such multivalent culinary symbol. In *The Tryal of the Lady Allurea Luxury* (Chapter 4) and *Vanity Fair* (Chapter 5), it is explicitly associated with a hale and hearty form of English national identity; similarly, in Chaucer's 'Summoner's Tale' (Chapter 1) and *The Woman Hater* (Chapter 2) it is considered substantial fare. However, when cooked 'en daube' in *To the Lighthouse* (Chapter 6), beef is evocative rather of French sophistication; indeed, the assembled company agrees that 'what passes for cookery in England is an abomination' (Woolf 2006, 82). Although certain literary foodstuffs appear to attain a measure of semantic constancy – apples, for instance, enjoy a fairly stable cultural currency as symbols of appetitive desire, despite never being specified in Genesis as the fruit that tempted Adam and Eve – representations of food more often furnish us with a record of shifting conceptions of taste, enabling us to map intricate patterns of socio-economic and geopolitical change. The sudden explosion of references to turtle (a West Indian import) in eighteenth-century fictions such as *Robinson Crusoe* and *Tom Jones* (Chapter 3) and *Lady Allurea Luxury*, *Humphry Clinker* and *Desmond* (Chapter 4), for example, attests to the transformative effect of British colonialism on the contents of the nation's dining tables. In similar vein, the metamorphosis of 'spice' from costly medicine or flavouring in medieval and early modern literature (Chapters 1 and 2), to icon of oriental luxury in the poetry of Byron and Keats (Chapter 4), to figure of cross-cultural fusion in postcolonial fiction (Chapter 6) bespeaks a history of ever-expanding global trade and international culinary exchange.

The historical approach to food in literature adopted in this book reveals that even apparently universal themes such as 'hunger' are constructed differently over time. As James Vernon points out, 'we imagine that the horrible experience of hunger has been the same for all humans throughout time and in all places', but, in fact, 'hunger has a cultural history that belies its apparently consistent material form' (2007, 7–8). In medieval works such as *Piers Plowman* (Chapter 1), hunger tends to feature as a depersonalized, allegorical entity; providentially ordained, it is depicted as an inexorable part of the human condition, a form of divine punishment for original sin, and a necessary spur to labour. By the literature of the late eighteenth and nineteenth centuries, however, hunger has been (largely) ideologically reconceived as a social problem: a matter of humanitarian concern. Affect-inducing representations of starving children and women in *Desmond* (Chapter 4) and the fiction of Dickens and the Brontës (Chapter 5) are purposefully designed to individuate the experience of hunger and elicit an empathetic response from the reader. Of course, this shift from providential to compassionate understandings of hunger is by no means straightforward or linear; notably, in Chapter 4, Charlotte Smith's humanitarian response to exigency co-exists with Hannah More's more traditional attitude to food shortage as the manifestation of divine will. A correspondingly uneven hermeneutic transition can be detected in relation to hunger's counterpoint – gluttony – a theme which also recurs throughout literary history. As we have seen, anxieties over physical health have long coincided with moral concerns in representations of gluttons (see, for instance, the portrayal of Gluttony in Spenser's *Faerie Queene* in Chapter 2); nevertheless, the discursive balance between hamartiological and medical constructions of excessive consumption has altered gradually over time, as immoderation has come to be viewed less in terms of Christian sin and more in terms of individual pathology.

Temporal and epistemic changes have also affected representations of the various social practices associated with food. Within the period considered in this study, female fasting or food refusal emerges as a persistent motif; however, though it is possible to identify interesting resonances in the abstemious behaviours of women such as Margery Kempe (Chapter 1), Marianne Dashwood (Chapter 4), Caroline Helstone (Chapter 5) and Marian MacAlpin (Chapter 6), it would be reductive to conflate the predominantly spiritually motivated fasts of medieval literary figures with the proto-anorexic self-denial depicted in more recent writings, as a number of critics have pointed out. In her careful and nuanced analysis of the fasting behaviours of medieval women, Caroline Walker Bynum argues that cultural context is crucial to interpretation (1987, 198, 206). Similarly, in her important study *Fasting Girls*, Joan Jacobs Brumberg cautions that 'we should avoid easy generalizations about the existence in past times of the modern disease entity anorexia nervosa or about "women's nature" . . . Even as basic a human instinct as appetite is transformed by cultural and social systems and given new meaning in different historical epochs' (2000, 5). The complex socio-historical picture around food refusal is further complicated by the fact that the abstemious female body is an inherently unstable signifier, subject to a variety of competing meanings: as Helen Malson notes, in Western societies it typically signifies both 'a multiplicity of femininities *and* a rejection of femininity', 'a conformity to patriarchal femininity' but also 'a differing from, and a deferring of, prescribed gender positions' (1998, 113).

A comparable semantic fluidity marks other customs and rituals surrounding food, such as commensality. The communal knightly feasting represented in *Sir Gawain and the Green Knight* (Chapter 1), which both reflects and upholds the value structures of feudal society, inevitably signifies differently from the cross-class Christmas festivities depicted by Dickens in *The Pickwick Papers* and *A Christmas Carol* (Chapter 5) and the disorderly tea-party found in *Alice's Adventures in Wonderland* (Chapter 5). Elsewhere, a mounting scepticism towards the idea of commensality as socially cohesive can be identified: in the modernist fictions of Joyce and Woolf (Chapter 6), the fragmentation of social and familial bonds jeopardizes the possibility of achieving positive communion through food, while, in *The Magic Toyshop* (Chapter 6), communal dining is associated as much with the exercise of asymmetrical power relations as with affirmative alimentary experience. The semiotics of hunting, likewise, undergo a perceptible cultural shift over time. From being conceived of as a noble and morally legitimate form of food-gathering in medieval literature, hunting comes to be associated more and more with social inequality or predatory gender relations in later fictions, such as *Tom Jones* (Chapter 3), *The Tenant of Wildfell Hall* (Chapter 5) and *The Edible Woman* (Chapter 6), although, again, this transition is not entirely smooth or even. Sir Gawain is implicitly represented as the prey of Lady Bertilak in *Sir Gawain and the Green Knight* (Chapter 1), while in *The Beth Book* (Chapter 5) the female protagonist's trapping of animals for food is configured as a necessitous and rightful form of restitutory justice against patriarchal oppression, rather than a socially elitist form of 'sport' or an act of gratuitous cruelty.

While mapping such evolutions in the meaning of food-related practice, it is important to remember references to food in literature are not simply *reflective* of changes within the social field; they can also work dynamically to *produce* new forms of consumer and culinary relations. Evocations of blood-stained sugar and the brutality of meat-eating in the works of Mary Birkett and Percy and Mary Shelley (Chapter 4), for instance, do not merely echo existing Romantic ethical concerns, but rather help actively to construct a series of distinctive political identities, such as the 'anti-saccharite' and the 'vegetarian'. Literary representation has also had a palpable influence on the conception of the 'cannibal' in the popular cultural imaginary; as a number of critics have pointed out, stereotypical notions of 'man-eating savages' are more indebted to the cannibalistic images located in works such as *Robinson Crusoe* (Chapter 3) and *Heart of Darkness* (Chapter 6) than to historical or anthropological fact (although, as this book has shown, Defoe's and Conrad's texts have a more complex relationship to cannibalism than might at first appear, working ultimately to subvert some of the anthropophagic assumptions they set up).

What kinds of consumers and modes of consumption might literary works help to construct in the future? Given the close links between food, culture and society, it seems likely that culinary and alimentary tropes will continue to adapt and transmute in relation to shifting ideological values and cultural anxieties. Although reasons of space preclude a full examination of contemporary engagements with food and consumption in this volume, emerging literary themes in recent years have included the obesity crisis that looms over developed, Western nations – a subject central to Lionel Shriver's *Big Brother* (2013) and Jami Attenberg's *The Middlesteins* (2013) – and the food security issues that threaten a rapidly increasing global population – a problem addressed in texts as diverse as Suzanne Collins's popular dystopian novel *The Hunger Games* (2008) and Jim Crace's ecofiction *Harvest* (2013), where it features in more allusive form. In Ben Lerner's *10:04* (2014) – a novel set in a world of extreme weather events and anti-corporate protests – contemporary middle-class concerns around food additives, high-sugar diets and the need for 'clean eating' generate 'a new bio-political vocabulary for expressing racial and class anxiety', in which unhealthy fast foods – 'high-fructose carbonated beverage[s]' and 'deep-fried, mechanically processed chicken' – function as eloquent non-verbal markers of social inferiority (2014, 97–98). Meanwhile, in Han Kang's prize-winning novel *The Vegetarian* (2015), a more existential set of anxieties arises in relation to ingestion; here, Yeong-hye's decision to stop eating meat is linked to her desire to cast off human selfhood in favour of a less violent, vegetal state of being, a rejection of anthropoid subjectivity that explodes the complacent assumptions of her husband and immediate family. Kang's deliberate use of food (and its refusal) to explore ethical and ontological crises indicates that, while engaging with historically and culturally specific events and alimentary ideas, future texts will also likely continue to deploy dietary motifs as a means to construct, negotiate and contest the wider, philosophically complex questions of identity (and non-identity) that have long dominated literary history. Whatever the final direction of future literary engagements with food, cooking, eating and not-eating, one thing seems clear: the writers of literary cookbooks in years to come will not want for new sources of creative material.

References

Attenberg, Jami. 2013. *The Middlesteins*. London. Serpent's Tail.

Barclay, Jennifer. 2015. *A Literary Feast: Recipes Inspired by Novels, Poems and Plays*. Chichester. Summersdale.

Brumberg, Joan Jacobs. 2000. *Fasting Girls: The History of Anorexia Nervosa*. New York. Vintage.

Bynum, Caroline Walker. 1987. *Holy Feast and Holy Fast: The Religious Significance of Food to Medieval Women*. Berkeley, CA, and London. University of California Press.

Collins, Suzanne. 2008. *The Hunger Games*. New York. Scholastic Press.

Crace, Jim. 2013. *Harvest*. London. Picador.

Forster, E. M. 1990. *Aspects of the Novel*. Ed. Oliver Stallybrass. London. Penguin.

Fried, Dinah. 2014. *Fictitious Dishes: An Album of Literature's Most Memorable Meals*. New York. Harper Design.

Gilbert, Pamela K. 1997. 'Ingestion, Contagion, Seduction: Victorian Metaphors of Reading'. *LIT: Literature Interpretation Theory* 8.1. 83–104.

Joyce, James. 1993. *Ulysses* (1922 text). Ed. Jeri Johnson. Oxford. Oxford University Press.

Kang, Han. 2015. *The Vegetarian*. Trans. Deborah Smith. London. Portobello Books.

Kolb, Jocelyne. 1995. *The Ambiguity of Taste: Freedom and Food in European Romanticism*. Ann Arbor. University of Michigan Press.

Lerner, Ben. 2014. *10:04*. London. Granta.

Malson, Helen. 1998. *The Thin Woman: Feminism, Post-structuralism and the Social Psychology of Anorexia Nervosa*. London and New York. Routledge.

Milton, John. 1993. *Paradise Lost. Complete English Poems, Of Education, Areopagitica*. Ed. Gordon Campbell. London. J. M. Dent.

Morton, Mark and Andrew Coppolino. 2008. *Cooking with Shakespeare*. Westport, CT. Greenwood.

Morton, Timothy. 2006. 'Food Studies in the Romantic Period: (S)mashing History'. *Romanticism* 12.1. 1–4.

Nicoletti, Cara. 2015. *Voracious: A Hungry Reader Cooks Her Way Through Great Books*. New York. Little, Brown and Company.

Scrafford, Barbara. 2005. *Literary Feasts: Recipes from the Classics of Literature*. New York. iUniverse.

Shriver, Lionel. 2013. *Big Brother*. London. HarperCollins.

Vernon, James. 2007. *Hunger: A Modern History*. Cambridge, MA, and London. Harvard University Press.

Vogler, Pen. 2013. *Dinner with Mr Darcy: Recipes Inspired by the Novels and Letters of Jane Austen*. London and New York. CICO Books.

Watson, Matt. 2013. 'Materialities'. *Food Words: Essays in Culinary Culture*. Eds. Peter Jackson and the CONANX group. London. Bloomsbury. 127–130.

Woolf, Virginia. 2006. *To the Lighthouse*. Ed. David Bradshaw. Oxford. Oxford University Press.

INDEX